D0544688

# Bangladesh

Marika McAdam

# Contents

RAJSHAHI DIVISION p97

DHAKA DIVISION p68

SYLHET DIVISION p142

DHAKA ✪ p41

KHULNA DIVISION p77

CHITTAGONG DIVISION p119

BARISAL DIVISION p92

Lonely Planet books provide independent advice. Lonely Planet does not accept advertising in guidebooks, nor do we accept payment in exchange for listing or endorsing any place or business. Lonely Planet writers do not accept discounts or payments in exchange for positive coverage of any sort.

লোনলি প্ল্যানেট (Lonely Planet) প্রকাশিত বইয়ে নিরপেক্ষ উপদেশ থাকে। লোনলি প্ল্যানেটের বইয়ে প্রকাশের জন্য কোন বিজ্ঞাপন গ্রহন করা হয় না। কোন প্রতিষ্ঠানের নাম বইয়ে উল্লেখ করার জন্য লোনলি প্ল্যানেট কোন অর্থ গ্রহন করে না। কোন প্রতিষ্ঠান বা জায়গার প্রশংসনিয় উল্লেখের জন্য লোনলি প্ল্যানেটের লেখকরা কোন প্রকার মুল্য গ্রহন করে না।

# Destination Bangladesh

For all of its forests, temples, mosques, islands and beaches, the highlight of Bangladesh is Bangladesh. Once evoking images of war, overcrowding, floods and poverty, Bangladesh has largely fallen off the radar of Western consciousness into obscurity. But while the international psyche may not extend beyond ambivalence towards Bangladesh, this dynamic country proudly and progressively considers itself to be an active participant in an increasingly global community. In defiance of its stuttering development and the weight of historical tragedy that it bears, it is a nation charged with insatiable perseverance and promise.

The secrets that Bangladesh unintentionally harbours from the world include the Sundarbans: a stunning repository of wildlife masquerading as a mangrove and imbued with surreal otherworldliness. There is also Sylhet division, carpeted with lush and lurid tea plantations, Cox's Bazar, with its seemingly infinite beaches, and the Chittagong Hill Tracts – a bounty of natural beauty and home to indigenous peoples who typify the unexpected colour and diversity of Bangladesh.

As a traveller you offer Bangladesh an insight into the rest of the world and an opportunity to give the rest of the world an insight into it. For this reason it is one of the last frontiers where genuine cultural interaction is not only possible, but unavoidable. Every exchange you have is significant. Each impression you leave will remain, and each impression you get will join with a thousand others and culminate in wonderment that the whole world isn't talking about Bangladesh, where extraordinary kindnesses are ordinary occurrences.

A visit to this overwhelming country is not just a travel experience – it's a life experience.

RICHARD I'ANSON

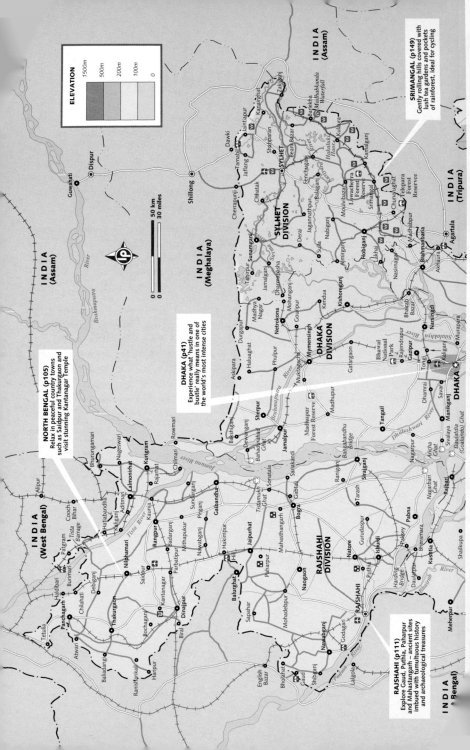

ELEVATION

1500m
500m
200m
100m
0

50 km
30 miles
0
0

SRIMANGAL (p149)
Gently rolling hills covered with
lush tea gardens and pockets
of rainforest, ideal for cycling

NORTH BENGAL (p105)
Relax in peaceful country towns
such as Saidpur and Thakurgaon and
visit stunning Kantanagar Temple

DHAKA (p41)
Experience what 'hustle and
bustle' really means in one of
the world's most intense cities

RAJSHAHI (p111)
Explore Gaud, Puthia, Paharpur
and Mahastangarh – ancient sites
imbued with tumultuous history
and archaeological treasures

INDIA
(Assam)

INDIA
(Assam)

INDIA
(Meghalaya)

INDIA
(West Bengal)

INDIA
(Tripura)

INDIA
( Bengal)

Guwahati

Dispur

Shillong

Dawki

Tamabil

Jaflang

Jaintiapur

Kanairghat

Zakiganj

Barlekha

Bean Bazar

Maulvibhazalbunda
Waterfall

SYLHET

Shahporan

Chhatak

Cherrapunji

Fenchuganj

Balaganj

Lawacherra
Forest
Reserve

Srimangal

Kulaura

Kamalganj

Tepepara
Forest
Reserve

Chunaghat

Madhabpur

Brahmanbaria

Agartala

Akhaura

SYLHET
DIVISION

Jagannathpur

Derai

Sulla

Nabiganj

Hobiganj

Lakhai

Ajmirganj

Nasirnagar

Sunamganj

Tahirpur

Jamalgan

Dharmapasha

Mohanganj

Goupur

Kendua

Kishoreganj

Bhairab
Bazar

Nasingdi

Muradpur

Derai

Madhya
Nagar

Netrokona

Durgapul

Haluaghat

Askipara

Phulpur

Mymensingh

Gafargaon

DHAKA
DIVISION

Bhawal
National
Park

Rajendrapur

Gazipur

Tongi

DHAKA

Kaligani

Sutakhya River

Sherpur

Bakshiganj

Dewanganj

Bahadurabad
Ghat

Jamalpur

Madhupur
Forest Reserve

Madhupur

Tangali

Dhamrai

Savar

Sivataia Manikganj

Daulatia
(Golundo) Ghat

Dholeshwari River

Bangbandhu
Bridge

Sakandi

Rangiort

Tarash

Sirajganj

Nagarpur
Ghat

Aricha
Ghat

Raibari

Rowmari

Chilmari

Tistamukh
Ghat

Sonatala

Gabtali

Bogra

Gurudaspur

Pabna

Bheramca

Kushtia

Shailkupa

Meherpur

Jumana River

Brahmaputra River

Jamuna River

Nageswari

Kurigram

Bhurungamari

Alipur

Cooch
Bihar

Patgram

Tista
Barrage

Haldibari

Burimari

Hatibandha

Kaliganj

Aditmari

Lalmonirhat

Rajarhat

Nilphamari

Rangpur

Badargan

Pirgani

Gaibandha

Debiganj

Chilahati

Saidpur

Thakurgaon

Panchagarh

Atwari

Tetulia

Ballatangj

Ranisingkal

Haripur

Bochaganj

Birol

Dinajpur

Kantanagar

Bochaganj

Sundirganj

Mithapukur

Nawabganj

Parbatipur

Hakimpur

Hili

Jaipurhat

Mahastangarh

Mahadebpur

Naogaon

Sapahar

Balurghat

Paharpur

Kauria

Badargan

RAJSHAHI
DIVISION

Natore

Puthia

RAJSHAHI

Ishurdi

Godagari

Nawabganj

Harding
Bridge

Daulatpur

Shibganj

Lalgola

Gaud

Bhojdhat

English
Bazar

Padma River

Mahananda River

Tista River

Brahmaputra
River

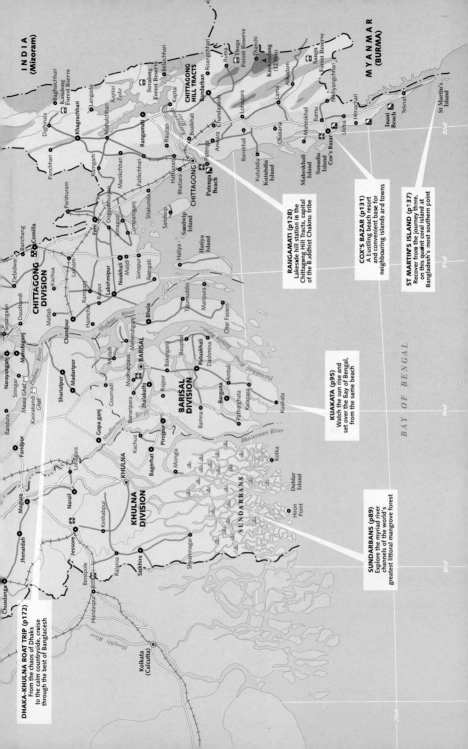

**INDIA**
(Mizoram)

**MYANMAR**
(BURMA)

**CHITTAGONG HILL TRACTS**

**CHITTAGONG DIVISION**

**BARISAL DIVISION**

**KHULNA DIVISION**

**SUNDARBANS**

BAY OF BENGAL

**DHAKA-KHULNA BOAT TRIP (p172)**
From the chaos of Dhaka
to the calm countryside, cruise
through the best of Bangladesh

**SUNDARBANS (p89)**
Explore the myriad river
channels of the world's
greatest littoral mangrove forest

**KUAKATA (p95)**
Watch the sun rise and
set over the Bay of Bengal,
from the same beach

**RANGAMATI (p128)**
Lakeside hill station in the
Chittagong Hill Tracts, capital
of the Buddhist Chakma tribe

**COX'S BAZAR (p131)**
A bustling beach resort
and convenient base for
neighbouring islands and towns

**ST MARTIN'S ISLAND (p137)**
Recover from the journey there,
on this quaint coral island at
Bangladesh's most southern point

Kolkata
(Calcutta)

There are more temples and palaces in Bangladesh than most people realise. Two must-see temples are **Paharpur** (p101) from the 4th to 8th centuries and **Kantanagar Temple** (p109) from the 12th and 13th centuries.

**Shait Gumbad Mosque** (p86) illustrates the stylistic influences of the Turkistan Khilijis period (13th to 15th centuries). **Lalbagh Fort** (p49) and **Sat Gumbad Mosque** (p51) show Mughal embellishment of the simple architectural designs that preceded their rule.

Terracotta floral scroll details on Atia Mosque, Tangail (p72)

RICHARD I'ANSON

TONY WHEELER

The Pink Palace of Ahsan Manzil (p47) offers amazing views of and from Sadarghat

Dhaka's National Assembly building (p51) is an impressively imposing sight by day or night

CHRISTINE OSBORNE

Bangladesh is said to float. It sits atop the world's largest river delta, a vast flood plain where an intricate system of rivers and tributaries weave like a network of roads, reshaping the terrain on their way to the Bay of Bengal. As much water flows through Bangladesh as through all of Europe.

For the traveller, numerous ferry crossings, a visit to the **chars (islands) of the Brahmaputra** (p102) and a **Rocket ride** (p172) from Dhaka to Khulna will reveal the power of water in shaping a nation.

RICHARD I'ANSON

Crops of deep water rice and water hyacinths line the Meghna River at Sonargaon (p69)

Vessels of all sizes ply the Buriganga River, Dhaka (p46)

TONY WHEELER

CRAIG PERSHOUSE

If Bangladesh's rivers were roads, Sadarghat (p46) would be its main bus terminal

Streets everywhere pulsate and overflow with activity. The ebb and flow of daily life is metaphorically and literally epitomised in the movement of people on buses, boats, trains and rickshaws. From the moment you step on to the street, onto a rickshaw or into a bus, you will be immediately swept up in the maelstrom of commotion.

RICHARD I'ANSON

A rickshaw ride (p176) is the quintessential Bangladeshi experience

Hang out at the markets (p63) to shop and talk

RICHARD I'ANSON

The rural town of Pabna (p116) offers glimpses of a slower-paced lifestyle

JERRY GALEA

# Getting Started

The fact that there are so few tourists in Bangladesh means that you won't have to contend with crowds at hotspots or with booked-out accommodation. However, it also means that there is very little tourist infrastructure. It can be rough going, though the more you pay the more comfortable things get. But even if it's just you and a backpack, the worst it gets is a rough ride or a bad night's sleep. Once you figure it out, there is even some method to the madness of the public transport system, and there is always help at hand. Unless you are planning to go on an organised tour, there is very little that you can arrange in advance other than visas and immunisations. All you really need to do is get excited and go!

See the Climate Charts (p156) for more information.

## WHEN TO GO

Bangladesh has three main seasons: the monsoonal or wet season from late May to early October; the cool season from mid-October to the end of February; and the hot season from mid-March to mid-May. Despite the fact that these are the only observable seasons in Bangladesh, locals commonly refer to six.

**Basanto (spring)** February to April
**Grishma (summer)** April to June
**Barsha (rainy)** June to August
**Sharat (autumn)** August to October
**Hemanto (misty)** October to December
**Sheet (winter)** December to February

Between October and February is the best time to go. The winter isn't as *sheet* as it sounds: skies are blue, days are sunny and the weather is dry, with daytime temperatures of around 21°C. By April the temperature rises to around 40°C, the humidity can be intolerable and hailstorms aren't uncommon. On average, Bangladesh is hit by one major cyclone every three years. The worst times for these are May to June and October to November.

The occurrence of festivals can also change your travel experience. If you plan purely to avoid the crowds (good luck in Bangladesh), you will also miss out on some interesting experiences. The only event that may really inconvenience you is Ramadan. During this month-long period of

---

### DON'T LEAVE HOME WITHOUT...

Given that the safety situation in parts of Bangladesh is *particularly* subject to change, don't leave home without checking some reputable travel advisories. Although you can buy almost anything if you know where to find it, there are a couple of things you might want to bring:

- Loose-fitting clothes to dress modestly until you can make the transition into local gear.
- Earplugs for inconceivably loud bus rides and neighbouring passengers.
- Sunglasses for sun and stare protection.
- Glasses in case contact lenses become irritated by the pollution.
- Torch (flashlight) for power failures.
- Appropriate visa (p164) and a passport valid for six months after you intend to leave Bangladesh.
- An open mind and more patience than you think you'll need.

fasting, getting food, especially in small towns, can be embarrassing if not difficult. Some budget hotels actually stop operating altogether.

## COSTS & MONEY

Bangladesh can be as dirt-cheap or as decadent as you want. If you're the type of traveller who just sees a cockroach-infested room as a dorm, then you'll enjoy Bangladesh. For around Tk 50 you can have a room all to yourself, for Tk 25 you can get an enormous meal, and for around Tk 5 you can get a meal on the street. At the 'you only live once' end of the spectrum, you can pay a couple of hundred US dollars for a lavish room, and buy a meal of the same price and quality that you would expect at home.

In between these two extremes is a healthy spectrum of mid-range options. For between Tk 200 and Tk 600 a night you will be able to find a nice place to stay with all the necessary amenities. A Tk 40 meal is large and tasty. In the way of transportation there is a range of classes on trains and boats and different types of buses, which offers enormous flexibility when weighing up value and comfort.

### HOW MUCH?

Litre of petrol Tk 35

Litre of bottled water Tk 20

Can of Heineken Tk 160

Souvenir T-shirt Tk 100

Boiled egg Tk 4

Sundarbans tour Tk 10,000

Cup of cha Tk 2

Bottle of Coke Tk 10-25

Newspaper Tk 7

Toilet paper Tk 10

## TRAVEL LITERATURE

Budding writers will be happy to hear that there is very little travel literature on Bangladesh published in the West. However, there is a growing range of books that will give the traveller an insight into the people and culture.

Jhumpa Lahiri's Pulitzer Prize–winning *Interpreter of Maladies*, an engaging collection of diverse stories that orbit the theme of displacement, is not so much concerned with travel in Bangladesh as with the travels of Bangladeshis. Paul Ryder Ryan's *Bangladesh 2000: On the Brink of Civil War* is an animated and engaging work, part 'behind the scenes' investigation into the political tumult of Bangladesh and part travel memoir.

*Postcards from Bangladesh* by Sudeep Sen is the sort of coffee-table book designed to be treasured. It is a stunning collection of lovingly composed and compiled photos that artfully capture the humanity of Bangladesh. In the same vein is Lonely Planet's *Chasing Rickshaws,* by Tony Wheeler and Richard I'Anson, which affectionately documents the plight of the rickshaw-wallah and has a chapter devoted solely to Dhaka.

*On the Brink in Bengal* by Francis Rolt is a travelogue with a strong focus on encounters with the minority tribal populations. It's out of print but worth reading if you can get a copy.

## INTERNET RESOURCES

As Bangladesh becomes more tech-savvy, the Internet is becoming an increasingly useful tool for pre-trip planning. It is also more up-to-date than printed material, which is particularly important for an ever-changing destination such as this. Good places to start surfing:

**Bangladesh Development Gateway** (www.bangladeshgateway.org) An extensive guide to the numerous development projects, organisations and activities in Bangladesh.

**Bangladesh Parjatan Corporation** (www.bangladeshtourism.org) The national tourism organisation website is user-friendly and has a wealth of information on all things travel-related.

**Daily Star** (www.thedailystar.net) The Internet edition of the country's major newspaper is a good place to check what's going on each day.

**Discovery Bangladesh** (www.discoverybangladesh.com) A great place to start getting an idea about the place and its people and tips on how to tackle Bangladesh.

**Lonely Planet** (www.lonelyplanet.com) Succinct information, useful links and the popular Thorn Tree bulletin board, which puts you in touch with some of the few people who have been to Bangladesh.

**Virtual Bangladesh** (www.virtualbangladesh.com) Regularly updated, this is an extremely extensive resource for both basic facts and bigger issues.

# TOP TENS
## Top Reads
Reading is a great way to get into the mindset of the nation. There are some great books that touch on various issues that have shaped Bangladesh.

- *Brick Lane* by Monica Ali (2003; p30)
- *Interpreter of Maladies* by Jhumpa Lahiri (1999; p10)
- *The Departed Melody* by Raja Tridiv Roy (2003; p24)
- *Rabindranath Tagore: An Anthology* Krishna Detta & Andrew Robinson (eds; 1998)
- *Shame* by Taslima Nasrin (1997)
- *Seasonal Adjustments* by Adib Khan (1995)
- *A Quiet Violence: View from a Bangladeshi Village* by Betsy Hartmann & James Boyce (1983)
- *Midnight's Children* by Salman Rushdie (1981)
- *Such a Long Journey* by Rohinton Mistry (1981)
- *Life of Pi* by Yann Martel (2001)

## Who's Who of Bangladesh
On your travels through Bangladesh you will see portraits prominently displayed in family homes and shops throughout the country. Here is a list of people you should have heard of.

- Rabindrath Tagore (Nobel Prize–winning poet)
- Sheikh Mujibur Rahman (founder of Bangladesh)
- General Zia Rahman (head of the army during the Liberation War, former president)
- Begum Khaleda Zia (present prime minister and General Zia's widow)
- Sheikh Hasina Wajed (Awami League president, former prime minister and daughter of Sheikh Mujibur)
- General Ershad (former president, jailed for corruption and illegal possession of weapons)
- Kazi Nazrul Islam (national poet)
- Taslima Nasrin (exiled author)
- Khaled Mahmud (captain of the cricket team)
- Popi (Dhallywood's answer to Julia Roberts)

## Top Museums
- National Museum (Dhaka; p51)
- Liberation War Museum (Dhaka; p51)
- Ethnological Museum (Chittagong; p123)
- Ahsan Manzil (Pink Palace; Dhaka; p47)
- Salban Vihara Site Museum (Comilla; p141)
- Mahasthangarh Site Museum (Mahasthangarh; p101)
- Somapuri Vihara Site Museum (Paharpur; p102)
- Nawab Syed Abdus Sobhan Chowdhury Memorial Museum (Bogra; p98)
- Varendra Research Museum (Rajshahi; p111)
- Sadarbari Folk Art Museum (Sonargaon; p70)

# Itineraries

## CLASSIC ROUTES

### CITY TO SUNDARBANS                                      One week

A well-spent week in Bangladesh can be enough to give you an overview of the country's scenery and culture. To really get the most out of your time, though, you will need to put in some thought.

Start with couple of days in **Dhaka** (p41). On the first day absorb as much information as you can at the **National Museum** (p51) and the **Liberation War Museum** (p51). At night check out the surreally lit **National Assembly Building** (p51) on your way to **Gulshan** (p61) for some fine dining. Spend the next day meandering through **Old Dhaka** (p46) towards **Sadarghat** (p46), from where you will leave Dhaka on the (in)famous **Rocket** (p172).

Your third day may be the week's most memorable, as the countryside scrolls past as the Rocket makes its way gently south towards **Khulna** (p82). In Khulna wander through markets and bazars, which burst into life at night. On a day trip to the landmark-filled historical town of **Bagerhat** (p85) you will experience bus travel, rickshaw rides, serene scenery and one of the most famous buildings in Bangladesh – **Shait Gumbad Mosque** (p86).

From Khulna try to do a short expedition into the **Sundarbans** (p89).

A week spent heading from Dhaka to the Sundarbans will give you a general overview of the best of Bangladesh. This 360km trip incorporates some of the country's highlights – the epic Rocket ride, the historical town of Bagerhat and the extraordinary Sundarbans.

## MONTH IN MOTION                                  One month

You can squeeze a lot into a month. If you pace yourself sensibly you
will be able to cover the gamut of highlights without cramming too much
into your memory banks.

Take your time in **Dhaka** (p41), doing things described in the Dhaka in
Two Days boxed text (p45). Ease yourself into the rhythm of rural life with
a Rocket ride to **Barisal** (p93), then catch a bus down to **Kuakata** (p95) to
experience beach life at the Bay of Bengal. Head back to Barisal and continue
by Rocket to **Khulna** (p82) and incorporate the suggestions of the City to
Sundarbans itinerary. Be sure to take your time in the **Sundarbans** (p89).

Make your way back to Dhaka overland by bus, with a break in **Kushtia**
(p81) to visit **Tagore Lodge** (p81).After soaking up city life again, retreat to
the relative quiet of **Sylhet** (p143). The scenic seven-hour bus ride from
Dhaka is worth doing during the day. After visiting the **Shrine of Shah Paran**
(p148) and the surrounding **Jaflang area** (p147), loop your way around to
**Srimangal** (p149), maybe via **Madhabkunda Waterfall** (p148). In Srimangal
hire a bicycle and peddle through **tea plantations** (p147) and villages.

From Srimangal catch the train to **Chittagong** (p120). If you're an archaeology buff, get off en route at Comilla to visit the **Mainimati Ruins** (p140). Spend
a couple of days exploring Chittagong, and maybe do some adventurous
side trips (p125). Check out the safety situation and ensure you have the
necessary permits (p128) before venturing into the **Chittagong Hill Tracts**
(p126); then try to get to **Rangamati** (p128) and **Bandarban** (p131).

If you still have time left, finish off by doing the beach Bangladeshi style
at **Cox's Bazar** (p131), four hours by bus from Chittagong.

This month of
steady travel will
show you the
breadth and beauty
of Bangladesh, from
its tea plantations
and beaches to its
tribal hill tracts and
cities. After this
2500km journey
on buses, boats,
trains and bicycles
you will be able to
say with absolute
confidence that you
have experienced
Bangladesh.

# ROADS LESS TRAVELLED

## BUSES, BOATS & BORDERS                    One month

Though none of Bangladesh is saturated with tourists, there are some trips that are more challenging than others.

In Rajshahi division spend a couple of weeks exploring some hard-to-get-to archaeological sites. From **Rajshahi** (p111) visit **Puthia** (p114), **Natore** (p115) and **Pabna** (p116). You could also head out to **Gaud** (p117) on the Indian border; it's a messy journey but the scenery makes it worthwhile.

**Bogra** (p98) is used as a base from which to travel to **Mahasthangarh** (p100) and **Paharpur** (p101). From here you can also make the trip to **Sariakandi** (p100) and hire a boat to explore life on the Jamuna River.

Further north in Rajshahi division you could explore **Panchagarh**, 40km from **Thakurgaon**. Though it may be a challenge to travel, northern Rajshahi is laid-back – a nice kind of reality to immerse yourself in. Make your way over to **Rangpur** (p102), then to Chilmari via Lalmonirhat and Kurigram. While you're in Chilmari explore the **chars of the Brahmaputra River** (p102).

Head back to Dhaka then take a train to **Chittagong** (p120), stopping on the way to check out the ruins at **Comilla** (p138). From Chittagong try to visit the **Chittagong Hill Tracts** (p126) for some trekking. You can also catch a launch boat over to Hatiya Island, a busy fertile char with a paved road running through its centre, or head down south to **St Martin's Island** (p137). On your way you could stop in at **Cox's Bazar** to visit some nearby islands.

Juggle buses, boats and borders on a quest to reach the remote corners of Bangladesh. This 1860km trip is a real rural experience, and your visit might be a major event for the population of a far-flung village.

# The Author

## MARIKA MCADAM

At the age of four, while still travelling with a passport signatured 'unable to write', Marika's fascination for developing countries was born. An after-school job in Lonely Planet's marketing and communications department fuelled her dream of becoming a Lonely Planet writer when she grew up. At the age of 24, realising that she would never grow up, Marika jumped at the chance to update Lonely Planet's guide to Bangladesh – a destination that perfectly marries her studies and interests in human rights, indigenous law, international relations and economic, cultural, social, civil and political development. Marika has recently graduated from university with degrees in law and political science, and now travels with a passport she signed herself.

### Life on the Road

Finding a simple piece of information in Bangladesh can easily turn into an epic quest. Was it possible to anticipate how long it would take to find a train timetable in a country where everything happens at Allah's will? Hardly. But nor was it possible to anticipate how much of an adventure this gig would be.

At times I felt like a contestant in some farcical subcontinental game show. There was a challenge: gather information. There was an audience: everywhere. There was an obstacle: Bangladesh. And there was a prize: Bangladesh.

So I'm standing in a crowd of protestors and police in riot gear, asking directions to a cybercafé and wondering where the hell I am. Then I remember: I'm exactly where I want to be.

## CONTRIBUTING AUTHOR

**Dr Trish Batchelor** wrote the Health chapter (p179). Trish is a general practitioner and travel-medicine specialist who works at the CIWEC Clinic in Kathmandu, Nepal, and is also a medical advisor to the Travel Doctor New Zealand clinics. Trish teaches travel medicine through the University of Otago, and is interested in underwater and high-altitude medicine, and in the impact of tourism on host countries. She has travelled extensively through Southeast and East Asia and particularly loves high-altitude trekking in the Himalayas.

# Snapshot

Bangladesh is a revelation of the many shades of grey that exist between black and white. Terrorism is a cause of increased consternation for Bangladesh, along with a concern that many in the West aren't distinguishing between Islam and terrorism. Meanwhile homage is paid to Osama bin Laden in the form of rickshaw art and collectable cards swapped by school kids.

Bangladesh keeps an attentive eye on troubles in the Middle East. American President George W Bush is arguably one of the most talked-about characters in the country; everyone has an opinion and you will no doubt hear many of them.

Bangladeshis are self-professed US-ophiles. The United States' Diversity Immigrant Visa Program (DV) throws the entire nation into a frenzy as *everyone* seizes the opportunity to enter the annual lottery for American residency. Internet cafés do big business touting the application form as their homepage and DV banners hang like festoons in the streets of even the most remote towns.

The political activism that gave birth to an independent Bangladesh (p20) has left a legacy of activism. Systemic corruption (the worst in the world, according to the UN) is a source of acute anger; people regularly take to the street in protest. The subversion of free expression in the form of attacks on and assassinations of journalists is also a growing issue.

The ruling BNP (Bangladesh Nationalist Party) and the opposing AL (Awami League) are ever vocal in their criticisms of each other. This 'Battle of the Begums' (p22) rages at its highest level between the leaders of the two parties, and at the loudest level in the form of organised hartals (strikes), which spark more hartals, and round it goes. To add confusion to the already confusing, numerous minor parties use a similar blend of propaganda and protest. Opinions flow thick and fast, but getting an objective grasp of the basics is something of a challenge.

The rights of the Adivasis (tribal people) of the Chittagong Hill Tracts and the debate surrounding the implementation of the 1997 Peace Accord (p127) looks as though it will be as topical in the next decade as in the past. The situation seems to fluctuate from hot to cold to boiling, almost on a weekly basis.

The rights of women (p27) are increasingly an issue, particularly for the educated classes. While daily newspaper reports of rapes and acid attacks don't augur well for the treatment of women, the fact that such reports are made is arguably indicative of the growing concern for these problems.

## FAST FACTS

Population: 140.9 million

Children that are underweight for their age: 48%

Population living on less than US$2 per day: 82.8%

GDP per capita: US$1610 (USA: US$34,320)

Life expectancy at birth: 60.5 years (USA: 76.9 years)

Female adult literacy (over 15 years old): 30.8%

Male adult literacy (over 15 years old): 49.9%

Year women received the right to vote: 1972

# History

The history of Bangladesh has been one of extremes: turmoil and peace, prosperity and destitution. It has thrived in the glow of cultural splendour and suffered the ravages of war. Throughout its tumultuous history it has known internal warfare, suffered invasion upon invasion, witnessed the rise and fall of mighty empires, and benefited from the trade and culture brought from foreign lands.

Virtual Bangladesh (www .virtualbangladesh.com /history/overview.html) gives a simple overview of a complicated history.

## EARLY HISTORY

The earliest mention of the region is in the 9th century BC Hindu epic *Mahabharata*, which tells of Prince Bhima's conquest of eastern India, including Varendra, an ancient kingdom in what is now Bangladesh.

By the 5th and 6th centuries BC, Aryan culture had spread eastward from the Indus River in Pakistan to dominate most of northern India.

In 325 BC, Alexander the Great set upon India. Alerted to this formidable threat, troops from the lower Ganges united under a native king of the Nanda dynasty. Alexander's troops were overwhelmed and retreated without entering into battle.

Chandragupta Maurya ascended the Magadhan throne and created an empire, then known as Pundravardhana Bhukti, now Mahasthangarh (p100). It spread across northern India under his grandson, the emperor Ashoka, whose conversion to Buddhism in 262 BC had a lasting effect.

In the 4th century AD northern India came under the imperial rule of the Guptas, during whose reign Buddhism reached its zenith. The Guptas succumbed to a wave of White Hun invasions. In the 6th century, Sasanaka founded the Gauda empire in Bengal, which was eventually overthrown by the warrior king Sri Harsa, who ruled the Bengal area until the 8th century.

Gopala, a Kshatriya tribal chief from Varendra, became the founding figure of the Buddhist Pala dynasty (8th to 11th centuries). He was succeeded by his son Dharmapala, who established the gigantic Somapura Vihara in Varendra, known today as Paharpur (p101).

In the 12th century Hindu Senas came to rule Bengal, and crushed Buddhism. Surviving Buddhists retreated to the Chittagong area, where a Buddhist community still exists today. In less than a century the Senas were swamped by the tide of Islam.

**DID YOU KNOW?**

The army, known to the Greeks as Gangaridae, that chased Alexander the Great from India in 325 BC, was supported by 4000 trained elephants and horses.

## THE MUSLIM PERIOD

With only 20 men, Mohammed Bakhtiar (a Khilji from Turkistan) captured Bengal in 1199, bringing the area under the rule of the sultanate of Delhi, the centre of Muslim power.

For a short period the Mameluk sultanate was established in Bengal, until the Tughlaq dynasty overthrew it in 1320. The Tughlaqs were defeated by another wave of Muslim invaders in 1398.

Under the Muslims, Bengal entered a new era. Cities developed, palaces, forts, mosques, mausoleums and gardens sprang up, roads and bridges were constructed and new trade routes brought prosperity and a

| TIMELINE | 13th–17th century | 1600 |
|---|---|---|
| | Muslim period; in 1575 Akbar defeats Bengali sultan Daud Karrani at the Battle of Tukaroi | Queen Elizabeth I grants royal charter giving British East India Company a monopoly over British trade with India |

new cultural life. The city of Gaud (p117), on the Indian border, emerged as a cosmopolitan metropolis, remaining the centre of power in Bengal until the capital was moved to Dhaka in 1608.

In 1576 Bengal became a province of the Mughal empire, which ushered in another golden age in India, only to be outdone by the country's final great empire – the British Raj.

## THE EUROPEAN PERIOD

For decades the Portuguese, Dutch, British and French tussled for influence over the subcontinent, but it was the British East India Company that prevailed.

In 1740 Sarfaraz Khan, the viceroy of the three provinces of Bengal, Orissa and Bihar, was overthrown by Ali Vardi Khan. This heralded the rise of the independent dynasty of the nawab (Muslim prince) of Bengal. In 1756 Suraj-ud-Daula, the 21-year-old nawab of Bengal, attacked the British settlement of Calcutta. British inhabitants were packed into an underground cellar, the infamous 'Black Hole of Calcutta', where most of them suffocated during the night.

A year later, Englishman Robert Clive defeated Suraj-ud-Daula, effectively making the British de facto rulers of Bengal. The British East India Company's control over Bengal aroused concern in London, leading to the passage of an act regulating its power. Following the Indian Uprising of 1857 the British government took control of India from the British East India Company.

### BRITISH RAJ

It has been said that the British Raj ushered Bengal into a period of growth and development, but historians hotly dispute this. The dictatorial agricultural policies of the British and the establishment of the zamindar (feudal landowner) system have been considered responsible for draining Bengal of its wealth, damaging its social fabric and directly contributing to today's desperate conditions in Bangladesh.

Hindus cooperated with the British, entering British educational institutions and studying the English language. Muslims, on the other hand, refused to cooperate, preferring to remain landlords and farmers. This religious dichotomy formed a significant basis for future conflict.

The Indian National Congress, founded in 1885, was initially supported by both Hindus and Muslims. But the division of Bengal in 1905 by Lord Curzon (into two provinces: East Bengal and Assam; and West Bengal, Bihar and Orissa) was seen as a religious partition, prompting the formation of the All India Muslim League to protect Muslim interests, as Congress was increasingly perceived as a Hindu power group.

When the province was reunited in 1912, Muslims feared a return to Hindu dominance and sought the formation of a Muslim state separate from India.

In 1943 five million people starved to death in the Great Bengal Famine. Natural disaster was only part of the problem. Crops had failed due to drought, and Raj authorities were buying up all the food grain for Allied forces fighting in WWII. Cities were overwhelmed with starving refugees and the last shreds of respect for the British administration disappeared.

**DID YOU KNOW?**

Originally a mere clerk for the British East India Company, Robert Clive rose to become local head of the company and, eventually, the effective ruler of Bengal.

In his 1987 book *Heroes*, the ever-emotive John Pilger discusses ordinary people in extraordinary situations. The words he dedicates to Bangladesh luridly evoke the fervour of its formation and the passion of the people involved.

| 1857 | 1943 |
|---|---|
| Indian Uprising leads to the winding up of the British East India Company and the British government assuming direct control | Great Bengal Famine; five million people starve to death |

# INDEPENDENCE

At the close of WWII it was clear that European colonialism had run its course. The Indian National Congress continued to press for Indian self-rule and the British began to map out a path to independence.

Despite Mahatma Gandhi's even-handed approach, Muslims were concerned that an independent India would be dominated by Hindus. The country was divided on religious grounds, with the Muslim League, headed by Mohammed Ali Jinnah, representing the Muslims, and the Indian Congress Party, led by Jawaharlal Nehru, commanding the Hindu population. Realising the impossibility of agreement between the two factions, viceroy Lord Mountbatten decided to partition the subcontinent.

## EAST PAKISTAN

The Muslim League's demand for an independent Muslim home state was realised with the creation of Pakistan in 1947. Its two regions were on opposite sides of the subcontinent, in the Punjab and Bengal, the latter becoming East Pakistan. For months, an epic and bloody exodus took place as Hindus moved to India and Muslims moved to East or West Pakistan.

Though support for the creation of Pakistan was based on Islamic solidarity, the two halves of the new state had little else in common. Furthermore, the country was administered from West Pakistan, which tended to favour itself in the distribution of revenues.

The final straw for the Bengalis came when the Pakistani government declared that 'Urdu and only Urdu' would be the national language, a language that virtually no-one in Bangla-speaking East Bengal knew. This resulted in the creation of the Bangla Language Movement – the real beginning of the move towards independence. There were riots in Dhaka and on 21 February 1952, 12 students were killed by the Pakistani army. Pakistan's waning democracy gave way to military government and martial law.

A catastrophic cyclone in 1970 killed around 500,000 people in East Pakistan. The Pakistani government appeared to do little. The Awami League, led by Sheikh Mujibur Rahman, had emerged as the national political party in East Pakistan, with the Language Movement as its ideological

*Bangladesh: A Legacy of Blood* (1986) and *The Rape of Bangladesh* (1971) by Anthony Mascarenhas are well-respected works. Bengali historians and critics praise Mascarenhas for his courageous and realistic approach to the horror of Bangladesh's birth.

### POLITICS & STUDENTS

Probably nowhere in the world do students play such a pivotal role in politics as in Bangladesh. Students today are empowered by recent tradition, stemming largely from the key role they played in the Liberation War. When the war started it was no mistake that the Pakistanis aimed their tanks first at Dhaka University. Many students were among the intellectuals targeted for death.

Today, the main political parties view students' support as crucial and court their allegiance by supporting student activists. Most of these 'permanent students', who live on campus for years, are paid political activists.

As a result, many state universities have become the scene for ongoing clashes between the major parties. After every bloody clash the universities close down, sometimes for weeks, invariably followed by public outcry for the government to 'do something' – which it rarely does. None of the major parties want to lose such an important source of street muscle. Under these conditions it's quite normal for students to take eight or 10 years to complete what should be a three-year degree.

| 1947 | 1971 |
|---|---|
| British colonial rule ends; East and West Pakistan established, separated by more than 1500km of Indian territory | Bangladesh becomes the world's 139th country |

underpinning. The 1971 national elections saw the Awami League win with a clear majority; in East Pakistan it won all seats but one (held by Tridiv Roy, the raja of the Buddhist Chakma tribe of the Chittagong Hill Tracts). Constitutionally, the Awami League should have formed the government of all Pakistan, but faced with this unacceptable result, President Khan postponed the opening of the National Assembly.

Visit Dhaka University (www.univdhaka.edu) – the setting of significant moments in history and now a repository of historical records.

## THE LIBERATION WAR

At the Race Course rally of 7 March 1971 in Dhaka (at what is now Ramna Park), Sheikh Mujibur (Mujib) stopped short of declaring East Pakistan independent. In reality, however, Bangladesh (land of the Bangla speakers) was born that day. Sheikh Mujib was jailed in West Pakistan, igniting smouldering rebellion in East Pakistan.

When the Mukti Bahini (Bangladesh Freedom Fighters) captured the Chittagong radio station, Ziaur Rahman, the leader of the Mukti Bahini, announced the birth of the new country and called upon its people to resist the Pakistani army. President Khan sent more troops to quell the rebellion.

General Tikka Khan, the 'Butcher of Balochistan', began the systematic slaughter of Sheikh Mujib's supporters. Tanks began firing into the halls of Dhaka University. Hindu neighbourhoods were shelled and intellectuals, business people and other 'subversives' were hauled outside the city and shot.

By June the struggle had become a guerrilla war. More and more civilians joined the Mukti Bahini as the Pakistani army's tactics became more brutal. Napalm was used against villages. Rape was so widespread and systematic that it appeared to be an attempt to change the racial make-up of the nation. Clouds of vultures cast ghastly shadows all over the country.

By November 1971 the whole country suffered the burden of the occupying army. During the nine months from the end of March 1971, 10 million people fled to refugee camps in India.

**DID YOU KNOW?**

In July 2002, Pakistani president Musharraf visited Bangladesh and expressed his regret at excesses carried out by Pakistan during the Liberation War.

With border clashes between Pakistan and India becoming more frequent, the Pakistani air force made a pre-emptive attack on Indian forces on 3 December 1971, precipitating a quick end. Indian troops crossed the border, liberated Jessore on 7 December and prepared to take Dhaka. The Pakistani army was being attacked from the west by the Indian army, from the north and east by the Mukti Bahini and from all quarters by the civilian population.

By 14 December the Indian victory was complete. Pakistan's General Niazi surrendered on 16 December, and Sheikh Mujib, on his release from jail, took over the reins of government.

## BANGLADESH

The People's Republic of Bangladesh was born into chaos: it was shattered by war, with a ruined economy and a totally disrupted communications system.

Seeming fated to disaster, the famine from 1973 to 1974 set the war-ravaged country back one more. A state of emergency was declared in 1974 and Sheikh Mujib proclaimed himself president. However, Sheikh Mujib and his entire household were slaughtered during a military coup on 15 August 1975. Only two of his daughters survived: they were out

| 1975 | 1981 |
|---|---|
| Sheikh Mujibur is assassinated in an attempted military coup | President Zia assassinated |

of the country at the time. One, Sheikh Hasina, would become prime minister in 1996.

After a couple of years of tumultuous power struggles, General Ziaur Rahman, now the head of the army, took over as martial-law administrator and assumed the presidency in late 1976.

The overwhelming victory of President Zia (as Ziaur Rahman was popularly known) in the 1978 presidential poll was consolidated when his party, the newly formed Bangladesh Nationalist Party (BNP), won two-thirds of the seats in the parliamentary elections of 1979. Martial law was lifted and democracy returned to Bangladesh. Zia proved to be a competent politician and statesman. Assistance began pouring in and over the next five years the economy went from strength to strength.

But, alas, during an attempted military coup in May 1981, President Zia was assassinated. Justice Abdul Sattar was appointed as acting president and, as candidate for the BNP, won 66% of the vote in the general election.

On 24 March 1982 General Hossain Mohammed Ershad seized power in a bloodless coup. Bangladesh was again placed under martial law, with

In *Bangladesh: From a Nation to a State* (1997), Craig Baxter discusses the development of national identity throughout history. A comprehensive and ambitious work that contextualises the nationalistic pride evident in Bangladesh today.

---

## DEVELOPMENT CULTURE IN BANGLADESH

Bangladesh's micro-credit models are setting an example for the rest of the developing world.

The Grameen Bank, founded in 1976 by Mohammad Yunus, operates under the principle that if financial resources are available to poor, land-less people at existing commercial terms, millions of small families can create a development wonder.

Under its lending formula, prospective borrowers form groups of five neighbours, who vet each others' loan requests. If one member fails to pay, the group receives no further loans; peer pressure tends to keep things straight. Interest rates are 20%. Loans can vary from US$65 to around US$1000, but the average is US$120, typically enough to purchase a cow, a sewing machine or a silkworm shed. Most loans go to women because Yunus believes they are more likely to plough money into the needs of the family, while men more often spend it on themselves. Loaning to women also has the effect of raising their status in communities. By the bank's statistics, the default rate is around 2% and about a third of the borrowers have crossed the poverty line.

The programme is not without its sceptics. The bank's claims are difficult to verify and, with so much foreign money pouring into the bank, it's unclear whether it is sustainable and thus a viable model for other countries and institutions.

A similar programme is the Bangladesh Rural Advancement Committee (BRAC). Founded by Fazle Hasan Abed in the early 1970s as a relief organisation during the Liberation War, BRAC later expanded its activities into development work, including rural credit, education and health care. BRAC is best known for its informal primary-education programme, which supplements the government primary system by catching those in rural areas, particularly girls. The teaching method is participatory, with students divided into groups of six. Students learn from each other, with the teacher (usually a woman) acting as a facilitator.

Today, BRAC has an enormous presence. There are 34,000 schools in operation with around 1.1 million enrolments. A significant number of BRAC graduates enter public schools at an advanced level. However, not everyone is happy with BRAC. Some conservative Muslim clerics have accused the programme of being Christian and have even instigated the tearing down of schools. Their real gripe seems to be that BRAC is educating women. Despite this, the programme's success has drawn such international attention that BRAC is now branching out to help organisations in other developing countries, especially in Africa, to do the same.

---

| 1982 | 1991 |
|---|---|
| General Ershad assumes presidency in coup, stepping down in 1990 following mass protests | Tidal wave kills between 140,000 and 200,000 people |

Ershad pledging a return to parliamentary rule within two years. As Zia had done, he formed his own political party, the Jatiya Party. The pledge to hold elections was never honoured. Though the country progressed economically during the late 1980s, in early 1990 the economy began to unravel and massive rallies and hartals (strikes) were held.

See Amnesty International (www.amnesty.org) for reports on human rights in Bangladesh.

Zia's wife, Begum Khaleda Zia, who had no political experience, was put forward as the head of the BNP. Her steadfast call for Ershad's resignation created support. Ershad resigned and soon after was jailed and convicted for corruption and illegal possession of weapons.

The ensuing election campaign was reasonably free and open. The Awami League won about 33% of the vote compared to the BNP's 31%, but the BNP won about 35 more seats in parliament. Begum Khaleda Zia became prime minister in 1991.

David Bornstein's *The Price of a Dream* is an ambitious and lively insight into the Grameen Bank's creditors and critics. It's a good choice if you want to learn about micro-credit, development, the workings of Grameen and the tapestry of issues surrounding it.

Never fully accepting the election result, the Awami League, headed by Sheikh Hasina, began to agitate against the BNP. A long and economically ruinous period of hartals eventually brought down the BNP government in June 1996, and the Awami League took power.

## CURRENT EVENTS

Khaleda Zia's Nationalist Party and its three coalition partners won the 2001 elections. Arguing that the elections were rigged, the now-opposition Awami League began parliamentary boycotts. Meanwhile, there were signs of internal fragmentation in the BNP, with President Chowdhury accused of taking an antiparty line. He resigned and was succeeded by Iajuddin Ahmed in September 2002.

In December 2002, two simultaneous bomb blasts in Mymensingh killed 17 people. In August 2003, two opposition Awami League politicians were murdered, triggering a spate of hartals. In February 2004, the opposition called a series of general strikes in an attempt to force the government from power.

The 'Battle of the Begums', as the conflict between Sheikh Hasina and Begum Khaleda is sometimes called, shows no sign of abating. It may be democracy but the endless hartals and demonstrations have prevented the country from achieving the sort of economic growth needed to reduce poverty and allow Bangladesh to join the ranks of the Asian tiger economies.

| 1998 | 2001 |
|---|---|
| 16 million people are made homeless by floods | Sheikh Hasina Wajed, daughter of Sheikh Mujibur Rahman, steps down as prime minister; Khaleda Zia sworn in |

# The Culture

## THE NATIONAL PSYCHE

It is Bangladeshi curiosity that you will encounter first, in the form of awestruck stares and a line of questioning that begins with your country, ends with your marital status and takes in your academic qualifications, opinion about Bangladesh and prediction for the state of the world. Enter another much-revealed characteristic: Bangladeshis are opinionated. It's almost as if Bangladesh keeps its finger on the pulse of the world to spite the world's apathy towards it. From American politics to Australian cricket, there are opinions aplenty.

Addacafe (www.addacafe .com) and Bangladesh Chat (www.bdchat.com) are frivolous sites dedicated to chat, gossip, showbiz and music.

The streets are the economic, social and political veins of human activity and engagement. Markets burst into life on back streets at night, students and businessmen stand on street corners to exchange ideas over cha, and politicians are held accountable by protestors on the main roads.

This eagerness to squeeze the juice out of all endeavours comes hand in hand with Bangladeshi pride. Bangladesh's bloody history is indeed a proud one. The legacy of ordinary people turned heroes resonates today to spur Bangladeshis on to shape their country's identity. You will be frequently asked, 'what do you think of Bangladesh?'. Regardless of your answer, you will be run through a check list of national assets from Sylhet to the Sundarbans, and regaled again with the history of the country's birth.

Fortunately, this national pride is not of the ilk that gives license to rest on the laurels of previous triumphs. Rather, it is a pride that is driven by a sense that while Bangladesh is economically poor it is intellectually rich. The right to an education is valued along with a duty to be educated. It isn't uncommon to be asked, 'What is your country?', followed immediately by, 'What is your academic qualification?'.

But, to the unprepared visitor, these traits can be as much overbearing as they are endearing, and the barrage of impertinent questions may blur the line between curiosity and intrusiveness.

Your 'all men are equal' sensibilities will be thrown into turmoil when a self-righteous businessman commands an employee to move an ashtray

---

### STARING

For most of us, Bangladesh is the closest we'll come to celebrity status. Anything unusual is a crowd magnet, be it a gruesome road accident, an angry protest or a humble foreigner. After a few minutes, you get the feeling that you wouldn't be met with more dumbstruck looks if you were dressed in drag and moon walking down the street (though I wouldn't test this).

It is not uncommon to have the entire population of a train platform mesmerised at the sight of you waiting for a train. A group of 20 spectators crowding into a restaurant to watch as you eat isn't out of the question. The 'saviours' who come to the rescue can be just as trying; they'll disperse the crowd only to stand there and stare for themselves. To put it frankly, all of this can be downright frustrating.

Keep it in perspective. You may be the most interesting thing that's happened for a long time. Every move you make is leaving an impression – make sure it's a good one.

Believe it or not, the best way to gain control of the situation can be to engage with the audience. Start to interact and you may discover that what was once a crowd has become company. But if you don't have the energy for conversation and can feel your rage-o-meter creeping into red, seek refuge in a shop. Chances are the shopkeeper will offer you cha…or summon his entire family to come and have a look at you.

slightly left of its current location. You will question the value of the Internet as an educational and communication tool when you are surrounded by mesmerised porn junkies in a cybercafé. Your Zen-like patience will morph into rage as a request that should take three minutes sucks away precious hours of your life.

But, above all, the prevailing impression you will have about Bangladeshis is their overwhelming and sincere hospitality. In a country where it is a privilege and honour to welcome you, it is indeed a privilege and an honour to be welcomed.

## DAILY LIFE
### Poverty
Circumstance always seems to be stacked against Bangladesh in its bid for economic security. The nation had to bear the cost of rehabilitating 10 million refugees and 20 million internally displaced people in the aftermath of the 1971 Liberation War. Crop failure, population growth, corruption, cyclones and floods continued to devastate the country, pushing the number of people living below the poverty line to around 83% by 1975. Today, nearly half the population still lives in poverty. Problems of inequality and unemployment are rife for Bangladesh's rural poor, who comprise the majority of the population. The current national unemployment rate is said to be around 40%, while 63% of workers are in agriculture. Unskilled workers make an average of Tk 80 per day, which in some way explains why 82.8% of Bangladeshis survive on less than US$2 (Tk 118) per day.

### Family
Even for city dwellers, there is a strong connection to the 'home village', to which they return on weekends or holidays. This is so pervasive that a likely excuse for your laundry not being returned on time is 'the room boy has gone to his home village'.

The extended family forms the basis of social and economic life in Bangladesh and remains a cornerstone despite the recent shift towards nuclear families. The head of the household assumes much of the responsibility and provides for parents, children and other relatives. All may occupy one house or compound area, establishing separate kitchens as the family grows and more independence is sought. When a son marries, his wife is brought to the family home and assumes the duties outlined by her mother-in-law. The family is a tightly knitted group, not only for economic and protective reasons, but as a major centre of both recreational and social activities.

Though rural lifestyles have remained largely unchanged for millennia, the small urban middle class live much like their Western counterparts. Young people from richer families are under great pressure to get a good education at a prestigious university.

## POPULATION
Bangladesh is the most densely populated country in the world, with a population of around 140 million. It is the 8th most populated country in the world, though one of the smallest in area: Bangladesh is 57 times smaller than Australia, but has seven times its population. By 2015 it's estimated that Bangladesh's population will be 183.2 million.

Despite these frightening figures, Bangladesh has actually done a reasonable job at reducing its birth rate. Where women of the 1970s were having around seven babies, today the average birth rate is around three.

**DID YOU KNOW?**

The subcontinental head waggle is a ubiquitous form of nonverbal communication. Waggling the head from side to side in response to a question may mean 'no', or 'not sure', while a single tilt to one side is a sign of assent or agreement.

Tiziana Baldizzoni's *Tales from the River: Brahmaputra* (1998) is a lavish coffee-table travelogue. Sumptuous photos and text capture the Indian, Tibetan and Bangladeshi lives that shape and are shaped by the Brahmaputra.

## TRIBAL PEOPLE

The tribal population of Bangladesh numbers almost one million. They generally live in the hilly regions north of Mymensingh, the Sylhet area, and more than 500,000 are concentrated in the wooded Chittagong Hill Tracts. Others live in urban areas such as Chittagong and Cox's Bazar.

The tribes living in the Chittagong Hill Tracts include the Chakma, Mogh, Mru, Murung, Mizo, Kuki, Bam, Tripura, Sak, Tangchangya, Shandu, Banjugi and Pankhar. The Chakmas constitute the major tribe here, and next to them are the Moghs, who are also found in Cox's Bazar and the Khepupara region near Kuakata. These tribes are sometimes collectively known as Jhumias, from *jhum*, their method of slash-and-burn agriculture.

The tribes that live in the Sylhet Hills – the Khashias, Pangous and the Manipuris – usually have their settlements on the hilly frontier areas. Some of them have become business people and jewellers in Sylhet.

The Garos (or Mandi, as they call themselves), Hanjongis, Hadis, Dahuis, Palais and Bunas live in the hilly regions north of Mymensingh, and in Haluaghat, Sreebardi, Kalmakanda and the Garo Hills. Some also live west of Mymensingh, around the Madhupur Forest.

Many of the workers on the tea gardens and estates are Santal and Oraon tribal people, brought by the British from the hills of eastern and central India. They are sometimes referred to as the 'tea tribes'. Their religion is a mixture of animism and simple forms of Hinduism.

Other tribal groups, such as the Kochis, Hus, Mundus and Rajbansis, are scattered in urban settlements in Rangpur, Dinajpur, Bogra, Rajshahi, Noakhali, Comilla and Bakerganj.

The tribes in the Mymensingh Hills were originally nomads from the eastern states of India, and those in the Chittagong Hill Tracts originate from Myanmar (Burma). They have distinct cultures, art, religious beliefs, superstitions, farming methods and attire. Many of the tribes are Buddhist, though some still retain their Hindu-influenced animist religion.

Many of the tribes still have very little contact with the outside world, but as modern civilisation encroaches on their territories, more and more of the younger villagers are moving to urban areas for employment. The Chakmas, for instance, now make saris and tribal jewellery and have established or joined weaving industries. They have begun to accept Western education and clothing, and even use Western medicine in lieu of herbs and mantras.

Found within the broad racial group of the plains people, who make up the vast majority of Bangladeshis, are subgroups who, although apparently integrated into the culture, continue to pursue strikingly different lives. The Bauls, for example, are wandering beggar-minstrels, whose sexual freedom and fondness for bhang (marijuana) are abhorred by the mainstream, but they are good musicians and are welcomed at weddings and parties.

Urbanisation is a big problem as job-seekers flock to the cities. Currently around 25% of people live in cities, and the three largest cities – Dhaka, Chittagong and Khulna – are starting to burst at the seams. Still, rural Bangladesh is only just beginning to feel crowded and, thus far, remains relatively free of slums and industrial wastelands.

The least populated area in the country is the Chittagong Hill Tracts, though the government is arguably trying to change this with policies designed to promote an influx of Muslim Bangladeshis to the area. Currently, the population of this 13,180-sq-km area is estimated at between one and 1.5 million people.

# RELIGION

Only Indonesia, Pakistan and perhaps India have a larger Muslim population than Bangladesh. Around 83% of Bangladeshis are Muslim, 16% are Hindu, leaving Christians and Buddhists to make up the remaining 1%.

## Islam

Bangladesh's Muslim majority is almost entirely Sunni. Although there is a vocal fundamentalist minority, the Liberation War affected the general attitude towards fundamentalist Islam. This is because some fanatics collaborated with the Pakistanis because they believed that rebelling against Pakistan, the 'land of the pure', was a crime against Islam.

On the Indian subcontinent, Islam was mostly spread by Sufis, followers of a branch of Islam from Central Asia. Sufism is a philosophy that holds that abstinence, self-denial and tolerance – even of other religions – are the route to union with God. Sufi missionaries were able to convert Hindus in Bangladesh with beliefs that have similarities to some branches of Hinduism. Major Sufi sects in Bangladesh include the Naqshbandhis, originally from Central Asia, and the Chishtis, which was founded in Ajmer, India.

*The Departed Melody* by former Chakma chief and member of the legislative assembly Raja Tridiv Roy is an all-encompassing account of the history, culture and political dispossession of the people of the Chittagong Hill Tracts.

## Hinduism

The Hindu minority was persecuted during the Pakistani era, and targeted by the murderous Pakistani army during the Liberation War. Since 1971, relations between Hindus and Muslims have by and large been peaceful, with respect shown for the sufferings of Hindu Bangladeshis during the struggle for independence. One notable exception was in 1992, when the destruction of India's Babri mosque by Hindu fanatics unleashed a wave of violence against Bangladeshi Hindus, an event captured in Taslima Nasrin's book *Shame*. Since Partition in 1947, many Hindus have emigrated to India.

It's worth checking out Hindu temples you come across in case something is happening, or just to meet people whose colourful cosmos is such a contrast from that of the austere Muslim majority.

## Buddhism

Buddhists today are mostly tribal people in the Chittagong Hill Tracts. A small ethnic Bangladeshi community also exists. The once-flourishing Buddhist culture faded under pressure from Hinduism before the arrival of Islam, but its influence lingered in styles of sculpture and the generally relaxed way of life. Some scholars claim that Tantric Buddhism, now largely confined to Himalayan countries, began here. Most temples and monasteries in Chittagong division reflect the influence of neighbouring Myanmar (Burma) rather than Bangladesh's Buddhist past.

## Christianity

Although there is a small Christian population, mostly descendants of Portuguese traders, there is quite a strong Christian presence courtesy of foreign aid organisations and missionary groups. Since overt pros-

---

**BEHAVIOUR IN MOSQUES**

One person's tourist attraction is another person's place of worship, so it is important to respect religious etiquette.

You may not be permitted to enter a mosque either because you are foreign or female (or perhaps both). Sometimes you may simply have to forgo close inspection during prayer times. If in doubt, ask, and be respectful of the answer.

If you *are* granted admittance, behave with appropriate solemnity and decorum. Displays of affection are highly inappropriate, as is smoking. Never step over or walk in front of someone praying. Ask permission before taking photographs.

A way of showing respect and increasing your chances of gaining entry is by dressing appropriately. Women, if not wearing *salwar kameez* (long, dress-like tunic over baggy trousers), should at least wear long pants, long sleeves and a headscarf. Shorts and singlets are inappropriate for men. Both sexes should take care not to rock up in dirty and/or tatty clothing.

elytising is forbidden by the Muslim government, these groups focus on providing aid and serving Christians in the community rather than attempting to make converts.

## WOMEN IN BANGLADESH

One thing you may notice quite quickly is the absence of women on the streets and in the marketplaces. All the shopkeepers, produce sellers and hawkers are men, and the outright majority of those doing the buying, the tea sipping, and the standing around are men.

Strict purdah, the practice of keeping women in seclusion in keeping with the Quranic injunction to guard women's modesty and purity, is not widely observed in Bangladesh. It is sometimes found in middle- to lower-class families, who tend to be the most conservative element of society, but most of the poorer segment cannot afford the luxury of idle females. The generally progressive upper class, with the benefit of an urban education, consider themselves too sophisticated to put up with it. Even in the absence of purdah, however, cultural tradition and religious custom serve to keep women 'under wraps', and relationships between men and women outside of the family are very formal.

The birth of a daughter is met with less fanfare than that of a son. The sum of a girl's training is usually directed towards the family, home, and eventually motherhood. Formal education is not a given, especially if there are sons who require the family's financial resources in order to be schooled. In rural areas, only 25% of primary-school students are female; a large percentage of girls are not enrolled at all. Most marriages are arranged by parents, and in rural villages the general marriageable age for girls is well below the legal minimum of 18 years.

Poorer Bangladeshi women bear the brunt of many of the country's problems. Numerous pregnancies, hard work and a poor diet mean that many women suffer ill health. Among the wealthier classes many women go to university and there are many professional women.

There are a number of development projects that are directed at women's concerns. These focus on training programmes about health care and legal representation and are intended to foster independence and self-sufficiency. There are also signs that the government is taking women's rights increasingly seriously. In response to increased public anger over violence against women, the government introduced a law in 2002 making acid attacks (usually committed by family members over marital disputes) punishable by death.

## MEDIA

The press in Bangladesh is relatively free. Newspaper ownership and content are not subject to government restriction and there are hundreds of daily and weekly publications, mostly in Bangla. However, the government does seek to influence newspapers through the placement of its advertising, one admitted criterion being the supposed objectivity of the reporting.

There are eight English-language daily newspapers. The ones with the most international news and, reputedly, the most unbiased reporting are the *Daily Star* and the *Independent*. The *Bangladesh Observer* is also fairly good, as is the newly launched *New Age*. Others include the *New Nation*, the *Financial Express* and the *Bangladesh Times*. Most cost Tk 7.

Satellite TV has revolutionised local television viewing habits, bringing up to 30 channels into the country, mostly entertainment channels from India such as Star (which brings *Knight Rider* to Bangladesh), Zee TV and Sony, but also CNN, Discovery, BBC and other European channels.

**DID YOU KNOW?**

The annual Biswa Ijtema, an international Muslim gathering second in size only to the hajj (pilgrimage) to Mecca, is held on the outskirts of Dhaka, usually in January.

Aamibangali (http://bangladesh.aamibangali.com) is a professional and informative site dedicated to the serious side of Bangladesh society and culture.

---

**RESPONSIBLE TRAVEL**

The relatively small number of foreigners in Bangladesh means that you are something of an ambassador, not just for your own country but for anyone belonging to the often homogenised category of 'foreigner'. Do your bit to make visitors to Bangladesh worthy of the respect and hospitality they currently receive.

Travellers should be sensitive to their impact on the local environment and society. Try to spend money in ways that benefit local communities. If you plan to visit Bangladesh on an organised tour, ask how the money is spent and whether companies employ local guides and staff.

Tribal people are quite vulnerable, not only to encroachment on their land but also to the undermining of their societies and cultures by insensitive visitors. Travellers should get the permission of local chiefs and elders to stay overnight in tribal villages, ask permission to take photographs and pay fair prices for handicrafts.

The Sundarbans (p89) is a particularly sensitive environmental region. Don't dispose of non-biodegradable waste by simply throwing it overboard, and try to ascertain in advance how the tour operator plans to deal with rubbish.

A few tourist-oriented shops still sell products from endangered animals. Think of how this item will be replaced if you buy it. Souvenirs made of tortoise shell, ivory and animal pelts will be confiscated by customs in your home country, and you could be fined or even jailed.

There has long been an illegal trade in antiquities from the country, in particular relics from the Hindu or Buddhist eras. Again, think of how these items will be replaced – by looting more of the country's heritage.

Prostitution is quite common in areas of Dhaka frequented by foreigners and the local elite. Because it is illegal it is entirely unsupervised by health authorities. Be warned that besides the health risks of such exploitation, the racket is controlled by the local Mafia. If you get robbed or worse, no-one is going to feel sorry for you.

Child prostitution also exists. Many countries now have extraterritorial child-sexual-abuse laws. This means that sex offenders can be prosecuted in their home country for crimes committed against children in other countries. At the same time, countries that have traditionally attracted sex tourists are now prosecuting foreigners for abusing children.

If you suspect that child sex offences are being committed by someone, you should act immediately. Check the End Child Prostitution and Trafficking (ECPAT) website (www.ecpat.net) for reporting procedures.

---

The national television broadcaster is ATN Bangla. It has nightly news in English, as does Radio Bangladesh. Bangladesh's first private television channel, Ekushey TV (ETV), commenced broadcasting in June 2000 but has struggled to stay on air. Check local newspapers for broadcast times.

Bangla2000 (www .bangla2000.com) is a popular portal to entertainment, sport, business and lifestyle links.

## SPORT

Cricket is enormously popular in Bangladesh, and Indian satellite TV broadcasts it practically nonstop. The national team qualified for the 1999 World Cup for the first time in 20 years, and became national heroes by beating Pakistan. This rare victory was the cause of national rejoicing, and the prime minister described it as the greatest day in the country's history. In June 2000 Bangladesh was granted Test-playing status by the International Cricket Council, allowing it to take its place alongside the other subcontinental teams – India, Pakistan and Sri Lanka.

The popularity of football (soccer) waxes and wanes. Football crowds can get as unruly as those in the West, with minor skirmishes escalating into major brawls.

The national sport of Bangladesh is kabaddi, in which two teams battle each other by capturing members of the opposing team. The 'raider' enters the opposition's half and has to 'tag' as many opponents as he can, while continuously chanting 'kabaddi-kabaddi' to prove he is not taking any breaths. If the opposing team manages to detain the raider in its half until he takes another breath, the raider is declared out.

Women don't play much sport, except for badminton, which is one of the country's most popular sports.

# ARTS
The people of the Bengal region share a similarity of language, dress, music and literature across the national boundaries. Weaving, pottery and terracotta sculpture are some of the earliest forms of artistic expression and the necessities of clothing and cooking utensils also provided a medium for aesthetic creation.

Literature, too, had an early place. Hindu and Buddhist translations and local mythology were preceded by theatre groups, whose rural wanderings date back 2000 years.

Sirajul Islam's multivolume *Banglapedia* covers history, politics and government, as well as the obvious and not so obvious elements of Bangladeshi culture. This complete library will adorn the bookshelf but encumber the backpack.

## Architecture
### PRE-MAURYAN & MAURYAN (4TH–2ND CENTURY BC)
The term *bangla* is associated with the indigenous architecture of this period. The bamboo-thatched hut with a distinctively curved roof, still seen in villages today, is known as a *bangla* and is the most ancient architectural form known in the country.

### GUPTA BUDDHIST (4TH–7TH CENTURY AD)
The traditional design of a stupa for this period consisted of a square plinth surmounted by a circular one and topped by a dome, which tapered off sharply near the top. Although excavation of sites at Mahasthangarh (p100), Comilla (p138) and Paharpur (p101) has uncovered evidence of Gupta occupation, the great brick temples and monasteries at Mahasthangarh and Comilla were already in existence during this time, and it is not known whether those at Paharpur date from this period.

### SENA DYNASTY (12TH–13TH CENTURY)
During this period Hindu temples were constructed with a pronounced Indian influence. Perfect specimens can be found in Puthia (p114). Much later, the Indian design of Hindu temples was replaced by purely local architecture. The temple in Kantanagar (p109) near Dinajpur is a good example.

### THE MUSLIM PERIOD (13TH–17TH CENTURY)
The Turkistan Khiljis period from the 13th to 15th centuries is noted mainly for its mosques, including the famous Shait Gumbad Mosque (p86) near Bagerhat and the Goaldi Mosque (p70) at Sonargaon. From 1576 to 1757 the Mughals ruled Bengal and altered the simple design of preceding Muslim architecture, without following the traditional designs employed in India. The best examples are Dhaka's Lalbagh Fort (p49) and Sat Gumbad Mosque (p51).

### BRITISH RAJ PERIOD
The most notable buildings constructed during the British Raj were the Hindu rajbaris – the generic name for palaces built by the zamindar (feudal landowners) – and public buildings constructed during the first two decades of the 20th century.

Although rajbaris are essentially very large Georgian or Victorian country houses, the cosmopolitan ideas of their owners were often expressed in a barrage of neo-Renaissance features, creating a mixture of styles. Many rajbaris are in ruins after being vacated at Partition. Two rajbaris are in excellent condition: in Dhaka, Ahsan Manzil (p47), which is now a museum, and in Natore, Dighapatia Palace (p115), now a government building.

*The Art of Kantha Embroi-dery*, by Naiz Zaman, uses drawings and photographs to explain the technique of *kantha* and give a face to the women involved in its production.

Most public structures built during the British era combined Renaissance and Mughal styles. Examples of this include Curzon Hall (p51) at Dhaka University, and Carmichael College (p103) in Rangpur.

Many government circuit houses resemble the British bungalow style, with high-pitched corrugated-iron roofs and low verandas. A good example is that in Chittagong, at what is now the Zia Memorial Museum (p122).

### MODERN BUILDINGS

The most notable modern building in Bangladesh is the National Assembly building (p51), designed by American architect Louis Kahn to incorporate bold geometrical patterns. The orthodox Islamic architecture of Baitul Mukarram Mosque (p50) is interpreted with very sharp and spare lines. At night it looms out of the darkness, looking a little like a drive-in movie screen.

## Folk Art

Weaving has always held a special place in the artistic expression of the country. In the 7th century, the textiles of Dhaka weavers found their way to Europe, where they were regarded as *textiles ventalis* – fabrics woven of air.

The most artistic and expensive ornamental fabric is the *jamdani* (loom-embroidered muslin or silk), which was exclusively woven for the imperial household centuries ago and evolved as an art form under the influence of Persian design.

Monica Ali's *Brick Lane* has received international acclaim. A beautifully written novel set in London and Bangladesh, the trials and tribulations of its multidimensional characters reveal the complexity of both Bangladeshi culture and human nature.

Needlework has become a cottage industry. Most well known are *nakshi kantha*, embroidered and quilted patchwork cloths that hold an important place in village life, the embroidery recording local history and myth. There are women's cooperatives that produce *kantha* commercially.

## Modern Art

The most pervasive form of popular culture, the paintings on rickshaws and trucks, are purveyors of history and myth. Many paintings are just rehashes of film posters, but some are fine examples of native art. Make an effort to look at some, before you get overwhelmed by the sheer quantity.

The turbulence of life in Bangladesh has given artists much to express, which they do with wondrous artistry and diversity. The Shilpakala Academy (p62), just next to the National Museum in Dhaka, showcases some of the finest contemporary work. The Osmani Auditorium, on Abdul Ghani Rd, also has good examples, such as Zianul Abedin's powerful depictions of famine.

## Literature

Best known in the literature of Bangladesh are the works of the great Bengali poets Rabindranath Tagore and Nazrul Islam, whose photos are displayed in restaurants and barber shops. Tagore received international acclaim in 1913, when he was awarded the Nobel Prize for Literature for his book *Gitanjali*. Despite his Hindu upbringing, Tagore wrote from a strong cultural perspective that transcended any particular religion. He celebrated 'humble lives and their miseries' and supported the concept of Hindu-Muslim unity. His love for the land of Bengal is reflected in many of his works, and a portion of the lyrics in one of his poems was adopted as the national anthem.

**BANGLADESH & THE NOBEL PRIZE**

In 1913 Rabindranath Tagore won the Nobel Prize for Literature – a momentous achievement that still resonates in the national pride. Years later, Amartya Sen received the 1998 Nobel Prize for Economics, largely for his contribution to welfare economics, including his work on Bangladesh.

Sen grew up in Dhaka, but was born in a school established by Tagore in Santiniketan. Sen claims to have been greatly influenced by the poet's rationalist and universalist approach.

In his Nobel Prize acceptance speech, Sen quoted Tagore as saying, 'Whatever we understand and enjoy in human products instantly becomes ours, wherever they might have their origin'. It would therefore seem justified to argue that while India considers these great men to be Indian, and Bangladesh considers them to be Bangladeshi, the contributions made by each transcend national boundaries.

The 'rebel poet' and composer Nazrul Islam is considered the national poet. When the country was suffering under colonial rule, Islam employed poetry to challenge intellectual complacency and spark feelings of nationalism.

## Cinema

Dhaka, or Dhallywood as the local movie fanzines call it, has a thriving film industry that produces 150 to 200 films annually. Every commercial movie follows the immortal formula of romance, comedy, violence and song-and-dance, often spliced together in ways gloriously free of Western notions of plot continuity. Given the ban on anything sexually explicit, movie makers are pushing the boundaries of what sexually implicit entails. They may not be high art but they are certainly entertaining, both for the audience participation and the fact that an understanding of Bangla probably wouldn't make them any less obscure.

Bangladesh Showbiz (www.bangladeshshowbiz.com) is a magazine-style gateway to entertainment gossip.

# Environment

## THE LAND

Although some geographers have divided Bangladesh into as many as 54 distinct geographical regions, the country's most obvious features are that it's very, very flat and the rivers are correspondingly vast. The two exceptions are the hills of sedimentary rock around Sylhet, which mark the beginnings of the hills of Assam, and the steep parallel ridges of the Chittagong Hill Tracts, which run along the Myanmar (Burma) border.

Bangladesh has a total area of 143,998 sq km, roughly the same size as England and Wales combined. It is surrounded to the west, northwest and east by India, and shares a southeastern border with Myanmar for 283km. To the south is the Bay of Bengal.

The topography is characterised by alluvial plains, bound to the north of Bangladesh by the submontane regions of the Himalaya. The piedmont areas in the northeast and the eastern fringes adjacent to Assam, Tripura and Myanmar are broken by the forested hills of Mymensingh, Sylhet and Chittagong. The great Himalayan rivers, the Ganges and Brahmaputra, divide the land into six major regions, which correspond to the six governmental divisions: northwest (Rajshahi), southwest (Khulna), south-central (Barisal), central (Dhaka), northeast (Sylhet) and southeast (Chittagong).

The alluvial river plains, which cover 90% of the country, are very flat, never rising more than 10m above sea level. The only relief from these plains occurs in the northeastern and southeastern corners of the country, where the hills rise to an average of 240m and 600m respectively. These hills have a north-south alignment. The highest peak in Bangladesh is Keokradang (1230m), which is about 80km southwest of Chittagong in the Hill Tracts.

Almost all the Bangladesh coastline forms the Mouths of the Ganges, the final destination of the Ganges River, and the largest estuarine delta in the world. The coastal strip from the western border to Chittagong is one great patchwork of shifting river courses and little islands. Over the whole delta area, which extends into India, the rivers make up 6.5% of the total area.

In all of Bangladesh the only place that has any stone is a quarry in the far northwestern corner of Sylhet division, bordering India. That's one reason you'll see bricks being hammered into pieces all over the country: the brick fragments are substituted for stones when making concrete.

## WILDLIFE
### Animals

Bangladesh is home to the royal Bengal tiger and other members of the cat family such as leopards and the smaller jungle cat. Tigers are almost exclusively confined to the Sundarbans, but their smaller relations prey on domestic animals all over the country. There are three varieties of civet, including the large Indian civet, which is now listed as an endangered species. Other large animals include Asiatic elephants (mostly migratory herds from Bihar), a few black bears in Chittagong division, wild pigs and deer. Monkeys, langurs, gibbons (the only ape on the subcontinent), otters and mongooses are some of the smaller animals.

Reptiles include the sea tortoise, mud turtle, river tortoise, pythons, crocodiles and a variety of venomous snakes. The voluble gecko, named for the sound it makes, is known here as *tik-tiki*.

## ENDANGERED SPECIES

The royal Bengal tiger is endangered and the government recently set aside three specific areas within the Sundarbans as tiger reserves, but numbers are low. See p89 for more information about these tigers.

Other species that are rare or under threat include Indian elephants, hoolock gibbons, black bears and the Ganges River dolphin. Reptiles under threat include the Indian python, the crocodile and various turtles.

Many of the diverse bird species are prolific, but some are vulnerable, including Pallas' fishing eagle and Baer's pochard.

Bird-watchers will enjoy *A Photographic Guide to the Birds of India and the Indian Subcontinent* by Bikram Grewal and Bill Harvey. It has useful maps and pictures and is compact enough to take with you.

## Plants

About 10% of Bangladesh is still forested. Half of the forest is in the Chittagong Hill Tracts and a quarter in the Sundarbans, with the rest scattered in small pockets throughout the country.

The forests fall into three distinct regional varieties: the tidal zones along the coast, often mangrove but sometimes hardwood, in much of the Sundarbans; the sal trees around Dhaka, Tangail and Mymensingh; and the upland forests of tropical and subtropical evergreens in the Chittagong Hill Tracts and parts of Sylhet.

Away from the forests, Bangladesh is still a land of trees. Lining the old trunk road in the west are huge rain trees, and every village is an arboreal oasis, often with spectacular banyan or *oshot* trees. The red silk-cotton, or kapok, tree is easily spotted throughout the countryside in February and

### BIRD-WATCHING

Between the natural and human problems of Bangladesh, it's difficult to imagine that the country is the habitat of more than 650 species of birds – almost half of those found on the entire subcontinent.

Tucked between the Indian subcontinent and the Malayan peninsulas, Bangladesh attracts both Indian species in the west and north of the country, and Malayan species in the east and southeast. It is also conveniently located for migrants heading south towards Malaysia and Indonesia, and those moving southwest to India and Sri Lanka. In addition, there are a number of Himalayan and Burmese hill species that move into the lowlands during the winter.

The Madhupur Forest (p75) is an important habitat for a variety of owls, including the rare brown wood owl, wintering thrushes and a number of raptors. The Jamuna River floods regularly, and from December to February provides winter habitats for waterfowl, waders and the occasional black stork.

The low-lying basin of Sylhet division has extensive natural *haors* (how-ars; wetlands), and during winter it is home to huge flocks of wild fowl, including Baer's pochard and Pallas' fishing eagle, along with a great number of ducks and skulkers. The remaining fragments of evergreen and teak forests are also important habitats, especially along the Indian border near the Srimangal area, where the blue-bearded bee-eater, red-breasted trogon and a variety of forest birds are regularly seen.

One of two important coastal zones is the Noakhali region, particularly the islands near Hatiya, where migratory species and a variety of wintering waders find suitable refuges. These include large numbers of the rare spoon-billed sandpiper, Nordman's greenshank and flocks of Indian skimmers.

The Sundarbans (p89), with its miles of marshy shorelines and brackish creeks, supports a number of wetland and forest species, along with large populations of gulls and terns along the south coast. Eight varieties of kingfisher have been recorded here, including the brown-winged, white-collared, black-capped and the rare ruddy kingfisher.

Overall the most exciting time of year for bird-watching is during winter, from November to March.

March, when it loses its leaves and sprouts myriad red blossoms. Teak was introduced into the Hill Tracts in the 19th century and the quality approaches that of Myanmar; it's much better than Indian teak.

Flowering plants are an integral part of the beauty of Bangladesh. Each season produces its special variety of flowers. Among them is the prolific water hyacinth, its carpet of thick green leaves and blue flowers giving the impression that solid ground lies underneath. Other decorative plants that grow easily are jasmine, water lily, rose, hibiscus, bougainvillea, magnolia and an incredible diversity of wild orchids in the forested areas.

*Intellectual conservationists will appreciate* Deforestation, Environment & Sustainable Development: A Comparative Analysis *by Dhirendra K Vajpeyi. As a part of its global analysis, this academic work takes a look at deforestation in the Sundarbans.*

## NATIONAL PARKS & FOREST RESERVES

There is a dismal lack of designated national parks, reserves and conservation areas in Bangladesh overall. With millions of people to feed, perhaps it's asking too much to lock away good agricultural land but, as always, the dilemma is that in many ways survival depends on intact natural areas. Unfortunately, due to intense human pressure, these are disappearing fast. To make matters worse, designated parks and reserves are not strictly controlled and blatant misuse, even by those paid to protect them, is an everyday occurrence.

**Bhawal National Park** (p72) Also known as Rajendrapur National Park, it comprises regrowth sal forest and open picnic spots. There are a few walking trails.

**Lowacherra Forest Reserve** (p152) A hilly sal forest similar in size to Madhupur Forest, though the species of wildlife varies slightly.

*ElNnews (www.einnews .com/bangladesh) is up to the minute, and has environmental and social links.*

**Madhupur Forest Reserve** (p75) A degraded sal and mixed forest with some remaining old growth. Over the past 20 years its size has been cut in half, but it continues to be a very interesting forest rich with wildlife.

**Singra Forest Reserve** In the Rajshahi division, well north of Dinajpur, this reserve is a fairly uniform sal forest with mixed woodland on the boundary.

**Sundarbans National Park** (p89) The finest natural area in the country, mostly due to its impenetrable jungle and maze of rivers. Located in the southern half of the Khulna division, it's part of the world's largest mangrove forest and home to the Bengal tiger.

**Telepara Forest Reserve** (p153) A mixed evergreen/teak forest featuring a sandy basin that is excellent for bird-watching.

## ENVIRONMENTAL ISSUES

Preserving the environment is not as much a priority as human survival in Bangladesh. The ever-swelling population and the growing scarcity of land forces landless peasants onto marginal forest lands and temporary river islands. Farmland soils are also being damaged by overuse, and rivers are being polluted by chemical pesticides used to boost crop yields. The water table is under threat as deep tube wells extract clean water for

### WORLD HERITAGE–LISTED SITES

Bangladesh is home to three World Heritage–listed sites. The historical mosque city of Bagerhat (p85) and the ruins of the Somapuri Vihara (p101) at Paharpur were placed on the list in 1985. Unesco considered Bagerhat a worthy addition to the World Heritage list because of the technical skill exemplified by the ancient city's infrastructure. Similarly, Paharpur, a renowned intellectual centre until the 12th century, was deemed a unique artistic achievement with its simple lines and carved decoration. The architecture of Paharpur has been credited with influencing styles as far away as Cambodia.

The most recent Bangladeshi addition to the World Heritage list is the Sundarbans (p89). The largest remaining mangrove in the world, and supporting exceptional biodiversity, the Sundarbans became Unesco's 798th World Heritage–listed site in December 1997.

## ARSENIC POISONING

As if war, floods and famine weren't tumultuous enough for Bangladesh, the 1970s also marked the beginning of its exposure to arsenic poisoning.

In the early 1970s people were relying on ponds and rivers for drinking water. The lack of sanitation at these sources was killing around 250,000 children annually. To address this, NGOs instigated massive tube-well projects to tap into underground water sources but, in doing so, neglected to test arsenic levels in the water. The presence of arsenic is a natural phenomenon, likely originating from the Himalayan headwaters of the Ganges and Brahmaputra Rivers. Bangladesh's special receptivity to dangerously high levels of arsenic has been attributed to its high quantity of arsenic-absorbing mud.

The battle over who is to blame for this crisis rages on. Meanwhile, more people than anyone seems to be able to count are dying every year. The social impact of this manifests itself in ostracism of affected people – children are turned away from school, and women are divorced and deserted. Physical symptoms (which often only show after a decade or so of drinking poisoned water) often begin with blisters on palms and soles, which may later become cancerous.

Needless to say, when you buy bottled water, always check that it reads 'arsenic free' and the seal is unbroken.

drinking, while in certain areas these wells are affected by arsenic leaching into the water table from the underlying bedrock (see above).

Annual flooding during the monsoonal season is part of life in Bangladesh. Some experts speculate whether the flooding is getting worse, and whether deforestation in India and especially Nepal, which causes increased runoff, may be the reason. Another theory holds that the river beds have become choked with silt from once-forested land, making flooding more severe. Regardless, there has been increased pressure to 'do something' and find a 'permanent solution'. Part of the problem of doing anything, however, is that the country depends for its fertility on regular flooding, and simply building massive dykes along river banks could be disastrous for agricultural output.

With the continuance of global warming, Bangladesh, as one of the 10 countries most vulnerable to a rise in sea level, will be drastically affected. Present predictions indicate the sea will rise by 8cm to 30cm by 2030, and 30cm to 110cm by 2100. A 1m rise in the Bay of Bengal would result in a loss of 12% to 18% of the country's land.

The Sustainable Development Networking Programme (www.sdnbd.org) is one of the most valuable sources of environmental, agricultural, social and developmental information.

Loss of land is just one consequence – severe flooding and reduced agricultural potential are almost inevitable. Seasonal flooding will become wider, deeper and more prolonged because a higher sea level will retard drainage. This will increase the salinity of ground water. Tidal waves during cyclones are likely to be more severe as well.

This is indeed a cruel twist of fate, since Bangladesh, as a poor, agricultural society, has contributed very little to global warming. Even with assistance from the Dutch, who are helping to devise a strategy to cope with rising water levels, the question remains whether Bangladesh will have the capacity to develop and apply the appropriate technology.

# Food & Drink

Bangladeshi food is influenced, like that of the rest of the Indian subcontinent, by the regional variations of its history. Bangladesh, once an outpost of the Mughal empire, now retains part of this heritage through its cuisine. Spicy kebabs, *kofta* (meatballs cooked in gravy) and biryani (rice mixed with chicken, beef or mutton) of all kinds are available. This tradition has combined to form a mix with the more vegetarian, southern cuisine.

*Bengali Cooking: Seasons & Festivals* by Chitrita Banerji and Deborah Madison has the approval of Bengali food aficionados. It contains a smorgasbord of recipes and authoritative insights into the historical and cultural role of Bengali food.

## STAPLES & SPECIALITIES

Overall, Bangladeshi food is not nearly as varied as Indian food, and many dishes begin to look and taste the same after a while. A typical meal would include a curry made with beef, mutton, chicken, fish or egg and vegetables, cooked in a hot spicy sauce with mustard oil and served with *dahl* (cooked yellow lentils) and plain rice. Rice is considered a higher-status food than bread – therefore, at people's homes you will generally be served rice rather than bread.

*Bhuna* (or *bhoona*), which is food fried for a long time over high heat, is seen on lots of menus and is usually meat in a rich, spicy gravy. Another common dish is *dopiaza* (literally 'double onions'), which is served with meat or fish. Finding purely vegetarian dishes can be quite difficult because in Bangladesh meat is highly prized. Ask for *bhaji*, which can be any kind of fried vegetable, such as squash or green beans. A mixed vegetable dish would probably be *shobji bhaji*. At fancy dinners an all-vegetarian meal would not be well received.

The three main forms of rice dishes that you're likely to encounter are biryani, *pulao* (fried and spiced like the biryani but without the meat) and *bhat* (plain rice). Rice and lentils mixed together and cooked is called *khichuri*. In restaurants chicken tikka is also common and usually served with Indian-style naan, a slightly puffed whole-wheat bread cooked in a tandoori oven.

Fish is part of the staple diet but as river fish become scarce, more sea fish is appearing on menus. During the summer, when storms keep fishers from the Bay of Bengal, sea fish served in restaurants is likely to be frozen and a little suspect. Make sure river fish is properly cooked, and beware of heads and entrails as they can contain some nasty parasites.

The fish you are most likely to eat – broiled, smoked or fried – is *hilsa* or *bhetki*. Smoked *hilsa* is very good, and is mainly available at five-star prices in big hotels. *Bhetki* is a variety of sea bass with lots of flesh and few bones. It's one of the best fish you'll eat and is served in mid-range restaurants along with prawn and crab dishes.

Beef is widely available, although the quality is low. Some cows are rumoured to have been smuggled across from India, leaving their 'sacred' status at the border, while others are imported.

Kebabs come in a wide variety including *shami kebab*, made with fried minced meat, and shish kebab, which is prepared with less spice and usually with mutton or beef.

A Bengali breakfast is usually *bhaji* or *dahl* on *rooti* or chapati. It's not always vegetarian, though – sometimes there's a lump of bone served on top.

The Bangladeshis have a sweet tooth, and there are many sugar-loaded desserts. One popular dessert is *misti doi* (sweetened yoghurt).

## DRINKS

There are very few sources of drinking water in the country that are guaranteed to be safe. Some expatriates say they brush their teeth in Dhaka tap water without problems; others abhor the very idea. People in Dhaka are advised to boil and filter tap water. In a restaurant, even if the water comes from a tube well, it can easily be contaminated by the glass.

It's possible to buy bottled water nearly everywhere. Because it's locally bottled, the price is not high (Tk 15 to Tk 20, Tk 25 in restaurants), but local newspapers have revealed that quite a few brands are made by companies that don't actually filter the water all the time. If the filter breaks, for example, they might choose not to jeopardise their business by stopping production. When buying bottled water from outdoor stalls, make sure that the plastic cap has not been tampered with in any way. Recycling takes many forms, including 'rebottling' water.

*Tea: Addiction, Exploitation and Empire by Roy Moxham is a sweeping and disturbing behind-the-scenes look at the tea industry. It reveals the blood that was spilt in Sylhet to make your cuppa.*

### Nonalcoholic Drinks

The milky sweet tea known as cha costs Tk 2 or Tk 3 a cup and is available everywhere. It's slightly better than the Indian version, as each cup is made individually, rather than stewing all day. This also means that it's no problem getting tea without sugar (say *chini na* or *chini sera*), but as sweetened condensed milk will be used it doesn't make much difference.

The magic words to get a pot of tea, usually with just one weak tea bag, are 'milk separate'. Miming a tea bag produces hilarity but not much else. Coffee is difficult to find and those who can't do without should consider buying a jar of the instant stuff in Dhaka.

International soft drinks, such as Pepsi, Coke and Sprite, are quite readily available throughout the country and cost between Tk 10 and Tk 20. Specify 'cold' if you want it refrigerated.

Fresh lime sodas are generally available at the better restaurants in Dhaka and at some of the top-end hotels outside Dhaka. Sometimes it's no more than antacid – highly recommended for an upset stomach.

Green coconut water is a safe and refreshing drink, and is helpful in treating diarrhoea. A whole young coconut costs about Tk 5.

Lassi, the refreshing yogurt drink found throughout India, is not as common in Bangladesh.

### Alcoholic Drinks

Every major town has at least one government-owned shop selling alcohol, but they're invariably hidden in very discreet locations (to avoid upsetting Islamic sensibilities). The 'selection' is usually only hard liquor such as whisky. In Dhaka, Chittagong, Cox's Bazar and Teknaf you can sometimes find Asian whisky and cans of Heineken or Tiger beer sold on the sly; the price is at least Tk 160 per can.

Hindus and Adivasis are generally not averse to drinking alcohol, typically their own brews made of rice. On the tea estates, which are worked predominantly by Hindus, the drinking of local brew, especially during festival time, is quite common. The liquor made in the Chittagong Hill Tracts kicks like a mad mule.

In the countryside you may encounter a drink called *tari*, made from coconut palms. When it's fresh it is cool and sweet, but when fermented it becomes the local beer. Many palm trees have a decidedly notched appearance due to repeated tapping. It is known as 'coconut toddy', but is only found in tribal areas like the Chittagong Hill Tracts. Kesare rose is the rural liqueur, made from date molasses. It is mixed with hot water and tastes like brandy or cognac. A bottle costs about Tk 10.

## WHERE TO EAT & DRINK

Budget restaurants are all very similar: they're plain rooms where men shovel down rice, *dahl* and maybe a meat curry, as quickly as possible. Notions of hygiene are pretty basic; extra rice might be served by hand, for instance. In low-end restaurants, it's rare to see women eating, but they are welcomed. Some restaurants have family rooms, often just a curtained booth, where women and families are supposed to eat. These offer a welcome opportunity for both men and women to go 'off stage'.

In Dhaka you can also find excellent Indian, Thai, Chinese and Korean restaurants, but outside Dhaka the only cuisine that you'll find besides Bangladeshi food is Chinese, or rather a Bangladeshi interpretation of Chinese, which you'll find everywhere, even in small towns. The prevalence of Chinese restaurants is something of a mystery, given that there are estimated to be only around 700 Chinese people in Bangladesh! Prices at these establishments typically cost from Tk 60 a dish, but can cost almost triple that in Dhaka.

BengaliSpice (www .bengalispice.com) is a well-maintained, colourful site with recipes and information for Bengali food lovers.

### Quick Eats

Breads and biscuits are available everywhere, and in some small towns they might be all that you feel like eating. 'Salt' biscuits are usually not salty, just not the usual extremely sweet variety.

Local fast foods are plentiful and rarely cost more than Tk 4 or Tk 5. Try to find them freshly cooked and hot.

## VEGETARIANS & VEGANS

Sutapa Ray's Bengali Cooking site (http://milonee .net/bengali_recipes/intro .html) exudes a contagious love of Bengali food and cooking.

The Bengali culinary tradition evolved on the basis of what was available and, given the scarcity of meat, vegetarianism was often necessary. This means that if you can make yourself understood, you should be able to find some delicious meatless meals. You may have to explain that by 'no meat' you mean any kind of animal, including fish, and that just a little bit isn't OK. Some vegetarians have complained of finding traces of meat in alleged vegetarian meals.

If in doubt you can always resort to fresh fruit, which isn't so poor a consolation, given the range. Major fruit-growing areas include the hilly fringes of Sylhet division, the Chittagong Hill Tracts and Rajshahi division.

Oranges and bananas are the most common fruits on sale in winter. Mango orchards along the banks of the Padma in Rajshahi division are said to grow the best mangoes.

## HABITS & CUSTOMS

Traditionally, Bengali meals are served on the floor. Each person sits on a *pati*, a small piece of straw carpet. In front of the *pati* is a large platter or banana leaf, around which bowls are placed. Tables and chairs are being used more and more, and certainly in restaurants.

For the uninitiated, eating in the proper Bengali fashion involves disregarding everything you've ever been taught about table manners. *Do* slurp, *do* burp and, above all, *do* play with your food. Eating with your hands is not only functional, but is also said to allow for an appreciation of textures before they are enjoyed by the tongue. Everyone has a different style of eating, some more graceful than others. Food is meticulously masticated and unchewable components like bones are discarded on the table. Try not to think of how your mother would react to the sight of a formally attired businessman licking his hands from his wrists to his finger tips. Just roll up your sleeves and get into it.

**DOS & DON'TS**

- It is courteous to use only the right hand to receive or give things. This is especially important when it comes to food. The left hand is considered unclean, given its use in the bathroom.
- You may break bread with both hands, but *never* put food into your mouth with the left.
- Water may be drunk from a glass with the left hand because it is not being directly touched.
- Always wash your hands before you eat – for the sake of courtesy as well as of hygiene.

## EAT YOUR WORDS

It's hard to get what you want if you can't explain what it is. For more on the Bengali language, including pronunciation tips, see the Language chapter (p188). See also the Food Glossary (p40) for more Bengali terms.

### Useful Phrases

| | |
|---|---|
| Do you have an English menu? | *ingraJlte lekha menu ache ki?* |
| I'm a vegetarian. | *ami shudhu shobji khai* |
| I don't eat (meat/chicken/fish/eggs). | *ami (mangsho/murgi/mach/dim) khete parina* |
| Could I have what that person is having, please? | *uni ja khachen sheta den?* |
| Is this bottled water? | *eta ki botoler pani?* |
| Not too spicy, please. | *moshla kom* |
| No more, thank you. | *aar na, dhon-nobad* |
| This food is delicious. | *khabar khub moja* |
| May I have the bill, please? | *amar hishabta deben?* |

### Menu Decoder

#### MAINS

**bhuna/bhoona** – food fried for a long period over high heat
**biryani** – a rice casserole, often cooked with chicken, beef, mutton and/or vegetables
**dahl** – yellow watery lentils
**dopiaza** – cooked with lots of onions
**hilsha/ilish** – national fish
**kalia** – a rich spicy meat curry, often with potatoes
**kebab** – small pieces of meat, skewered and usually cooked over charcoal
**kofta/bora** – ground meat or vegetables bound by spices and egg
**korma** –meat cooked in a mild yoghurt sauce and butter

#### SNACKS

**alur chop** – a fried potato cutlet
**chapati** – round, thin bread made from grilled unfermented dough
**chotpoti** – hot chickpeas with potato, egg, spices and tamarind sauce
**luchi** – deep-fried flatbread
**moghlai paratha** – a *paratha* stuffed with egg, vegetables and spices, delicious for breakfast
**paratha** – thick flatbread, lightly fried in oil or ghee
**puri** – deep-fried bread stuffed with *dahl*
**samosa** – a wheat-flour pastry triangle stuffed with spiced vegetables or minced meat
**shingara** – similar to a samosa but round and with a slightly heavier filling, typically spiced potatoes or liver

#### DESSERTS

**firni/paish** – rice pudding cooked with milk, sugar, flavouring and nuts, popular at Eid celebrations
**halua** – a common dessert made with carrot or pumpkin, butter, milk and sugar
**jorda** – yellow sweet rice with saffron, almonds and cinnamon

**DID YOU KNOW?**

In a Bengali meal flavours are usually fused by introducing the more delicate-tasting dishes first, followed by the stronger ones.

Bengali Food on the Web (www.angelfire.com /country/bengalifood/) offers easy-to-find and easy-to-make recipes.

**kalojam** – fried milk-and-flour balls, soaked in syrup
**kheer** – rice pudding with thick milk
**molidhana** – a milk-based dessert similar to *halua*
**pitha** – a blanket term for all kinds of cakes or pastries, including specific varieties such as *chitoi, dhupi, tokti, andosha, puli, barfi* and *pua*
**rosh malai** – *roshogulla* floating in a thick milk
**roshogulla** – soured-milk balls boiled in syrup
**shemai** – vermicelli cooked in milk and sugar
**shirni** – rice flour with molasses or sugar
**shondesh** – a milk-based dessert, one of the best available
**shooji** – semolina and almond and pistachio nuts

## Food Glossary

**bhat** – rice
**chamoch** – spoon
**churi** – knife
**dim** – egg
**glas** – glass
**gorur mangsho** – beef
**kata** – fork
**khasir mangsho** – mutton

**lebu** – lemon, lime
**mach** – fish
**mangsho** – meat
**morich** – chilli
**murgi** – chicken
**pani** – water
**rooti/naan** – bread
**shobji** – vegetable

# Dhaka

**CONTENTS**

## HIGHLIGHTS

- Spying on the river life in Old Dhaka by taking a boat ride from **Sadarghat** (p46)

- Taking a whirlwind tour of architecture through the ages at **Lalbagh Fort** (p49), **Sat Gumbad Mosque** (p51), **Ahsan Manzil** (p47), Dhaka University's **Curzon Hall** (p51) and the **National Assembly Building** (p51)

- Furthering your understanding of the country's past trauma and present pride at the **Liberation War Museum** (p51) and **National Museum** (p51), a multistorey insight into the cultural heritage of Bangladesh

- Shopping for handicrafts, cheap clothes and books while immersing yourself in the vibrant commercial and cultural life of Dhaka's many **bazars** (p63)

- Getting the hell outta there

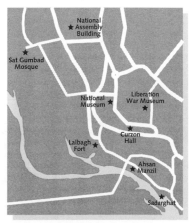

| ■ TELEPHONE CODE: 02 | ■ POPULATION: 12 MILLION |
|---|---|

Dhaka is charged with a raw energy that is at once enraging and engaging. Millions of individual pursuits constantly churn together into a frenzy of collective activity – it is an urban melting pot bubbling over. Nothing seems to stand still. Even the art moves, paraded on the back of the city's sea of 600,000-plus rickshaws, which throb with colour and restlessness even when gridlocked.

Many visitors find their first moments in Dhaka overwhelming. For sure, if you stand by passively and watch while Dhaka rages on, you will certainly become vertiginous with the unstoppable activity surging past. But if you move with it, if you climb onto a rickshaw and go with the heady flow of things, you may be surprised at how comfortable you can feel in a city that seems perpetually uncomfortable with itself.

If Dhaka was a man, you might not instantly warm to him, but he would linger in your mind as one of the most dynamic characters you had the good fortune to meet.

## HISTORY

Once a small town dating from the 4th century, Dhaka first received principal status in 1610, when the Mughals transferred the capital from Rajmahal to Dhaka, and renamed it Jahangirnagar. During the Mughal period Dhaka became the chief commercial emporium. In 1626 Mogh pirates and their Portuguese allies briefly took Dhaka, and from 1639 to 1659 the capital was moved to Rajmahal, leaving Dhaka as the administrative centre. This had the effect of encouraging a much greater concentration of commerce: maritime trade brought industry, Islamic education and increasing sophistication in the arts.

Dhaka remained the capital under the Mughals until 1704, when they moved it to Murshidabad. Under the Mughals Dhaka's prosperity was considerably enhanced – they built mosques, palaces, caravanserais (accommodation for camel caravans), bazars and gardens. This development began to attract European traders from southern India.

The Portuguese, the Dutch and the French all vied for influence with the Mughals. Armenian and Greek merchant families also arrived on the scene. Armenians concentrated on inland trade and pioneered the jute trade in the second half of the 19th century, until they were overtaken by British monopolies.

In 1666 the British East India Company established a trading post in Dhaka; however, Dhaka's decline as a trading maritime centre had already begun. The British East India Company extended its power to such an extent that by 1757 it controlled all of Bengal except Dhaka, which it took eight years later. It was under the British, during the late 18th and early 19th centuries, that the dominant forms of current economic development were established: indigo, sugar, tobacco, tea and, of course, jute. At the same time the other European powers were eased out – the Dutch surrendered their property to the British in 1781. In 1824, after almost six decades of indirect rule, the British finally took over direct control and administration of the city.

In 1887 Dhaka became a district capital of Bangladesh, and in 1905 Bengal was divided into east and west, the eastern section incorporating Assam (with Dhaka as its winter capital). From this point on Dhaka again began to assume some measure of importance as an administrative centre. Government buildings, churches, residential enclaves and educational institutions transformed it into a city of prosperity. During the existence of East Pakistan, Dhaka was classed as a subsidiary capital, and it was not until Independence in 1971 that Dhaka once again achieved its former capital-city status.

## ORIENTATION

Dhaka is not too difficult to figure out, though you'll probably have a different opinion when you're standing in the street.

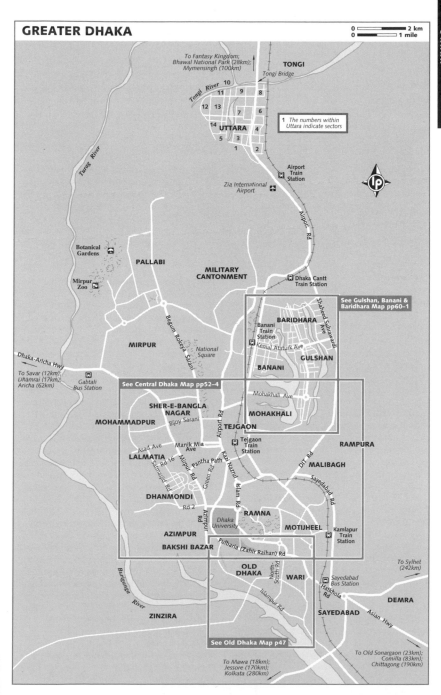

# GREATER DHAKA

0 ———— 2 km
0 ———— 1 mile

To Fantasy Kingdom;
Bhawal National Park (28km);
Mymensingh (100km)

TONGI
Tongi Bridge
Tongi River

10
11    9    8
12  13
7    6
14
UTTARA    4
5    3
1    2

**1** *The numbers within
Uttara indicate sectors*

Airport
Train
Station

Zia International
Airport

Airport Rd

Turag River

Botanical
Gardens

PALLABI

MILITARY
CANTONMENT

Mirpur
Zoo

Dhaka Cantt
Train Station

Begum Rokeya Sarani

See Gulshan, Banani &
Baridhara Map pp60–1

Banani
Train
Station

BARIDHARA

Shaheed Suhrawardi Ave

MIRPUR

National
Square

Kemal Ataturk Ave

GULSHAN

BANANI

Dhaka-Aricha Hwy

To Savar (12km);
Dhamrai (17km);
Aricha (62km)

Gabtali
Bus Station

See Central Dhaka Map pp52–4

SHER-E-BANGLA
NAGAR

Mohakhali Ave

MOHAKHALI

MOHAMMADPUR

Bijoy Sarani

Airport Rd

TEJGAON

Tejgaon
Train
Station

RAMPURA

Asad Ave

Manik Mia
Ave

Mirpur Rd

Pantha Path

Green Rd

Kazi Nazrul

Islam Rd

DIT Rd

MALIBAGH

Sayedabad Rd

LALMATIA

Rd 16

Satmasjid Rd

DHANMONDI

Rd 2

Azimpur Rd

Dhaka
University

RAMNA

MOTIJHEEL

Kamlapur
Train
Station

AZIMPUR

BAKSHI BAZAR

Fulbaria (Zahir Raihan) Rd

To Sylhet
(242km)

OLD
DHAKA

North-
South Rd

WARI

Sayedabad
Bus Station

Hathola Rd

Buriganga River

Islampur Rd

DEMRA

ZINZIRA

SAYEDABAD

Asian Hwy

See Old Dhaka Map p47

To Mawa (18km);
Jessore (170km);
Kolkata (280km)

To Old Sonargaon (23km);
Comilla (83km);
Chittagong (190km)

**DHAKA**

The city can be divided into three areas. Old Dhaka is a maze of crowded bazars and equally crowded narrow streets lying between the northern bank of the Buriganga River and Fulbaria Rd. It's brimming with points of interest for tourists, but not many facilities. The much larger 'modern' city begins about 2km to the north. The heart of Central Dhaka is Motijheel (moh-tee-*jeel*), which is also the commercial district. Major landmarks that can be found here include the National Stadium, the Shapla (Lotus Flower Fountain) Circle on Inner Circular Rd and the Raj-era Supreme Court, just north of Dhaka University. Beyond are the suburbs, including the cantonment and the upmarket quarters of Banani, Gulshan and Baridhara. These three quarters have the best restaurants, guesthouses and almost all of the embassies. There are also bookshops, travel agencies, banks and Internet cafés in this part of the city.

Most major arteries run north–south. Starting in the east these include: DIT Rd/ Shaheed Suhrawardi Ave, Airport Rd, Kazi Nazrul Islam Ave, the shorter Begum Rokeya Sarani, and Mirpur Rd. The airport is on Airport Rd between Uttara to its north and the rest of the city to its south.

An important road connecting Old Dhaka and the central area is North-South Rd, heading south from Kakrail Rd past the main post office and the Gulistan (Fulbaria) bus station into Old Dhaka, and leading almost all the way to the Buriganga River. The intersection of North-South and Fulbaria Rds is known as Gulistan Crossing.

Travelling around Dhaka is complicated by the fact that the main roads are known by the names of the areas through which they pass, and rarely by their official name. Adding to the confusion is the fact that side streets and lanes often take the same name as the nearby main road. If the driver of your rickshaw (three-wheeled bicycle-driven passenger vehicle), bus or baby taxi (mini three-wheeled auto-rickshaw) doesn't speak English, you'll be better off giving sections of the city or landmarks, and addresses only after you get there.

Between 5pm and 8pm the traffic jams are phenomenal. Friday morning is the best time for wandering around. Although few commercial businesses are open, a number of public markets and tourist sites can be visited. Some shops reopen in the afternoon, when traffic on the streets picks up.

## Maps
The best map of Dhaka is produced annually by **Mappa** (Map pp52-4; 112 Green Rd, Farmgate); you will be able to find it at most bookshops and occasionally at markets. The **Parjatan Corporation** (Map pp52-4; 233 Airport Rd) also has a map of Dhaka, which has enough detail to enhance your sightseeing experience.

## INFORMATION
### Bookshops
There is a great literary culture in this city. The Sheraton and Pan Pacific Sonargaon Hotels both have bookshops that carry international newspapers, maps and a few interesting books on Bangladesh, plus some recent blockbusters, though you will pay more here than elsewhere. There is a host of small but well-stocked bookshops on **Mirpur Rd** in Dhanmondi.

Other recommended bookshops:

**Boi Bichitra** (Map pp60-1; Kemal Ataturk Ave) Wide range of novels, blockbusters and arty tomes.

**Bookworm** (Map pp52-4; ☎ 912 0387; Airport Rd) Mostly fiction.

**Etcetera** (Map pp60-1; Gulshan Ave) Specialises in English-language titles. Also sells CDs.

**Narigrantha Prabartana** ( ☎ 811 465; 5/4 Ring Rd, Shamoli) A feminist bookshop and restaurant. For a nice change men must be accompanied by women.

**New Market complex** (Map pp52-4; Azimpur Rd) The bibliophile's fantasy. When entering through the main entrance, turn left and walk as far as you can: you will be surrounded by great bookshops.

**Omni Books** (Map pp60-1; ☎ 988 346; Gulshan Ave) Enormous range of English-language titles from Harry Potter to Kafka as well as Bangladesh-related non-fiction, maps and Lonely Planet books. Staff don't mind the long-term browser.

**University Press Bookshop** (Map pp52-4; 2nd fl, Red Crescent Bldg, 114 Motijheel, Dilkusha I Circle; ☾ 9am-5pm Sat-Thu) Also sells non–University Press publications, including a great range of titles from the excellent London-based publisher Zed Books.

## Emergency
**Fire** ☎ 955 6666
**Gulshan Police Station** ☎ 988 0234
**Holy Family Hospital** ☎ 831 1721-5
**International Centre for Diarrhoeal Disease Research in Bangladesh Hospital (ICDDRB)** ☎ 881 1751-60
**Police** ☎ 999

## DHAKA IN TWO DAYS

Ease yourself into the pace of Dhaka with a quiet breakfast in **Banani**. Head over to **Zia Uddyan** and the striking **National Assembly building** (p51). To get prepped for tomorrow's activities, head to the **National Museum** (p51), via Dhanmondi's **Mirpur Rd** for lunch. In the afternoon spend some time wandering around nearby **Ramna** and **Suhrawardi Parks** (p50), and check out the sights of **Dhaka University** (p51). At night head to **DIT II Circle** in Gulshan and choose one of the many fine restaurants as the setting for the post-mortem of your day.

Exploration of **Old Dhaka** is the only way to spend your second day. Start with an hour or so of boating on the Buriganga River from the chaotic **Sadarghat boat terminal** (p46). Then wander leisurely through **Ahsan Manzil** (Pink Palace; p47). From here walk in any direction and you'll find sights and unexpected adventures at every turn. Pace yourself with cha breaks and street snacks. Don't miss out on **Shankharia Bazar** (p48), the home of Hindus, and **Nazira Bazar**, the birthplace of rickshaw art.

Allow yourself some shopping time in the afternoon. Head to **Banga Bazar** (p63), the **Stadium Arcade** (p64) or **New Market** (p64). Wind down with an indulgent dinner on **Gulshan Ave**.

## Internet Access

There are several small **business centres** (Map p47) offering fax, telephone and photocopying. Some also have one or two computers with Internet access. However, you may have to wait and you're likely to have people trying to engage you in conversation as you type.

**Adda** (Map pp60-1; 3rd fl, Banani Super Market, Kemal Ataturk Ave; per hr Tk 24) Serves coffee.

**Big-B** (Map pp60-1; 2nd fl, Banani Super Market, Kemal Ataturk Ave; per hr Tk 30)

**Cyber Café** (Map pp52-4; Dewan Complex, cnr Elephant & New Elephant Rds; per hr Tk 50) Overpriced.

**Speednet** (Map pp60-1; 1st fl, Banani Super Market, Kemal Ataturk Ave; per hr Tk 25)

## Medical Services

**International Centre for Diarrhoeal Disease Research in Bangladesh Hospital** (ICDDRB; Map pp60-1; ☎ 881 1751; 68 Shahid Tajuddein Ahmed Sharani, Mohakhali) Has a traveller's clinic.

**Japanese-Bangladesh Friendship Hospital** (Map pp60-1; ☎ 818 7575; House 27, Rd 114, Gulshan)

**Pharmacy** (Map pp60-1; Banani Mall, Kemal Ataturk Ave; ☽ 24hr)

**Prescription Aid Pharmacy** (Map pp60-1; ☎ 885 0999; info@prescription-aid.com; 67/C, Rd 11, Block E, Banani; ☽ 8am-midnight) Friendly and professional.

There is a plethora of dentists in Banani, most of which are situated south of Kemal Ataturk Ave. We haven't had bad reports about any of them, and we've had good reports about those at **House 52, Rd 11** (Map pp60-1; ☎ 818 6789) and **House 28, Rd 17A** (Map pp60-1; ☎ 818 5107).

## Money

**American Express** (Map pp52-4; ☎ 956 1751; Inner Circular Rd, Motijheel)

**American Express** (Map pp60-1; Gulshan Ave, Gulshan) North of DIT II Circle. ATM.

**Citibank** (Map pp52-4; ☎ 955 0060-9; 122-4 Motijheel) North of Dilkusha II Circle.

**Eastern Bank** (Map pp52-4; ☎ 955 8391; Dilkusha II Circle, Motijheel)

**HSBC** (Map pp60-1; ☎ 881 7604-6; cnr Gulshan Ave & Rd 5, Gulshan) ATM.

**HSBC** (Map pp52-4; ☎ 711 3711-2; 1/C DIT Ave, Motijheel) ATM.

**Janata Bank** (Map pp52-4; ☎ 956 1593; Dilkusha I Circle, Motijheel)

**Pubali Bank** (Map pp52-4; ☎ 955 1614; 26 Dilkusha Rd, Motijheel)

**Sonali Bank** (Map pp52-4; ☎ 955 0426-34; Shapla Circle, Motijheel)

**Standard Chartered Bank** (Map pp52-4; ☎ 956 1465; Inner Circular Rd, Motijheel) ATM.

**Standard Chartered Bank** (Map pp60-1; ☎ 882 1718; 14 Kemal Ataturk Ave, Banani) ATM.

## Post

**DHL** (Map pp60-1; ☎ 988 1703-7; House 1, Rd 95, Gulshan) Courier service.

**FedEx** ( ☎ 956 5114; 95 Motijheel)

**Main Post Office** (Map pp52-4; ☎ 955 5533; cnr Abdul Ghani & North-South Rds) Near Baitul Mukarram Mosque. Parcel-wallahs (who sew up large parcels) can be found in a small shelter on the left of the building. Closed on Friday.

## Tourist Information

**Parjatan** (Map pp52-4; ☎ 811 7855-9; Airport Rd) National tourism organisation. Tourist brochures, car rentals and a couple of local tour options.

## Travel Agencies

**Bengal Airlift** Motijheel (Map pp52-4; ☎ 956 8277; 54 Motijheel Ave); Gulshan II (Map pp60-1; ☎ 988 6634-37; Landmark Building, DIT II Circle)

**Hac Enterprise** Motijheel (Map pp52-4; ☎ 955 2208; 5 Inner Circular Rd)

**Pacific Overseas Travel** Motijheel (Map pp52-4; ☎ 955 4661; 21 Topkhana Rd)

**Regency Travels** Banani (Map pp60-1; ☎ 882 4760; 18 Kemal Ataturk Ave)

**Unique Tours & Travel** Banani (Map pp60-1; ☎ 988 5116-23; 51/B Kemal Ataturk Ave)

**Vantage Tours & Travel** Mogh Bazar (Map pp52-4; ☎ 811 7134-9; Pan Pacific Sonargaon Hotel, Kazi Nazrul Islam Ave)

**Zoom Travel** Motijheel (Map pp52-4; ☎ 956 3505; Adamjee Court Bldg, Dilkusha II Circle)

## DANGERS & ANNOYANCES

The biggest annoyance in Dhaka is air pollution, which is up there with the worst in the world. On some days the city's air is a chewable cloud of filthy brown smog – a dense soup of lead, partially unburned hydrocarbons and construction dust. After a few hours in the central city or Old Dhaka you will have a new-found understanding of the constant spitting of the city's inhabitants. People react differently but itching eyes, sore throats and headaches aren't uncommon. Though the situation has improved since the phasing out of two-stroke baby taxis, the traffic that remains is horrendous and likely to get worse as the number of vehicles inexorably rises.

Bag-snatchings and muggings aren't unheard of. One trick is for a baby taxi driver to snatch the belongings of the unsuspecting rickshaw passenger, often through prior arrangement with the rickshaw-wallah. As in the rest of the world, pickpockets operate in crowds, of which there are plenty in Dhaka. Be a little cautious, particularly in markets.

Take particular care when withdrawing money from an ATM; it's a good idea to use Standard Chartered Bank's private booths so you can stuff your money down your pants before you hit the streets. Train and bus stations can be dodgy after dark, so try to avoid leaving or arriving at night.

Hartals (strikes) and accompanying violent demonstrations are common. During hartals it is safe enough to drive around the Gulshan area, and it is usually possible to move around the central city area by rickshaw; rickshaw-wallahs usually know which areas to avoid. Don't let your photojournalistic fantasies get the better of you – be curious from a safe distance. If you happen to arrive at the airport during a hartal, believe it or not, ambulances will be there to take you wherever you want to go (shame about the people who might actually need to go to hospital).

See also p157 for more about scams.

## SIGHTS
### Old Dhaka

Long after you've left, when you're retrospectively romanticising Bangladesh in your head, Old Dhaka is what you will think of. Time spent getting lost in its streets is time spent falling in love with this city.

### SADARGHAT & BADAM TOLE

If you have time to do only one thing in Dhaka, take a small boat out on the Buriganga River from **Sadarghat boat terminal** (Map p47; Ahsanullah Rd; admission Tk 4). The panorama of river life is fascinating. In the middle of the river, which is roughly 500m wide, you'll see an unbelievable array of boats in which people are bathing, cooking or just resting and observing, while hordes of people cross in small canoes, and ships ply up and down.

Along the river's edge you may also spot some of the ancient houseboats called *baras*. These worn-out boats, some half a century old, are popular floating restaurants catering to the poorest of the poor, where meals are served from 8am until midnight.

You'll find large ferries stationed there during the day, many heading south to Barisal in the evening. Among the large ships are the tiny wooden ones that you can hire. These are almost anywhere along the waterfront, so it isn't essential to enter the boat

---

**TAKA TOUR**

A good way of seeing the sights of Dhaka is to do a 'taka tour'. Visit Dhaka University's **Central Shaheed Minar** (p51), as depicted on the Tk 2 note, **Baitul Mukarram Mosque** (p50), which is on the Tk 10, the **National Assembly Building** (p51), as seen on the Tk 50 note, and the **Sitara Mosque** (Star Mosque; p48), as seen on the Tk 100. You could say it will be time well spent.

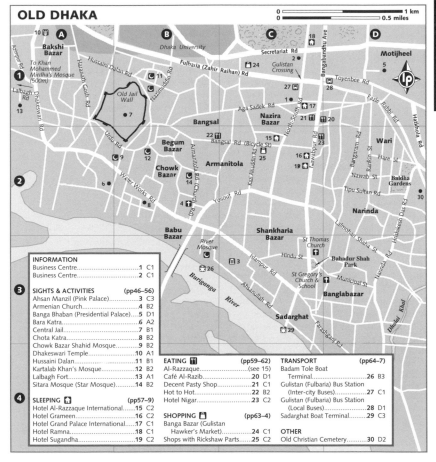

OLD DHAKA

INFORMATION
Business Centre...................................1 C1
Business Centre...................................2 C1

SIGHTS & ACTIVITIES           (pp46–56)
Ahsan Manzil (Pink Palace).................3 C3
Armenian Church................................4 B2
Banga Bhaban (Presidential Palace)....5 D1
Bara Katra...........................................6 A2
Central Jail..........................................7 B1
Chota Katra.........................................8 B2
Chowk Bazar Shahid Mosque............9 B2
Dhakeswari Temple............................10 A1
Hussaini Dalan...................................11 B1
Kartalab Khan's Mosque.....................12 B2
Lalbagh Fort.......................................13 A1
Sitara Mosque (Star Mosque)............14 B2

SLEEPING                        (pp57–9)
Hotel Al-Razzaque International.......15 C2
Hotel Grameen...................................16 C2
Hotel Grand Palace International......17 C1
Hotel Ramna......................................18 C1
Hotel Sugandha.................................19 C2

EATING                          (pp59–62)
Al-Razzaque.............................(see 15)
Café Al-Razib...........................20 D1
Decent Pasty Shop..................21 C1
Hot to Hot...............................22 B2
Hotel Nigar..............................23 C2

SHOPPING                        (pp63–4)
Banga Bazar (Gulistan
  Hawker's Market)..............24 C1
Shops with Rickshaw Parts......25 C2

TRANSPORT                      (pp64–7)
Badam Tole Boat
  Terminal..............................26 B3
Gulistan (Fulbaria) Bus Station
  (Inter-city Buses).................27 C1
Gulistan (Fulbaria) Bus Station
  (Local Buses).......................28 D1
Sadarghat Boat Terminal.........29 C3

OTHER
Old Christian Cemetery...........30 D2

terminal, but it is interesting. Bargaining can be difficult because the boat owner is unlikely to understand your itinerary. A reasonable price would be Tk 50 per hour. Foreigners are rarely seen doing this, so not all boat operators will demand an outrageous fee. Still, expectations may be rising.

## AHSAN MANZIL
About 600m west of Sadarghat is **Ahsan Manzil** (Pink Palace; Map p47; Ahsanullah Rd; admission Tk 2; 10.30am-4.30pm Sat-Wed, 4-7pm Fri), one of the most interesting buildings in Dhaka and a must see. The interior of the building is one of the few to be furnished in the style of the era in which it was built, but the exterior of the building is the real highlight, and

the views over the busy Buriganga River are superb.

Dating from 1872, Ahsan Manzil was built on the site of an old French factory by Nawab Abdul Ghani, the city's wealthiest zamindar (landowner). Some 16 years after the palace's construction, it was damaged by a tornado. It was altered in the restoration, becoming even grander than before. Lord Curzon stayed here whenever he came to visit. After the death of the nawab and his son, the family fortune was dispersed and the palace eventually fell into disrepair. It was saved from oblivion by massive restoration in the late 1980s, aided by photos of each of the 23 rooms, taken during the high point of the palace's history. The photos are still on display.

The admission fee will be the best Tk 2 you spend in Dhaka (although the tea is also very good).

## SHANKHARIA BAZAR

Often called **Hindu St** (Map p47) by foreigners, this is without doubt the most fascinating street in Dhaka. It contains an interesting row of ancient houses sheltering countless *shankharis* (Hindu artisans), most notably the conch-shell bangle makers. Bright coloured saris hang overhead like a multicoloured sky and bright orange marigold chains hang about like curtains, giving Shankharia a perpetual air of festivity.

*Shankharis* first came here over 300 years ago, but these days their art is slowly dying out. If you pass a shop and hear some faint grinding sounds out the back, ask to see the tiny quarters where they make the jewellery; some owners will be delighted to show you around. Other artisans on the street include drum makers, gravestone carvers, wedding-hat vendors and kite sellers. Any day is good for visiting, including Friday, which is a work day for *shankharis*.

To find it head north along Nawabpur Rd from Sadarghat. After two long blocks you'll pass a small square on your right called Bahadur Shah Park, which has a cenotaph to commemorate the Indian Uprising of 1857. From the northwestern corner, cross the street and head west, parallel to the river. After 100m you'll come to some small shops selling tombstones – that's the beginning. It continues for about 400m until it merges with Islampur Rd.

## ARMENIAN CHURCH

About 1km northwest of Sadarghat, and north of Badam Tole, is an area called Armanitola, named after the Armenian colony that settled here in the late 17th century.

The **Armenian Church of the Holy Resurrection** (Map p47; Armanitola Rd), which dates from 1781, is an oasis of tranquillity in the heart of the crowded city. During the course of the Liberation War, the silver setting and organ were stolen and many of the graves were desecrated. Mr Martin ( ☎ 731 6953), who took over as caretaker in the mid-1980s, has done much to restore it, and delights in giving personal tours. There are postcards of the church that can be taken in exchange for a donation, but there is no pressure placed on you to do so.

The Armenian archbishop from Australia comes here about twice a year to hold ceremonies, which is by far the best time to visit. It is open so long as the caretaker is around. From Badam Tole head north for two blocks to Islampur Rd, then left for one block and right for another. If it's locked when you arrive, be patient and passers-by will fetch the caretaker.

## SITARA MOSQUE

About 350m north of the Armenian church, on the same street, you'll come to **Sitara Mosque** (Star Mosque; Map p47), one of the

---

### NAWAB ABDUL GHANI

Nawab Ghani, born in 1830 of Kashmiri descent, was the most influential person in East Bengal in the last half of the 19th century. Unlike most zamindars, the nawab was Muslim. Ghani, his son, Nawab Ahsanullah, and his grandson, Salimullah Bahadur, contributed greatly to Dhaka's development. Along with elephants, horses, boats and other materials donated to the British government, they also contributed large sums to local colleges. As Ghani's land holdings grew to include most of Dhaka, he ruled like a king.

Politically astute, Ghani participated in both Hindu and Muslim festivals and both groups admired him. He also introduced professional horse racing to Dhaka. When he returned from a voyage to Calcutta by steamer, flags were flown along the river, a band played lively tunes and guns were fired.

The demise of the family occurred when Ahsanullah, for whom Ahsan Manzil (Pink Palace) was named, died suddenly in 1901 without a will. Under Islamic law the monolithic estate was broken into nine parts and his son, Salimullah, received only one. Salimullah, although residing at the Pink Palace, was reduced to being a relatively poor man. Nevertheless, he contributed more to Muslim schools than anyone in the city's history, and founded Dhaka Medical School. Because of this he is revered today perhaps even more than his illustrious grandfather.

city's most popular tourist attractions because of its striking mosaic decoration of coloured glass set in white tiles. The mosque dates from the early 18th century, but has been radically altered. It was originally built in the typical Mughal style, with four corner towers. Around 50 years ago a local businessman financed its redecoration with Japanese and English china tiles and the major addition of a new veranda. If you look hard you can see tiles illustrated with pictures of Mt Fuji. Sitara Mosque is pictured on the Tk 100 note.

### BARA KATRA & CHOTA KATRA
These are two of the oldest buildings in Dhaka, which is why they're in most tourist brochures. These Mughal-era structures are very dilapidated, especially Chota Katra. **Bara Katra** (Map p47), once a palace of monumental dimensions, was built in 1644 and now has a street running through its arched entrance. While only a small portion of the original structure is still standing, the building is still occupied and has a small prayer room on top. If you walk up to the roof, three storeys up, you can get some excellent views of Old Dhaka.

**Chota Katra** (Map p47), which dates from 1663, was a caravanserai for visiting merchants. It was similar in design to Bara Katra, but there's not much left.

To find Bara Katra head west along Water Works Rd (the continuation of Islampur Rd) to the landmark **Chowk Bazar Shahid Mosque**, which has a very tall red-brick tower – you can't miss it. Bara Katra is located 100m south of the mosque, towards the river. Finding Chota Katra is a little more difficult. From Bara Katra head south and take the first left. Follow this road for a few hundred metres and Chota Katra is along a street to your left.

### LALBAGH FORT
Along with Sadarghat, **Lalbagh Fort** (Map p47; admission Tk 10;  10am-5pm Sun-Wed, 2.30-5.30pm Fri Nov-Mar, 10.30am-5.30pm Sun-Wed, 3-6pm Sun Apr-Oct, closed holidays) is one of the best places to begin a tour of the old city. It appears larger on the inside than its walled exterior would suggest. The grounds themselves also offer surprising views of the surrounding city.

Construction of the fort began in 1677 under the auspices of Prince Mohammed

Azam, third son of Aurangzeb, who handed it to Shaista Khan for completion. The death of Khan's daughter, Pari Bibi (Fair Lady), was considered such a bad omen that the fort was never completed. However, three architectural monuments within the complex – Diwan (Hall of Audience), Mausoleum of Pari Bibi and Quilla Mosque – all in the *bangla*-Mughal style of architecture, were finished in 1684.

On the eastern side of the fort, to your far left as you enter, is the residence of the governor containing the Hall of Audience. It's an elegant two-storey structure. Inside there's a small museum of Mughal paintings and calligraphy, along with swords and firearms. Beyond the Hall of Audience, on the western side, a massive arched doorway leads to the central square *hammam* (a place for having baths and massages, and going to the toilet).

The middle building, the Mausoleum of Pari Bibi, is the only Bangladeshi building in which black basalt and white marble (from Bangladesh), and encaustic tiles of various colours have been used to decorate an interior. The inside central chamber, where Pari Bibi is buried, is entirely veneered in white marble.

You'll find Lalbagh Fort near the intersection of Dhakeswari and Azimpur Rds.

### KHAN MOHAMMED MIRDHA'S MOSQUE
Some 500m west of Lalbagh Fort, on Lalbagh Rd, is **Khan Mohammed Mirdha's Mosque**. Erected in 1706, this Mughal structure is stylistically similar to Lalbagh Fort. It is built on a raised platform, up a flight of 25 steps. Three squat domes, with pointed minarets at each corner, dominate the rectangular roof. To get a good view of this walled mosque, enter the main gate off the main road. Unfortunately, unless you're here during prayer times (around 1 pm), you'll probably find the gate locked.

### DHAKESWARI TEMPLE
About 1km northeast of Lalbagh Fort, up a short alley off Dhakeswari Rd, is the city's main **Hindu temple** (Map pp52–4), dating from the 12th century. There are two sets of buildings. The one often seen in tourist photos consists of four adjoining *rekha* temples (buildings with a square sanctum on a raised platform with mouldings on the

walls) covered by tall pyramidal roofs of the typical curvilinear *bangla* (bamboo-thatched hut with curved roof) style. It's nothing special, but it is colourful and you are likely to find some long-haired sadhus (itinerant holy men) hanging around smoking ganja.

### HUSSAINI DALAN

A block north of the Central Jail, on Hussaini Dalan Rd in Bakshi Bazar, is a **historic building** (Map p47) that looks more like a Hindu rajbari (zamindari palace) than an Islamic building. It was built in the 18th century, near the end of the Mughal period, as the house of the imam of the Shi'ia community; the Ashura festival, on the 10th day of the Islamic month of Muharram, is celebrated here (see p159).

Though the architecture seems baroque in inspiration, the original building was purely Mughal. It changed somewhat with restorations after the 1897 earthquake, when the roof collapsed. You can see a silver filigree model of the original building in the National Museum (p51).

### BANGA BHABAN

The **official residence** (Map p47) of the president, the country's titular head, is just south of the modern commercial district of Motijheel. It's a grand palace built in Mughal-style architecture, which unfortunately you will only be able to glimpse from the outside. Photography, even of the gate, is forbidden.

### BALDHA GARDENS

At the eastern end of Tipu Sultan Rd, and a block south of Hatkhola Rd, the **Baldha Gardens** (Map p47; admission Tk 5; ☿ 9am-5pm Sat-Thu, closed at lunch) in Wari provide a nice break from the rest of the sightseeing you'll be doing in the area. The two walled enclosures, Cybele and Psyche, were once the private gardens of Narendra Narayan Roy, a wealthy zamindar whose grandson gave them to the government in 1962 as a tribute to his family.

Started in 1904, these gardens have housed about 1500 plants and 672 species. Many of these are rare plants procured from about 50 different countries, including an Egyptian papyrus plant such as was used to make paper millennia ago, and a century plant that apparently blooms once every 16 years. The gardens are a bit whimsical – you can't help wondering how all that Royal Doulton got

smashed to make the free-form mosaic. Psyche has a lovely lily pond, while inside Cybele are the tombs of Roy and his son.

### BANGSAL RD (BICYCLE ST)

For a souvenir of Bangladesh, you can't beat rickshaw art. The place to find this art is in Nazira Bazar on **Bangsal Rd**, popularly known as Bicycle St (see also p64). This is also the best place to buy cheap Chinese bikes (about Tk 3500) and spare parts.

The street begins 700m south of Gulistan bus station, heading west from North-South Rd, a block south of the well-marked Hotel Al-Razzaque International.

## Central Dhaka

North of Old Dhaka is the old European zone, now the modern part of town.

### BAITUL MUKARRAM MOSQUE

West of Motijheel on Topkhana Rd, the modern **Baitul Mukarram Mosque** (Map pp52–4) is designed in the style of the holy Ka'aba of Mecca. The national mosque only rarely permits non-Muslims to enter.

### DHARMARAJIKHA BUDDHIST MONASTERY

The largest Buddhist cultural centre in the country is the **Dharmarajikha Buddhist Monastery** (Map pp52–4), located east of Sayedabad Rd. It contains an enormous bronze statue and one marble statue of Buddha. There's a peaceful pond here too; bring a book and get some reading done. The monastery is open during daylight hours (vague, but true). Take off your shoes before entering the temple and don't take photos of shrines without permission.

### OLD HIGH COURT

This **imposing white building** (Map pp52–4), once the governor's residence, is just north of Dhaka University's main campus. It's the finest example in Dhaka of the European Renaissance style, with few or no Mughal features. Nearby is the newer **Mausoleum for Three Martyrs** (Map pp52–4) and, to the east, the better-maintained **Supreme Court**.

### SUHRAWARDI PARK

Beginning near the Old High Court and stretching all the way to the National Museum, **Suhrawardi Park** (Map pp52-4; ☿ 6am-10pm) covers an enormous area. This was once the race course where both the Bangladeshi Declaration of Independence and the surrender of Pakistani occupation forces took place in 1971. At night the park turns into something of an open-air market. Keep your wits about you – it's a family atmosphere but lurking seedy characters can quickly turn things nasty.

Northeast of Suhrawardi Park is **Ramna Park**, which is well tended and has a boating lake.

### DHAKA UNIVERSITY & CURZON HALL

Dating from 1921, **Dhaka University** (DU; Map pp52–4) has some fine old buildings. North of the Engineering University campus is the **British Council Library** (Map pp52–4) and further north, on Kazi Nazrul Islam Ave, is the **Institute of Arts & Crafts** (Map pp52–4), which has an art gallery.

On the main campus, south of the Old High Court, **Curzon Hall** (Map pp52–4) is the university's architectural masterpiece and science faculty. It's a fine example of the European-Mughal style of building erected after the first partition of Bengal in 1905. A red-brick building with many eye-catching details, it has an elegant façade.

Two blocks west, on Secretariat Rd and just north of the **College of Medicine**, is **Central Shaheed Minar** (Map pp52–4), built to commemorate the historic Language Movement of 1952.

### NATIONAL MUSEUM

A visit to the **National Museum** (Map pp52–4; Kazi Nazrul Islam Ave; admission Tk 5; ☺ 10.30am-4.30pm Sat-Wed, 3.30-7.30pm Fri) is a good way of downloading information about Bangladesh. If you're short of time, skip the top floor, which displays reproductions of Western paintings (no nudes, of course) and portraits of historical figures. Some of the exhibits are a little stale – the stuffed birds are looking more stuffed and less bird with every passing year. The cynic might also chortle at the unintentional comic value of displays like the 'Life of the Middle-Class Farmer', depicting two women labouring in the yard, while the middle-class farmer has a smoke on the veranda.

There are displays from Bangladesh's Hindu, Buddhist and Mughal past, and an extensive collection of folk art and handicrafts. One of the highlights is the collection of paintings and charcoal drawings by Zainul Abedin, depicting the 1943 Great Bengal Famine. The stark images of stick-thin figures in a scorched landscape, stalked by carrion birds, are very powerful. There's also a simple but moving display on the Liberation War. Exhibits include the first Bangladeshi flag (made by hand) and a Pakistani torture box, evil in its bland hi-tech design.

### LIBERATION WAR MUSEUM

This **museum** (Map pp52–4; ☎ 955 9091; 5 Segun Bagicha Rd; admission Tk 3; ☺ 10.30am-6.30pm) has been put together with enormous pride and respect. This moving display on the 1971 War of Independence is arranged chronologically, with English and Bangla newspaper reports, photographs (some of which are quite graphic) and various memorabilia. You can wander through at your own pace and will certainly come out having had an educational and revelational experience.

From Topkhana Rd head north up Segun Bagicha Rd; it's on the second street on the right. Contact the museum to find out about its cultural events.

### NATIONAL ASSEMBLY

In 1963 the Pakistanis commissioned Louis Kahn, a world-renowned American architect, to design a regional capital for East Pakistan. Due to the liberation movement and ensuing war, the **National Assembly Building** (Map pp52–4) wasn't completed until 1982. The building often features in books on modern architecture, and is regarded as among Kahn's finest works.

A typical Kahn structure, it's a huge assembly of concrete cylinders and rectangular boxes sliced open with bold, multistorey circular and triangular apertures instead of windows. The marble strips between the concrete layers have been likened to pinstripes on a finely tailored suit. The interior, which includes the octagonal Assembly Hall, features bizarre Piranesi-inspired spaces.

Tours are only by special appointment. If Parliament is in session, ask for a seat in the visitor's gallery; if you're lucky, you might be given one for a session several days later.

### SAT GUMBAD MOSQUE

Dating from 1680, **Sat Gumbad Mosque** (Map pp52–4) is the finest example of the pure Mughal-style mosque in Dhaka. The mosque's most notable features are its seven

# CENTRAL DHAKA

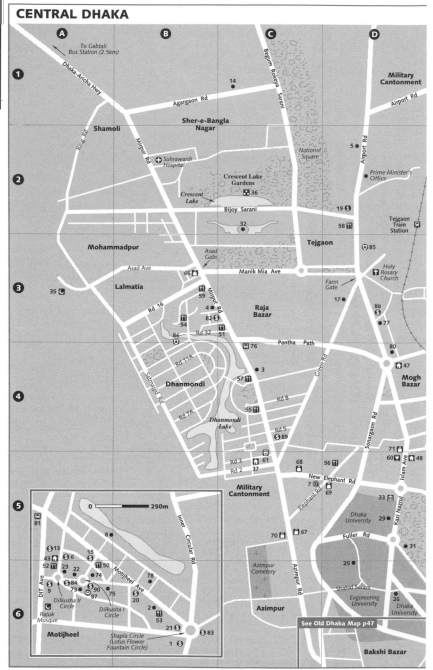

DHAKA

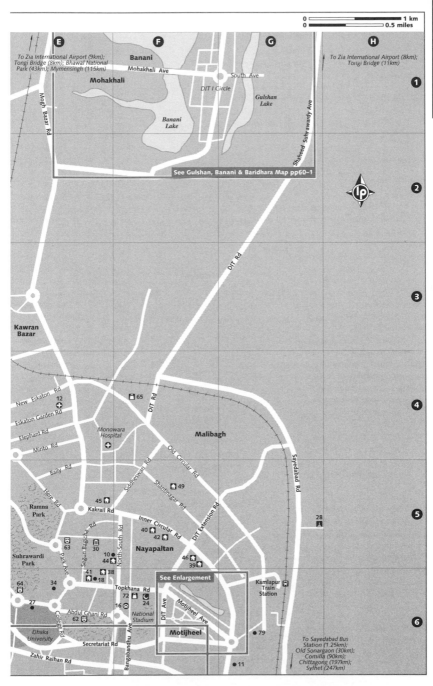

0 ——————— 1 km
0 ——————— 0.5 miles

To Zia International Airport (9km);
Tongi Bridge (8km); Bhawal National
Park (43km); Mymensingh (115km)

To Zia International Airport (8km);
Tongi Bridge (11km)

**E**   **F**   **G**   **H**

**1**

Banani

Mohakhali Ave

Mohakhali

South Ave

DIT I Circle

Gulshan
Lake

Mogh Bazar Rd

Banani
Lake

Shaheed Suhrawardy Ave

**2**

See Gulshan, Banani & Baridhara Map pp60–1

DIT Rd

**3**

Kawran
Bazar

**4**

New Eskaton Rd   12

DIT Rd   65

Eskaton Garden Rd

Elephant Rd

Minto Rd

Monowara
Hospital

**Malibagh**

Bally Rd

Hera Rd

Ramna
Park

45

Sidheswar Rd

Old Circular Rd

Shantinagar Rd   49

Sayedabad Rd

**5**

Kakrail Rd

Sagun Bagicha Rd

North-South Rd

Inner Circular Rd

40

DIT Extension Rd

Suhrawardi
Park

Park Ave

63

30

42

**Nayapaltan**

10
44

28

64

34

41   38

18

46
39

27

Topkhana Rd   72

24

Kamlapur
Train
Station

**6**

College Rd

Abdul Ghani Rd

16

62

National
Stadium

See Enlargement

DIT Ave

Motijheel Ave

Dhaka
University

Secretariat Rd

Bangabandhu Ave

**Motijheel**

79

To Sayedabad Bus
Station (1.25km);
Old Sonargaon (30km);
Comilla (90km);
Chittagong (197km);
Sylhet (247km)

Zahir Raihan Rd

11

bulbous domes crowning the roof and covering the main prayer hall.

Unfortunately, few travellers see Sat Gumbad because of its somewhat remote location. Getting here is quite simple. Head north from Dhanmondi on Mirpur Rd, turn left through Asad Gate and go to the end of the road (1.5km). Then begin asking; it's nearby, towards the river. Suitably clothed women are admitted.

## Suburban Dhaka
### MIRPUR ZOO
On the northwestern outskirts of Dhaka, 16km from the city centre, is **Mirpur Zoo** (Map p43; admission Tk 10; ☺ 8am-6pm), containing over 100 species of animals. As with many zoos in the developing world, this one is rather depressing, particularly given the animal teasing that goes on, which only adds insult to injury. But if you want to see a royal Bengal tiger, come here.

Take a bus from Farm Gate or Gulistan bus station to Mirpur via Begum Rokeya Sarani. You may have to take a rickshaw from the point that the bus drops you off, which will cost about Tk 5.

### BOTANICAL GARDENS
These shady tranquil **gardens** (Map p43; admission Tk 5; ☺ 9am-5pm), next to the zoo, stretch over 40 hectares and contain over 1000 species of local and foreign plants. It's a nice respite from the city's mass of humanity. In the distance you'll see the Turag River.

These gardens are probably the best place in the city for bird-watching. The quiet early mornings are especially good.

## ACTIVITIES
### Cycling
Because of the relative flatness of Bangladesh, cycling can be a relaxing way of soaking up the atmosphere, though cycling in Dhaka

itself is not advised, and is hardly relaxing. But not far out of Dhaka you'll feel as though you're in the rural heart of Bangladesh.

### TONGI-KALIGANJ RD

The crowded town of Tongi, 5km north of Zia International Airport, is a good starting point for a cycling trip. When you cross the Tongi River Bridge on the main road north to Mymensingh, go about 1km further north into town and turn right. Head east from there. For the first kilometre or so you'll ride past shops and at the 3km point you'll cross over the railway tracks, where you'll leave the town behind. The road follows the railway line, so you can cycle all the way to Kaliganj (20km) on the Sitalakhya River. From there the easiest way back is to retrace your path.

### TERMOUK RD

This is a somewhat more adventurous backroad cycling route that connects with the Tongi-Kaliganj Rd route via Termouk (tair-mouk). Heading north towards Tongi, about 1km south of the Tongi River Bridge, you'll pass the last red-light intersection before the bridge. Take a right (east) for Termouk (7km), which is a major crossing point (not a village) on the Tongi River. The brick-road route is not direct, so you'll have to ask directions along the way. At Termouk you can get a canoe to take you across the river; get off on the eastern bank. From there have someone point you towards Ulukala (ou-look-ah-lah), on the same bank several kilometres north. From Ulukala continue northward, heading for the Tongi-Kaliganj Rd, which runs east–west. That portion will take about half an hour and you must ask for directions (for Tongi Rd). During the rainy season it could be slippery.

## Language Courses

See Courses in the Directory chapter (p156) for information about learning Bangla.

## Rickshaw Rides

One of the best ways to see the sights of Dhaka is by rickshaw. The going rate is about Tk 40 per hour. Rickshaw-wallahs who speak English can generally be found outside five-star hotels, but charge around Tk 75 to Tk 100 per hour and expect a tip. Convincing them that sex and drugs aren't on the itinerary can be difficult. You may

find that you'll get bullied less into seeing things you don't want to see if you approach a rickshaw-wallah away from these tourist hubs, but you will have to do more navigating. An efficient way of arranging this is to find an English-and-Bangla speaker to convey where you want to go to your wallah before you set out. You can also approach a tour company to organise a sightseeing tour on a rickshaw. Most tour companies are amenable to this, and Guide Tours even suggests it.

## River Trips

There are several companies offering trips on the rivers encircling Dhaka.

**Contic** ( ☎ 881 4851; mail@contic.com; House 183, Rd 69, Gulshan II) is a river-cruise specialist with an elegant boat, the *Fleche D'Or*, which cruises along the Turag River, west of the city, down to the Buriganga River. Tour prices are US$35 for a half day and US$44 for a full day, including lunch and transport. Contic cruises get excellent reviews.

**Guide Tours** (Map pp60-1; ☎ 988 6983; 1st fl, Darpan Complex, DIT II Circle, Gulshan) offers a 4½-hour cruise Monday, Friday and Saturday, along the Sitalakhya River on its yacht, the *SB Ruposhi*, departing from Demra, a river town about 15km east of Dhaka. You'll get to stop at a village of *jamdani* (muslin-cloth) weavers en route. Swimming is also possible. The US$30 cost includes food and transport to/from Dhaka (minimum six people). On Sunday, Tuesday and Thursday the trip starts at 4pm, returning to Demra at 9.30pm with dinner served on board.

### TONGI RIVER BOAT RIDE

If you are keen to do some river exploration on your own, then Tongi is a scenically impressive and logistically simple place to do it. Amid the expanses of greenery you'll never sense how close you are to the city.

The motorised passenger boats plying the river are called *tolars* (toh-*lars*) and can take up to about 50 passengers. The launching point for the *tolars* is on the northern bank, about 300m west of Tongi Bridge (Map p43). Most *tolars* are headed to Ulukala (Tk 5, 1½ hours). From Ulukala you can return to Tongi by boat or take a rough rickshaw ride to Kaliganj (Tk 50, 70 minutes).

From there you can take a bus or train back to Dhaka or another *tolar* to Demra

(Tk 15, 4½ hours) on the wide Sitalakhya River. You could shorten the journey by getting off in Murapara (Tk 10, three hours) and catching a local bus back to Dhaka (Tk 10, one hour).

## Swimming

Nonguests can use the pools at the Pan Pacific Sonargaon (Map pp52–4) and Sheraton Hotels (Map pp52–4) for Tk 600.

## TOURS

**Guide Tours** (Map pp60-1; ☎ 988 6983; fax 988 6984; 1st fl, Darpan Complex, DIT II Circle, Gulshan), the company with the best reputation, offers half- and full-day tours in and around Dhaka. Half-day tours cover Sadarghat, Lalbagh Fort, the Liberation War Museum and other sights, and cost US$20 per person; full-day tours include Savar or Sonargaon and cost US$30 per person (minimum four people). Guide Tours also runs day trips to a pottery village near Savar (US$40 per person, minimum two people) and overnight stays in a village (US$75 per person).

**Parjatan** ( ☎ 811 7855-9; Airport Rd) offers three- and four-hour city tours by minibus. The three-hour tours focus on the commercial area, (including Gulshan, National Assembly, Dhaka University and various mosques), while the four-hour tours go on to parts of Old Dhaka including Lalbagh Fort and Sadarghat. Both are US$10 per person.

There are several other companies offering city tours and, at this stage in Bangladesh's foray into tourism, it's a good idea to give some of the smaller up-and-coming operators a go.

## FESTIVALS & EVENTS

One of the most exciting events to be part of in Dhaka is the colourful festival of **Durga Puja**, which occurs around the second week of October at Dhakeswari Temple to commemorate the victory of the mighty warrior goddess, Durga.

At around 5pm on the last day of the five-day festival, devotees parade their colourful clay-and-bamboo effigies through the streets toward Sadarghat. At nightfall the statues of Durga are immersed in the Buriganga, ending the festivities.

Around Durga Puja there's a colourful boat race on the Buriganga near Postagola. It's quite a spectacle and is inaugurated each year by the president of Bangladesh. Each longboat is crammed with roughly 60 oarsmen and the competition ensues amidst continuous clapping by the spectators. Advance publicity is poor. Contact **Parjatan** ( ☎ 811 7855-9) for details.

Another interesting experience in Dhaka is 21 February. **International Mother Language Day** commemorates the martyrs who fought in the 1952 Language Movement. Blood was shed at the Central Shaheed Minar to establish Bangla as the national language. Mourners gather at the monument at midnight each year to pay their respects with songs, prayers and the laying of wreaths.

---

**FANTASY KINGDOM**

**Fantasy Kingdom** ( 10am-10pm Fri & public holidays, noon-9pm weekdays; admission plus some ride coupons around Tk 200), the fantasy world of Prince Ashu and Princess Lia, is a US$600 million theme park that opened in 2002 to a storm of cynicism. Critics have expressed abhorrence at the worthlessness and inaccessibility of so lavish a venture to the scores of people who earn less than its entry fee in a day.

It is indeed easy to be pessimistic about the juxtaposition of Prince Ashu's castle with the rundown apartment blocks surrounding it. But Fantasy Kingdom is here to stay, much to the delight of the growing middle class.

A visit to this 50-acre theme park with its model dinosaurs and pizza restaurants may well be one of the most surreal experiences you have in this country. When wandering around this pristine pastel-coloured complex, it's easy to forget that you're in Bangladesh; until the sight of a woman in *hijab* (head scarf) on a Dodgem car reminds you. The roller coaster is the clear favourite. It doesn't go upside down but goes close enough to be almost as hair-raising as a Bengali bus ride.

There are bus-ticket booths at various locations in Dhaka that will take you on the hour-long drive to the toon-town gates of Fantasy Kingdom.

Bangladeshi New Year's Day falls in mid-April.

## SLEEPING

Accommodation is more expensive in Dhaka than elsewhere in Bangladesh, but it's still cheap by international standards. The highest concentration of budget and mid-range hotels is in the area extending from Inner Circular Rd down to Old Dhaka. Unfortunately most budget hotels in this area don't accept foreigners. There aren't any top-end hotels in Old Dhaka.

The best-value top-end accommodation is in the Gulshan area, but you won't find budget options there.

### Old Dhaka
**BUDGET**
Hotels accepting foreigners:
**Hotel Grameen** (Map p47; ☎ 956 2422; Nawabpur Rd; s/d with shared bathroom Tk 60/130, s/d with bathroom Tk 80/150) Near the Bangsal Rd intersection, Grameen is well signed and extremely friendly.

**Hotel Sugandha** (Map p47; ☎ 955 6720; 24 Nawabpur Rd; s/d with shared bathroom Tk 90/180, s/d with bathroom Tk 120/350) Characterless, but by no means unpleasant. The bathrooms aren't dry but they're clean.

**Hotel Al-Razzaque International** (Map p47; ☎ 956 6408; 29/1 North-South Rd; s/d with bathroom Tk 160/270) Cleanliness is encouraged by signs that read 'Cleanliness is part of the faith' and 'Do not spit everywhere'. Women have felt outnumbered and uncomfortable in this devout male environment.

**MID-RANGE**
**Hotel Grand Palace International** (Map p47; ☎ 956 1623; 11-12 North-South Rd; s Tk 200-600, d Tk 300-900) All rooms have attached bathroom, most have TV and pricier rooms have sit-down toilets and a fridge. Try to get a room with a window; if you can put up with the noise, the views over the busy intersection make for great people-watching.

**Hotel Ramna** (Map p47; ☎ 956 2279; 45 Bangabandhu Ave; r Tk 325-800) The more expensive rooms at the Ramna come with AC and TV. The hotel is big enough to escape street noise, and the balconies offer wide views over the city. Reception is on the 2nd floor but it can be difficult to find in the maze of tailor shops.

## Central Dhaka
**BUDGET**
**Asia Hotel** (Map pp52-4; ☎ 956 0709; 34/1 Topkhana Rd; s with shared/attached bathroom Tk 180/250, d with/without TV Tk 450/350) One of the few hotels on Topkhana Rd that accepts foreigners, the Asia Hotel is in a quiet location, is well maintained and has relatively large rooms. Doubles have a bathroom.

**New Hotel Yeameni International** (Map pp52-4; ☎ 831 8337; 2 Fakirapool, Rajib Mansion, Motijheel; s/d/t/q Tk 250/240/550/650) Rooms at this popular hotel are generally spacious, bright and airy and bathrooms are tiled and have squat toilets. Signs that read 'Be courteous' and 'Maintain your dignity' set the tone. You can also pay more for AC.

**MID-RANGE**
**Hotel Pacific** (Map pp52-4; ☎ 955 8148; www.hotelpacificdhaka.com; 120/B Motijheel; d with/without AC Tk 900/600, deluxe d Tk 1200) Hotel Pacific is the best mid-range place to stay in Central Dhaka; you walk in and feel instantly comfortable. Reception staff are as personable as they are professional and room staff quickly figure out how much space you need. Rooms can vary in size, but all are carpeted and have a hot water bathroom. Some even have a desk and a chair. The deluxe rooms have more space and slightly better furniture and linen. The Hotel Pacific's restaurant is popular with businessmen and families.

---

**THE AUTHOR'S CHOICE**

**French Inn** (Map pp60-1; ☎ 882 9474, 881 8733; House 97, Rd 4, Block B, Banani; economy/standard/deluxe r US$20/25/32, ste US$45) With its rare balance of class and character, the French Inn is one of the nicest places to stay. Just off Kemal Ataturk Ave on tree-lined Rd 4, it's a three-storey white building marked only by a small blue sign that reads 'French Catering'. The building is laid out in such a way that rooms are all different but similarly homely. If you can afford it, the suite is superb. It has a large bedroom, a sitting room and a separate eating area, two private balconies and a fridge. Staff are extremely unimposing characters, who give great service while also respecting your privacy. The French Inn also prides itself on its food. The rooms here are great value and, best of all, it feels like home.

**Hotel Eastern** (Map pp52-4; ☎ 831 4695; 12 Inner Circular Rd; s/d/q Tk 200/300/600, deluxe r Tk 800) This seven-storey establishment isn't outstanding but the beds are comfortable and the bathrooms are well maintained. The Green Line bus (to Chittagong) has its office here.

**Hotel Midway International** (Map pp52-4; ☎ 831 9315; hotelmid@aitlbd.net; 30 Inner Circular Rd, Nayapaltan; r Tk 500-1200) Staff can sometimes be apathetic, but the rooms are clean, comfortable and furnished. It's a few more taka then you'll pay elsewhere, but the difference shows.

**Hotel Mrigaya** (Map pp52-4; ☎ 955 4049; Topkhana Rd; s/d Tk 600/1200) This hotel has small rooms, but the bathrooms are tiled and the sheets are clean. Solo women cannot stay and staff aren't overly communicative if you ask.

**White House Hotel** (Map pp52-4; ☎ 832 2973-6; fax 831 7726; 155 Shantinagar Rd; s/d with fan US$12/15, deluxe s/d with AC US$25/30) This hotel has a business centre and restaurant.

**Hotel Royal Palace** (Map pp52-4; ☎ 966 6962; fax 956 6588; 31/D Topkhana Rd; s US$13-21, d US$18-40) Peculiarly located for such a nice establishment, the Royal Palace is clean and friendly. Bedrooms and bathrooms are tiled and have basic furniture.

**Ambrosia Guest House** (Map pp52-4; ☎ 836 1409; ambrosia@bdmail.net; House 17, Rd 3; r US$45) On the quiet corner of Rd 2 and Rd 3 in Dhanmondi, a convenient distance from Mirpur Rd, rooms here have a certain wooden-slatted colonial charm, though they're overpriced.

You could also try **Hotel Pritom** (Map pp52-4; ☎ 955 4564; fax 988 4339; North-South Rd; s Tk 400-800, d Tk500-1000).

**TOP END**

The big boys in town are the Pan Pacific Sonargaon and the Sheraton Hotels, both of which manage to create secluded worlds sheltered from the chaos of Dhaka while planted in the heart of it. There are new hotels opening in the area, which are quick to discount in a bid to build a client base.

**Pan Pacific Sonargaon Hotel** (Map pp52-4; ☎ 811 1005; www.panpacific.com; 107 Kazi Nazrul Islam Ave; s/ste US$170/760) Amenities include a pool, a tennis court, a squash court, a health club, car rental, a disco and a shopping arcade. The corridors (which are something of a let-down after the majesty of the reception) are equipped with security cameras, apparently remaining from a visit by former US president, Bill Clinton. Prices don't include tax.

**Sheraton Hotel** (Map pp52-4; ☎ 861 1191; www.sheraton.com/dhaka; 1 Minto Rd; standard/deluxe r US$194/625) The 256-room Sheraton is grand from the moment you step through the metal detectors and see the glass-domed ceiling. The shopping arcade is pleasant, and the collection of restaurants is diverse and inviting. Tea by the pool lives up to the colonial fantasy. Prices don't include tax.

**Hotel Orchard Plaza** (Map pp52-4; ☎ 933 0829; www.hotelorchardplaza.com; r US$70-110) One of the new kids on the block, the Orchard is open to offering discounts. Its spacious rooms are decked out with mod cons geared to the technologically demanding businessperson. There is also a nice restaurant on the 11th floor.

## Gulshan Area

The greater Gulshan area, including Banani and Baridhara, is the heart of the diplomatic zone and hence something of a foreigners ghetto. This can be a pro or a con, depending on what you're looking for, but it is hard to see the peace, quiet and cleanliness of this area as a negative. The 50 or so guesthouses scattered around offer cosy ambience and much cheaper rates than the Pan Pacific Sonargaon or Sheraton. All offer discounts for stays of more than a week or so. If you're staying for a while, or splashing out for a stint, look around until you find a place that suits.

**MID-RANGE**

**Tropical Inn Guest House** (Map pp60-1; ☎ 881 3313; tropical@citechco.net; House 19, Rd 96, Gulshan; s $US35, d$US40-50) There's a nice feel to the Tropical Inn. Some rooms have a serviceable desk and a full-sized fridge. Prices include breakfast, local calls, laundry and a real rarity – Internet access. There's a nice restaurant with a garden setting.

**Hotel Golden Deer** (Map pp60-1; ☎ 882 6259; gdeer@bdmail.net; Rd 35/A, House 31/B, Gulshan II; s/d with breakfast US$40/50) One of many hotels in the pocket between Banani Lake and Gulshan Ave with a penchant for animal names, the Golden Deer takes full advantage of its lakeside location to offer fantastic views from its balconies. The kitchen turns out some great Bangladeshi dishes.

**Hotel De Castle** (Map pp60-1; ☎ 881 2888; fax 881 0182; House B/72, Rd 21, Banani; r/ste US$70/110) Just around the corner from the French Inn, but smelling more like a hotel, the De Castle has somewhat overpriced rooms. However, discounts are offered before you even hint.

**Golden Goose Guest House** (Map pp60-1; ☎ 608 222; golden@coronait.com; Rd 41, House 46, Gulshan II; r Tk 1400-4500) Suffering with the competition, the tastelessness of the fake deer at reception is outdone only by the leopard-skin shower curtains.

Also recommended:

**Eastern House** (Map pp60-1; ☎ 988 2216; www .eghousedhaka.com; House 4, Rd 24, Gulshan I; r US$55-80)

**Excelsior Guest House** (Map pp60-1; ☎ 882 5139; fax 882 3007; House 38J, Rd 18, Banani; r US$20-65)

**Golden Inn** (Map pp60-1; ☎ 881 0239; fax 882 3849; House 30, Rd 10, Baridhara; r Tk 2240-4200)

**Green Goose Guesthouse** (Map pp60-1; ☎ 882 1928; fax 882 6432; Rd 38, Gulshan; r Tk 2000, with kitchenette Tk 3000)

**Uniconsult Guest House** (Map pp60-1; ☎ 988 2608, 882 3268; www.uniconsultguesthouse.com; House 34, Rd 18, Block J, Banani; r US$40-70)

**TOP END**

**Hotel Lake Castle** (Map pp60-1; ☎ 881 2812; www .hotellakecastle.com; House 1A, Rd 68A, Gulshan II; r/ste US$70/125) As classy as the hotels around Gulshan get. Some rooms have a view, and all have the generic comfort of the archetypal good hotel room. The foyer is a busy testament to its popularity.

**The Chalet** (Map pp60-1; ☎ 881 5689; fax 881 2773; House 5/A, Rd 32, Gulshan I; r US$40-60, ste US$85) One of the newest and nicest places to stay, all rooms are light and airy. A real asset of this hotel is its labyrinthine restaurant, partly in a glass enclosure and partly private rooms with tasteful and imaginative decorations. The whole place has real ambience and attention to detail.

Also recommended in the Gulshan area:

**Asia Pacific Blossom Hotel** (Map pp60-1; ☎ 988 0406, 988 8512; www.blossomhotel.com; House 27, Park Rd, Baridhara; r US$65-140)

**Asia Pacific Hotel** (Map pp60-1; ☎ 881 5461; fax 881 4125; House 2, Rd 2, Block K, Baridhara; r/ste US$65/130) The suite has an exotic harem feel to it.

**Civic Inn** (Map pp60-1; ☎ 881 7461; civicinn@dhaka .net; House 4B, Rd 67, Gulshan II; r US$80-100)

**Hotel de Crystal Garden** (Map pp60-1; ☎ 882 3147; www.degardenhotel.com; House 28, Rd 63; Gulshan II; r US$70-100)

**Marino Guest House** (Map pp60-1; ☎ 988 1585, 882 9647; marino@bdonline.com; House 46, Rd 18, Block J, Banani; r US$50-90)

# EATING
## Old Dhaka

**Al-Razzaque** (Map p47; 29/1 North-South Rd; meals Tk 50) Travellers have raved about Al-Razzaque, under the hotel of the same name. The women's booths provide a nice refuge, the staff are friendly and the food is fabulous.

**Café Al-Razib** (Map p47; Nawabpur Rd; mains Tk 30) A nice place with well-spaced tables. You'll get plenty of attention from patrons and plenty of service from staff. You could always escape to a booth, but the crowd of cockroaches therein will make the human crowds comparatively bearable.

**Hotel Nigar** (Map p47; Nawabpur Rd) Much the same as Al-Razib.

**Hot to Hot** (Map p47; Bangsal Rd, Bangsal) For a quick escape from the packed streets of Old Dhaka, duck into the laid-back Hot to Hot. There is no English sign or menu, but the manager, Mr Titu, will happily give you a rundown of the fast-food and Chinese selections on offer. An interesting feature here is Mr Titu's prized birds' nests hanging on the wall.

**Decent Pastry Shop** (Map p47; Nawabpur Rd) Lives up to its name.

## Central Dhaka

There is a great range of food for a great range of prices in Central Dhaka.

**Mango Café** (Map pp52-4; mains Tk 50) A favourite of young, opinionated and well-to-do Bangladeshis, this nonsmoking café has an extremely hip ambience, with a courtyard and a rooftop area for eating. It does great breakfasts (everything bar bacon). To find it, turn onto Rd 32 from Mirpur Rd and take the first right. It's a block up on the left.

**Bengal Food Restaurant** (Map pp52-4; ☎ 957 0863; 99 Motijheel Ave, Motijheel; mains Tk 50) For some truly great Bangladeshi fare, try Bengal Food Restaurant, tucked away in the business district. It's unusually clean and extremely well-priced, though the fish will clock up the bill. The food is fresh and tasty, and there is a set of cutlery anticipating your arrival. It's open for lunch and dinner.

**Jimmy's Kitchen Chinese Restaurant** (Map pp52-4; Motijheel Ave, Motijheel; 🕙 11am-4pm) The soft drinks are cold and most of the food is tasty. Beef with oyster sauce and vegetables costs Tk 110. Sit at the window to watch the manic traffic below.

DHAKA

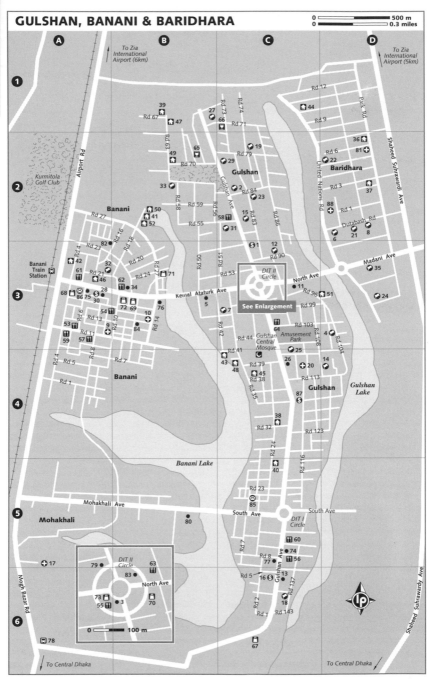

# GULSHAN, BANANI & BARIDHARA

0 ————— 500 m
0 ————— 0.3 miles

**DHAKA**

**Santoor** (Map pp52-4; Mirpur Rd) The high prices are justified on the basis of the ambience. If you need a brief escape to some staged civility, this is a great place to come to. Steaks cost around Tk 1000, the Tandoori chicken is Tk 150 and a lassi is Tk 60.

For some upmarket Chinese try **Xian** (Map pp52-4; Elephant Rd) or **Xinxian** (Map pp52-4; Mirpur Rd). Both have identical menus and the same manicured environment. Mains cost around Tk 200. Both are open for lunch between 12pm and 3pm and dinner from 6pm to 10.30pm. In the same vein, though with a slightly more demure atmosphere, is **Chilis Chinese Restaurant** (Map pp52-4; Mirpur Rd).

For a fast-food snack, there's a **Helvetia** (Map pp52–4) on Mirpur Rd and another in Motijheel next to the Hotel Pacific. Both have a clean efficient feel, the sterility of which is made up for by the enthusiasm of its numerous patrons. Pastries are upwards of Tk 40, a beef burger is Tk 90 and cappuccinos (yes, cappuccinos) are Tk 50. The two branches of **Yummy Yummy** (Map pp52–4), on Mirpur Rd and Airport Rd, and **Wimpy's** (Map pp52-4; Mirpur Rd) will offer you similarly efficient deep-fried delicacies.

## Gulshan Area

There is no shortage of fine eateries and choice of cuisine in Gulshan.

**Spitfire's Barbeque and Grill** (Map pp60-1; ☎ 885 1930; cnr Rd 55 & Gulshan Ave; mains Tk 450; ⏰ 11.30am-3pm & 6-11pm) This place is a favourite among expats. Local steaks, from local cows, cost Tk 400 and imported steaks (from American cows) cost Tk 1200. There are only a couple of vegetarian options on the largely carnivorous menu. The setting is Alaskan log cabin meets Jamaican bar.

**Khazana** (Map pp60-1; Gulshan Ave) Spitfire's white-linen neighbour also gets good reports.

**Spaghetti Jazz** (Map pp60-1; ☎ 882 2062; ⏰ 12.30-3pm & 6.30-10pm) This Italian restaurant, just off DIT II Circle, is a long-time favourite. The atmosphere is jazz-inspired and the food is spaghetti-inspired. The average pizza or pasta costs around Tk 280 and desserts Tk 130.

**Topkapi** (Map pp60-1; ☎ 881 0886; 134 Gulshan Ave) For the best lunch in town head to Topkapi. For Tk 250, you'll be let loose on cold meats, soup, salads, and beef, chicken and vegetable dishes – all top-quality Bangladeshi food. It's all you can eat under a roof

DHAKA

### THE AUTHOR'S CHOICE

**El Toro** (Map pp60-1; ☎ 861 6343; House 1A, Rd 138, Gulshan I; 🕙 11.30am-10.30pm) The only Mexican restaurant in Bangladesh, and surely the best on the Indian subcontinent. The gazpacho (Tk 70) and burritos (Tk 100 to Tk 170) are both recommended. The chunky chicken quesadilla (Tk 130) is a Trojan Horse of flavour – it looks benign on the plate but stages a coup in your mouth. Vegetarian options are available on request. The ambience is sombreros and ponchos aplenty but, mysteriously, the mock mud-brick walls and obligatory neon cactuses don't detract from the ultra-cool feel of this place. In fact the only thing missing is *cerveza* (beer). El Toro is open for lunch and dinner.

that could grace a mosque. Topkapi is also open for dinner, but a sensible menu replaces the outlandish buffet.

**Don Giovanni's Sizzler Restaurant** (Map pp60-1; ☎ 989 6855; Plot 11, Rd 46, Gulshan II) A popular place for pizza and pasta. The surprisingly good pizzas cost between Tk 250 and Tk 280, and the spaghetti bolognaise Tk 210. There are also some good steak choices. The décor is what an Italian John Wayne would seek out in Germany.

**Dhaba** (Map pp60-1; Rd 11, Banani) You can enjoy genuine street food, away from the street, at this self-proclaimed roadside eatery. Chicken tikka kebab is Tk 50, and there are two set Chinese menus for Tk 100 and Tk 120.

**Kebab-E-Q** (Map pp60-1; Rd 11) Fairy-lit rooftop dining, albeit only two stories high, is on offer here. The most expensive choice on the thesis-sized menu is around Tk 250. There are two whole pages of vegetarian options. There are also lots of tandoori meals, soups and desserts. The service isn't fast but it's worth the wait.

**King's Confectionary** (Map pp60-1; ☎ 989 4321; House 25, Rd 11, Block F, Banani; 🕙 7am-10.30pm) A spectacular range of pastries, donuts and cakes, all for prices that are rendered irrelevant at first smell. The Portuguese tartlet (Tk 30) is fabulous, and the Tk 120 *nasi lemak* (coconut rice) set makes a delicious and diverse lunch. There is a pleasant outdoor eating area.

For fine Korean fare, try **Koreana Restaurant** (Map pp60-1) or **Lotterea** (Map pp60-1; Kemal

Ataturk Ave, Banani). Authentic Korean mains at both cost around Tk 350. The latter has an attached bakery.

For some 'what-you-see-is-what-you-get relief', head to **FFC** (Map pp60-1; Gulshan Ave) next to Spitfire's, **Dominous Pizza** (Map pp60-1; Rd 10) or **Helvetia** (Map pp60-1; Tower Hamlet, 16 Kemal Ataturk Ave, Banani). There's also the **New Yorker Café** (Map pp60-1; Kemal Ataturk Ave, Banani), which turns into something of a landmark at night. Don't get excited about the beer taps at the bar – they're just for show.

## DRINKING

Various embassy social clubs including the **American Club** (Map pp60-1), **Bagha (British) Club** (Map pp60-1), **Swedish Club** (Map pp60-1) and the **Australian Club** (Map pp60-1) in Gulshan have happy hours on Thursday nights. These clubs are open only to ticket holders, but it is possible to get temporary membership or to enter under the auspices of a member, if you can find an expat willing to befriend you. Security is increasingly tight, so bring your passport.

There are licensed bars at the **Pan Pacific Sonargaon Hotel** (Map pp52-4) and the **Sheraton Hotel** (Map pp52-4). For a cheaper beer you could try **Hotel Peacock** (Map pp52-4), down an alleyway opposite the Sheraton, where a cold Heineken costs Tk 160. A discreet mutter at other similarly shady establishments might also prove fruitful.

## ENTERTAINMENT
### Cinemas

Midst the plethora of Bengali movies (p31), cinemas only very occasionally play mainstream Western films. Check newspapers. Expats find the range of pirated DVDs is adequate compensation for the lack of variety on the big screen.

### Sport

There are often cricket, soccer or hockey matches at the National Stadium. Women usually don't go to sporting events – it's considered unseemly. Check English-language newspapers for details.

### Traditional Music & Dance

The best place for cultural performances is **Shilpakala Academy** (Map pp52-4; ☎ 9562801), in a side street off Segun Bagicha Rd, next to the **National Art Gallery**. This is the national academy of fine art and the performing arts. The major cultural event of the year is the month-long **Asian Art Biennial** in November (held odd-numbered years). The exhibition, which spills over into the National Museum, attracts top artists and the quality is very high. Contact the Shilpakala Academy for details of other upcoming events.

Cultural events are also held at **Shishu Academy** (Map pp52-4; Old High Court Rd), southwest of the Supreme Court; the **National Museum** (Map pp52-4; Kazi Nazrul Islam Ave), 1km northwest of the Supreme Court; **Osmani Auditorium** (Map pp52-4; Abdul Ghani Rd), 1km southeast of the Supreme Court; and **Dhaka University** (Map pp52–4). Finding out about events is a challenge — they seem to be advertised only among the cultural elite. Your best option is to ask at the Shilpakala Academy or the **Alliance Francaise** (Map pp52-4; Mirpur Rd).

## SHOPPING
### Clothing

Dhaka is a fantastic place for purchasing cheap ready-made garments, all of which are produced locally for export. If you're ready to haggle, then head for **Banga Bazar** (Map p47; Fulbaria Rd), a block west of Gulistan bus station. Although some of the clothes are seconds, with small flaws, most are over-runs. Items for sale include cotton shorts (Tk 40), cotton pants (Tk 100), winter jackets (Tk 300) and blue jeans (up to Tk 200).

You can usually get things to a third of the asking price. Speaking a few words of Bangla will help. The kids who hang around the market are experts at seeking out particular garments – for a tip of course. Banga Bazar is usually closed on Friday, but always double check.

For easier but pricier purchasing try the upmarket clothing shops around the Gulshan area. For an interesting and socially aware designer purchase try **Essentials** (Map pp60-1; ☎ 989 2127; House 20, Rd 24, Block K, Banani). This is the latest project of the much-revered designer and former model Bibi Russel. Bangladeshi-born Russel uses local materials and skills to create gorgeous clothes and global awareness, and has walked Bangladesh down the world's most prestigious catwalks with her label 'Fashion for Development'. New designs can be bought from the showroom out the front, which opened its doors in Banani in January 2004.

## Handicrafts

Many handicraft shops accept credit cards. Most open at 9am and close between 7pm and 9pm, and are closed on Friday.

The Pan Pacific Sonargaon and Sheraton Hotels have handicraft shops in their malls and are probably the best places for purchasing jute carpets. You can pay less elsewhere, including at the row of shops on **New Elephant Rd**, but the selection won't be as good.

If you're looking for jewellery, consider items made of white conch shells, particularly bangles. They're made by Hindu artisans in Shankharia Bazar (p48) and are sold at most handicraft shops.

Bangladesh is also noted for its pink pearls. They are sold individually and set in jewellery, all over the city.

Leading handicraft shops and reliable jewellery shops:

**Aarong Handicrafts** (www.brac-aarong.com) Gulshan (Map pp60-1; Gulshan-Tejgaon Link Rd, Gulshan I); Lalmatia (Map pp52-4; 1/1, Block A, Mirpur Rd); Mogh Bazar (Map pp52-4; 4 New Circular Rd) The biggest name in quality handicrafts. Aarong is the retail branch of the Bangladesh Rural Advancement Committee (BRAC), which aims to create employment for economically and socially marginalised people through the promotion of traditional Bangladeshi handicrafts.

**Gem World** Banani (Map pp60-1; 42 Kemal Ataturk Ave)

**Halima Handicrafts** Mohammadpur (11/20 Iqbal Rd, Block A) A project to help abandoned and widowed women support themselves and their children by producing goods such as wall hangings, bedspreads, cushions and tablecloths.

**Karika Handicrafts** Dhaka (Map pp52-4; Paribagh Super Market, Kazi Nazrul Islam Ave); Dhaka (Map pp52-4; Sheraton Hotel Shopping Arcade, Kari Nazrul Islam Ave) One of the cheaper options, it has Bangladeshi fabrics and jute products as well as bronze work, leatherwork, purses, handbags and jewellery.

**Kumudini** Gulshan (74 Gulshan Ave); Mogh Bazar (Map pp52-4; Pan Pacific Sonargaon Hotel, Kazi Nazrul Islam Ave) Specialises in jute products.

**Mona Jewellers** Nayapaltan (Map pp52-4; 13 Baitul Mukarram Market)

**Monno Ceramics** Mogh Bazar (Map pp52-4; 334 New Elephant Rd) For modern ceramics.

**Monno Fabrics** Gulshan (Map pp60-1; DIT II Circle)

**Shetuli Handicrafts** Banani (Map pp60-1; House 104, Rd 12, Block E)

## Markets

It's a good idea to check newspapers to confirm whether a market is open or not on a given day.

**NEW MARKET & CHANDNI CHOWK BAZAR**
The city's largest market is **New Market** (Map pp52–4), at the southern end of Mirpur Rd. You can find almost anything here including maps, material, saris and household items. A great place to get kitted up in local gear, you can find pre-made *salwar kameez* (a long dress-like tunic worn by women over baggy trousers) for as low as Tk 150. **Chandni Chowk** (Map pp52–4), east across the street, is best for local fabrics.

Both markets are closed on Monday afternoon and all day Tuesday.

**OTHER MARKETS**
**Stadium Arcade** (Map pp52–4), north of the National Stadium, has an array of electrical goods, CDs and DVDs. There are also interesting restaurants on the ground floor. It's closed Thursday afternoon and all day Friday.

**DIT II Market** (Map pp60–1), with its intense but friendly atmosphere, is particularly fascinating for its ground-floor fish and livestock market. The cockroaches look healthier than the chickens, and are even more free-range. Tucked away on the first floor are a couple of framing stores that sell Bengali art.

**Rickshaw Art**
**Bangsal Rd** (Bicycle St; Map p47), in Old Dhaka's Bangsal, is the place to buy rickshaw parts. For rickshaw art try further along Bangsal Rd in Nazira Bazar, or Bangla Duair Lane. The art is painted on strips of tin and vinyl that fit within most suitcases and cost only around Tk 40, sometimes more if it's special. Bargaining is required, of course. For a personalised piece of rickshaw art, visit Syed Ahmed Hossain, whose pen name 'Ahmed' can be spied on the back of many a rickshaw. If you give him some idea of what you want and a couple of photos, the reliable and imaginative Mr Hossain ( ☎ 730 0236; 17 Hossaini Dalan Rd) will give you a bona fide Bangladeshi interpretation for around Tk 2000. It's best to see him between 7am and 11am, a couple of weeks before you would like your piece.

**GETTING THERE & AWAY**
**Air**
The two major airlines in Bangladesh are **Biman** (Map pp52–4; ☎ 955 9610; Dilkusha II Circle, Motijheel) and **GMG Airlines** (Map pp52–4; ☎ 711 4155–7;

Sena Kayan Bhaban, 13th fl, Motijheel). The latter is slightly more stylish. Routes and prices vary little between the two competitors.

At the time of writing, there were services to Barisal (Tk 1400, 35 minutes), Chittagong (Tk 2600, 50 minutes), Jessore (Tk 1500, 40 minutes), Rajshahi (Tk 1400, 40 minutes), and Sylhet (Tk 2600, 45 minutes).

See regional chapters and p166 for more details.

**Boat**
Book 1st- and 2nd-class Rocket (paddle-wheel) tickets at the **Bangladesh Inland Waterway Transport Corporation office** (BIWTC; Map pp52–4; ☎ 955 9779, 891 4771) in Motijheel, a block east of Dilkusha Circle I. It's open Sunday to Wednesday until around 5pm, Thursday until 2pm, and is closed Friday and Saturday. It's well marked on the outside, but not at all inside. You may be told that only 1st-class tickets can be booked from this office. A smile and some persistence should change this policy.

The Rocket departs from Sadarghat, and on rare occasions from Badam Tole ghat, 1km north of Sadarghat. Get there in plenty of time. The trip to Khulna takes anything from 27 to 30 hours. Fares to Khulna are roughly Tk 1000/600/150/100 for 1st/2nd/inter/deck class, depending on which Rocket you catch. Prices are sequentially less, depending on where you want to jump off along the way. For an explanation of classes see p171.

Boats depart for Khulna every day except Sunday at 6pm sharp.

Those travelling deck class (good luck convincing someone to sell you a deck-class ticket) may want to stake a place before the hordes arrive. You could pay a local to occupy a place for you, sitting all day for a fee of around Tk 30.

Private launches operate up and down the major rivers but most head south. Short-distance destinations reached by services from Dhaka include Bandura (30km west), Munshiganj (25km southeast) and Srinigar (20km southwest). Long-distance destinations include Barisal (110km south), Bhola (110km south), Chandpur (60km southeast), Madaripur (60km southwest) and Patuakali (40km south).

Short-distance launches travel during the day. The large long-distance launches travel at night, arriving at Sadarghat in the morning and remaining there all day, until departing at around 6pm or 7pm. Tickets are usually sold on board on the day of departure and require some bargaining.

## Bus

The bus 'system' in Bangladesh teeters between mind-bogglingly chaotic and surprisingly organised. When you arrive at a bus station, you will be swamped by panic-stricken men shouting like auctioneers. When you so much as mutter your intended destination you will be frantically shunted onto a bus as if it's going to leave at any second, only to wait for it to leave in its own sweet time. Though confronting at first, trust that there is method in the madness. The only thing you really need to do is get to the right bus station.

### GABTALI BUS STATION

The largest bus station in Dhaka, Gabtali (Map p43) is on the northwestern side of town on Dhaka-Aricha Hwy (an extension of Mirpur Rd), 8km from the heart of the city (Tk 5 by bus from Gulistan bus station). It's a madhouse; be on guard for pickpockets (particularly after dark), but in general people are very friendly and helpful.

Gabtali serves destinations in the northwest and southwest such as Savar (Tk 10, one hour) and Kusthia (express/chair coach Tk 130/220, 6¾ hours) between 8am and 10.30pm. Buses to Jessore (express/chair coach Tk 210/350, 6½ hours) and Khulna (Tk 170/240, eight hours) leave between 7am and 4.30pm.

Between around 7.30am and 11pm buses leave for Barisal (Tk 220, 12 hours), Pabna (Tk 130, four hours), Bogra (Tk 170, five hours), Rangpur (Tk 200, eight hours), Saidpur (Tk 200, 8¾ hours), Dinajpur (Tk 200, 9½ hours), Rajshahi (express/chair coach Tk 180/200, six hours) and Jessore (Tk 150/230, six hours).

Buses for most destinations leave every 20 minutes or half an hour. Travel times vary considerably depending on traffic in Dhaka.

Long-distance chair coaches increasingly leave during the day to avoid bandits who attack at night. One of the best coach companies at Gabtali is Metro Paribahan. It runs AC coaches on various routes including Jessore (Tk 280) and Khulna (Tk 300).

Many AC coach companies serving Rajshahi and Khulna divisions also have offices on Mirpur Rd, around the Pantha Path junction, across from Dhanmondi Lake. A good one is **National Bus Company** (cnr Mirpur Rd & Pantha Path), which has frequent services to Rajshahi (Tk 200, 4½ hours, almost hourly between 7.15am and 11pm).

### SAYEDABAD BUS STATION

Sayedabad bus station (Map p43) is on Hatkhola Rd, 1km before Jatrabari Circle, on the southeastern side of town. Buses leave every half an hour or so to destinations in the south and west, such as Comilla (express/chair coach Tk 40/60, three hours, between 5.30am and 10.30pm), Chittagong (Tk 110/180, six hours, between 5am and 12pm) and Sylhet (Tk 150/200, five hours, between 5am and 11.30pm).

For coaches to Sylhet check SylCom at Sayedabad bus station. Fares to Barisal, Jessore, Khulna and Kushtia are the same as those from Gabtali.

For Chittagong the best coach companies are along a one-block stretch on Inner Circular Rd in the Nayapaltan area near the New Hotel Yeameni International. They all charge around the same for chair coaches (Tk 190, six hours) and up to twice as much with AC.

There are also buses from here to Cox's Bazar (Tk 300, 10 hours). Comparable companies serving Chittagong Division are **Soudia** ( ☎ 933 1864), **Hanif** ( ☎ 831 3869) and **Green Line** (933 9623). Private chair coaches usually leave from around 7am onwards.

### MOHAKHALI BUS STATION

Mohakhali bus station (Map pp60–1) is on Mogh Bazar Rd, 2km south of Banani. From here buses head north for Mymensingh (Tk 125, 4½ hours), Tangail (Tk 55, 2½ hours) and Jamalpur (Tk 140, four hours) every 20 or 30 minutes between around 6am and 8.30pm.

### GULISTAN (FULBARIA) BUS STATION

Finally, there's Gulistan (Fulbaria) bus station (Map p47), in the heart of town on North-South Rd at Gulistan Crossing. Most buses depart from a block east at the chaotic intersection of Bangabandhu Ave and Toyenbee Rd. It's extremely crowded and traffic jams in the area are constant. Most buses are local and people are stuffed into them like sardines. Destinations include greater Dhaka as well as many towns within 30km or so of Dhaka, such as Mograpara (Old Sonargaon).

The government **Bangladesh Road Transport Corporation** (BRTC; Map pp52-4; DIT Ave) leaves from Kamlapur station. It's best forgotten as the service is far inferior to that of the private lines, although its recently introduced bus service to India has received compliments about its ease and efficiency (see p170).

## Train

Dhaka's main train station is the modern Kamlapur station (Map pp52–4) in Motijheel. Buying tickets is easy and there's a large timetable in English. Double-check it for accuracy because the schedules change slightly in the summer and the board may not reflect this. The inquiry counter, which is open until 11pm, and the chief inspector are both helpful. The following table shows some examples of express trains from Dhaka.

| Destination | Departure | Approximate Duration (hr) |
| --- | --- | --- |
| Sylhet | 6.40am | 7 |
| Sylhet | 12.30pm | 8 |
| Sylhet | 9.30pm | 7 |
| Chittagong | 7.40am | 7 |
| Chittagong | 3.15pm | 7 |
| Chittagong | 4.30pm | 6 |
| Chittagong | 11.00pm | 8 |
| Comilla | 6.00am | 4 |
| Khulna | 6.20am | 10 |
| Rajshahi | 2.40pm | 6 |

## GETTING AROUND
### To/From Zia International Airport

The cheapest way to get to the city centre from the airport (Map p43) is by bus. They're extremely crowded, so it's possibly not a viable option if you have a lot of luggage. You'll find buses out on the main highway (Airport Rd), a five-minute walk from the airport. The fare is less than Tk 10 to most places. After 8pm you may have difficulty finding one.

Coming out of the airport you'll be surrounded by scores of young men offering you rides. This is not a dangerous situation, just a confusing one. Most are not taxi drivers; they simply help drivers make arrangements. There's a fixed-rate taxi booth just

---

### THE MUSTANS

If you get a baby taxi from one of the larger taxi stands, you may see the driver give a young man a Tk 2 note before departing. This money ultimately goes to one of the *mustans* who wield Mafia-like power over their territories. Baby-taxi drivers have to pay for the privilege of using a public space to park. A man carting cargo through an area controlled by a *mustan* may be stopped by one of his lieutenants and forced to pay a small fee for the right to pass on a public street. Roadside food vendors also have to pay regular tolls to *mustans*. These thugs levy similar tolls on slum-dwellers occupying public lands. Refusal often draws a beating.

*Mustans* operate all over the country. Popular belief is that the most powerful *mustans* are connected with the major political parties.

---

outside the airport but Bangladeshis never use it, preferring to bargain down the price with the drivers. Fares to most places in the city seem to be around Tk 400 for foreigners, which is outrageous. You can call **Capital Cabs** ( ☎ 935 2847), but you'll save tonnes of taka if you walk out onto the main road and hail down a taxi or baby taxi with a meter.

To get to the airport, buses and tempos leave Gulistan bus station throughout the day and cost around Tk 7. A baby taxi will probably cost a little over Tk 60 and a taxi around Tk 80. Rickshaws aren't allowed at the airport or on the major highway (Airport Rd) passing the airport.

### Baby Taxi

Travel by baby taxi is as efficient as it gets in Dhaka, and can be great fun (or hair-raising). Though pricier than rickshaws over short distances, they have the added advantage of a meter, which avoids the hassle of bargaining. Meters start at Tk 12 and only start to rise after a few kilometres, explaining why drivers are often reluctant to take you short distances. A baby-taxi fare from, say, Motijheel to Gulshan will cost around Tk 60.

### Bus

Cheaper than cheap, buses have no signs in English and their numbering is in Bangla. Furthermore, they are always overcrowded

---

### COUNTING RICKSHAWS

The Dhaka police estimate there are something like 600,000 rickshaws in the city. However, the revenue department of Dhaka City Corporation, the body responsible for collecting licence fees from rickshaw-wallahs, has a different figure. When a newspaper reporter asked a top official from the department about the number of rickshaws in Dhaka, the official replied, 'There are 88,700 and something rickshaws in the city'. When the reporter pointed out that other estimates were somewhat higher, the official replied, 'As far as we are concerned there are only 88,700 and something rickshaws in the city. If you disbelieve me, why don't you start counting.'

---

so boarding between major bus stops is virtually impossible. Fares vary a lot but around Dhaka you won't pay much more than Tk 7.

BRTC buses have become outnumbered and outdated by private bus lines.

Buses to the towns of Narayanganj, Mograpara (Old Sonargaon), Murapara and other outlying towns and villages can be found at Gulistan bus station and will cost closer to Tk 10 or Tk 15. If you're heading northwest for Savar and Dhamrai, you must go to Gabtali bus station.

### Car

Unless you have an International Driver's Licence, self-driving isn't an option, and even if you do, it isn't a good option. However, hiring a car or van with a driver can make a lot of sense (see p175).

There are numerous car-hire establishments scattered around Dhaka. One is **Dhaka Tours Rent-A-Car Association** ( ☎ 966 3134; 3 Link Rd), 1½ blocks southwest of the Sonargaon, and also with an office opposite the Sheraton, just off Kazi Nazrul Islam Ave (Map pp52-4; ☎ 408 499). It charges Tk 1200 for a driver

and car (slightly more for a minibus). This doesn't include petrol, and if you venture outside of Dhaka, you will have to pay extra each day for the driver's food and accommodation. A rule of thumb is that a car, driver and petrol will cost you around Tk 1500 per day. When you are negotiating with any company, make sure you are clear on what is included in the price.

The more upmarket option is to approach a **Hertz** (Map pp60-1; ☎ 988 4311; cnr Rd 14 & Kemal Ataturk Ave) or equivalent office, where prices are higher but cars are shinier (Hertz even hires Mercedes Benz!). Two hours for a Hertz car and driver will cost you roughly what you would pay a small operator for a day, plus Tk 300 a day for your driver's expenses, if going outside Dhaka.

### Rickshaw

You will find rickshaws everywhere and when the streets are crowded (as they usually are), they're not much slower than anything else that moves, except pedestrians. Aim for a basic fare of about Tk 5 for the first kilometre and Tk 4 per kilometre after that, and make your own judgments with regard to baksheesh (tip).

### Taxi

There are two types of taxis on the roads of Dhaka. The yellow taxis are more spacious and usually cleaner than their black counterparts, but you pay for the difference. Meters in yellow taxis start at Tk 20 and clock more quickly and at a higher rate than the black taxis, which start at Tk 15.

### Tempo

Fast and cheap, tempos (auto-rickshaws) are a convenient way to travel if you aren't carrying much luggage and don't mind rib-cage compression. The close quarters might make women (and those around them) uncomfortable. A trip from Gabtali bus station to Farm Gate costs around Tk 5.

# Dhaka Division

**CONTENTS**

To say that Dhaka division, home to one of the world's most intense cities and some 25,244 villages, epitomises the diversity of this surprising country is an understatement. You don't have to travel far out of the crazy capital to be transported out of the hustle and bustle and into the rural soul of Bangladesh. Dhaka division, the most densely populated area of the country, is surrounded to the west, south, and east by the other five divisions, with the Indian state of Meghalaya to the north. All of Dhaka division lies east of the mighty Jamuna and Padma Rivers and north of the wide Meghna, except for the Faridpur region, which is south of the Padma. Most of the division is closely settled farmland – only in the far north can you find some of the gradually shrinking woodland.

The northern part of Dhaka division reaches the Indian border at the base of the low, wooded Garo Hills chain. It is the largest district of Bangladesh, located in the heart of the deltaic region of the Jamuna and the Meghna Rivers. Neglected by its Mughal overlords, the region boomed and became one vast jute plantation under the British. Jute was an important crop and it grew better here and was of a higher quality than anywhere else.

## HIGHLIGHTS

- Snapping photos of regal **Sadarbari** (p70), now the folk-art museum in the old capital of Sonargaon

- Paying homage at the **National Martyrs' Memorial** (p71) in Savar, where the expanse of space is thick with reverie

- Encountering monkeys, langurs and numerous bird species on your way to tribal Mandi villages through the **Madhupur Forest Reserve** (p75)

- Admiring the attention to detail on **Atia Mosque** (p72) and verifying its depiction on the Tk 10 note

## SONARGAON

One of the best day trips from Dhaka is an excursion to Sonargaon (sometimes known as Old Sonargaon), the country's first capital. An hour away from Dhaka, it's just off the Dhaka-Chittagong Hwy, some 23km southeast of Dhaka. Today it is nestled between the Meghna and the modest Sitalakhya Rivers, but when it was the capital the Sitalakhya was the main channel of what is the now the Jamuna River. These days the Sitalakhya is a relatively minor river, and the mighty Jamuna has changed course, flowing into the Padma, which is some 90km away.

Many visitors to Sonargaon mistakenly believe that its buildings are remnants of the ancient capital city. Except for several mosques, a bridge, a few tombs and stupas (Buddhist monuments), and some indistinguishable mounds scattered around the area, nothing remains of the original city. The area also has two newer but much smaller villages: Mograpara and Painam Nagar.

Unfortunately the government's archaeological department has done precious little to preserve the buildings of Sonargaon. Reportedly some of the poorer occupants sell the bricks from these ramshackle buildings to be broken into gravel for construction work. Since Independence, only Goaldi Mosque, a pre-Mughal bridge and a single rajbari (zamindari palace) called Sadarbari have been restored.

### History

By the 13th century the ancient capital of Sonargaon ('Golden Town' in Hindi) was the Hindu seat of power. With the Muslim invasion and the arrival of the sultan of Elhi in 1280, its importance was magnified as the region's de facto Islamic capital. Some 42 years later the first independent sultan of East Bengal, Fakhruddin Mubarak Shah, officially established his capital here.

For the next 270 years Sonargaon prospered as the capital of East Bengal. In 1558 famous traveller Ralph Fitch noted that it was an important centre for the manufacture of *kantha* (traditional indigo-dyed muslin), reportedly exported to wrap ancient Egyptian mummies.

When the invading Mughals ousted the sultans, they regarded Sonargaon's location along the region's major river as too exposed

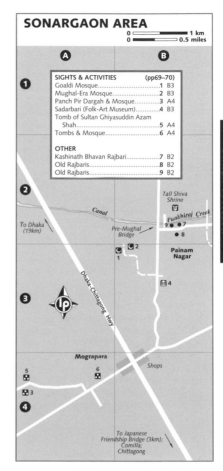

**SONARGAON AREA**

| SIGHTS & ACTIVITIES | (pp69–70) |
|---|---|
| Goaldi Mosque | 1 B3 |
| Mughal-Era Mosque | 2 B3 |
| Panch Pir Dargah & Mosque | 3 A4 |
| Sadarbari (Folk-Art Museum) | 4 B3 |
| Tomb of Sultan Ghiyasuddin Azam Shah | 5 A4 |
| Tombs & Mosque | 6 A4 |

| OTHER | |
|---|---|
| Kashinath Bhavan Rajbari | 7 B2 |
| Old Rajbaris | 8 B2 |
| Old Rajbaris | 9 B2 |

to Portuguese and Mogh pirates. So in 1608 they moved the capital to Dhaka, initiating Sonargaon's long decline into oblivion.

### Sights & Activities
#### MOGRAPARA

A thriving village located on the Dhaka-Chittagong Hwy, Mograpara claims most of the remains of the old capital, including the **Tomb of Sultan Ghiyasuddin Azam Shah**, which is the oldest surviving Muslim monument in Bangladesh, the **Panch Pir Dargah** and **Fateh Shah's Mosque**. Most of these are 1km or 2km west of Mograpara. These monuments aren't very impressive and most visitors, believing only Painam Nagar to be Old Sonargaon, don't even know they exist.

## SADARBARI

Built in 1901, this beautiful rajbari is an appropriate building for a **folk-art museum** (admission to compound Tk 4, museum Tk 3). This two-storey building has two façades. The one facing the street, with steps leading down to the water and life-size English horsemen in stucco on either side, is one of the most picturesque in Bangladesh. The other, at the museum's entrance, is profusely embellished with a mosaic of broken china and stucco floral scrolls.

Inside are unadorned rooms with various objects and handicrafts on display, some of which are looking quite stale. There is also a new building with more exhibits.

If you're really tight on taka, just paying the entrance fee for the compound will afford close-up inspection of the folk-art museum's beautiful exterior (far more impressive than its interior anyway) and access to the popular grounds for some lakeside lolling.

## GOALDI MOSQUE

Built in 1519, the **Goaldi Mosque** is the most impressive of the few extant monuments of the old capital city. This graceful single-domed mosque is a good example of pre-Mughal architecture.

The single-domed mosque 50m beyond Goaldi, built in 1704 during the Mughal period, is historically less-important. Yet another single-domed mosque in the Mograpara area is Fateh Shah's Mosque, which predates Goaldi Mosque by 35 years. It has been renovated rather than restored and is consequently not so interesting.

## PAINAM NAGAR

Continue past the folk-art museum and you'll come to Painam Nagar. Constructed almost entirely between 1895 and 1905 on a small segment of the ancient capital city, this tiny settlement consists of a single narrow street, lined with around 50 dilapidated mansions built by wealthy Hindu merchants. At the time of Partition, many owners fled to India, leaving their elegant homes in the care of poor tenants, who did nothing to maintain them. The remaining owners pulled out during the anti-Hindu riots of 1964, which led up to the 1965 Indo-Pakistan War.

Today Painam Nagar has a delightful ghost-town quality, with its buildings choked with vines and their façades slowly crumbling away. One mansion, marked **Sonargaon Art Gallery**, is rented from the government by artist Aminul Islam, whose paintings are on display.

## Getting There & Away

From Dhaka's Gulistan bus station, say the buzz word 'Mograpara' (around Tk 15, 40 minutes). If you ask for Sonargaon, you will likely end up at the Pan Pacific Sonargaon Hotel. Once you're in Mograpara, a short rickshaw ride will get you to the museum and other sights. Rickshaw-wallahs will guess what you're there to see.

## MURAPARA

For a full-day outing from Dhaka, you can combine a trip to Sonargaon with a visit to the rajbari at Murapara, which is 20km up the Sitalakhya River from Narayanganj, on the eastern bank. Built in 1889, this rajbari now houses a small tertiary college.

In the front of the main building you'll see two small Hindu shrines, both still in reasonably good condition. Built largely in carved red stone, the attractive stucco

---

**CYCLING AROUND OLD SONARGAON & MURAPARA**

For a delightful bicycle day trip that combines peaceful rural scenery with some interesting historical sights and good river views, try the areas around Sonargaon and Murapara. Take your bike by baby taxi to Sayedabad bus station in Dhaka and catch a Comilla bus (departing every five minutes). Tell the driver you want to get off at Mograpara – he will not know what you mean by Sonargaon.

As you pedal around the greater Sonargaon area, don't limit yourself to Painam Nagar.

Afterwards head north along the Dhaka-Chittagong Hwy to the long bridge over the Sitalakhya River (11km). Just before crossing it, turn right (north) onto the Sylhet road and peddle to Murapara junction (11km). Cycle west to Murapara (5km) and south along the scenic eastern bank of the river, passing Murapara Palace, and back to the junction with the Chittagong road (10km more). If you can't hail a Dhaka-bound bus there, go over the bridge and catch one at the crowded intersection just beyond.

decorations and ornate roofs make good backdrops for photographs.

## Getting There & Away

Buses to Murapara (Tk 10, 45 minutes) leave from Dhaka's Gulistan bus station. Murapara is 26km from Jatrabari Circle in Dhaka.

## SAVAR
☎ 06626

A popular day excursion for Dhaka locals is a trip to Savar (*shar*-var). The town, called Savar Bazar, is on the Dhaka-Aricha Hwy, 15km north of Gabtali bus station in Dhaka. Tuesday is market day in Savar Bazar, which becomes very animated, especially along the banks of the Bangsi River just west of town.

The main attraction is the historic **National Martyrs' Memorial** (Jatiya Sriti Saudha), which is 8km further along the Dhaka-Aricha Hwy, just off the road. The tapering 50m-high structure is a memorial to the millions who died in the struggle for independence. The beautifully kept grounds contain a number of grassy platforms that cover the mass graves of some of those slaughtered in the Liberation War. This is an important place for Bangladeshis, who wander the grounds with an air of reverence.

## Eating

Across the road from the National Martyrs' Memorial is a large Parjatan (government tourist organisation) restaurant. Downstairs the food is fast and cheap; upstairs it's more expensive and tasty. There is a well-marked Chinese restaurant on the main drag in the centre of Savar Bazar.

## Getting There & Away

Buses for Savar (Tk 10, one hour) leave from Gabtali bus station. You can also go to Savar Bazar by baby taxi for Tk 80, or to the actual memorial for slightly more. Alternatively you can take an Aricha-bound bus from Gabtali or Farm Gate and get off at Savar, but you'll pay a little bit more. If you want the actual town, ask for 'Savar Bazar', otherwise the driver will probably think you want to go to the memorial further on.

## DHAMRAI
☎ 011

If you're in the Savar area, make a side trip to Dhamrai, 5km west of the monument

and 1km north off the Dhaka-Aricha Hwy. Known for artisans who work with brass and *jamdani* (embroidered muslin or silk) weavers, it's a predominantly Hindu town with a friendly atmosphere. Most of its Raj-era buildings are in good shape and are inhabited by some of the town's wealthier citizens.

On market days, including Saturday, the main drag is lined with vegetable stands, behind which are artisans' shops. One that has received high praise is **Dhamrai Metal Craft** ( ☎ 832 620). Further on sits the town's multi-storey wheeled Jagannath (chariot) that has images from Hindu mythology painted on the sides and is paraded down the street during **Rath Jatra**, the mela (festival) held here during the full moon in late June/early July (see p160).

## Getting There & Away

Buses to Dhamrai (Tk 15, one hour) leave from Dhaka's Gabtali bus station. A baby taxi will be quicker but costs around Tk 150. Buses between Savar and Dhamrai cost about Tk 5 – just hail one going in the right direction and do the 'run and jump'.

## MANIKGANJ
☎ 0651

If you have the means to explore further, you could check out two rarely visited rajbaris further west in the Manikganj district, 30km beyond the Savar memorial. The first, **Baliati Palace**, is the largest rajbari in Bangladesh with a frontage of approximately 125m, an area of about eight hectares and over 200 rooms. The impressive Renaissance frontage is reminiscent of a neoclassical English country house.

Further west, on the banks of the Jamuna River, is **Teota Palace**, built in 1858 by the zamindars of the Joy Sankar estate. The highlights are the large Hindu temple and the smaller family shrine. The well-preserved temple resembles the impressive Shiva temple in Puthia (see p115).

## Getting There & Away

Baliati Palace is about halfway between Savar's National Martyrs' Memorial and Aricha ghat. Turn left (south) at Kalampur, which is about 8km before (east of) Manikganj on the Dhaka-Aricha Hwy. Teota Palace is 30km or so further west at Sivalaya, which is several kilometres south of Aricha ghat by tarred road and along the Jamuna River.

## BHAWAL NATIONAL PARK

Located at Rajendrapur, and only one hour north of Dhaka, **Bhawal National Park** (admission per person Tk 6, per car Tk 30, per minibus Tk 50) is far less interesting than Madhupur Forest Reserve (see p75). However, its accessibility ensures it is more frequented, especially as a weekend picnic spot.

There's angling and boating on the long meandering lake and pleasant walking through stands of young sal trees. It's no wilderness, but in a country with so few forests, it's a welcome sight.

### Getting There & Away

The park is on the Dhaka-Mymensingh Hwy, 38km north of Dhaka and 15km beyond Shandana (shan-dah-*nah*), the four-way intersection west of Gazipur. From Mohakhali bus station in Dhaka (p65), buses headed for Mymensingh run right past the well-marked park entrance, on your right. The trip takes an hour.

---

**CENTRE FOR THE REHABILITATION OF THE PARALYSED (CRP)**

An inspiring organisation that has been operating since 1979, **CRP** ( ☎ 771 0464-5; www.crp-bangladesh.com) helps paralysed people develop skills that enable them to become self-sufficient and productive. While its founder, Valerie Taylor, continues to keep the organisation going with donations, the CRP aims to become more economically independent.

In addition to selling fish, fruit, poultry, handicrafts and wheelchairs, CRP's funding is also derived from the guesthouses it runs in the tea gardens of Moulvibazar.

The centre has branches in Gonokbari, Gobindapur and Mirpur, but its headquarters is on the northeastern outskirts of Savar Bazar on the Dhaka-Aricha Hwy, from where you can buy postcards, stationery and other trinkets produced by CRP patients.

Visitors are most welcome at this sprawling complex; various training sessions and workshops are held daily from 8am to 1pm and from 3pm to 6pm. The centre is closed Thursday afternoon and Friday.

---

## TANGAIL

☎ 0921

Tangail has one of the country's real gems – Atia Mosque. Other than that, though, there is nothing much to see in this singularly unattractive city.

You will find the **District Forestry Office** ( ☎ 53524) for Madhupur Forest Reserve (p75) on the 3rd floor of the well-marked Water Development Board building, a block north of the post office on Victoria Rd. It is no longer possible to stay overnight in the forest, but if for some reason you require access to one of the guesthouses during the day, this is where you seek permission to do it.

There is an Internet café, City Cyber Café, on the Victoria Rd junction.

### Sights & Activities

#### ATIA MOSQUE

Built in 1609, this fascinating transitional-phase **mosque**, depicted on the Tk 10 note, blends pre-Mughal elements with imperial Mughal architectural features. It has been diligently restored to its former glory, and is well worth a visit.

This well-known mosque is located 5km south of Tangail on the tarred road to Nagarpur. Coming from Dhaka you'll have to go completely through Tangail, along Victoria Rd and the crowded Six Annas Market Rd, before coming to the intersection of Delduar and Nagarpur Rds. Veer to your right into Nagarpur Rd and continue for around 4km. The turn-off, to your left, is marked by a sign in Bangla; the mosque is several hundred metres down that dirt road, by a pond.

### Sleeping & Eating

Tangail supports only a few hotels.

**SSS Rest House** (BB Girl's School Rd; s/d with breakfast Tk 600/1000) Extremely clean and quiet but insanely overpriced, rooms here have attached bathrooms with cold-water showers, and TV.

**Polashbari Hotel** ( ☎ 53154; Masjid Rd; s Tk 90-100, d Tk 250) This four-storey establishment is near the heart of town and east of the market, with a sign in Bangla. It's decent enough, with reasonably comfortable mattresses and attached bathrooms.

If the Polashbari is full, a decent alternative is the Residential Hotel across the road. Rooms are similarly priced.

There are some friendly local restaurants in this area, and more serving similar chicken, fish and mutton dishes at the intersection of Dhaka and Mymensingh Rds.

## Getting There & Away
Ordinary buses leave Tangail every 20 minutes or so between 5am and 7pm to Dhaka (Tk 55, 2½ hours), Mymensingh (Tk 60, 2½ hours) and Madhupur (Tk 30, one hour). All leave from the main bus station on Mymensingh Rd, 2km north of the intersection with Dhaka Rd. There are also less frequent buses to Bogra (Tk 80, four hours).

Buses for Tangail depart from Mohakhali bus station in Dhaka (p65).

## MYMENSINGH
☎ 091
The outskirts of Mymensingh are slightly deceptive. Many modern buildings greet the newly arrived visitor but the further you go into the town, the more this original impression diminishes. The scene reverts to the usual chaos of Bangladeshi urban life. Despite this the town has a comfortable,

unhurried atmosphere. The local rickshaw owners are in fierce competition to see who has the most colourfully decorated fleet.

There are some Internet cafés on Station Rd. A good one with a reliable connection is **Millenium Computers** (Mymensingh Online; 1st fl, Alimun Plaza; per hr Tk 20). E-View Cyber Café is further west on the same side of the road.

## Sights & Activities
Built between 1905 and 1911, the **Mymensingh Rajbari** is a well-kept building in the middle of the city, and overlooks the Brahmaputra River. It is now occupied by an organisation that trains female teachers, but much of the original structure remains. An ornamental marble fountain with a classical statue of a seminude nymph lies just beyond the arched gateway entrance. Behind the main building is the Jal-Tungi, a small two-storey bathhouse once used as the women's bathing pavilion. You can politely ask the security guard for admittance to the grounds, but it is doubtful whether he will grant you a glimpse of the interior, unless you befriend a passing staff member or student.

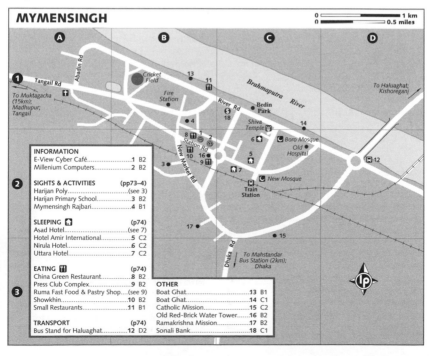

The **Harijan Poly** is a community of members of the Hindu untouchable caste, known today as Harijans (meaning 'God's children') or Dalits (meaning 'the oppressed'). It's an interesting area to walk through, if only to experience being among Hindus in a predominantly Muslim culture. By following the main track leading into the community to the end and taking a left, you'll come to a small Hindu shrine and see a red metal gate opposite. Behind the gate lies the interesting **Harijan Primary School**, which aims to empower its students through education.

## Sleeping & Eating

**Hotel Amir International** ( ☎ 54030; Station Rd; s/d Tk 400/650, with AC Tk 600/950) A stand-out building and the nicest place to stay, prices here are unduly high but it is the cleanest place in town. There's also a particularly nice foyer area where you can unwind with a drink. Rates don't include taxes.

**Nirula Hotel** (s Tk 100-150, d Tk 150-200) This five-storey building in Chowk Bazar near the Boro Mosque is a good budget option. Rooms are mostly clean, though windowless, and some have attached bathrooms.

**Uttara Hotel** ( ☎ 54455; Station Rd; s/d/t Tk 100/200/300) Not far west of the railway station, the Uttara has some quite spacious rooms with chairs and desks. Look before you commit, though – some rooms aren't that clean and could get noisy.

**Asad Hotel** ( ☎ 55692; s/d with bathroom Tk 90/150) Just around the corner from the Uttara is the unmarked Asad, with smaller rooms. Staff may prefer you to stay elsewhere, and you might too.

There are some nice low-key Bangladeshi restaurants in the numerous side streets off Station Rd. There are also a couple of Chinese options for lunch and dinner, such as **China Green Restaurant** ( ☎ 53331; Station Rd) and **Showkhin Restaurant** ( ☎ 52675; Station Rd); the latter has a nice enclosed balcony for dining.

There are also some restaurants in the Press Club complex, just off Station Rd. One is the recently opened **Ruma Fast Food & Pastry Shop**, where teenagers snack on vegetable rolls (Tk 15), club sandwiches (Tk 22), milkshakes (Tk 20) and the like. Some of the food is of the fresh-from-the-microwave variety.

For some ultra-cheap food and priceless atmosphere, head to the gaggle of small **restaurants** along River Rd.

## Getting There & Away

Buses take the shortest route to Dhaka, which goes directly south, passing west of Gazipur and parallel to the railway line. The Old Dhaka Hwy through Tangail is more circuitous, but offers interesting side trips along the way, including Madhupur Forest. Connections with Rajshahi division have improved since the completion of the Bangabandhu Bridge, but the Tangail road is much busier.

Train connections to Rajshahi division involve a three-hour ferry crossing, at least until the rail link over the Bangabandhu Bridge is completed.

### BUS

The main bus terminal is Mahstandar bus station, about 3km from the Station Rd Circle. Between 6am and 6pm you can get a bus to a zillion places including Tangail (Tk 60, 2½ hours), Madhupur (Tk 30, 45 minutes) and Dhaka (Tk 80, 4½ hours).

At the rear of the bus terminal is the United Transport coach service, which has buses going to Dhaka (Tk 85, five hours), Sylhet (Tk 220, 12½ hours) and Chittagong (Tk 250, 11 hours) every half-hour or so between 7am and 8pm. Their buses are more spacious than the local alternative. Make sure you raise an eyebrow if they try to charge you extra for your baggage.

The bus stand for Haluaghat and other destinations on the other side of the Brahmaputra River is, logically, at the bridge. Buses to Haluaghat (around Tk 25, one hour) leave regularly between 8am and 7pm.

### TRAIN

Mymensingh is on the Dhaka–Rangpur route and there are four intercity (IC) trains, which operate six days a week (with different days off for each train) in either direction. From Dhaka trains leave at 7am, 9.20am, 4.50pm and 5.10pm and take three hours. The fare is Tk 110/60 for 1st/*sulob* (upper-2nd) class. From Mymensingh there are two early-morning trains and two late-afternoon trains headed for Dhaka.

## AROUND MYMENSINGH

To the north the hill country of the Indian state of Meghalaya beckons enticingly, but there is no border crossing here. The area may be divided politically, but culturally it shares a common heritage among the tribal hill people – Mandi (known as Garos across the border in India), Hanjongis and Kochis – all of whom are ethnically distinct from the others around them.

## Haluaghat

This is the end of the line, so to speak – the sealed road ends here, but a number of pot-holed dirt roads take off in various directions for smaller villages along the Indian border. Haluaghat, one of the Mandi tribal centres for the area, is a typical bustling town less than two hours north of Mymensingh. It is one big market, with vendors selling a variety of rice, dried peppers, melons in season and so on. Blacksmiths work in small shops next to silversmiths and cloth dealers.

### OXFORD MISSION

Founded in 1910, the **Oxford Christian Mission** welcomes visitors. It operates a boys and girls high school, with a combined enrolment of about 1000. If you're interested in getting out further into some of the smaller Mandi villages, such as Askipara, staff at the mission may be able to help.

The spacious compound is tucked away off the main street. Many locals don't seem to know where it is – asking directions may prove futile. Follow the main road north through town past some modern-looking buildings (grain-storage warehouses) on your left (west). About 50m further is a large mosque; take the narrow road leading west and follow it for about 300m. The red metal gate on your left past the grain warehouses is the entrance to the mission.

### GETTING THERE & AWAY

Buses for Haluaghat (Tk 25, one hour) leave from the bus stand near the Brahmaputra Bridge in Mymensingh.

## Askipara

This Mandi village is in a beautiful area north of Haluaghat, near the Indian border, and is about as remote as you can get in Bangladesh. The predominantly tribal area is officially 'restricted', and to visit you must get permission from the district office in Haluaghat, although you may be able to get around that. A local guide could be your 'host', or you could get lucky and not be checked going into the area. At worst, without permission you could be turned back.

There are wonderful walks in the area, and some distance away right on the border is Pani Hata, an Anglican mission surrounded by beautiful teak trees. On the hilltop above the mission is a wonderful view looking out over the plains to the hills of Meghalaya.

There is no public transport to Askipara, but a rickshaw can be hired from Haluaghat (roughly Tk 100, two hours).

## Muktagacha

Situated 12km west of Mymensingh on the old Tangail-Dhaka Hwy is the little village of Muktagacha. It is said that sometime during the early 18th century, a local smith named Muktaram presented the eldest son of the region's ruler with a brass *gacha* (lamp) as a sign of loyalty. In recognition of the gift, the son named the town Muktagacha.

The rajbari here draws the occasional visitor, but the town is best known for its famous sweet shop, Gopal Pali Prosida Monda, which makes the best *monda* (grainy, sweetened yogurt cake) in the country. Two hundred years ago the Pal family cooked these delicious sweetmeats for the zamindar, who liked them so much that he employed the family. When the landowner's family left during Partition, the Pal family opened up shop and have been in business ever since.

Coming from Mymensingh on the Tangail road, take the second road leading northeast (right) into Muktagacha. Go down about three blocks and the shop will be on your right. Look for the lion motif over the door.

Twenty feet past the shop are old concrete pillars marking one of the entrances to the Muktagacha Rajbari – definitely worth seeing if you're in the area. This palace, dating back to the early-to-middle 19th century, is now mostly in ruins. It includes several different blocks and spreads over 10 acres. It is a very special estate, even in disrepair, bedecked with Corinthian columns, high parapets and floral scrolls in plaster. The Rajeswari temple and the stone temple, believed to be dedicated to Shiva, are two of the finer temples within the complex.

## Madhupur Forest Reserve

The town of Madhupur (*mode-uh-poor*) is nothing special, but the surrounding area is definitely unique. The biggest attraction is Madhupur Forest Reserve, a tract of land roughly 50 sq km, just northeast of town.

MANDI SETTLEMENTS

Far into the Madhupur Forest, where there are fewer trees, are some small Mandi settlements. The atmosphere of these enclaves is quite distinct from that of Muslim villages. A matrilineal group, the Mandi (or Garo as they are commonly called by outsiders), may have originally migrated from Myanmar (Burma). They are peaceful and accustomed to living in a spacious forest. Primarily Christians or animists, they seem to be more at ease with foreigners than your average Bangladeshi.

Unfortunately for the Mandi, neighbouring Bengalis are slowly encroaching on their lands and cutting down their forests. Accustomed to having their own space, the Mandi, although the original inhabitants of this region, are selling off their lands and heading to more remote areas further north. The rate of deforestation is high and poorly paid forestry officials are turning a blind eye to the destruction. If something doesn't change, this reserve is doomed.

About 8km from Madhupur town, on the highway to Mymensingh, you'll arrive at the forest's southwestern edge. It continues for around 8km along both sides of the highway, but the principal section lies to the north.

This is the last remnant in Bangladesh of the moist deciduous old-growth forest, which at one time extended for hundreds of kilometres across Dhaka division. Unfortunately government conservation efforts have been ineffective and there has been considerable felling in the area.

This area was once famous for tigers. Now explorations of the forest will likely turn up some rhesus monkeys and golden-coloured capped langurs, which look like bushy-tailed monkeys. There are also three species of civets here. Madhupur is also very good for bird-watching. There are numerous species, but serious bird-watchers will be most interested in spotting the dusky owl, the brown fish owl, the spotted eagle owl and the famous brown wood owl, which is a speciality of the forest.

The hiking is best after the high-water (monsoonal) season, when the lower swampy areas dry up.

GETTING THERE & AWAY

There are frequent buses between Mymensingh and Tangail; Madhupur (Tk 60, 45 minutes) is about halfway between the two. From Madhupur town the entrance to the forest is about 15km to the northeast along the Mymensingh Hwy. Take a tempo or hop on any bus heading for Mymensingh.

The main entrance to Madhupur Forest is on the northern side of the Mymensingh–Madhupur road at the eastern end of the forest, just before it abruptly ends and paddy fields begin. At the entrance you'll find the main forestry headquarters; those driving must register their vehicles here.

## Dhanbari Nawab Palace

Some 15km north of the town of Madhupur is the old **Dhanbari Nawab Palace**. It was originally owned by a Hindu, Dhanwar Khan, but it fell into the hands of Muslims, which explains the presence of a mosque. Within the complex there is also a main palace and a large *kutchery* building (clerks' office) in poor-to-fair condition, but still intact.

The interior of the elegant three-domed mosque, renovated in 1901, is marvellous – the inner walls are covered from floor to ceiling with mural decorations made from broken china pieces.

To get here from the town of Madhupur, take the tarred road north towards Jamalpur and after about 15km you'll see the palace on your right, just off the highway.

# Khulna Division

Khulna division, in the southwest of the country, is made up of marshland, dense jungle and numerous rivers, which once formed natural barriers against invasion from the west or east. Even after its late settlement, Khulna division remained relatively neglected by the Mughals. It was not until the arrival of the British that it started to develop.

Today, the city of Khulna is the country's third-largest urban centre. Products from the nearby Khulna Export Processing Zone are shipped out from the country's second international port at Mongla.

Khulna division proudly claims the Sundarbans (Beautiful Forest), an enormous network of waterways through waterlogged jungle that is a haven for wildlife. Many travellers consider the Sundarbans the highlight of their visit to Bangladesh. The monuments and mosques scattered around Bagerhat also make a worthwhile excursion.

**KHULNA DIVISION**

## HIGHLIGHTS

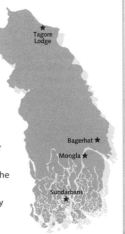

- Drifting surreally through the **Sundarbans** (p89), the world's largest littoral mangrove, and home to the royal Bengal tiger
- Pretending you're Indiana Jones while traipsing through lush rural settings in search of ancient monuments and shrines hidden at **Bagerhat** (p85)
- Being inspired to write a literary masterpiece while visiting **Tagore Lodge** (p81), the former home of Nobel laureate Rabindranath Tagore
- Speculating on the underhand goings-on in the port town of **Mongla** (p87)
- Revelling in the otherworldliness of the sturdy bowels of **Shait Gumbad Mosque** (p86) in Bagerhat

## JESSORE

☎ 0421

Of the country's modern cities, which include Khulna, Dhaka and Sylhet, Jessore (*josh*-or) is the oldest.

At first glance Jessore is an uninteresting town with nothing but the Bhairab River to slice through its ordinariness, but turn enough corners and you will discover its true character. Narrow winding backstreets overcrowded with shops and activity give Jessore a bizarre bazar feel – the perfect town in which to get lost and find adventures.

Jessore was the scene of a decisive event in the 1971 Liberation War. The city had been an important stronghold for the Pakistani army, and after India declared war on 3 December a huge battle was expected here. The Pakistani army at Jessore gave up on 7 December with little resistance, and the war was over less than 10 days later.

### Orientation & Information

To the north, the Bhairab River meanders through town, and the city's principal bazar begins just east of the roundabout that intersects High Court, MK and Benapole Rds. A further 1.5km along MK Rd is the Moniher Cinema intersection, where the bus stations are located. You'll find most hotels, restaurants and banks between these two intersections.

There's a **cybercafé** (High Court Rd) at the western end of town.

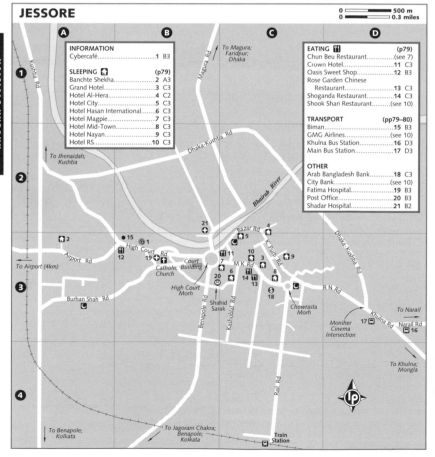

**JESSORE**

0 ——————— 500 m
0 ——————— 0.3 miles

| INFORMATION | |
| --- | --- |
| Cybercafé...................................1 | B3 |

| SLEEPING | (p79) |
| --- | --- |
| Banchte Shekha.........................2 | A3 |
| Grand Hotel...............................3 | C3 |
| Hotel Al-Hera.............................4 | C2 |
| Hotel City..................................5 | C3 |
| Hotel Hasan International.......6 | C3 |
| Hotel Magpie............................7 | C3 |
| Hotel Mid-Town.......................8 | C3 |
| Hotel Nayan..............................9 | C3 |
| Hotel RS...................................10 | C3 |

| EATING | (p79) |
| --- | --- |
| Chun Beu Restaurant............(see 7) | |
| Crown Hotel............................11 | C3 |
| Oasis Sweet Shop...................12 | B3 |
| Rose Garden Chinese | |
| Restaurant.......................13 | C3 |
| Shoganda Restaurant............14 | C3 |
| Shook Shari Restaurant.........(see 10) | |

| TRANSPORT | (pp79–80) |
| --- | --- |
| Biman......................................15 | B3 |
| GMG Airlines..........................(see 10) | |
| Khulna Bus Station................16 | D3 |
| Main Bus Station....................17 | D3 |

| OTHER | |
| --- | --- |
| Arab Bangladesh Bank...........18 | C3 |
| City Bank................................(see 10) | |
| Fatima Hospital......................19 | B3 |
| Post Office..............................20 | B3 |
| Shadar Hospital......................21 | B2 |

KHULNA DIVISION •• Jessore 79

## Sleeping

### BUDGET

**Hotel Mid-Town** (s/d/t Tk 85/120/150) This is one of
the best budget hotels in town. It has clean
rooms with lots of windows, all with attached squat-toilet bathrooms. Some even
have balconies. The hotel is visible from
MK Rd but accessed just off it.

**Grand Hotel** ( ☎ 73038; grand@khulna.bangla.net; MK
Rd; s/d Tk 150/350) This budget hotel is managed
like a mid-range one. Don't be fooled by
the crumbling staircase – it leads to some
well-kept rooms.

**Hotel City** (s/d Tk 45/130) Close to the major
roundabout, in a roundabout sort of way.
There is little English spoken at reception,
but this hotel is cheap in any language.

Tucked away in lively market-lined back-
streets, **Hotel Al-Hera** (Tk 130) and **Hotel Nayan** (s/d
Tk 200/300) both have character. To find them,
ask directions from K'Purti Rd. Nayan has
sit-down toilets, and TV. The devout Muslim management of the Al-Hera may be
averse to solo women staying.

There are some more budget options
near the bus station at the east end of town,
on Khulna Rd.

### MID-RANGE

**Hotel Hasan International** ( ☎ 67478; cnr Kashoblal &
Shahid Sarak Rds; s/d Tk 300/500) By far the best place
to stay, enormous Hotel Hasan is so new you
can smell the paint. Rooms are extraordi-
narily good value, with comfortable beds,
sparkling clean bathrooms, hot water and
TV. There's even a business centre. Unfortunately, the staff aren't as nice as the hotel.

**Banchte Shekha** ( ☎ 6436; Airport Rd; dm Tk 65,
r Tk 250-800) Just east of the bypass road to
Benapole, Banchte Shekha (*bach*-tah *shay*-
kah) is a voluntary organisation that aims
to socially and economically empower des-
titute women. Double rooms are carpeted,
spotless and well lit, and the bathrooms
have hot showers. If you let staff know in
advance, you can join in their family-style
meals for a small fee.

**Jagorani Chakra** ( ☎ 72218; 44 Mujib Sarak; r Tk 400)
Another good option for the socially aware,
Jagorani Chakra is a highly active development organisation. Rooms have hot water
and lots of space, and staying here offers an
insight into the workings of this interesting
NGO. Look for the pink building a short
rickshaw ride out of town.

**Hotel Magpie** ( ☎ 72162; MK Rd; s/d Tk 250/400, with
AC Tk 1000) Though no longer the best place in
town, Hotel Magpie is still as central as you
can get. Rooms are nicer then the building's
exterior suggests, but they're tired.

**Hotel RS** (RS Tower, MK Rd; r Tk 300-1500) Rooms
here are clean enough and have hot water
but, as with the Magpie, show their age.

## Eating

**Chun Beu Restaurant** (4th floor, Hotel Magpie, MK Rd;
dishes around Tk 100) Come here for decent Chinese food in big servings; if you can't go
with company, try to arrange half-serves.

**Rose Garden Chinese Restaurant** (Jess Tower,
MK Rd; dishes around Tk 100) Similar to the Chun
Beu, the well-hidden Rose Garden has an
extensive menu.

**Shook Shari Restaurant** (RS Tower, MK Rd) One of
the nicest (and darkest) places to eat, this is
a local 'special occasion' eatery. You won't be
able to see what you're eating, but you'll certainly be able to taste it. Anything tandoori is
spectacular; anything Chinese is overpriced.

Two inexpensive and central places serving typical Bangladeshi food are the clean
**Crown Hotel** (Bazar Rd), east of High Court Morh,
where a Coke, ample *dahl*, spinach, rice and
salad costs around Tk 25, and the unmarked
**Shoganda Restaurant** (MK Rd), 1½ blocks east of
the same circle.

For a good range of sweetmeats, try the
**Oasis Sweet Shop** (High Court Rd), opposite Biman.
The K'Purti Rd area is a great place for
street food, fresh produce and a carnival-
like atmosphere.

## Getting There & Away

### AIR

The airport is around 6km west of the city
centre.

**GMG Airlines** ( ☎ 73280; RS Tower) flies from Jessore to Dhaka (Tk 1495, 40 minutes) daily
at 11am and 6.25pm. There are also flights
at 3.25pm every day except Thursday and
Saturday. **Biman** ( ☎ 75023; High Court Rd) has daily
flights to Dhaka (Tk 1575, 45 minutes) at
12pm, plus a 5.40pm flight on Saturday, Sunday, Monday and Wednesday.

### BUS

From Dhaka, buses for Jessore (Tk 210, eight
hours) leave from Gabtali bus station.

Buses leave for Dhaka (ordinary/AC
coach Tk 180/280, seven to 10 hours, 6am to

10.30pm) from the main bus station. Several companies have offices around the main bus station. The trip can drag out, with a long wait for the ferry across the Padma River.

There are buses for Benapole (Tk 20, 1½ hours, periodically from 6am), also from the main bus station, and if you're headed to Kolkata count on about six hours for the entire trip.

There are also buses to Khulna (Tk 30, 1½ hours), Barisal (Tk 120, eight hours), Rajshahi (Tk 95, six hours), Bogra (Tk 115, eight hours) and Kushtia (Tk 50, three hours). Most buses leave every 10 minutes or so from 6am onwards.

### TRAIN
The **train station** ( ☎ 5019; Rail Rd) is 2km south of the central area. There's an express to Rajshahi (1st/*sulob* class Tk 215/75, daily at 7.56am).

It's simpler to travel by bus on the short journey to Khulna, although there are inter-city (IC) trains (1st/*sulob* class Tk 85/35, 1½ hours, daily at 3.30am, 2.50pm, 4pm and 6.35pm).

There is also a daily train to Benapole (Tk 15, 8.45am).

## BENAPOLE
Benapole (also spelt Benapol) is the border town situated on the overland route from Kolkata. The town is essentially a 2km-long road lined with trucks waiting to cross the border. It's a friendly enough place, but not one you'd visit unless you were crossing the border.

### Sleeping & Eating
If you've arrived at a reasonable time, it's probably best to spend your first night in Jessore. Failing that, there is some accommodation in Benapole.

**Hotel Haque International** (Tk 100-700) This is a good choice. The most expensive room, a triple, has AC and TV. Some rooms even have sit-down toilets.

**Parjatan Hotel** (r with/without AC Tk 1000/500, ste Tk 2000) The Parjatan corporation set up camp in Benapole in September 2003. The suites have two bathrooms and two bedrooms. There's also a decent restaurant here.

---

### CROSSING THE BORDER

Border officials see quite a few travellers crossing at Benapole and things are relatively efficient. Travellers have been surprised by the friendliness of Bangladeshi border officials after dealing with their Indian counterparts. The border is open every day between 6am and 6.30pm. The changing of the guards on the Indian side adds an air of officialdom to the area and certainly attracts a crowd of interested observers on the Bangladesh side.

Travellers who've arrived in Bangladesh by air have been asked for a 'change of route' permit when trying to leave by land. These can be obtained for free at the Immigration and Passport Office (p164).

#### Changing Money

Sell your excess taka to moneychangers before leaving Bangladesh. Rates aren't the best, so avoid having to change large amounts. You'll do better waiting to change other currencies into Indian rupees on the Indian side, where you'll get better rates from 'authorised moneychangers'.

If you're coming into Bangladesh, be sure to have cash on you, as you'll be hard pressed changing travellers cheques and won't find an ATM. Watch out for minor rip-offs when changing money.

#### Entering & Exiting

Formalities can take a couple of hours, so be sure to start the process with plenty of time. The quietest (and therefore speediest) time to cross is in the middle of the day.

Travelling from the railway station at Bangaon in India to the border costs Rs 30 by baby taxi. It may be easier to take a rickshaw (Rs 15, 30 minutes). Take a rickshaw or three-wheeler cart to the bus stand in Benapole (between Tk 5 and Tk 10). From here you can get a local bus to Jessore (Tk 20, 1½ hours).

If you're going into India, from Bangaon you can take the local train to Kolkata (Rs 15, 2½ hours).

If you're really on a budget, you'll find a small, unmarked **residential hotel** (dm/r Tk 20/60) not far from the centre of town (on the right side of the road if you're facing India). The grubby hovel consists of windowless bunk rooms with five or six beds crammed one against the other.

Also on the right side of the road, there's a well-marked **Chinese restaurant** (meals Tk 80) with cold drinks and an extensive menu. There are also plenty of ordinary restaurants with meals from around Tk 25.

### Getting There & Away

Minibuses ply between Benapole and Jessore, as do local buses (Tk 20, 1½ hours). A minibus will cost you twice as much as, but won't stop en route nearly as much.

Ask for both 'Benapole' and 'border' to avoid confusion. The word 'India' may also come in handy.

## KUSHTIA

☎ 071

Kushtia is a bustling town just south of Rajshahi division. The only 'sights' are a lively Hindu Jagannath temple on the main street (Nawab Sirajuddula Rd) and Tagore Lodge outside of town. This is one of the poorest areas in the country and, to make things worse, the deep tube wells in the area are affected by high arsenic levels.

### Sights

#### TAGORE LODGE

It's a worthwhile trip to **Tagore Lodge**, as much for the journey there as for the lodge itself. A ride to the lodge on a three-wheeler affords the privilege of witnessing village life candidly unfold in front of you. Villagers will find you just as fascinating as you find them as you unexpectedly glide through their day.

This picturesque home was built in the mid-19th century and the world-famous Bengali poet Rabindranath Tagore lived here for over 10 years from 1880, composing some of his immortal poems, songs and short stories. He returned in 1912 for several years, translating his works into English and earning the Nobel Prize for Literature (1913) in the process (see p30).

Photos on display in this elegant building show Tagore in the company of Gandhi and Einstein, amongst others.

The estate is perched on the south bank of the Padma River, outside Shelaidaha, east of Kushtia. To get here, cross the Gorai River (which should not cost more than a few taka, but probably will), then hire a three-wheeler to take you the remaining 8km to the lodge. The cart should cost around Tk 100 return if you bargain successfully.

Opening hours depend on what the groundskeepers feel like doing, but if you rock up at a sensible time you'll generally be able to have a look.

#### SHAILKUPA MOSQUE

This extensively renovated six-domed **mosque** dates from the late 15th or early 16th century. It's one of Bangladesh's better-preserved examples of pre-Mughal architecture. The main entrance, now heavily covered with plaster, was originally decorated with terracotta panels. The mosque is on the eastern edge of the town of Shailkupa, a 28km bus ride southeast of Kushtia.

### Sleeping & Eating

**Circuit House** (Jessore Rd; Tk 200) Unquestionably the best place to stay, this attractive circuit house in the southern part of town has well-maintained, spacious rooms with twin beds, fans and attached bathrooms. The manager will hopefully call the district commissioner and get permission for you to stay.

**Azmiree Hotel** ( ☎ 3012; 107/1 RCRC Rd, Court Para; s/d Tk 150/250) The old Azmiree (aj-mee-ree), near Kushtia Halt, has some impressively clean rooms and shutters that look as though they could withstand a siege. It's poorly marked so you'll have to ask directions near the train station.

**Hotel Alamein** (s/d Tk 100/200) Rooms here aren't spacious but they're secure. If you're a light sleeper, get a room away from reception or you'll be kept awake by Bangladeshi soap operas.

**Pritom Hotel** (Tk 100-500) The Pritom Hotel has rooms that are clean and cosy (read: small).

There are the usual local eateries, and a couple of Chinese restaurants.

### Getting There & Away

Coming into Kushtia, you'll likely be dropped off on a main road away from the main drag. It might be worth getting a rickshaw to Nawab Sirajuddula Rd so you can get your bearings.

Those travelling north by bus must cross the Padma by ferry between Bheramara and Paksey. The ferry takes 20 minutes and runs next to Harding Bridge, the longest railway bridge in Bangladesh.

The bus ride to Jessore (Tk 50, three hours) can be punctuated with stops, but the roads are reasonably well maintained. There's also a train to Jessore (4½ hours).

There are a few luxury coach companies on Babar Rd, at College Gate, that service Dhaka (Tk 220, 6½ hours). One is the friendly **Hanif Enterprises** ( ☎ 913 5018).

## KHULNA
☎ 041

Khulna is the major starting point for trips to the Sundarbans, which start about 50km to the south. While there aren't any sights or activities to speak of in Khulna, the streets burst into life at night, with endless markets and bazars to explore.

### Orientation & Information

Most hotels and restaurants are located in the city's heart. Khan A Sabar Rd, also known as Jessore Rd, is the main drag through the city, and KDA Ave is the major thoroughfare on the western side.

**Bengal Tours** ( ☎ 724 355; 236 Khan Jahan Ali Rd)
**Café.net** (2/2 Babu Khan Rd; per hr Tk 30) A cybercafé that actually has a café.
**Guide Tours** ( ☎ /fax 731 384; www.guidetours.com; KDA Building, KDA Ave)
**Hotel Royal International** ( ☎ 721 638/9; royal@bttb .net.bd; 33 KDA Ave) General tourist information and car rentals. Also does package tours to the Sundarbans.
**New Market** (Upper Jessore Rd; per hr Tk 20) The best place for Internet access, with a few different establishments on the 1st floor. New Market is also a great place to shop; the environment is pressure-free and prices are fixed.
**Standard Chartered Bank** (KDA Ave) Changes money and has an ATM; near Shiv Bari Circle.

For information about Sundarbans tours, and other operators, see p91.

### Sleeping
#### BUDGET

Khulna's cheap hotels are concentrated in the heart of the city in an area 1km south of the train station. Most are well marked in English.

**Society Hotel** ( ☎ 720 995; Helatala Rd; s/d Tk 50/80) One of the best places for the price, it has

### PERMITS FOR THE SUNDARBANS

Permits for travel to the Sundarbans are issued by the **Divisional Forestry Office** ( ☎ 720 665; cnr KD Ghosh & Circuit House Rds; ☼ 10am-5pm Sat-Thu). Staff can be helpful, though some travellers have reported being misinformed. The magic words to write on the application are: 'I will avail the Port Authority vessel' (to get to Hiron Point and back).

If you do manage to get a permit, you will have to take it to the Dhangmari Forestry Station (p91) in the Sundarbans for the 'real permit'; you also may be issued with an armed guard for a small fee.

You don't need a permit if you just do a day trip from Mongla, though you are technically supposed to register at Dhangmari. The downside to doing such a day trip, other than the anguish of organising anything from Mongla, is that you won't see much of the Sundarbans.

If this all sounds confusing, that's because it is. The easiest way to go about seeing the Sundarbans is to pay the money to take an organised tour. For more information on arranging trips to the Sundarbans, see p91.

tiny, reasonably clean rooms with attached bathrooms, fans and mosquito nets.

**Khulna Hotel** ( ☎ 724 359; s/d Tk 120/150) Another decent option for the not-so-discerning, the Khulna Hotel is 30m from the Society Hotel in the same alley.

**National Hotel** (s Tk 60, d Tk 100-150) Down a narrow market lane off Clay Rd, the National has cell-like rooms with common squat-toilet bathrooms.

**Hotel Basundhara** (24 Clay Rd; s/d Tk 150/300) The relatively average beds will look luxurious after you've hiked up the stairs to get to them.

#### MID-RANGE

**Hotel Babla** ( ☎ 731 374; 65 Khan A Sabar Rd; s/d/t Tk 150/190/290, d with AC Tk 650) A great new place, Hotel Babla is extremely clean, and the uneven floor plan gives it character. The friendly manager speaks English and German. The AC doubles have sit-down toilets.

**Hotel Park** ( ☎ 720 990; 46 KD Ghosh Rd; s/d/t Tk 150/220/400, r with AC Tk 750) A good option with laundry service and a refrigerator stocked

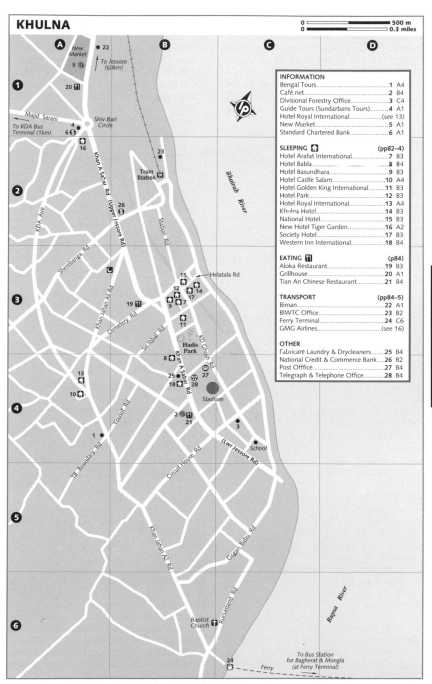

# KHULNA

0 — 500 m
0 — 0.3 miles

**INFORMATION**
Bengal Tours.................................1 A4
Café.net.....................................2 B4
Divisional Forestry Office.................3 C4
Guide Tours (Sundarbans Tours)..........4 A1
Hotel Royal International...............(see 13)
New Market.................................5 A1
Standard Chartered Bank.................6 A1

**SLEEPING** (pp82–4)
Hotel Arafat International................7 B3
Hotel Babla.................................8 B4
Hotel Basundhara..........................9 B3
Hotel Castle Salam.......................10 A4
Hotel Golden King International.......11 B3
Hotel Park.................................12 B3
Hotel Royal International................13 A4
Khulna Hotel..............................14 B3
National Hotel............................15 B3
New Hotel Tiger Garden.................16 A2
Society Hotel.............................17 B3
Western Inn International...............18 B4

**EATING** (p84)
Aloka Restaurant..........................19 B3
Grillhouse.................................20 A1
Tian An Chinese Restaurant............21 B4

**TRANSPORT** (pp84–5)
Biman.....................................22 A1
BIWTC Office.............................23 B2
Ferry Terminal...........................24 C6
GMG Airlines...........................(see 16)

**OTHER**
Fabricare Laundry & Drycleaners.......25 B4
National Credit & Commerce Bank....26 B2
Post Offfice................................27 B4
Telegraph & Telephone Office.........28 B4

KHULNA DIVISION

with cold drinks in the reception area. There is also a restaurant on the roof. The standard rooms are a better buy than the pricier options; if you're prepared to pay the AC price, you might as well pay it elsewhere.

**Hotel Golden King International** ( ☎ 725 917; 25 Sir Iqbal Rd; s/d Tk 160/600) It's reasonably well kept, with some larger-than-average rooms and funky 1970s décor.

**New Hotel Tiger Garden** ( ☎ 721 108; 1 KDA Ave; Tk 180-950) This is the sort of place where staff suggestively whisper to single male guests that they can arrange 'anything'. The place could certainly do more to justify having added 'new' to its name, starting with the sheets and carpets.

**Hotel Arafat International** ( ☎ 721 780) A contender for 'last resort' category, this dingy hotel, down an alley off Sir Iqbal Rd, has seen better days (one hopes). Prices seem to be made up on the spot – generally upwards of Tk 200, for which you could do better.

### TOP END

**Western Inn International** ( ☎ 733 191; western@bttb .net.bd; 51 Khan A Sabur Rd; Tk 800-2000) The ritziest place in town and arguably the best value for its type, the new Western Inn is extremely well managed. There are even meeting rooms and business centres. Rooms have every mod con imaginable and are display-home clean. Some rooms have secluded balconies. The fantastic restaurant (right) on the ground floor is also a big tick in favour of this hotel.

**Hotel Royal International** ( ☎ 721 638/9; royal@ bttb.net.bd; 33 KDA Ave; Tk 500-1200) The most expensive rooms have a balcony, satellite TV and a minibar. Rooms are reasonably big, and bathrooms have Western toilets and hot water. Staff are hospitably engaging. There's a travel agency in the lobby where you can make arrangements for car rental and guided trips to the Sundarbans. The restaurant offers European and Chinese selections.

**Hotel Castle Salam** ( ☎ 730 725; castle@khulnanet .net; cnr Khan Jahan Ali Rd & KDA Ave; Tk 800-1200) Across the road from the Royal, Castle Salam is a step up in class but a step down in personality. Rooms are decked out with all mod cons, including IDD phones, and are unusually large. The enormous restaurant offers Western and Chinese dishes. This hotel feels more home-grown than the Western Inn, but for this reason you might opt against it. Check them both out to see which fits.

## Eating

**Western Inn International** ( ☎ 733 191; dishes around Tk 200) The Bengali/European/Chinese/Thai restaurant at the Western Inn is not as expensive as you might expect, and the French onion soup would hold its own in Paris.

**Aloka Restaurant** ( ☎ 733 342; 1 Khan A Sabar Rd) Simply lovely. There is no menu but the waiters won't rest until you're adequately fed. A feast of quality Bangladeshi *dahl*, vegies, rice and salad will set you back around Tk 60.

**Grillhouse** ( ☎ 760 245) People rave about the kebabs, thick *dahl* and naan at the Grillhouse, near New Market. It also has a secluded outdoor eating area.

**Tian An Chinese Restaurant** (dishes Tk 60-150) There's a good range of Chinese dishes here.

For really cheap food, head for the food stalls around the train station. There's also good street food in the Dak Bangla area, near Hadis Park.

## Getting There & Away

### AIR

The nearest airport is at Jessore. **Biman** ( ☎ 731 020) and **GMG Airlines** ( ☎ 732 273) provide direct bus services between Jessore airport and their Khulna offices.

### BOAT

The **Bangladesh Inland Waterway Transport Corporation** (BIWTC; ☎ 721 532) office looks like a small house. It's just behind the train station and opens every day at around 9am.

Between Khulna and Dhaka (1st/2nd/ inter/deck class Tk 915/555/139/94) there are four Rockets per week in each direction. They stop at Mongla (1st/2nd/inter/deck class Tk 126/75/24/16), Barisal (1st/2nd/inter/ deck class Tk 479/290/92/61) and several smaller ports. Reserve several days in advance to ensure a 1st-class cabin.

Departures from Khulna are scheduled at 3am daily, though there can be delays.

### BUS

The main bus station is KDA bus terminal (also known as Sonadanga bus terminal), 2km northwest of the city centre. A rickshaw costs about Tk 10 from the city centre and Tk 20 from the Rupsa ghat. Inside KDA terminal, bus companies servicing common destinations are grouped in the same area. This station serves all points except Mongla and Bagerhat; buses for those towns leave from south of the city, just across the Rupsa River. The ferry over the Rupsa leaves regularly and is free for pedestrians. If you're in a hurry you could pay a small boat a couple of taka to take you over.

Buses headed to Mongla (Tk 22, one hour) and Bagerhat (Tk 18, 45 minutes) depart throughout the day.

Buses to Dhaka (Tk 100, 7½ hours) depart throughout the day also, until early evening. **Eagle Paribahan** ( ☎ 924583), across from Hotel Castle Salam, charges Tk 260/170 for an AC/chair coach; its buses leave from the Hotel Royal International intersection area nearby.

Buses for Barisal mostly leave in the early morning and early evening. SM Enterprise has buses bound for Barisal (Tk 130, eight hours), daily at 6.30am, 7pm and 7.30pm).

Buses for Jessore (Tk 15, one hour) leave frequently until the early evening; the fare is Tk 30 for coaches.

### CAR
You can rent a car through the Hotel Royal International or the Hotel Park; the cost is around Tk 1200 a day, including the driver but not petrol. The Hotel Castle Salam also rents cars to guests, charging Tk 1200 to Jessore, Mongla and Bagerhat, and up to Tk 6000 to Dhaka.

### TRAIN
The main **station** ( ☎ 723222) is near the city centre. There are four IC trains a day to Jessore (1st/*sulob* class Tk 85/35, 1½ hours) and three mail trains, which also take passengers but are slower. The 6.45am IC express continues on to Rajshahi (1st/*sulob* class Tk 265/90, 6½ hours), and the 8.45pm express goes to Saidpur (1st/*sulob* class Tk 355/170, nine hours) via Ishurdi.

There's a night train to Dhaka (1st/*sulob* class Tk 625/235, 9½ hours, departs 10.30pm), though buses are preferable given the disruptive need to switch trains en route.

## BAGERHAT
☎ 401
Bagerhat has more historical monuments in its surrounding area than any other town in Bangladesh (except Dhaka), including one of its most famous – Shait Gumbad Mosque.

Bagerhat was also home to one of the most revered men in Bangladeshi history, Khan Jahan Ali (p86), and is a significant cradle of Islam in Bangladesh.

The principal 15th-century mosques are in one large area 5km west of Bagerhat. The tranquil countryside is a joy to walk through, and locals will find you a joy to watch. There are lotus-filled ponds, which support a variety of bird life.

With the Sundarbans so close there are reportedly occasional attacks by crocodiles in the waterways around Bagerhat.

The town lacks decent hotels and restaurants, so it's sensible to visit Bagerhat as a day trip from Khulna or Mongla.

KHULNA DIVISION

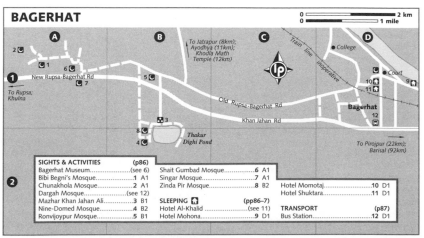

## Sights

### BAGERHAT MUSEUM

The **Bagerhat Museum** (admission Tk 2), opposite Shait Gumbad Mosque, is a good place to start. It gives a good overview of what you'll be seeing.

### MOSQUES

Built in 1459, the same year Khan Jahan died, the famous **Shait Gumbad Mosque** is the largest and most magnificent traditional mosque in the country. Shait Gumbad means 'the Temple with 60 Domes' – a misnomer given that there are actually 77. This fortress-like structure is an impressive sight from a distance, and equally fascinating inside. The 60 stone columns punctuating the single sanctuary emphasise how big the building is.

Around Shait Gumbad are three other mosques worth seeing, all single-domed and in reasonably good condition. These are **Bibi Begni's Mosque**, about 500m behind Shait Gumbad and across a large pond; **Chunakhola Mosque**, in a paddy field about 500m behind Bibi Begni's; and **Singar Mosque**, across the highway from Shait Gumbad.

On the western bank of the Thakur Dighi Pond, the recently repaired **Nine-Domed Mosque** is an impressive structure. Of the same period as the other religious buildings in town, it has massive walls and nine low hemispherical domes supported by four slender stone columns. The mihrabs are embellished with terracotta floral scrolls and foliage motifs, with a prominent chain-and-bell terracotta motif in the centre.

You might also want to check out **Zinda Pir Mosque** just north of the Nine-Domed Mosque.

About 2km east of Shait Gumbad is the splendid **Ronvijoypur Mosque**. It is singularly impressive, with the largest dome in Bangladesh, spanning 11m and supported by 3m-thick walls. Each side has three arched doorways, and on each corner is a circular tower.

### MAZHAR KHAN JAHAN ALI

Across the main highway from Ronvijoypur Mosque is **Khan Jahan's Tomb** – the only monument in Bagerhat that retains its original cupolas. The cenotaph at the entrance is apparently covered with tiles of various colours and inscribed with Quranic verses, but it is usually covered with a red cloth embroidered with gold threads. The mausoleum and the single-domed **Dargah Mosque** are enclosed by a massive wall with short towers at each corner and archways on the front and back.

#### KHAN JAHAN ALI

Khan Jahan was a Turkish Sufi – a Muslim mystic similar to Hindu sadhus or yogis in India. Khan Jahan settled in Bagerhat in the middle of the 15th century and became widely known as a holy man.

After arriving in Bagerhat with thousands of horsemen, clearing the jungle and founding Khalifatabad (as the town was originally named), this warrior-saint initiated an incredible construction programme. In just a decade or two, he had adorned his capital city with mosques, bridges, palaces and other public buildings, and brick-paved highways to neighbouring regions. Large ponds of water with staircase landings were built in various parts of the township to provide salt-free drinking water in this predominantly saline belt.

When Khan Jahan died, a mausoleum was raised in his memory. Today he is the patron saint of the area and his name equates with a major pre-Mughal architectural style in Bangladesh.

### KHODLA MATH TEMPLE

The 20m-high spire on this beehive-like **Hindu building** makes it one of the tallest Hindu structures ever built in Bangladesh. Built by a Brahman in the early 17th century, during Mughal times, legend has it that it was a memorial to a court adviser. The entrance façade is thought to have been decorated with moulded terracotta art, but it's now badly weathered.

Khodla Math is just outside the village of Ayodhya, about 11km from Bagerhat. Take a rickshaw or baby taxi to the market town of Jatrapur. From there ask directions to Ayodhya, 3km east along winding paved paths.

## Sleeping & Eating

Pickings are slim on the sleeping front.

**Hotel Mohona** (Khan Jalan-Ali Rd; s/d Tk 50/125) The best option is probably this place, which is clean but noisy given that it's on the main road.

**Hotel Momotaj** (Rail Rd; s/d Tk 70/120) It's poorly marked, but has attached bathrooms and is liveable.

**Hotel Shuktara** (s/d Tk 60/120) and **Hotel Al-Khalid** (s/d Tk 60/100) are on the same block. The latter has a restaurant and some interesting characters milling around. It could do with new mattresses, though.

There are some basic local restaurants and street stalls along the main road.

## Getting There & Away
### BUS
The bus from Khulna (Tk 20, 45 minutes) takes you through some enchanting countryside. The bus passes Shait Gumbad (5km before town) on the left, where you can disembark and start sightseeing.

If you're headed to Mongla, it may be faster to take a bus to the Khulna–Mongla Rd intersection and hail another bus there. You may have to stand, but the 33km trip from the intersection takes less than an hour. Buses from Khulna headed east to Pirojpur and Barisal also pass through Bagerhat, but finding a seat might be difficult.

### CAR
You can organise a hire car from Khulna to take you to and around Bagerhat (see p85). The bus ride is an easy one though, and it's the sort of scenery in which you don't mind being delayed.

## Getting Around
From the bus station, hire a rickshaw for a few hours to take you to the various sights and back to the bus terminal. You could start the bidding (and maybe be successful) at around Tk 70, but when you see the narrow bumpy roads that inflict wear and tear on the rickshaw, you may feel like upping the price.

## MONGLA
☎ 04658
Mongla, 42km south of Khulna, is large enough to be something of a melting pot, but small enough to feel like a community.

Despite being about 80km upriver from the Bay of Bengal, the port on the vast confluence of the Pusur and Mongla Rivers has a string of freighters riding at anchor waiting

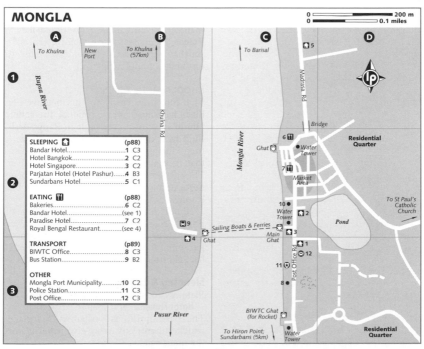

to be loaded or unloaded. It's a spectacular sight, especially towards the southern end where dense jungle lines the banks. The Sundarbans begins only 5km south.

Some of the locals have crewed foreign ships, and there are smuggled goods available for sale in the market, including beer and 'Burmese whisky'. All of this excitement brings with it some not-so-savoury elements, so it's wise to be guarded after dark. If the intensity of Mongla becomes too much, a walk on the outskirts of town will yield surprisingly serene scenery and sincere smiles.

## Sights & Activities
### BOAT CRUISE
At the outset, it's worth saying that despite Mongla's proximity to the Sundarbans, Khulna is the better place from which to organise a **boat trip**.

Many travellers have reported bad experiences in the form of hostile negotiations, overcharging and/or failure to deliver on what was promised. Some companies get bad reports about overcharging and cutting tours short, and it is hard to get a sensible quote from an independent operator. To determine whether a boatman is independent of Mongla's mafia elements, ask for a business card. If he doesn't have one, he's more likely to be. You really need to do your research. When you're shopping around for quotes, be clear on what is included in the price, where the boat will go and how long it will go for. Don't pay everything up front; arrange to pay a percentage of the negotiated price on delivery of what was promised.

A day trip can cost as much as Tk 2000 (when even Tk 1000 is high) and there is no guarantee that you will see much of the Sundarbans. You're better off spending more money to arrange a proper trip from Khulna or even Dhaka. For more information see p91.

Having said that, there are some good operators in Mongla (Jahangir Enterprises has been recommended) and if you are a shrewd bargainer, you may be able to get a price you're comfortable with, support a local business, and have a fun taster tour of the Sundarbans.

### ST PAUL'S CATHOLIC CHURCH
Built in 1992, **St Paul's Catholic Church** is a fascinating marriage of Catholic and Islamic

design. Skilfully embroidered wall hangings depict a Bangladeshi Christ. The church grounds, home to the legendary Italian priest who has been living here for 50 years, are something of an oasis in messy Mongla. St Paul's also operates a hospital, a high school and a sewing school. If you drop by the church grounds, someone will probably be able to show you around and may even arrange a visit to the hospital and high school. You can purchase stunning embroideries from the **sewing centre** ( 9am-noon & 2-4pm, closed Sun).

## Sleeping
**Parjatan Hotel** (Hotel Pashur; ☎ 801 698; r with/ without AC Tk 1200/600) Without a doubt, the nicest place to stay is the Parjatan, across the river from town. Rooms are bright and clean, with a small balcony overlooking Mongla River and the busy port beyond. Staff can help you track down a boatman for the Sundarbans.

**Hotel Bangkok** (s/d Tk 75/200) Locals will all direct you to Hotel Bangkok. Singles have shared bathroom and doubles have attached. Some doubles have mosquito nets. Staff are friendly and keen for your patronage.

**Hotel Singapore** (s with shared bathroom Tk 50, s/d Tk 70/120) The sheets are not changed as often as they should be, but mosquito nets are provided. Though relatively indistinguishable from each other, Hotel Bangkok seems to be preferred to Hotel Singapore.

If for some reason you can't get a room in any of these, there's also the **Bandar Hotel** (s/d Tk 60/100). The **Sundarbans Hotel** (Madrasa Rd) will have plenty of rooms, unoccupied but for the cockroaches. It's a dark place at a dark end of town, but it's there.

## Eating
Mongla isn't overflowing with eating options. The best appears to be **Bandar Hotel** (Post Office Rd), which is located on the main drag, across from Hotel Singapore. Also on the main drag is the **Paradise Hotel** (Post Office Rd). If you need an escape, head across the river to the **Parjatan Hotel** (Hotel Pashur, Khulna Rd), where you'll find the **Royal Bengal Restaurant** ( breakfast, lunch & dinner), with a decent selection of Bangladeshi and European options at tolerable prices.

At the north end of town, before the bridge, there are a couple of bakeries with some basic snack foods.

## Getting There & Away
### BOAT
The BIWTC office is 150m south of the ferry ghat, and the Rocket ghat is 100m further south. You may have difficulty booking 1st- and 2nd-class Rocket tickets here; if possible, book in Khulna or Dhaka.

The Rocket goes to Dhaka (1st/2nd/inter class Tk 870/530/95, departs 6.20am), Khulna (Tk 145/85/20, departs 5am) and Barisal (Tk 390/240/50, departs 6pm), daily except Sunday.

Rockets coming in from Dhaka often arrive late, so even if you think you've missed the boat, check anyway.

### BUS
Almost all buses leave from the bus station across the Mongla River, just outside the Parjatan Hotel (Hotel Pashur). It costs Tk 2 to cross the river on the public wooden boats.

Buses for Khulna (Tk 22, one hour, 6.40am to 7pm) leave every 20 minutes.

## SUNDARBANS NATIONAL PARK
The Sundarbans is the largest littoral mangrove belt in the world, stretching 80km into the hinterland from the coast. The forests aren't just mangrove swamps; they include some of the last remaining stands of the mighty jungles that once covered the Gangetic Plain.

The Sundarbans begin about 5km southwest of Mongla along the Pusur River, and cover an area of nearly 3600 sq km in Bangladesh and another 2400 sq km in India. This is still thought to be half the size it was 200 years ago. About one-third of the total area of this forest is covered in water – river channels, canals and tidal creeks varying in width from a few metres to a few kilometres. The land is constantly being reshaped by tidal action, and cyclones wreak havoc.

The ecological balance of these impenetrable forests is extremely delicate and influenced greatly by tidal shifts that affect the salinity, and hence the growth rates, of the surrounding vegetation. The eclectic inhabitants of the Sundarbans range from deer, pigs and crabs to the mighty Bengal tiger. The Divisional Forestry Office supervises activities to protect the delicate ecological balance and botanists, zoologists, environmentalists and conservationists around the world keep eager eyes on this ecological repository.

---

**WARNING**

In addition to the logistical hassles involved in mounting your own expedition into the Sundarbans, another big reason to be wary of doing so is the presence of bandits in the area. The danger is often exploited by amateur boat operators who try to charge you for additional 'security' or, conversely, don't inform you of the dangers but give you an abbreviated tour to avoid them.

The truth is that people have been held up at gunpoint in the Sundarbans. You may save money by mounting your own trip, but it could end up costing you more. You're safer and more likely to experience the Sundarbans properly if you employ the services of a guide (see p91).

---

The dry season, November to April, is the most popular season for visiting the Sundarbans.

## History
The first record of settlement in the region is from the 13th century. Hindus fleeing the Muslim advance sought refuge in the forests, eventually settling and building a number of temples (one of which was memorably fictionalised by Salman Rushdie in *Midnight's Children*). They were later joined by the Khiljis, who were fleeing the Afghans. In the 17th century, Portuguese-Mogh pirates probably caused the population to leave the area, although lack of fresh water and an unhealthy climate must have been contributing factors.

The Sundarbans has been a wildlife sanctuary since 1966 and was added to the World Heritage list in 1997.

## Wildlife
The Sundarbans is home to some unique subcontinental wildlife, though spotting them in the thick mangrove forests is difficult. Most visitors report seeing little, but many argue that it is the pristine environment and not the wildlife that is the real attraction of the Sundarbans. Elevated viewing towers have been constructed to help visitors spot wildlife.

### ROYAL BENGAL TIGERS
Royal Bengal tigers, the pride of Bangladesh, have been known to grow to a body length

## LIFE IN THE SUNDARBANS

There are no permanent settlements within the forest, apart from a few government camps housing the labour force for the extraction of timber. These camps are either built on stilts or 'hang' from the trees because of the soft muddy ground and the 2m-high tides that course through the coastal areas.

From November to mid-February thousands of fishermen from Chittagong converge on Dublar Island, at the mouth of the Kunga River, a Sundarbans estuary, to harvest schooling shrimp that come here to breed, and to catch fish and sharks.

During the same period, thousands of low-caste Hindus from Khulna, Barisal and Patuakhali come to the island for a three-day mela (festival). They set up statues of deities in makeshift temples, bathe in the holy waters and release or sacrifice goats. During the mela, sweetmeats, dried fruit, toys, hookahs, wooden clogs and religious paraphernalia are sold in the market. A few weeks after their departure, the fishermen also return to Chittagong. For the next nine months the island is deserted.

You might also see fishing families who live like sea gypsies in the Sundarbans. They have large boats with thatched roofs and cabins. Some woodcutters working in the Sundarbans also live in boats or temporary dwellings on the edge of the forest, usually at a height of 3m or so, for protection from tigers.

Besides yielding fish in great quantities, the region produces the *sundari* tree (see opposite). Other forest products include *gol* leaves (from a local shade tree of that name), reeds, snails and honey. Indeed, the Sundarbans is one of the country's richest sources of honey (*madhu* or *mau*), producing over 250,000kg annually. About 90% comes from the far western area called Satkhira, where certain flowering trees thrive on the higher salinity.

The people who gather honey, known as *maualis*, occasionally constitute a part of the diet of the royal Bengal tiger. Locals say that each season five to 10 *maualis* are attacked and eaten by tigers. Indeed, they are far more vulnerable to tiger attack than anybody else. The *maualis* carry no protection and in the frenzy of following the bees to their hives, can't keep an eye out for tigers as well. Tigers attack from the rear, and in a matter of seconds can crush a victim's head or break his neck. On the Indian side of the Sundarbans, the forest department has developed iron head-masks for the *maualis*, which have proven quite effective. But in Bangladesh, honey collectors continue to work unprotected.

of more than 2m. They have a life span of 16 years and prey on deer, boars and fish stranded on river beds at low tide. It is only in old age, when they have lost their physical agility and canine fangs, that they sometimes prey on workers in the area.

There are thought to be roughly 400 tigers remaining in the Sundarbans and every year there are reports of people in the area getting eaten by tigers. Although they may not admit it, most guides, despite carrying rifles, are terrified of the tigers. Consequently, they make considerable noise during excursions, scaring them off and virtually ensuring that you won't encounter one. Nevertheless, there are just enough sightings to encourage visitors. One group reported seeing a tiger swim right by their boat.

### BIRDS

Over 270 different species have been recorded in this region, including about 95 species of water birds and 35 species of birds of prey. Birds found here include snipes, white and gold herons, woodcocks, coots, yellowlegs, sandpipers, common cranes, golden eagles and the *madan-tak* (adjutant bird), which always looks worried and dejected.

### OTHER WILDLIFE

Wildlife in the Sundarbans includes deer, wild boars, clawless otters, monkeys, crocodiles, 50 species of reptiles (including snakes and eight species of amphibians) and numerous river dolphins.

There are an estimated 30,000 spotted deer in the Sundarbans. They're relatively easy to find given that they use clearings and river banks to drink. Monkeys have curiously been observed to drop *keora* leaves whenever deer appear on the scene.

Even more curiously, otters are trained by fishermen to herd fish. Nets are placed at the mouths of streams or creeks, and the otters are released upstream to chase the fish down into the nets.

## Information

Officially, permits are required to visit the Sundarbans. They are issued by the Divisional Forestry Office (p82) in Khulna and validated at the Dhangmari Forestry Station, 4km southwest of Mongla across the Pusur River on the northern fringes of the Sundarbans.

If you have no permit because you are only doing a day-trip from Mongla, you are technically required to inform the Forestry Station. This is rarely done in practice, though. For overnight trips a permit, guides and guards are required.

To get to Dhangmari from Mongla, the 2½-hour round trip will cost around Tk 100 in a rowboat, which you can find on the waterfront near the BIWTC office. A motorised boat shouldn't cost much more, but it will.

## Organised Tours

For a motorised excursion into the Sundarbans, expect to pay up to Tk 1000 for a day trip that might only take you as far as Karamjal Wildlife Breeding centre – a boardwalked piece of mangrove with some bored-looking deer milling about. For information on organising trips in Mongla, see p88.

**Guide Tours** (Map p83; ☎ /fax 041-731 384; KDA Bldg, KDA Ave, Khulna) gets fantastic reports for all of its tours, and its Sundarbans trips are no exception. The more people in a group, the less you'll pay. A standard three-day, five-night trip will cost US$70 per person for a large group (44 people) and $165 for a small group (six people). A five-day, four-night trip costs US$95 (large group) or US$255 (small group). Fees include all food, accommodation (usually on board the boat) and transport, though there is usually an extra Tk 1000 to cover forestry entrance expenses

---

### THE SUNDARI TREE

The Sundarbans derives its name from the *sundari* trees that grow here. These 25m-high trees are very straight, have tiny branches and keep well in water – they become rock hard when submerged for a long time and are thus suitable for shipbuilding, electric poles, railway sleepers and house construction. Gema wood, also felled in the Sundarbans, is mainly pulped for the Khulna newsprint factory. Timber workers here are called *bawulis*.

---

such as permits and guards. You could organise these yourself for less money, but a lot more hassle. There is another **Guide Tours office** (Map pp60-1; ☎ 02-988 6983; 1st floor, Darpan Complex, DIT II Circle, Gulshan) in Dhaka, and also a **desk** at the Sheraton Hotel (Map pp52-4; 1 Minto Rd, Dhaka).

You can also easily arrange trips through the manager of the **Hotel Royal International** (Map p83; ☎ 041-721 638; royal@bttb.net.bd; 33 KDA Ave, Khulna), where customers are pooled with those from the Western Inn. While most visitors give positive reports, there have been complaints about less-than-eco-friendly practices. A two-day overnight trip to Hiron Point, including food, accommodation, transport, permits and guards, will cost upwards of Tk 7000, depending on how many people sign up for a trip.

If you have time, you could shop around for competitive prices:

**Bangladesh Expeditions** Dhaka (Map pp52-4; ☎ 018-227 387; www.expeditions-bd.com; 2nd fl, Sheraton Hotel, 1 Minto Rd)

**Bengal Tours** Dhaka ( ☎ 882 0716; www.bengaltours.com; house 66, Rd 10, block D, Banani); Khulna ( ☎ 724 355; 236 Khan Jahan Ali Rd)

**Unique Tours and Travels** Dhaka (Map pp60-1; ☎ 029 885 1168; unique@bangla.net; 51/B Kemal Ataturk Ave, Banani)

KHULNA DIVISION

# Barisal Division

Barisal division is marked by the branches of the Padma that braid through it to the Bay of Bengal, creating a maze of waterways. This wide, flat region has little to offer in the way of historical monuments but, in many ways, Barisal division is the quintessential Bangladesh. There is hardly any industrial development in this luxuriously green region fringed by rivers and the sea. The land is intermingled with ponds, marshes and streams, which keep the soft, fertile ground moist.

Barisal division lies south of Dhaka division, and Khulna division forms its western boundary. To the east flows the silt-laden lower Meghna River, building huge islands in its wide channel as it devours others. At the southern tip of the division is Kuakata – a wide, sandy beach boasting coconut groves, a Buddhist temple and tribal communities.

**BARISAL DIVISION**

### HIGHLIGHTS

- Meandering through quiet, temple-lined backstreets in **Barisal** (p93)
- Watching the sun rise and set over the Bay of Bengal from the beach in **Kuakata** (p95)

- POPULATION: 7,757,000

# BARISAL

☎ 0431

The capital of the division, Barisal (*bore*-ee-shal) is a major port city largely isolated from the rest of Bangladesh. It's one of the more pleasant cities in the country, with several ponds in the city centre and handsome buildings from the Raj era in quiet backstreets. Another interesting area is the busy river port, which is always teeming with activity.

## Information

**City Bank** (Sadar Rd) Change money here.

**Cybercafé** (Ali International Bldg, Sadar Rd) Erratic opening hours. Follow the signs up the stairs.

**Genius Café** (Sadar Rd; per hr Tk 20) Most of your money will be spent waiting for the computer to do something.

**Netcop Café** (Sadar Rd; per hr Tk 20) Next door to Genius and equally slow.

## Sleeping

### BUDGET

Quite a few of the cheaper hotels near BIWTC Ghat Rd are loath to accept foreigners.

**YMCA** (Iswar Bose Rd; dm Tk 25) Sometimes closed and almost always appearing as if it is, you may have to ask someone to track down the *chowkidar* (caretaker). Head down an alley across from the gateway to the Catholic church, then left down a lane (Iswar Bose Rd). Walk past a large maroon building, then follow the laneway to the right. At the end you'll find the YMCA.

**Hotel Park** ( ☎ 52678; with/without AC s Tk 120/80, d Tk 120/200) On a busy street between BIWTC Ghat and Sadar Rds, this hotel is a little overpriced but otherwise a reasonably good place to stay. Prices vary depending on the size and cleanliness of the rooms. A big downside is the lack of natural light.

**Hotel Golden Inn International** ( ☎ 53161; s/d Tk 110/200) Across the street from the Hotel Park, the Golden Inn isn't as roomy (twin beds are so close together they might as well be a double), but the staff are just as friendly. Rooms are reasonably clean and have fans, mosquito nets and decent bathrooms.

### MID-RANGE

**Hotel Ali International** ( ☎ 54122; Sadar Rd; s Tk 150-350, d 200-700) One of the best places to stay, it's an orderly, well-managed place with knowledgeable reception staff and hotel boys who don't pound the door down. Some rooms share a common bathroom,

while the pricier rooms are large and spotless with comfortable armchairs and beds, fans, coffee tables and sit-down toilets. The GMG Airlines office is on the 1st floor of the building.

**Paradise Hotel** ( ☎ 52009; Hospital Rd; s/d Tk 125/200, s/d with TV Tk 250/600, d with TV & AC Tk 750) It's almost as good as the Hotel Ali International. The exterior looks a bit shabby but there's private parking, a small garden and, besides some musty carpets, it's clean and well furnished. All rooms have attached bathroom.

**Circuit House** ( ☎ 56464; s/d Tk 200/400) An attractive old single-storey building on the main drag on the southern side of town. It has a relaxing atmosphere, with a comfortable sitting room. You must seek permission from the district commissioner ( ☎ 52040) and, as usual, this can be difficult.

**Hotel Hoque International** ( ☎ 54971; 54 Sadar Rd; s/d Tk 130/200, s/d with TV Tk 200/300, d with TV & AC Tk 600) The beds are comfortable, bathrooms are clean and management is helpful. One English sign reads Hotel Huq.

## Eating

There aren't many restaurants to speak of in Barisal. There are numerous small, cheap, seemingly makeshift restaurants in the area around the intersection of BIWTC Ghat Rd and Faisal Huq Ave. Some cha stalls around town specialise in 'red tea' – cardamom tea without milk.

**Rose Garden Restaurant** (Sadar Rd; ☽ lunch & dinner) This is a great place to dine. There is no menu but the Bangladeshi food is more often than not delicious. Female patrons soothe the atmosphere, and the nonsmoking rule makes for a refreshing change. It's almost opposite Faisal Huq Ave.

**South King Chinese Restaurant** (BIWTC Ghat Rd; dishes around Tk 100; ☽ dinner) Like so many

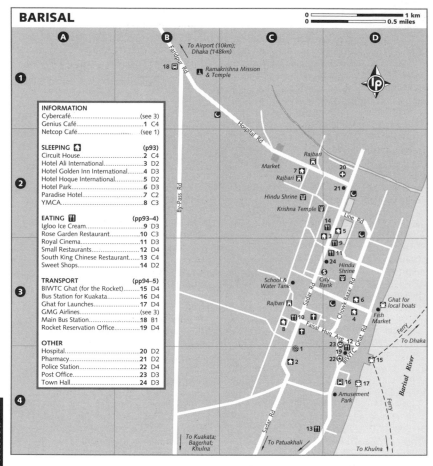

**BARISAL**

INFORMATION
Cybercafé.............................(see 3)
Genius Café..............................1  C4
Netcop Café.........................(see 1)

SLEEPING 🏠                        (p93)
Circuit House...........................2  C4
Hotel Ali International.............3  D2
Hotel Golden Inn International........4  D3
Hotel Hoque International.........5  D2
Hotel Park.................................6  D3
Paradise Hotel.........................7  C2
YMCA.......................................8  C3

EATING 🍴                        (pp93–4)
Igloo Ice Cream.......................9  D3
Rose Garden Restaurant.........10  C3
Royal Cinema.........................11  D3
Small Restaurants...................12  D4
South King Chinese Restaurant.....13  C4
Sweet Shops...........................14  D2

TRANSPORT                      (pp94–5)
BIWTC Ghat (for the Rocket)....15  D4
Bus Station for Kuakata..........16  D4
Ghat for Launches...................17  D4
GMG Airlines.......................(see 3)
Main Bus Station....................18  B1
Rocket Reservation Office........19  D4

OTHER
Hospital...................................20  D2
Pharmacy.................................21  D2
Police Station..........................22  D4
Post Office...............................23  D3
Town Hall................................24  D3

To Airport (10km);
Dhaka (148km)

Ramakrishna Mission
& Temple

Hospital Rd

Faridpur Rd

By-Pass Rd

Rajbari
Market
Rajbari
Hindu Shrine
Krishna Temple

Line Rd

Sadar Rd

Chowk Bazar Rd

School &
Water Tank

City
Bank

Rajbari

Faisal Huq Ave

BIWTC Ghat Rd

Hindu
Shrine

Ghat for
local boats

Fish
Market

Ferry

To Dhaka

Barisal River

Ferry

Amusement
Park

To Kuakata;
Bagerhat;
Khulna

To Patuakhali

To Khulna

Bangladeshi Chinese restaurants, the food at the South King Chinese Restaurant is far from fine cuisine. It does provide an isolated reprieve from the streets, and from sunlight.

There are some low-key but popular restaurants at the **Royal Cinema** (Sadar Rd). The larger restaurant at the end of the hall serves Bangladeshi food, while the **Mini Chinese** (dishes Tk 20-50) with its mini-prices offers the Chinese alternative. It's overly dark and warm inside, but some would call that cosy.

For ice cream and sweets there's **Igloo Ice Cream** (Sadar Rd), 30m to the north of Royal Cinema, and small sweet shops half a block further.

## Getting There & Away

### AIR

**GMG Airlines** ( ☎ 56510; 1st fl, Ali International Bldg, Sadar Rd) has flights from Barisal to Dhaka (Tk 1395, 35 minutes, daily at 9.15am) and from Dhaka to Barisal (Tk 1395, 35 minutes, daily at 8.25am). GMG offers a complimentary minibus service for the 20-minute ride to and from the airport. A baby taxi will cost around Tk 70.

### BOAT

The Rocket from Barisal to Dhaka (1st/2nd/deck class Tk 480/300/55, departs 6.30pm Monday to Saturday) is supposed to arrive in Dhaka at 6am the following morning, but during the high-water (monsoonal) season (July to August) it can take up to 16 hours.

The Rocket to Khulna (1st/2nd/deck class Tk 530/320/75, departs 6am Sunday to Friday) also stops at Mongla (1st/2nd/deck class Tk 390/240/50).

On Tuesday there is a Rocket to Chittagong (1st/2nd/inter/deck class Tk 850/560/175/120, departs 8.30pm).

It is also possible to get to Hatiya Island from Barisal. The boat leaves at 8:30pm on Friday and Tuesday, and arrives between 8am and 9am the following morning. The fare for this trip is Tk 375/255/60 for 1st/2nd/deck class, and around double this if you're going on to Chittagong.

For information and reservations for the Rocket, see the **BIWTC** (Barisal harbour) or the **Reservations Office** (BIWTC Ghat Rd).

There are also launches plying nightly between Barisal and Dhaka. Their 1st-class compartments are smaller than the Rocket's but are adequate, while deck class is just as good. There are four launches every evening (5.30pm, 6pm, 7pm and 7.30pm) in each direction. The departure point in Barisal is just south of the BIWTC terminal. The trip takes the same length of time as the Rocket.

### BUS
The principal Dhaka–Barisal overland route passes via Mawa (the Padma River crossing) and Madaripur. Rds are quite good, though ferry crossings can delay journeys. Day coaches depart each way, mostly in the morning from around 6.30am, while night buses depart mostly between 6pm and 9pm. Buses for Dhaka (Tk 110, seven to 10 hours) depart from the northern entrance to Barisal, 4km from the town centre. Chair coaches can cost up to Tk 200.

From Dhaka, **Eagle Paribahan** ( ☎ 710 1504) runs a coach to Barisal (Tk 200, six daily). You could do it cheaper, but probably not more comfortably.

There are also direct connections from Barisal to Khulna (Tk 100, eight hours). The trip, involving two ferry crossings, is via Bagerhat. There are also chair coaches for Tk 200.

Buses also travel south to Kuakata (Tk 100, two hours, 110km, hourly between 6am and 4.30pm). Buses for Kuakata leave from the southern end of town.

## MADHABPASA
The village of Madhabpasa, about 10km to the northwest of Barisal, has a **lake** that is known for attracting birds. There is also a medieval **Hindu temple** close to the village.

## KUAKATA
☎ 0441

This isolated beach at the southern tip of the delta, about 100km from Barisal, was named by the original Mogh (Rakhine) Buddhist settlers whose ancestors remain today. *Kua* means 'well', and *kata* means 'dug'.

The river mouths east and west of the beach ensure that the sea is rather murky, and sharks drying on racks along the beach similarly don't augur well for swimming. Though Kuakata isn't the archetypal turquoise tropical ocean, the vibe is right. Quieter and less developed than Cox's Bazar, Kuakata affords the opportunity to watch the sun both rise and set over the Bay of Bengal.

### Sights & Activities
There is a **Buddhist temple** close to the Parjatan Motel, about 100m from the beach on a slightly raised mound. The tin-walled shrine holds a 100-year-old statue of Buddha, said to be the largest in the country. The nearby **forestry reserve** is pleasant but succumbing to illegal logging. Some travellers report that hiring a fisherman to take you to nearby forested **islands** is a pleasant excursion.

### Sleeping
**Hotel Sunrise** ( ☎ 63945; s Tk 100, d Tk 250-300) A rickety beach shack with more atmosphere than amenities. The engaging manager organises package tours to nearby areas and the not-so-nearby Sundarbans.

**Parjatan Motel** ( ☎ 64433; d Tk 300-500, with AC Tk 1200) The rooms are decent but otherwise unremarkable. It is becoming outshone by the plethora of new establishments springing up along the main road.

**Golden Palace** ( ☎ 0171 441 622; d Tk 500) Rooms at the rear of the building (No 203, 205, 207 etc) have secluded balconies surrounded by greenery.

**Hotel Seaview** (d with/without AC Tk 800/500, ste Tk 1000) This hotel boasts a chef who can cook anything you can order, though you might not want to test this beyond Bangladeshi fare.

**Hotel Sekander** (d Tk 200) The friendly staff are relatively unaccustomed to foreign travellers. It's a decent budget option, though.

Very basic lodgings are also available in a **flophouse** (Tk 30) on the beach.

## Eating

**Hotel Smriti** (dishes Tk 50-100) Facing the beach (turn right at the main junction) but lacking a beach atmosphere, this is one of the best places in town for a feed.

**Shaphired Restaurant** (mains Tk 60) Directly opposite the Parjatan Motel, it doesn't have a menu, but does have a nice attitude.

**Parjatan Motel** (set Bangladeshi meal Tk 55) Be warned that 'eggs any style' means any style that is an omelette. French fries are Tk 10 and the tasty chicken corn soup is Tk 20.

## Getting There & Away

The road between Kuakata and Barisal isn't as good as that between Barisal and Dhaka, largely due to extensive renovations.

There is a small, barely identifiable ticket office diagonally opposite the Parjatan Motel that sells tickets for the bus to Dhaka (Tk 240, 14 hours, 277km, daily at 1pm). You'd be wise to book a day ahead. Bad roads, seemingly countless ferry crossings and hazardous fog can make the journey unpredictably tedious, so it may pay to break the trip in Barisal.

# Rajshahi Division

## CONTENTS

### HIGHLIGHTS

- Oohing and aahing over **Kantanagar Temple** (p109), the finest Hindu monument in the country

- Taking in the size of **Paharpur** (p101), once a Buddhist temple and now the most impressive archaeological site in Bangladesh

- Revelling in the age of **Mahasthangarh** (p100), the oldest known city in Bangladesh

- Decompressing in the laid-back northern towns of **Saidpur** (p105) and **Thakurgaon** (p109); as the temperature drops so does the pace

- Exploring old rajbaris and even older mosques in **Puthia** (p114), **Natore** (p115) and **Gaud** (p117); the journey from Rajshahi is part of the adventure

RAJSHAHI DIVISION

Rajshahi is one of the largest divisions in Bangladesh, with 16 districts and 25% of the country's population. Rajshahi division is overwhelmingly agricultural, with no large cities and little industrial development. It's the centre of the silk industry, produces wheat and grows almost half the country's mangoes.

As the northwestern division of the country, Rajshahi's borders are the major rivers. The powerful Jamuna cuts a swath between it and Dhaka division, while the Padma divides it from Khulna division. The Indian state of Bangla (West Bengal) lies at Rajshahi's jagged western and northern boundaries. On clear days the great Himalayan peak of Kanchenjunga can be seen from the northernmost district of Tetulia.

For travellers, the region offers some remote towns with a calmer pace than you're likely to find elsewhere in Bangladesh. There is also an enormous variety of historical monuments, including mosques, Hindu temples, rajbaris (Raj-era palaces built by landowners) and British-era buildings. As with much of Bangladesh, half the fun of visiting these places is seeing rural life on the way there and back.

# BOGRA
☎ 051
The small traffic circle (roundabout) at the heart of Bogra, Sat Mata, is a good place to begin exploring. The teeming Chandi Market is so crowded during the day that walking is often faster than taking a rickshaw.

Bogra is a good base for visiting two of the country's most famous archaeological sites – Mahasthangarh (p100) and Paharpur (p101). The former is 10km north of town, and the more-impressive latter, 53km to the northwest.

## Information
There is a **Standard Chartered Bank** (Sherpur Rd) just visible from Sat Mata. Other banks don't always change money. Further along the same road is a cybercafé. There is another, **Wait & Browse** (Nawab Bari Rd), nearby.

## Sights
Two blocks east of Sat Mata, the **Nawab Syed Abdus Sobhan Chowdhury Memorial Museum** (admission to grounds Tk 5, museum Tk 3; ⏲ 10am-7.30pm) is one of only a handful of furnished rajbaris in Bangladesh. The rooms have mannequins dressed to impress in both Bengali and British fashions. The last room you'll see is dedicated to modern art – it's a compelling display but the lack of English explanation leaves it somewhat obscure.

The grounds of the museum have been made into a quirky **amusement park** with rickety fairground rides and charmingly naive statues of peasants, bullock carts and wild animals.

Just next to the museum's entrance is a 'zoo' of **painted cement animals**, called a *carnapuli* (car-*na*-pou-luu); it seems that even inanimate animals are subject to degrading treatment.

About 1km north of Sat Mata, along busy Kazi Nazrul Islam Rd, just before the water tower, you'll find an old Hindu quarter including some **Hindu ruins**. In January and early February, you can watch the mass production of human-size statues of Saraswati for the *puja* (festival) celebrating this goddess.

## Sleeping
### BUDGET
**Mandolin Hotel & Chinese Restaurant** ( ☎ 65176; Shaptobari Market, Sat Mata; s/d Tk 100/170) On the top floor of the Shaptobari Market building, this hotel has a pleasant reception area and friendly staff. Rooms are clean and roomier than average, with fans, mosquito nets and lots of light. Singles with no windows and shared bathroom go for Tk 60.

**Naz Complex Hotel** (s/d Tk 125/190) In the Chandi Market area, look for a big yellow and red sign, then head up the stairs to the back of the building. The rooms are clean,

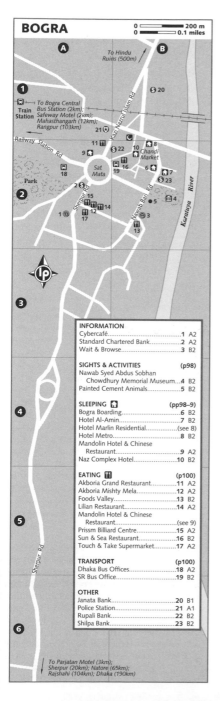

**BOGRA**

0 ——— 200 m
0 ——— 0.1 miles

**INFORMATION**
Cybercafé...............................1 A2
Standard Chartered Bank.........2 A2
Wait & Browse.........................3 B2

**SIGHTS & ACTIVITIES          (p98)**
Nawab Syed Abdus Sobhan
  Chowdhury Memorial Museum...4 B2
Painted Cement Animals............5 B2

**SLEEPING**                   **(pp98–9)**
Bogra Boarding.........................6 B2
Hotel Al-Amin...........................7 B2
Hotel Marlin Residential..........(see 8)
Hotel Metro.............................8 B2
Mandolin Hotel & Chinese
  Restaurant.............................9 A2
Naz Complex Hotel..................10 B2

**EATING**                      **(p100)**
Akboria Grand Restaurant........11 A2
Akboria Mishty Mela................12 A2
Foods Valley...........................13 B2
Lilian Restaurant......................14 A2
Mandolin Hotel & Chinese
  Restaurant..........................(see 9)
Prissm Billiard Centre...............15 A2
Sun & Sea Restaurant..............16 B2
Touch & Take Supermarket.......17 A2

**TRANSPORT**                   **(p100)**
Dhaka Bus Offices....................18 A2
SR Bus Office..........................19 B2

**OTHER**
Janata Bank............................20 B1
Police Station..........................21 A1
Rupali Bank............................22 B2
Shilpa Bank............................23 B2

with fans, mosquito nets and sit-down toilets. The area could be a little noisy but the prices are reasonable.

**Bogra Boarding** ( ☎ 65609; Nawab Bari Rd; s Tk 50-70, d Tk 90-120) A three-storey building with an English sign. The rooms are tiny but relatively clean, and come with fans and mosquito nets.

If your primary consideration is finance, try **Hotel Marlin Residential** (Nawab Bari Rd; s/d Tk 40/60), a block east of the tall landmark mosque, or the virtually identical **Hotel Metro** (Nawab Bari Rd; s/d Tk 40/60) next door. Only the Metro has an English sign. Rooms at both places are small and dark; they don't call them dirt-cheap for nothing. Rooms have fans, mosquito nets and common bathrooms.

### MID-RANGE & TOP END
**Parjatan Motel** ( ☎ 66753; r with/without AC Tk 1200/600, VIP ste Tk 2000) This crazily coloured building looks a little like a multistorey circus. Room are unfailingly clean and soothingly lit, with hot water and TV. If you are told that non-AC rooms are unavailable, don't necessarily believe it. There is also a pool table and a spacious restaurant. The Parjatan is at the southern entrance to town, 4km from the town centre.

**Safeway Motel** ( ☎ 66087; safeway@bogra.desh.net; r Tk 460-570, r with AC Tk 690-790) The three-storey Safeway is considered by many to be Bogra's best, but lacks the shiny newness of the Parjatan. Executive rooms are available, costing upwards of Tk 1000. All the rooms are spacious and have hot water and satellite TV. Some rooms have nicer bathrooms than others, so look before you book. It's an easy walk from the central bus station.

**Akboria Abasir** ( ☎ 65765; s Tk 100-200, d Tk 200-600) This is a decent mid-range option. It's down an unlikely alley left of the police station in the centre of town. Rickshaw-wallahs know where it is. The cheapest rooms are ordinary but clean, with fan and mosquito net. Larger rooms have small balconies. There's no hot water, but staff can bring it on request.

**Hotel Al-Amin** ( ☎ 72937; s Tk 300-500; d Tk 500-800) Corridors at the Al-Amin are dark but the rooms are spacious and bright. The more expensive rooms have carpets, chairs and TV, and some even have balconies. Cheaper options have squat toilets. It's opposite Bogra Boarding.

To Parjatan Motel (3km); Sherpur (20km); Natore (65km); Rajshahi (104km); Dhaka (190km)

## Eating
**Akboria Grand Restaurant** (Kazi Nazrul Islam Rd; mains Tk 30) It's overflowing with character. There's no English sign but you'll be able to pick it from all the activity. It's surprisingly relaxed for somewhere this crowded; patrons are more interested in gorging than gawking, and understandably so – the food is fantastic, though the Akboria offers a dining experience you'll remember long after you've forgotten what you ate.

**Safeway Motel** ( ☎ 66087; safeway@bogra.desh.net) One of the best restaurants by reputation, it's a nice, secluded place where the waiters take their service seriously. Vegetable fried rice is Tk 110. The chicken chilli with onion is Tk 148 and quite delicious.

**Mandolin Hotel & Chinese Restaurant** ( ☎ 65176) It's worth a try, despite the fact that it's too dark to really admire the lurid decor. 'Potato cheaps' are Tk 50; mixed fried rice Tk 80.

**Prissm Billiard Centre** (3rd floor, Sairul Complex, Sherpur Rd) This is a relaxed pool hall that also serves food and drink.

**Touch & Take Supermarket** Stock up on hard-to-come-by food-stuffs and toiletries; unfortunately, despite the name, you have to pay for items.

Other recommendations:

**Parjatan Motel** ( ☎ 66753) Bright and big. Standard Bangladeshi fare with a smattering of Western dishes.

**Lilian Restaurant** (mains Tk 150-250) Chinese, Thai and Sichuan dishes.

**Akboria Mishty Mela** A buffet of sweetmeats, coffee and chocolate, with a quiet dining area.

**Foods Valley** A clean snack shop.

**Sun & Sea Restaurant** Popular among locals for its tasty Bangladeshi fare, low-key Sun & Sea has nothing to do with the sun or the sea.

## Getting There & Away
### BUS
Buses usually arrive at Bogra's central bus station, 2km northwest of town at the junction of the Rangpur Bypass road and the road to Naogaon (close to the Safeway Motel). From here it's a Tk 15 rickshaw ride into town.

Ordinary buses travel to Dhaka (Tk 120, 4½ hours) via the Bangabandhu Bridge. Most coach offices for buses to Dhaka are west of Sat Mata, but the SR bus office is just to the east of Sat Mata. Deluxe AC buses cost between Tk 250 and Tk 280.

Buses leave the central station throughout the day for Natore (Tk 30, 2½ hours) and Rajshahi (Tk 70, three hours). There are several buses to Khulna (Tk 170, 8½ hours, depart around 9am) and Rangpur (Tk 60, 2½ hours, every 20 minutes from 5.30am to 6pm). Travellers to Paharpur can take regular buses throughout the day to Jaipurhat (Tk 30, 1½ hours) and a tempo (autorickshaw) on to Paharpur. Buses also run to Mahasthan (Tk 5, 30 minutes, 11km).

### TRAIN
There's an express to Dhaka (1st/*sulob* class Tk 310/105, 7.39pm daily except Tuesday) via Mymensingh (Tk 250/80). It arrives at Mymensingh at around 5am and Dhaka at around 7am. Few people bother with this lengthy train trip.

If you're coming from Dhaka, when you switch to the train waiting at the other side of the Jamuna River make sure you get into a carriage that goes to Bogra, as the rest of the train goes to Dinajpur.

There are no direct trains from Bogra to Dinajpur or Rajshahi.

## AROUND BOGRA
### Sariakandi
For a bit of good adventure, consider heading 20km east via Gabtali (General Zia's home town) to Sariakandi and hiring a motorised boat to take you out onto the Jamuna River. It will cost around Tk 40 for half an hour. During the monsoonal season you can see broken embankments, and people living on the tiny islands created by the massive annual flooding. The banks of the Jamuna are about the most erosion-prone places in the country, forcing farmers off their land during flood season. Many dispossessed farmers join the ranks of the rickshaw-wallahs.

### Hat Bazar
Every Friday in a village just south of Bogra there's a hat bazar, a small open-air market that attracts so many people that they spill onto the highway. Roaming around these bazars can be great fun. To get there, head out of town on a rickshaw (or a communal baby taxi heading in the right direction).

## MAHASTHANGARH
The oldest known city in Bangladesh, dating back to at least the 3rd century BC, Mahasthangarh (an easy half-day trip from Bogra) is an archaeological site consisting

largely of foundations and hillocks hinting at past riches.

The principal site, the Citadel, contains traces of the ancient city. Many other sites in the vicinity are lumped together under the name Mahasthangarh. The whole area is rich in Hindu, Buddhist and Muslim sites, but most have all but vanished. The Buddhists were here until at least the 11th century; their most glorious period was the 8th to the 11th centuries, when the Buddhist Pala emperors of North Bengal ruled. It is to this period that most of the visible remains belong.

## Sights
### MAHASTHANGARH SITE MUSEUM
This small but well-maintained **museum** (admission Tk 7; ☺ 10am-1pm & 2-6pm Sun-Thu, 10am-12.30pm & 2.30-6pm Fri Apr-Sep, 9am-1pm & 2-5pm Sun-Thu, 9am-12.30pm & 2.30-5pm Fri Oct-Mar) has some interesting Hindu and Buddhist pieces dating from the 6th to 13th centuries AD.

Inside you'll find recovered pieces that date back to the 2nd century BC, and some well-preserved bronze images mostly found in monasteries from the Pala period. Also on display are large black-stone carvings depicting Hindu deities.

### THE CITADEL
Adjacent to the museum, the **Citadel** forms a rough rectangle covering more than 2 sq km. It was once surrounded on three sides by the mighty Karatuya River. Hindus still make an annual pilgrimage to the Karatuya River in mid-April.

Probably first constructed under the Mauryan empire in the 3rd century BC, the site shows evidence of various Hindu empires and Buddhist and Muslim occupations – though it's doubtful the helipad dates back that far. The Citadel fell into disuse around the time of the Mughal invasions. Most of the visible brickwork dates from the 8th century, apart from that added during restoration.

Outside the Citadel, opposite the museum, the remains of a 6th-century **Govinda Bhita Hindu Temple** overlook a picturesque bend in the river.

## Sleeping & Eating
If it's not full, you could stay at the **Archaeology Department Rest House** (d Tk 200), across the road from the museum, overlooking the Karatuya River. The three rooms have a fan,
mosquito netting and bathroom. There's also a small dining room. The museum caretaker can hunt down the person in charge.

The town of Mahasthan, 1.7km from Mahasthangarh, has a few basic restaurants.

## Getting There & Away
Buses run from Bogra to Mahasthan (Tk 5, 30 minutes, 11km). From here you can take a rickshaw (Tk 5 to Tk 10) or walk the 1.7km to the Citadel and museum.

## PAHARPUR
The Somapuri Vihara at Paharpur was once the biggest Buddhist monastery south of the Himalaya. It dates from the 8th century AD. This is the most impressive archaeological site in Bangladesh; it was declared a protected archaeological site back in 1919, although the scholar-traveller Dr Buckman Hamilton had shown interest in it as far back as 1807.

## Sights
### SOMAPURI VIHARA
The temple complex at **Somapuri Vihara** is in the shape of a large quadrangle covering 11 hectares, with monks' cells making up the walls and enclosing a courtyard. The 20m-high remains of a stupa rise from the centre of the courtyard. Its cruciform floor plan is topped by a three-tier superstructure; the 3rd level has a large tower structure similar to that of Moenjodaro in Pakistan.

Some of the clay tiles of this *mahavihara* (great monastery) depict an animal that might be the variety of rhinoceros that is now extinct in Bangladesh.

Lining the outer perimeter are over 170 small monastic cells. Seventy-two of these contain ornamental pedestals, the purpose of which still eludes archaeologists. It is possible they contained the remains of saintly monks who had resided here.

On the east side of the courtyard you can make out the outline of what was once a miniature model of the temple. On the western wing of the north side are remains of structures that baffle archaeologists. On the eastern wing of the south side is an elevated brick base with an eight-pointed star-shaped structure that must have been a shrine. To the west lie the remains of what appears to have been the monks' refectory and kitchen.

Except for the guardhouse to the north, most of the remains outside the courtyard lie to the south. They include an oblong building, linked to the monastery by a causeway, which may have been the wash house and latrines. In the same area is a bathing ghat, probably of Hindu origin. Only 12m southwest of the ghat is the rectangular Temple of Gondeswari, with an octagonal pillar base in the centre and a circular platform to the front.

The monastery is thought to have been successively occupied by Buddhists, Jains and Hindus, which explains the curious mixture of artwork. The Jains must have constructed a *chaturmukhar*, a structure with all four walls decorated with stone bas-reliefs of deities. The Hindus replaced Buddhist terracotta artwork with sculptural stonework of their own deities, and terracotta artwork representing themes from the *Mahabharata* and the *Ramayana*. Artefacts discovered at the site range from bronze statues and bas-reliefs of the elephant-headed Hindu god Ganesh, to statues of the Jain god Manzuri, bronze images of the Buddha and statues of the infant Krishna.

### MUSEUM
The small **museum** (admission Tk 2; ☼ 10am-1pm & 2-6pm Sun-Thu, 10am-12.30pm & 2.30-6pm Fri Apr-Sep, 9am-1pm & 2-5pm Sun-Thu, 9am-12.30pm & 2.30pm-5pm Fri Oct-Mar) gives a good idea of the range of cultures that have used this site. Stucco Buddha heads unearthed here are similar to the Gandhara style of Indo-Hellenic sculpture from what is now northwestern Pakistan. Sculptural work includes sandstone and basalt sculptures, but the stonework of Hevagara in passionate embrace with Shakti is the collection's finest item. The most important find, a large bronze Buddha, is usually away on tour.

### Sleeping
The small white building between the museum and the temple is the **Archaeological Rest House** (per person Tk 200). Staff at the museum should be able to point you to the appropriate person.

### Getting There & Away
From Bogra, take a bus to Jaipurhat (Tk 40, 1½ hours, 44km). From there, buses leave regularly between 7am and 4pm for Paharpur (Tk 7, 25 minutes, 9km). To get to the sights from Paharpur village, take a three-wheeler (around Tk 20).

---

**CHARS OF THE BRAHMAPUTRA**

*Bruno De Cordier*

An adventurous side trip, and a good way to see how rivers affect people's livelihoods, is to visit one of the chars in the Brahmaputra River. Chars are large sandbank islands that once belonged to the mainland. There are literally hundreds of chars, but their number and position change with the process of silting and erosion. There are estimated to be 230,000 char-dwellers in North Bengal. They scratch out a living from agriculture, livestock and seasonal labour in towns on the mainland. When their makeshift villages flood and eventually disappear, they pack up and move to another sandbank.

To get to the chars, first go to the town of Kurigram and on to the village of Chilmari, about 40km south of Kurigram. There, take one of the long, engine-driven wooden 'service boats' that link the chars to the mainland. There are several possibilities, depending on the char you want to visit, but the one to the Ashtomir char leaves at 10am and returns at 1pm. The boat ride takes about two hours and costs Tk 20. The best time to visit is in winter.

---

You can always get a tempo back to Jaipurhat, but it will cost significantly more and you may have to wait a while. Don't count on getting a bus from Jaipurhat to Bogra after 6pm.

## RANGPUR
☎ 0521

Rangpur is a major transit point for the northern half of Rajshahi division, sometimes referred to as North Bengal. The town is home to several public buildings of the Raj era, including Carmichael College and Tajhat Palace. The town is also one place you may see members of the Kochi ethnic group, an Indo-Tibetan people related to the plains tribes of Assam, and recognisable by their rounder, more Southeast Asian faces.

### Orientation & Information
Most places of interest to travellers lie between Nawabganj Bazar (the centre of town on GL Roy Rd between Shinpara and Station Rds) and the train station, 3km south at the end of Station Rd.

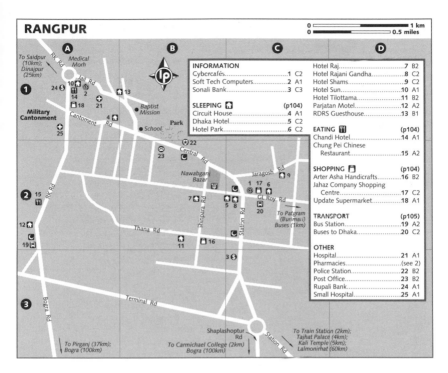

# RANGPUR

0 _____ 1 km
0 _____ 0.5 miles

**INFORMATION**
Cybercafés.................................1 C2
Soft Tech Computers..................2 A1
Sonali Bank................................3 C3

**SLEEPING** (p104)
Circuit House.............................4 A1
Dhaka Hotel...............................5 C2
Hotel Park.................................6 C2

Hotel Raj....................................7 B2
Hotel Rajani Gandha..................8 C2
Hotel Shams..............................9 C2
Hotel Sun.................................10 A1
Hotel Tilottama.........................11 B2
Parjatan Motel..........................12 A2
RDRS Guesthouse.....................13 B1

**EATING** (p104)
Chandi Hotel............................14 A1
Chung Pei Chinese
    Restaurant...........................15 A2

**SHOPPING** (p104)
Arter Asha Handicrafts..............16 B2
Jahaz Company Shopping
    Centre.................................17 C2
Update Supermarket.................18 A1

**TRANSPORT** (p105)
Bus Station...............................19 A2
Buses to Dhaka.........................20 C2

**OTHER**
Hospital....................................21 A1
Pharmacies.........................(see 2)
Police Station...........................22 B2
Post Office................................23 B2
Rupali Bank..............................24 A1
Small Hospital..........................25 A1

**Cybercafés** (cnr Station & GL Roy Rds; per hr Tk 20)

**Soft Tech Computers** (RK Rd Circle; per hr Tk 20)

**Sonali Bank** (Station Rd) About 500m south of Nawabganj Bazar, Sonali changes cash and travellers cheques. You need to show your passport for both.

## Sights

### TAJHAT PALACE

In the 19th century Manna Lal Ray, a Hindu, was forced to emigrate from the Punjab and found his way to Rangpur. He became a successful jeweller, acquired a lot of land and eventually won the title of raja. His crowning achievement was the construction of this huge mansion during the mid-19th century. Local villagers believe there is treasure hidden in its walls, which doesn't augur well for its long-term survival.

**Tajhat Palace** is one of the finest rajbaris in Bangladesh. During the regime of General Ershad (1982–91) it was used by the High Court division of Bangladesh's Supreme Court, but since 1991 has lain empty.

The palace is 5km south of Nawabganj Bazar and 2km south of the train station, outside the de facto city boundaries.

### KALI TEMPLE

The delightful architectural folly of **Kali Temple** is modelled on a Florentine dome, or at least a Bengali vision of an English adaptation of a Florentine dome. The Hindu family who live in the compound will be surprised to see you but happy for you to have a look. Their children and all of their friends will also be happy to let you take their photograph.

The temple lies about 1km south of Tajhat Palace. Take a rickshaw from High Court Rd and ask around the neighbourhood for 'Kali mondir'.

### CARMICHAEL COLLEGE

This famous old **college** is one of the largest in the country in terms of area. Some 18,000 students study here – more than can comfortably be accommodated in and around Rangpur. Situated on the outskirts of town, the college dates from 1916. Similar in inspiration to Curzon Hall in Dhaka and with a grand frontage of over 100m, it is a splendid fusion of classical British and Mughal architecture. Its domes rest on slender columns, and a series of arched openings all add to its

RAJSHAHI DIVISION

mosque-like appearance. It is spacious and rural, with cows grazing on the main lawn. A weekday visit might afford the chance to meet some students, who will no doubt have strong opinions about the growing demand to turn their college into a university.

## Sleeping

**RDRS Guesthouse** ( ☎ 62598; www.rdrsbangla.net /home/main/bookings/bookings.htm; s/d Tk 400/600, with AC Tk 800/1150) If you can afford it, there is no better place to stay than the guesthouse at the Rangpur Dinajpur Rural Services Project (RDRS) office. This well-respected NGO takes a professional but personal approach to its accommodation. Rooms have hot water, TV and balcony. There is a pool table, Internet access, laundry service and a collection of books to borrow. There are also some handicrafts, books and postcards on sale. The RDRS also has an inviting non-smoking **restaurant** (breakfast Tk 70, lunch & dinner Tk 130). The manager is unfailingly helpful.

**Parjatan Motel** ( ☎ 63681; RK Rd; r with/without AC Tk 1050/575, VIP ste Tk 1600) This is a modern establishment with balcony rooms and hot water. Standard rooms are well ventilated and come with carpet, fan, nice furnishings and attached bathroom. There is also a **restaurant** (fixed Bangladeshi meal Tk 85) with the usual mix of Chinese, Bangladeshi and Western dishes.

**Hotel Park** ( ☎ 66718; GL Roy Rd; s/d Tk 200/350, VIP with AC 850) This extremely clean establishment looks as though it will cost some serious taka, but not so. Rooms are light, airy and spacious. The sheets are crisp. All bathrooms are tiled and have squat toilets. The only thing missing is hot water.

**Hotel Tilottama** ( ☎ 63482; Thana Rd; s Tk 150, d Tk 210-375) This is on a quiet road, and rooms come with fan, desk, chair and a reasonably comfortable bed and bathroom, some of which have sit-down toilets. Management may be unwilling to let you stay in the cheaper rooms on the ground floor, so be prepared to be persistent. The business card boasts of a 'Lonely Atmosphere', which in Bangladesh can be a virtue indeed. The hotel restaurant has the usual Bangladeshi interpretation of Chinese dishes.

**Hotel Sun** ( ☎ 66912; s/d Tk 200/300) The septic cleanliness of the medical centre you must walk through to get to Hotel Sun has diffused up to the brightly lit corridors of this pleasant hotel. All rooms have attached bathrooms.

**Dhaka Hotel** (GL Roy Rd; s/d Tk 100/150) Expect small rooms with fans, mosquito nets and attached bathrooms that are the typical prison-style ablutions chamber. You may have to push for a room with a shared bathroom – staff may even try denying their existence. There's a popular restaurant downstairs. There is no English sign, so ask around.

**Circuit House** ( ☎ 63095; s/d Tk 200/400; Cantonment Rd) You will be hard-pressed staying here with so many options in town.

Other budget options:

**Hotel Rajani Gandha** ( ☎ 62669; cnr GL Roy & Station Rds; s Tk 80-125, d Tk 150-200) All rooms have attached bathroom. Nice-ish rooftop area to hang out in.

**Hotel Raj** ( ☎ 64202; Sinpara Rd; s/d Tk 100/150) Some rooms have access to a common balcony. Slightly bigger tiled rooms for Tk 250. Small English sign.

**Hotel Shams** ( ☎ 63768; Jaragosh Rd; s/d Tk 50/90) Aptly named – a bottom-end hotel if ever you saw one. Grubby walls, smelly bathrooms and lots of mosquitoes.

## Eating

The best way to pick a place to eat is to head into Nawabganj Bazar and wander down some side streets. As well as the local holes-in-the-wall, there are some slightly pricier restaurants in this area that serve sensational food in surprisingly clean surrounds.

**Chandi Hotel** ( ☺ lunch & dinner) This is a nice option in the Medical Morh area, just south of the roundabout. The enticing 'Ballness Chicken' costs Tk 100.

**Chung Pei Chinese Restaurant** (dishes around Tk 100) About 100m from the Parjatan Motel, Chung Pei is a place for well-to-do locals to be seen spending money.

## Shopping

**Arter Asha Handicrafts** ( ☎ 092 150; house 3, CP Sen Rd) This eye-catching boutique store specialises in handmade traditional clothes. Fashions and souvenirs at Arter Asha don't come cheap, but they do come classy.

**Jahaz Company Shopping Centre** (GL Roy Rd) The perfect place to splash out on the elaborate souvenir sari that you may wear once when you get home. As well as the overwhelming collection of clothes and jewellery, you'll also find electronic goods at the Jahaz.

**Update Supermarket** (PK Rd) There's a healthy range of groceries and toiletries at the Update Supermarket. There's also an attentive employee who will try to promote every product within a 2m radius.

## Getting There & Away

### AIR

**Biman** ( ☎ 63437) flies every day to Saidpur, 40km to the west. Most people take a bus from Saidpur to Rangpur, but an expensive taxi from the airport is an option.

### BUS

The **bus station** (RK Rd) is 3km southwest of the central area (about Tk 12 by rickshaw). There are regular buses for Bogra (Tk 40, two hours, every 20 minutes from 7am to 5.30pm). For towns such as Dinajpur and Thakurgaon you may have to change at Saidpur (Tk 30, 2½ hours, regularly until 7pm). Many buses leaving this bus station get to their final destination via Bogra.

Only a few buses make the journey to Rajshahi (Tk 120, 4½ hours); the last leaves at around 3pm. There are no chair coaches on any of these routes.

**JL Pariban** ( ☎ 63940) and **Hanif** ( ☎ 62462) both operate coaches to Dhaka (Tk 200, five hours, 325km) at various times between 7am and 11pm. **Agomony** ( ☎ 65133) has deluxe AC coaches (Tk 300, daily at 3.30pm and 11pm) and non-AC chair coaches (Tk 230, daily at 8am, 11am and 11pm). There are several companies alongside each other, so shop around until you get the right time for the right price.

Some Rajshahi-bound buses leave from this area too.

### TRAIN

There are two intercity (IC) trains to Dhaka (1st/*sulob* class Tk 340/165) but given the length of the trip to Dhaka it is understandable that most people catch a bus. One train leaves at 8.05am and arrives in Dhaka the following morning between 8am and 9am. The other leaves at 7.20pm. Sleeping berths are available on the night train for Tk 500.

There is also a mail train that leaves at 3.36pm and takes 20 hours.

## SAIDPUR
☎ 0552

Saidpur is a quiet backwater town where the atmosphere of the Raj lingers. Near the old train station is one of Bangladesh's few surviving **English-style churches**. The southern

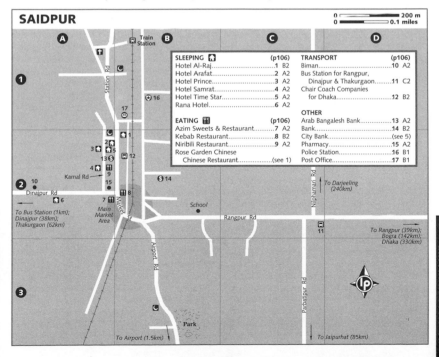

part of town has some impressive **red-brick buildings** from the latter period of the Raj.

There are a couple of banks that might be persuaded to change cash at bad rates, but you'll have to continue on to Rangpur or Dinajpur to change travellers cheques. There is no Internet access in Saidpur.

## Sleeping & Eating

Saidpur only has budget hotels.

**Hotel Arafat** (s/d Tk 150/250) One of the best places to sleep, rooms here are well lit, tiled and clean, with small tables and chairs. There are larger doubles available for Tk 350, or Tk 650 with AC.

**Hotel Samrat** ( ☎ 2105; s/d/VIP Tk 60/120/300) There's not much to recommend the standard rooms at the Samrat. However, the VIP room has chairs, a TV and a rooftop pretty much to itself. It's not pristine but it's private and has character.

**Rana Hotel** ( ☎ 2559; s with shared bathroom Tk 60, s/d Tk 80/165) The floors are grotty, but the ceilings are nice and high and the sheets are clean.

**Hotel Time Star** ( ☎ 2493; Station Rd; s/d Tk 50/100) This slightly grubby multistorey concrete establishment has the usual basic rooms with attached bathroom. If staff say it's full, they mean they'd rather you didn't stay. Women will find it's always full.

**Hotel Al-Raj** ( ☎ 3137; s/d Tk 60/150) All rooms at this friendly place have attached bathroom, adequate space and are comfortably secure.

**Hotel Prince** ( ☎ 2502; s Tk 60-70, d Tk 140-250) is similar but has a wider range of rooms.

There's a nice food culture on Market St; have a wander to see what's on offer. Directly opposite Dinajpur Rd is a cheap kebab restaurant with no English sign but impossibly good kebabs.

Other recommendations:

**Azim Sweets & Restaurant** (Market St; mains Tk 25) A veritable smorgasbord of street food, sweetmeats and cha.

**Niribili Restaurant** (Station Rd; Mains Tk 25) Not overly clean, but local families endorse it. Good *misti doi*.

**Rose Garden Chinese Restaurant** (Hotel Al-Raj; Station Rd) A nice escape, under the Hotel Al-Raj, where you may even be able to appropriate the TV. The coffee is unfathomably bad.

## Getting There & Away

### AIR

The airport is 2km to the south of town, beyond the old administrative area and next to the military cantonment. **Biman** ( ☎ 2007) is on the north side of Dinajpur Rd, 300m west of the city's main intersection. There are daily flights to/from Dhaka (Tk 1550, 50 minutes) and Rajshahi (Tk 825, 35 minutes).

The rickshaw fare from the airport into town is around Tk 10 with some hard bargaining. There are also taxis at the airport. Ask someone to help you distinguish a taxi from a private car.

### BUS

The main bus station is about 1.5km east of the town centre. There are departures every few minutes until around 7pm for Rangpur (Tk 30, 1¼ hours) and Dinajpur (Tk 13, one hour), and slightly less frequently for Thakurgaon (Tk 15, 1½ hours). If you're headed south for Jaipurhat (near the Paharpur ruins) you may have to wait so long for a direct bus that you're better off taking a series of buses.

There are chair coach offices for Dhaka (Tk 120 to Tk 180) in the centre of town along Station Rd, around Hotel Arafat. Coaches mostly leave after dark. Shop around – this changes quickly.

At the western end of town, a five-minute rickshaw ride from the centre, is a small bus stand from where some local buses leave for Dinajpur and Thakurgaon, both for around Tk 15.

### TRAIN

There are IC trains to Rajshahi (1st/*sulob* class Tk 190/65, 5½ hours, daily at 6.37am and 4.09pm) and Khulna (1st/*sulob* class Tk 525/170, 9½ hours, daily at 7.45am and 7.30pm).

## DINAJPUR

☎ 0531

Dinajpur, 50km south of Thakurgaon and 70km west of Rangpur, is the largest city in northwestern Bangladesh and is famous for its rice. There are some interesting old buildings in town, the most famous being Dinajpur Rajbari with an adjoining Krishna temple. There are also some interesting buildings in surrounding areas, including Kantanagar Temple. If you want to visit the temple, you'll have to come through here.

## Orientation & Information

The train station is in the heart of town. The market and most hotels and restaurants

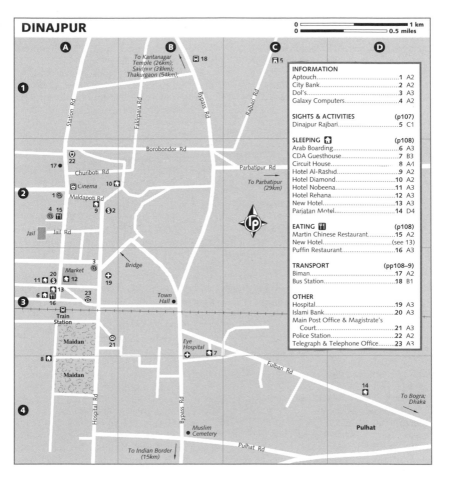

# DINAJPUR

0 ———————— 1 km
0 ———————— 0.5 miles

To Kantanagar
Temple (26km);
Saidpur (38km);
Thakurgaon (54km);

To Parbatipur
(29km)

To Bogra;
Dhaka

To Indian Border
(15km)

Borobondor Rd
Churiboti Rd
Maldapoti Rd
Jail Rd
Parbatipur Rd
Fulbari Rd
Pulhat Rd
Bypass Rd
Rajshahi Rd
Fakirpara Rd
Station Rd
Hospital Rd

Cinema
Jail
Bridge
Market
Town Hall
Train Station
Maidan
Maidan
Eye Hospital
Muslim Cemetery
Pulhat

| INFORMATION | | |
| --- | --- | --- |
| Aptouch | 1 | A2 |
| City Bank | 2 | A2 |
| Dol's | 3 | A3 |
| Galaxy Computers | 4 | A2 |
| **SIGHTS & ACTIVITIES** | | **(p107)** |
| Dinajpur Rajbari | 5 | C1 |
| **SLEEPING** | | **(p108)** |
| Arab Boarding | 6 | A3 |
| CDA Guesthouse | 7 | B3 |
| Circuit House | 8 | A4 |
| Hotel Al-Rashid | 9 | A2 |
| Hotel Diamond | 10 | A2 |
| Hotel Nobeena | 11 | A3 |
| Hotel Rehana | 12 | A3 |
| New Hotel | 13 | A3 |
| Parjatan Motel | 14 | D4 |
| **EATING** | | **(p108)** |
| Martin Chinese Restaurant | 15 | A2 |
| New Hotel | (see 13) | |
| Puffin Restaurant | 16 | A3 |
| **TRANSPORT** | | **(pp108–9)** |
| Biman | 17 | A2 |
| Bus Station | 18 | B1 |
| **OTHER** | | |
| Hospital | 19 | A3 |
| Islami Bank | 20 | A3 |
| Main Post Office & Magistrate's Court | 21 | A3 |
| Police Station | 22 | A2 |
| Telegraph & Telephone Office | 23 | A3 |

are just north. South of the train station is the administrative area, including the circuit house, some imposing Raj-era buildings (the post office, mapping office etc) and a maidan (grassed area) that hosts cricket and badminton matches as well as political demonstrations.

You may be able to change money at **City Bank** (Hospital Rd), about 1km north of the train station. There are a few cybercafés in town: **Dol's** (Hospital Rd); and Aptouch and Galaxy Computer off Station Rd.

## Sights

Though dilapidated, **Dinajpur Rajbari** is one of the country's most picturesque historic buildings. To the left of the entrance is a daintily painted Krishna temple. The rajbari itself lies through a second gate, facing another courtyard. Both structures date from the 1890s, when the 18th-century palace was rebuilt after the great earthquake of 1897.

The **Krishna Temple** is open only when the custodian cares to make an appearance, but someone will find him for you. Hindus still worship here, so the cows that wander among the ruins are probably as safe as their ancestors were when the terracotta scenes of Krishna and the *gopis* (milkmaids) were made.

The rajbari is about 4km northeast of central Dinajpur. A rickshaw will cost at least Tk 15.

RAJSHAHI DIVISION

## Sleeping

**BUDGET**

**CDA Guesthouse** ( ☎ 64428; Tk 100) It might be possible to stay at the Community Development Association (CDA) Guesthouse, an NGO on the eastern outskirts of town, just off Fulbari Rd. It's probably best to stay here only if you have an interest in the work that will be going on around you. Staff can also organise accommodation at their training centre near Kantanagar Temple (see p109).

**Hotel Rehana** ( ☎ 64144; Station Rd; s/d/VIP Tk 70/120/300) It's cosy but noisy (particularly the rooms at the back, which are adjacent to a cinema). Rooms have attached bathroom, and the VIP room is slightly bigger than the others and has TV.

**Hotel Nobeena** ( ☎ 64178; s/d Tk 70/120) The Nobeena is half a block west of Rehana and of comparable value. It has ventilated rooms and beds with mosquito nets. It's not very women-friendly.

**New Hotel** ( ☎ 64155; Station Rd; s/d Tk 60/120) The clean rooms have decent tiled bathrooms, fans, mosquito nets and basic furniture. They are surprisingly spacious for this price range.

**Arab Boarding** (s/d Tk 30/60, s/d with bathroom Tk 40/80) The most basic of them all is just west of the train station. The showers are the sort that make you feel dirtier than you did before.

**MID-RANGE**

**Parjatan Motel** ( ☎ 4718; Fulbari Rd; with/without AC Tk 1200/600) This new hotel has clean, modern rooms. It's on the edge of town, about 3km from the train station. There's a restaurant here as well.

**Hotel Diamond** ( ☎ 64629; s/d Tk 200/500) The reception is very dark, but the rooms are tiled, and have a desk and lots of space. It's about 200m from the Hotel Al-Rashid on a busy commercial road.

**Hotel Al-Rashid** ( ☎ 64251; r Tk 125-175) This hotel, 1km north of the train station, a block east of Station Rd, is clean and well run. The small rooms have attached wet bathrooms (which are 'cleaned' simply by hosing down).

**Circuit House** ( ☎ 63122; s/d Tk 300/600) It may be easier to get permission to stay by going directly there rather than to the district commissioner, though you will likely be directed to the Parjatan Motel.

## Eating

There is a range of small local restaurants, including some ultra-cheap choices around the Maldapoti Rd area.

**New Hotel** ( ☎ 64155; Station Rd; meals Tk 18) The best Bangladeshi restaurant in the town centre, New Hotel's restaurant is very popular and open almost till midnight. There are vegetarian dishes here, too.

**Puffin Restaurant** ( ☎ 64672) This is reputedly the city's best restaurant, so much so that rickshaw-wallahs may take you here even when you ask for the train station. There's more light in the fish tank than there is in the rest of the restaurant. It has the standard Chinese fare, plus some more exotic dishes, such as 'Hoot's Shower Soup' for Tk 85.

**Martin Chinese Restaurant** ( ☎ 64074; Station Rd) North of the Puffin, but slightly less popular, is Martin. Crab curry is Tk 120 and mixed vegetables with basil leaf, Tk 80. Martin does sensible half-serves.

## Getting There & Away

**AIR**

The nearest airport is at Saidpur, 40km away. There's a **Biman** ( ☎ 63340; Station Rd) office about 2km north of the train station.

**BUS**

The **station** (Rangpur Bypass Rd) is northeast of town. Buses go to Saidpur (Tk 30, one hour), Thakurgaon (Tk 40, 1¾ hours), Dhaka (Tk 160, 8½ hours) and Bogra (Tk 80, 3½ hours). There are some direct buses to Rangpur (Tk 60, 2½ hours), but you may have to change buses at Saidpur.

Chair coaches to Dhaka (Tk 200, 7½ hours) depart between 5pm and 7pm. Some companies have offices in town.

For information on buses to Kantanagar Temple see p109.

**TRAIN**

A number of trains serve Dinajpur, although there are better connections available at the nearby junction town of Parbatipur. There are two IC trains from Dinajpur to Parbatipur (30 minutes, 6.15am and 5.30pm). From here, going on to Dhaka (berth/1st/sulob class Tk 570/385/185, 14 hours) is a long haul.

If you are headed for Khulna (1st/sulob class Tk 385/185) or Rajshahi (1st/sulob class Tk 213/68), you will have to change in Parbatipur onto the 8.30am Khulna train or the 7.05am Rajshahi train.

There is also a decrepit mail train for Thakurgaon (three hours, daily at 8.15am).

## KANTANAGAR TEMPLE

One of the most spectacular monuments in Bangladesh, this Hindu **temple** (also known as Kantajees Temple) should not be missed. Built in 1752 by Pran Nath, a renowned maharaja from Dinajpur, it is the country's finest example of brick and terracotta style. Its most remarkable feature, typical of late-Mughal-era temples, is its superb surface decoration, with infinite panels of sculpted terracotta plaques depicting both figural and floral motifs.

The folk artists did not lack imagination or sense of humour. One demon is depicted swallowing monkeys, which promptly re-appear from his ear. Other scenes are more domestic, such as a wife massaging her husband's legs and a lady combing lice from another's hair. Amorous scenes are often placed in obscure corners. These intricate, harmonious scenes are like a richly embroidered carpet.

This 15-sq-metre, three-storey edifice was originally crowned with nine ornamental two-storey towers, which collapsed during the great earthquake of 1897 and were never replaced. The building sits in a courtyard surrounded by offices and pilgrims' quarters, all protected by a stout wall. Visitors can no longer go inside the temple, but the intricate detail of its exterior will keep you engaged.

### Sleeping & Eating

It is possible to stay at the **CDA training centre** (d/t/semi-VIP Tk 150/75/300) at Proshikhan Kendra, 3km from the temple in the village of Mukundupur. It's a large complex and all rooms have an attached bathroom. Food is also available. Arrange to stay here through the CDA Guesthouse (p108) in Dinajpur.

### Getting There & Away

You can get a bus from Dinajpur to Kantanagar (Tk 14, 26km, 45 minutes). It's on the route to Thakurgaon but request Kantanagar, otherwise you may end up paying more and/or missing your stop.

In Kantanagar village, take the unpaved path on your left (west) until you come to the boom gate, where you will have to pay

Tk 5 to cross the river. If the tide is high enough there will be a boat waiting to take you to the other side; otherwise, cross the rickety bamboo bridge. Walk up the small incline and turn left at the top. Follow this pleasant, winding path for 10 minutes through mustard, banana, rice and chilli fields until you reach the temple, which is marked by a small flag above the tree line that is visible from a distance.

## THAKURGAON

☎ 0561

Thakurgaon is one of the more pleasant towns in northern Bangladesh, with beautiful scenery and few motor vehicles.

It's relatively cool, so in December and January you will definitely need a jumper (sweater) at night. The town is small enough to cover on foot, provided you like to walk, but rickshaws are everywhere and at night you'll be charmed by the twinkling of their lanterns as they glide along the dark streets.

### Sights & Activities

If you're interested in seeing what local NGOs are doing, visit the office of the **Humanitarian Agency for Development Services** (HADS) and its farm on the southwestern edge of town. There's also a **Rangpur Dinajpur Rural Services Project** (RDRS) office here.

An interesting **cycling trip** would be north to Panchagarh via Atwari, and then north to the Indian border at Tetulia and Banglabandha. Alternatively, from Atwari take a narrow back road southwest to Baliadangi then head either east back to Thakurgaon or further south to Haripur, on the Indian border, and, from there, southeast to Dinajpur.

### Sleeping

**RDRS Guesthouse** ( ☎ 53670; s/d Tk 695/1050) The RDRS has recently set up a four-storey, 30-room guesthouse in a quiet area outside of Thakurgaon. All rooms have hot water and AC. Each room has ample space and a good-sized desk. The guesthouse **restaurant** (lunch Tk 130, dinner Tk 100) turns out some great meals, but nonguests must order in advance. Breakfast is free for guests. Long-term guests may be able to negotiate a discount.

**HADS Guesthouse** ( ☎ 53513; Sirajuddowlah Rd; d/t Tk 400/300) The double rooms are spacious and

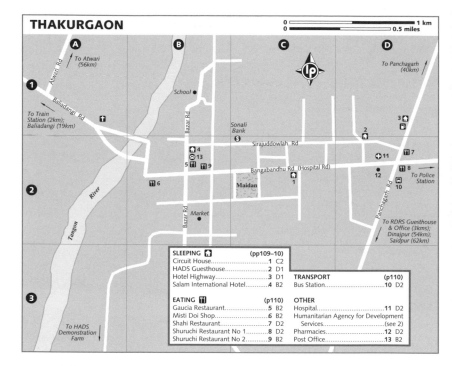

**THAKURGAON**

SLEEPING (pp109–10)
Circuit House.............................1 C2
HADS Guesthouse......................2 D1
Hotel Highway..........................3 D1
Salam International Hotel...........4 B2

EATING (p110)
Gaucia Restaurant.....................5 B2
Misti Doi Shop...........................6 B2
Shahi Restaurant.......................7 D2
Shuruchi Restaurant No 1..........8 D2
Shuruchi Restaurant No 2..........9 B2

TRANSPORT (p110)
Bus Station................................10 D2

OTHER
Hospital.....................................11 D2
Humanitarian Agency for Development
   Services..............................(see 2)
Pharmacies................................12 D2
Post Office.................................13 B2

airy, with fans, comfortable twin beds with mosquito nets, drinking water and spotless attached bathrooms. Staff can also arrange for meals to be brought to your room.

**Circuit House** (Hospital Rd; r Tk 200) If the guesthouses are full, the district commissioner may allow you to stay here.

Other options:

**Salam International Hotel** ( ☎ 52246; Howladar Market shopping centre, Bazar Rd; s Tk 50-200, d Tk 250-1200) Clean, reasonably well run and with a range of rooms.

**Hotel Highway** ( ☎ 52519; Panchagarh Rd; s/d Tk 40/100) Charmless, cell-like singles and dingy doubles. The building's exterior has just been given a fresh coat of green paint. Staff are extremely amiable.

## Eating

**Shuruchi Restaurant No 2** (Hospital Rd; mains Tk 20) This local restaurant is inexpensive and a notch better than other establishments.

Other eateries include the Gaucia Restaurant and several restaurants along Panchagarh Rd, at or near the intersection with Hospital Rd, including Shuruchi Restaurant No 1 and Shahi Restaurant. All serve typical Bangladeshi snacks and meals. You can get

sweet yogurt at a **misti doi shop** (Hospital Rd) at the baby taxi stand.

## Getting There & Away
### BUS

All buses listed here depart from the bus station on the Dinajpur–Panchagarh highway, 500m south of Hospital Rd. Buses go south to Dinajpur (Tk 40, 1¾ hours, depart between 7am and 7.30pm), Saidpur (Tk 60, 1¾ hours, depart between 6.30am and 5.30pm) and Bogra (Tk 145, five hours, depart between 6.30am and 5.30pm).

A chair coach to Dhaka (Tk 250, nine hours) is also available.

### TRAIN

The train station is 2km from the western edge of town. The 2nd-class trains connecting Dinajpur and Panchagarh depart from each town around 7am and pass through Thakurgaon two to three hours later.

## BURIMARI

Burimari is a major crossing point into India, though it's hardly busy.

## Information

The customs office at the border is open from 7.30am to 6.30pm. It should take about 20 minutes to have your passport processed, but all the socialising and cha-drinking will slow you down. There is a government travel tax of Tk 500 for Bangladeshis, but foreigners are not required to pay this.

There is nowhere to change money on the Bangladeshi side of the border, so make sure that before you leave India you grab enough taka to get you to your next destination.

## Sleeping

**Mahoroma Hotel** (s/d 100/200) If you arrive late at night at Burimari, you can stay at this hotel, around the corner from the customs office. It has small but clean rooms with attached bathroom.

**Hotel Paradiso** (Tk 200) in Patgram is a better choice for the restaurants that surround it.

## Getting There & Away

There is a direct bus from Rangpur through some stunning countryside to Patgram village (Tk 90, four hours, every 30 minutes between 6.30am and 7pm). Patgram is 13km from the border.

When you get to the small bus terminal in Patgram, wait for a bus to Burimari (Tk 5, 20 minutes). They come fairly regularly. There are also rickshaw-wallahs willing to take you, but they will want a hefty fee, and won't save you any time. Once you arrive in Burimari, catch a three-wheeler to the customs office (Tk 10).

On the Indian side, at the town of Chengrabandha, it is possible to get a bus to Siliguri (Rs 30, 3½ hours). They run irregularly between 9am and 4.30pm. From Siliguri you can travel to Nepal, Darjeeling and Sikkim. There are also taxis and minibuses milling about in Chengrabandha.

If you're coming from India, you can arrange a coach to Dhaka (Tk 200 to Tk 300, 15 hours) directly from Burimari. The scenery is a typical introduction to the varying landscapes of Bangladesh. It is also possible to get a bus from Burimari to Saidpur (Tk 75, 3½ hours, every hour between 7am and 3.30pm).

A good way to get yourself moving is to get a bus to Patgram (Tk 5, 20 minutes) and another bus from there to Rangpur (Tk 90, six hours).

## RAJSHAHI

☎ 0721

Built on the northern bank of the Padma River, Rajshahi is a laid-back and relatively prosperous university town.

The river bank by the Padma River affords one of the best river views in the country. Sunsets here are particularly worth seeing. In the late afternoon, walk south from the Parjatan Hotel and stroll along the river. It's almost carnival-like, with people strolling and chatting, children playing and vendors selling ice cream and other snack food.

Looking across the vast flood plain to the opposite bank you'll see India, where the river is called the Ganges. In the dry season it is sometimes possible to walk across the river bed, which aids the thriving smuggling trade along the border. The local trade in smuggled goods is most evident in Saheb Bazar. Indian beer can sometimes be found at very high prices.

## Orientation & Information

There are quite a few bookshops in New Market and to the north of Saheb Bazar. Rajshahi being a university town, they sell mainly academic texts, but the odd novel is available.

**Agrani Bank** (Greater Rd) The best place to change money.

**Syenthiya Computer** (Saheb Bazar Rd; per hr Tk 20) The best Internet café, with broadband access.

**Twenty-1 Cyber Café** (Saheb Bazar Rd; per hr Tk 20) Newly opened and far less crowded. Look for the blue sign.

## Sights

### VARENDRA RESEARCH MUSEUM

Founded in 1910 with the support of the maharaja of Dighapatia, the **Varendra Research Museum** (admission free; ☯ 10am-5pm Sat-Wed, 2.30-5pm Fri) is managed by Rajshahi University (RU), and is the oldest museum in the country. The predominantly British-style building has some interesting Hindu-Buddhist features, including a trefoil arch over the doorways and windows. A small *rekha* temple forms the roof.

Inside, artefacts from all over the subcontinent are on display, including some rare examples from the ancient city of Mohenjodaro in Pakistan, and a superb collection of local Hindu sculpture.

### MARTYRS' MEMORIAL MUSEUM

The collection of Liberation War mementos at the **Martyrs' Memorial Museum** (Shaheed

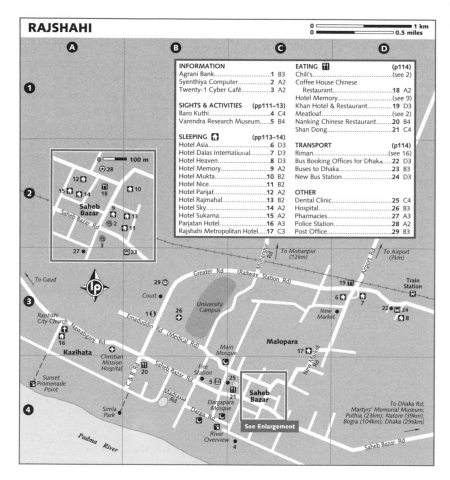

## RAJSHAHI

| INFORMATION | |
| --- | --- |
| Agrani Bank | 1 B3 |
| Synthiya Computer | 2 A2 |
| Twenty-1 Cyber Café | 3 A2 |

| SIGHTS & ACTIVITIES | (pp111–13) |
| --- | --- |
| Baro Kuthi | 4 C4 |
| Varendra Research Museum | 5 B4 |

| SLEEPING 🏠 | (pp113–14) |
| --- | --- |
| Hotel Asia | 6 D3 |
| Hotel Dalas International | 7 D3 |
| Hotel Heaven | 8 D3 |
| Hotel Memory | 9 A2 |
| Hotel Mukta | 10 B2 |
| Hotel Nice | 11 B2 |
| Hotel Parijat | 12 A2 |
| Hotel Rajmahal | 13 B2 |
| Hotel Sky | 14 A2 |
| Hotel Sukarna | 15 A2 |
| Parjatan Hotel | 16 A3 |
| Rajshahi Metropolitan Hotel | 17 C3 |

| EATING 🍴 | (p114) |
| --- | --- |
| Chili's | (see 2) |
| Coffee House Chinese | |
| Restaurant | 18 A2 |
| Hotel Memory | (see 9) |
| Khan Hotel & Restaurant | 19 D3 |
| Meatloaf | (see 2) |
| Nanking Chinese Restaurant | 20 B4 |
| Shan Dong | 21 C4 |

| TRANSPORT | (p114) |
| --- | --- |
| Biman | (see 16) |
| Bus Booking Offices for Dhaka | 22 D3 |
| Buses to Dhaka | 23 B3 |
| New Bus Station | 24 D3 |

| OTHER | |
| --- | --- |
| Dental Clinic | 25 C4 |
| Hospital | 26 B3 |
| Pharmacies | 27 A3 |
| Police Station | 28 A2 |
| Post Office | 29 B3 |

Smriti Sangrahashala) at RU is a reminder of the dreadful days of the 1971 war. Unfortunately, the dilapidated state of the museum, with its dusty collection of war artefacts, is more likely to make one feel that the country has forgotten its heroes. Among the exhibits are blood-stained uniforms, a pen used by a fighter to write his last love letter, the deed papers of surrender by the Pakistani forces, and remains recovered from a mass grave of victims, among whom were intellectuals from RU.

### BUILDINGS OF THE BRITISH RAJ

Near the centre of Rajshahi are some Raj-era buildings. **Rajshahi Government College**, which dates from 1873 when several maharajas donated money for its establishment, is an elegant two-storey edifice with beautiful semicircular arched windows. Others nearby include **Collegiate School** (1836), which consists of two single-storey structures east of the college, with verandas along the façades; and **Fuller House** (1909), a large two-storey red-brick building that is similar in appearance to the college.

### BARO KUTHI

A block southeast of Rajshahi Government College, on a high bank of the Padma River, is a historic structure known as **Baro Kuthi**. It's one of the last remaining examples of the indigo *kuthis* (factories) that once flourished in the region. The simple buildings are of little architectural interest but their history is fascinating.

In the early 19th century Baro Kuthi was built by the Dutch for the silk trade and served as a fort in times of emergency. Some rooms were probably used as a prison and for mounting cannons. After 1833, when Baro Kuthi was taken over by the British East India Company, it was used for the indigo trade (see right), which lasted about 25 years. It is reputed to have been the scene of countless crimes during that period, including murder and torture.

## Sleeping
### BUDGET
**Hotel Heaven** ( ☎ 775 054; s/d/t Tk 85/125/200) This multistorey establishment with friendly staff is close to train and bus stations. Standard rooms have attached bathroom and comfortable beds. There are also a couple of cramped singles with common bathroom for Tk 65, and larger doubles with couch, table and sit-down toilet for Tk 150. Look for the red sign with yellow Bangla script.

**Hotel Asia** (s/d with shared bathroom Tk 50/80, s/d with bathroom Tk 70/120, s/d with tiled bathroom Tk 100/150) A good budget option near the intersection of Railway Station and Airport Rds, it's clean and some rooms are spacious with small tables.

**Rajshahi Metropolitan Hotel** ( ☎ 772 861; New Market Rd; s Tk 60, d Tk 80-110) This well-marked hotel is close to the town centre. Rooms have a fan, mosquito net and attached bathroom. The hotel features a breezy reception area with comfortable chairs – good for relaxing.

**Hotel Parijat** ( ☎ 773 434; Emaduddin Rd; s/d with shared bathroom Tk 50/90, s/d with bathroom Tk 70/100) This is a poorly marked two-storey building facing the police station. Rooms are reasonably clean and well ventilated, although staff might try talking you out of staying by saying it's full.

**Hotel Rajmahal** ( ☎ 774 399; s/d Tk 140/190) Just east of New Market Rd, the Rajmahal has rooms with carpet, fan, mosquito net and attached bathroom. There are also singles with common bathroom for Tk 65.

**Hotel Memory** ( ☎ 774 742; s/d/t Tk 25/45/60) The impossibly small rooms with shared bathrooms are indeed hard to forget. Fractionally larger singles/doubles with attached bathrooms cost Tk 50/100.

### THE INFAMOUS INDIGO KUTHIS

In the 18th and early 19th centuries the trade in indigo – the plant that yields the indigo hue for dye – was highly profitable. By the mid-1800s the Rajshahi region alone had more than 150 indigo *kuthis*. The local zamindars even loaned money to peasants so they could plant more indigo. Indeed, trade was so lucrative and the *kuthis* so numerous that factory labourers had to be imported.

The farmers, however, didn't profit at all and began changing crops. Using oppression and torture to keep the peasants growing indigo, angry zamindars sometimes went as far as committing murder and burning whole villages. An adage at the time held that 'no indigo box was despatched to England without being smeared in human blood'.

In 1859 the peasants revolted. The Indigo Revolt lasted two years and brought the cultivation of indigo to a halt. Eventually the government had no choice but to decree that the peasants could no longer be forced to plant indigo. As a result, by the end of the century the indigo trade had completely disappeared. Some of the *kuthis* were converted into silk factories but most simply fell into ruin.

### MID-RANGE
**Hotel Dalas International** ( ☎ 773 839; s/d Tk 250/450) It's an easy walk from the main bus station, but nicely tucked away from its chaos. Standard doubles have carpet, TV, balconies, chairs and cosy bedding, with tiled hot-water bathrooms. AC costs an extra Tk 200.

**Hotel Sukarna** ( ☎ 771 817; s Tk 100-450, d Tk 300-600) A very clean mid-range option. Some doubles have hot water and sit-down toilets. You will get a nice carpeted single with TV for Tk 200. Renovations are underway to add Tk 1200 deluxe rooms. The location is great and the staff are obliging.

**Hotel Sky** ( ☎ 810 641; s/d Tk 70/150, with AC Tk 400/550) At this five-storey establishment near Saheb Bazar, AC rooms also have satellite TV. The hotel has unusually spacious hallways that give the place a very airy atmosphere. Rooms are bright and fairly large by local standards. Doubles have mirrors and comfortable reading chairs.

**Hotel Nice** ( ☎ 776 188; s Tk 100-350, d Tk 200-700) Rooms aren't as nice as the reception (and name) would suggest. Some smell like old carpet and old *dahl*.

**TOP END**

**Hotel Mukta** ( ☎ 771 100; with/without AC s Tk 700/250, d Tk 1000/750, ste Tk 1600) Somewhere between a mid-range and a top-end hotel, Hotel Mukta is conveniently around the corner from Saheb Bazar. All rooms have hot water.

At the time of writing, the Parjatan Hotel was undergoing heavy renovations, which will hopefully include alterations to staff attitudes. Rooms will likely be upwards of Tk 600, but perhaps worth it. The Parjatan's proximity to the river is an advantage. The Biman office is also here.

## Eating

**Hotel Memory** (meals Tk 26) There are two restaurants at Hotel Memory; the one at the end of the corridor is a nice respite. Come here for a feast of unrecognisable but tasty food.

**Khan Hotel & Restaurant** (cnr Airport & Railway Station Rds) Near the Dalas International, the Khan serves nice meals and great sweetmeats. Staff don't speak English but you can bet they'll all try to get you what you want. There are a few women patrons.

**Nanking Chinese Restaurant** (cnr Nawabganj & Greater Rds) Decent Chinese and Thai food can be found at Nanking. It has *tom yam* for Tk 90, beef fried rice for Tk 70 and the obligatory French fries for Tk 48. It's at the Monibazar crafts centre.

**Shan Dong** (Saheb Bazar Rd; dishes Tk 80-100) In an impossible-to-miss colourful building it shares with the community centre, this Chinese restaurant has standards such as prawn fried rice and chicken dishes.

**Coffee House Chinese Restaurant** (Emaduddin Rd) It's oddly named, but it does serve coffee in dim surrounds.

For fast food, try **Chili's** (Saheb Bazar Rd) or **Meatloaf** (Saheb Bazar Rd). You could also take a picnic to Simla Park, just beyond the circuit house on C&B Rd, overlooking the Padma River.

## Getting There & Away

### AIR

The airport is 10km from the centre of town. A baby taxi will cost around Tk 30. **Biman** ( ☎ 774 373; Parjatan Hotel) has daily flights

to Dhaka (Tk 1150), and flies to Saidpur (Tk 825) four days a week.

### BUS

**National Bus Company** (cnr Mirpur Rd & Pantha Path) in Dhaka operates coaches to Rajshahi (Tk 200, 4½ hours, almost hourly between 7.15am and 11pm).

From Rajshahi, buses for Dhaka (ordinary bus Tk 150 to Tk 170, AC coach Tk 260 to Tk 300, seven hours) leave from the town centre on Saheb Bazar Rd, though it may be more efficient to head straight to New Bus Station, across from the train station. Here you will find booking offices for the Dhaka-bound buses that leave from this area.

From New Bus Station you can also get ordinary buses to Bogra (Tk 80, three hours, every 15 minutes between 6.15am and 5.45pm), Natore (Tk 30, one hour, every 20 minutes between 5am and 9.30pm), Jessore (Tk 130, 5½ hours, every 30 minutes between 6am and 6.30pm) and Rangpur (Tk 140, 4½ hours, every 45 minutes between 6am and 4.40pm).

### CAR

Hire cars can be arranged through the Parjatan, Nice and Sky Hotels. The cost for a day drive to Gaud, Puthia and Natore (about 10 to 12 hours) should be around Tk 1000, not necessarily including petrol.

### TRAIN

IC trains depart from the **train station** ( ☎ 774 060) for Dhaka (1st/*sulob* class/AC berth Tk 290/140/630, 6½ hours, daily except Sunday at 7am).

There's a daily express to Jessore (1st/*sulob* class Tk 215/75, five hours) and Khulna (1st/*sulob* class Tk 265/90, 6¼ hours) that departs at 1.45pm. There is also a 7.30am mail train on this route. There are also IC trains to Saidpur (1st/*sulob* class Tk 190/65, 5½ hours) and Parbatipur (1st/*sulob* class Tk 175/60, five hours) that leave at 6.30am and 3pm daily except Friday.

## PUTHIA

Puthia (*pou*-tee-ah) has the largest number of historically important Hindu structures in Bangladesh. It also has one of the country's finest old rajbaris, which is in such poor condition that it's positively picturesque. Only 23km east of Rajshahi (16km west of Natore) and 1km south of the highway, it's very accessible. Coming from the highway, you'll pass a tall Hindu shrine to your left. Continue past it to a large grassy field, with the rajbari just beyond. As you walk around, ask for the mandir (temple), which may lead you to the discovery of some lesser Hindu structures in the area. The scarcity of decent places to sleep poses no problem, given Puthia's proximity to both Rajshahi and Natore.

## Sights
### PALACES
The stately two-storey **Puthia Palace** was built in 1895 by Rani Hemanta Kumari Devi in honour of his illustrious mother-in-law, Maharani Sharat Sundari Devi. She was a major benefactor in the Rajshahi region, having built a boarding house for college students and a Sanskrit college, for which she was given the title maharani in 1877. The building is in just good enough condition to serve as a college today. Most of the walls have political slogans scrawled over them.

**Tahirpur Palace** is 18km due north of Puthia, up a back road along the Baralai River in Tahirpur. Rebuilt after the great earthquake of 1897, it's an imposing two-storey structure that, despite the collapse of its roof, remains largely intact.

### TEMPLES
The most amazing monument in the village is the **Govinda Temple**, on the left-hand side of the rajbari's inner courtyard. Erected between 1823 and 1895 by one of the maharanis of the Puthia estate, it's a large, square structure with intricate terracotta designs embellishing the surface. In this sense, it's very similar in inspiration to the Kantanagar Temple (p109), which is about a century older. Most of the terracotta panels depict scenes from the love affair between Radha and Krishna as told in the Hindu epics.

Built in 1823, the photogenic **Shiva Temple** at the entrance to Puthia, overlooking a pond, is an imposing square structure and an excellent example of the *pancha-ratna* (five-spire) Hindu style common in northern India. Unfortunately, many of the stone carvings and sculptures were disfigured during the 1971 Liberation War, though there's still an impressive black-stone phallic image of Shiva.

One of Bangladesh's finest examples of the hut-shaped temple is the **Jagannath Temple**, about 150m to the right (west) of the rajbari. This nicely restored 16th-century temple, measuring only about 5m on each side, features a single tapering tower that rises to a height of about 10m. The temple's western facade is finely adorned with terracotta panels of mostly geometric design.

## Getting There & Away
There are numerous buses between Rajshahi and Natore (Tk 20, 30 minutes) throughout the day that pass through Puthia. On leaving Puthia, you can easily hail a bus travelling between the two towns on the main highway.

# NATORE
☎ 0771
Located on the Rajshahi–Dhaka highway, 40km east of Rajshahi and 75km southwest of Bogra, Natore (*nut*-or) is noted for having two of the most outstanding rajbaris in the country. Otherwise, there's not much reason to stop in this busy crossroads town.

## Orientation
The main drag runs east to west. A bus station and some cheap hotels are at a three-way intersection at the eastern end of town, with major highways heading east to Pabna and Dhaka and north to Bogra. The train station is at the city's opposite end, on the road west to Rajshahi.

## Sights
### UTTARA GANO-GHABAN
The building was once the palace of the Dighapatia Maharaja, the region's governor. It's now a government building called **Uttara Gano-Ghaban** (Dighapatia Palace; ☺ 10am-4pm Sat-Thu) and serves as one of the president's official residences. Situated 3km north of town, off the road to Bogra, the beautifully maintained complex occupies about 15 hectares of land. It's enclosed within a moat and a high boundary wall, and is approached from the east through an imposing four-storey arched gateway. The incongruous mosque-like dome covering the central hall was added in 1967.

### NATORE RAJBARI
One of the oldest rajbaris in Bangladesh, dating from the mid-1700s, the magnificent

but dilapidated **Natore Rajbari** is actually a series of seven rajbaris, four of which remain largely intact. The main block, called Baro Taraf, is approached via a long avenue lined with impressively tall bottle palms, the white trunks of which resemble temple columns.

To the rear of Baro Taraf is a second block called Chhota-Taraf, consisting of two rajbaris. The principal one faces a pond and is one of the most beautifully proportioned buildings in Bangladesh.

Natore Rajbari is at the northern edge of town, but to avoid getting lost it's easier to take the Natore–Bogra road and, 1km before the turn-off for Dighapatia Palace, take a left on an unmarked paved road that leads west towards the complex. It's 1.5km down that road, just beyond a school on your right.

### RANI BHAWANI GARDENS
For over 50 years until she died in 1791, Rani Bhawani, wife of the owner of the Natore Rajbari, managed the huge estate after her husband's death. She became a legendary figure because of her boundless charity; even today her name is recognised by many Bangladeshis. A **garden** bearing her name is now a popular picnic spot. To get there, take a right (north) at the *thana* office on the main east–west drag and start asking directions.

## Sleeping & Eating
**VIP Guest House** (s/d Tk 200/400) Even other hotel proprietors will probably direct you to the VIP Guest House, which is clearly the best place to stay. Rooms have TV and balconies. It's on the main road into town for Pabna-bound buses.

**Hotel Raj** (s/d Tk 50/100) One of the cheapest places is the unmarked Hotel Raj at the eastern end of town, 200m north of the three-way intersection. Rooms are tiny, with fans, mosquito nets and attached bathroom.

The main drag is the best place for finding street food and a couple of restaurants.

## Getting There & Away
### BUS
Buses headed north and east leave from the intersection at the eastern end of town, while those headed for Rajshahi (Tk 30, one hour) leave from the west. There's a bus to Pabna (Tk 40, 1½ hours).

### TRAIN
Trains run to Rajshahi (Tk 25), Saidpur (Tk 40) and Chilahati (Tk 55). Khulna is on the same line as Chilahati – mail trains to Khulna cost Tk 62 and IC trains Tk 105.

## PABNA
☎ 731
Between Rajshahi and Dhaka, Pabna, which dates from medieval times, features some fine old buildings, including a superb Hindu temple and two well-known rajbaris.

## Sights
### JOR BANGLA TEMPLE
Built in the 18th century in the form of two traditional village huts intertwined and standing on a platform, this **temple**, 2km east of the town centre, is the best remaining example of the *jor bangla* (twin hut) style. Before construction was completed something sacrilegious occurred on the site, so the temple was never used. While the building is not large or imposing, it is extremely elegant and has been beautifully restored.

### RAJBARIS
The **Taras Rajbari**, viewed from the street through an unusually impressive archway, is a few hundred metres south of the town centre on the main road. Dating from the late 19th century, it was evidently once an elegant palace, but it's now all too obviously the drab home of government offices. The building's most prominent feature is its two-storey front portico supported by four tall columns, resembling a pre-Civil War *Gone with the Wind* mansion in southern USA.

East of town, on the banks of the Padma River, **Sitlai Palace**, dating from 1900, is a grand rajbari that's fairly well preserved. Today it's occupied by a drug company, so you can't see the 30-room interior. The exterior is interesting, however, with a broad staircase flagged with white marble, leading to a 2nd-storey arched portico.

### SHAHZADPUR MOSQUE
Just outside of Pabna is this splendid 15-dome pre-Mughal **mosque**, built in 1528 in traditional *bangla* (Pre-Mauryan and Mauryan) style with thick walls and various arched entrances.

## Sleeping & Eating

**Birani House** (s/d Tk 50/100; Rupkatha Rd) The well-marked Birani House, opposite the cinema, also boasts fast food, by which it means Chinese and Bangladeshi food prepared in a hurry. Single rooms have shared bathrooms.

**Hotel Tripti Niloy** (s/d Tk 100/150) Towards the northern edge of town, on the main road, the Tripti Niloy is good value. Cheaper rooms are available with shared bathrooms. There is also a restaurant here, but it is a bit too gloomy to eat in.

**Birani Chayanirr Hotel** (s/d Tk 80/150) Diagonally opposite Birani House, the Chayanirr has clean and tidy rooms with attached bathrooms.

**Hotel Rohan** (s/d Tk 160/200) Facing the cinemas, the Rohan is on the right. It's not such good value as the Chayanirr but it's adequate.

There are lots of basic restaurants along Rupkatha Rd. The one beneath the Birani Chayanirr Hotel has piping-hot naan and a waiter with all the ancient charm of a human rajbari.

## Getting There & Away

Most buses leave from the main road just south of the town centre. There are buses to Dhaka via Aricha, although the expresses that originate in Rajshahi will probably be full.

Buses run west to Natore (Tk 40, 1½ hours) and Rajshahi (Tk 60, 2½ hours), and northwest to Ishurdi (Tk 14, 45 minutes), which has better bus and train connections. You have to go to Ishurdi to get to Kushtia in Khulna division; all buses leave from the Ishurdi town centre.

## GAUD

A site of great historical importance, Gaud (or Gaur) has more historic mosques than any area in Bangladesh, except Bagerhat. It's over 100km west of Rajshahi, right on Bangladesh's western border – some of its sights are in India, some in Bangladesh.

The Hindu Senas established their capital here, after which the Khiljis from Turkistan took control for three centuries, to be followed in the late 15th century by the Afghans. Under the Afghans, Gaud became a prosperous city surrounded by fortified ramparts and a moat, and spread over 32 sq km. Replete with temples, mosques and palaces, the city was visited by traders and merchants from all over Central Asia, Arabia, Persia and China. A number of mosques are still standing today, and some have been restored. None of the buildings from the earlier Hindu kingdoms remain.

## Sights

### MOSQUES

Built between 1493 and 1526, the well-preserved **Chhota Sona Masjid** (Small Golden Mosque) is a fine specimen of pre-Mughal architecture. The mosque's chief attraction is the superb decoration carved on its black-stone walls. On both the inner and outer walls, ornate stonework in shallow relief covers the surface. It also features an ornate women's gallery, arched gateways and lavishly decorated mihrabs (niches).

The single-domed **Khania Dighi Mosque** (also known as Rajbibi Mosque), built in 1490, is in Chapara village and is in reasonably good condition. It also has some ornately decorated walls, but here they are embellished primarily with terracotta floral designs. Like Chhota Sona, it also features some highly ornate stonework, primarily on the three arched entrances on the western wall.

Built around 1470, **Darasbari Mosque** is in poorer condition than Khania Dighi Mosque and is missing some of its original domes. It has two sections: a long oblong prayer hall measuring 30m; and a wide veranda on the east. The walls are 2m thick, and on the interior western wall of the prayer hall you'll see nine doorways with superb terracotta ornamentation in various floral and geometric patterns.

### MONUMENTS IN FIROZPUR

At nearby Firozpur you'll find several interesting structures that are all fairly well preserved and close to one another. One is the picturesque **Shah Niamatullah Mosque**, a three-domed mosque built in 1560 which overlooks a large pond. About 100m away is the **Mausoleum of Shah Niamatullah Wali**; it has three domes and four squat towers. The third structure, north of the mausoleum, is **Takhkhana Palace**, built by Shah Shuja in the early 17th century and the area's major Mughal-era building. A large two-storey brick edifice, it has a flat roof, which in those times was virtually unheard-of in Bangladesh.

## Sleeping

**Archaeology Department Rest House** (Tk 200) There are fairly basic but decent rooms here. If you just show up, chances are excellent that you'll be allowed to stay here because there is no other accommodation in Gaud, barring some extremely basic rooms above an equally basic restaurant where the bus stops near the Bangladeshi border post.

## Getting There & Away

Getting to Gaud can take so damn long that you'll forget how close you are to Rajshahi. From the main bus terminal in Rajshahi, take a bus to Nawabganj (Tk 25, two hours). From there it may be possible to get a bus directly to Gaud. If not, take another bus to Shibganj (Tk 10, 45 minutes). From here, either wait for an irregular bus to Gaud or get a baby taxi to take you the rest of the way. If you get blank looks when you ask for 'Gaud', try 'India' or 'border' instead.

The consolation of all of this messing about is that the scenery on the journey is quite unusual. There are fascinating expanses where village life takes place amid enormous expanses of trees with foot-worn pathways meandering between them. There are mud-brick huts interspersed throughout, and mustard fields so bright you almost have to squint.

On arrival in Gaud it is a good idea to call on the friendly soldiers at the border post. They can advise you where not to go; the strip of no-man's-land between the two countries is just as intensively farmed as surrounding areas, so it's easy to make a mistake.

# Chittagong Division

CONTENTS

Stretching down to the southeastern corner of the country, Chittagong division shares borders with Sylhet division to the north, India and Myanmar (Burma) to the east and Dhaka division along the Meghna River. Around Chittagong, particularly in the Chittagong Hill Tracts and south to the Myanmar border, hills are the dominant feature.

Chittagong's coastal strip is very narrow, and crowded against the sea by the hills to the east. This is the only coastal region of Bangladesh where the land is not fragmented by river deltas. The beaches are long and broad, and extend from Sitakunda to Patenga, where they are cut off by the estuary of the Karnaphuli River, and then continue to Teknaf. This last uninterrupted stretch (120km) is said to be the world's longest beach.

## HIGHLIGHTS

- Visiting Chakma villages from **Rangamati** (p128), a hill-tribe town scattered over countless unfathomably green islands

- Holidaying Bangladeshi style at the long beach of **Cox's Bazar** (p132)

- Revelling in the absence of cars while wandering through palm trees on **St Martin's Island** (p137), Bangladesh's only coral island

- Losing your bearings in the carnival-like streets of **Chittagong** (p120)

- Taking a boat ride on **Kaptai Lake** (p128), the country's largest artificial lake and one of its most beautiful

Kaptai Lake ★
Rangamati ★
Chittagong ★
Cox's Bazar ★
St Martin's Island ★

# CHITTAGONG

☎ 31

Chittagong city (the second-largest city in Bangladesh, with a population of around four million) is 264km southeast of Dhaka, on the north bank of the Karnaphuli River. The climate is pleasant year-round – cool in winter and only slightly humid in summer. Its annual rainfall is 2400mm (twice that of Dhaka). Chittagong is the initial jumping-off point for the Chittagong Hill Tracts to the east and Cox's Bazar to the south.

This strategic port is the country's busiest, making the city notoriously prone to demonstrations and hartals (strikes). Despite this, the urban environment is noticeably less

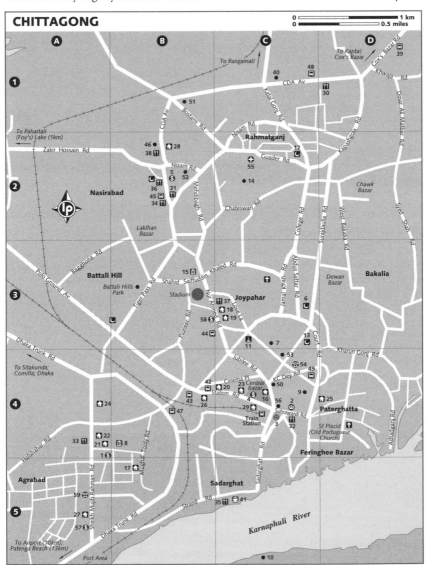

chaotic than Dhaka, and a strong local civic movement works hard to keep the streets reasonably clean and unclogged by traffic.

The Chittagong dialect of Bangla is somewhat different from that spoken in other parts of the country, incorporating words from Arabic, Portuguese, Arakanese and tribal languages.

## History

Locals say the word Chittagong originated from *chattagram* (small village), though it more likely comes from the Arakanese phrase *tsi-tsi-gong* ('war should never be fought') inscribed on a tablet brought by an invading Buddhist army.

Despite its name, Chittagong has been consistently fought over. In 1299 Muslims occupied the city, until the Arakanese retook it and retained it until 1660. The Mughals took possession next, only to be expelled by the Arakanese in 1715. Finally, in 1766 the British raised their flag.

By this time the Burmese had subdued the hill area of Arakan (now known as Rakhine), and many Arakanese fled into British-occupied territory south of Chittagong. Continuing friction between the British and the Burmese led to the first Anglo-Burmese War in 1824, and resulted in the British annexing Arakan. The Burmese were forced to give up any claims they previously had to the region around Chittagong.

The evolution of the city followed a similar pattern to Dhaka, except that the oldest parts, where the city of Sadarghat now stands, were wiped out during the British and post-Independence periods. The Pakistani navy shelled the city during the Liberation War.

## Orientation

Station Rd is basically the centre of town and is a good reference point. Towards its eastern end, on the corner of Jubilee Rd, is the large New Market building (Riponi Bitan).

The central bazar is a warren of lanes between the lower ends of Jubilee and Station Rds. It's almost impossible not to lose your way among the densely packed rows of clothing shops.

The more upmarket shopping area is along CDA Ave, at the intersection of Zakir Hossain and Nizam Rds, which is called GEC Circle. There are also a number of restaurants in this area.

Chittagong's business district is the Agrabad Commercial Area, the grid of streets between Sheikh Mujib Rahman Rd and the Hotel Agrabad, around which you'll find numerous international-airline offices.

### MAPS
Mappa publishes a good Chittagong city map. You may be able to find it at bookshops on CDA Ave or from street vendors.

## Information
### BOOKSHOPS
**Hotel Agrabad** (Agrabad Commercial Area)

| INFORMATION | |
|---|---|
| HSBC | 1 A4 |
| Main Post Office | 2 C4 |
| Parjatan | (see 29) |
| SM International Internet Cafe | 3 C4 |
| Standard Chartered Bank | 4 C4 |
| Standard Chartered Bank | 5 B2 |

| SIGHTS & ACTIVITIES | (pp122–3) |
|---|---|
| Chandanpura Mosque | 6 C3 |
| Circuit House | (see 15) |
| DC Hill | 7 C3 |
| Ethnological Museum | 8 B4 |
| Fairy Hill | 9 C4 |
| Fish Harbour & Market | 10 C5 |
| High Court | (see 9) |
| Marine Fisheries Academy | (see 10) |
| Nandankanan Buddhist Monastery | 11 C3 |
| Qadam Mubarak Mosque | 12 C2 |
| Shahi Jama-e-Masjid | 13 C3 |
| WWII Memorial Cemetery | 14 C2 |
| Zia Memorial Museum | 15 B3 |

| SLEEPING | (pp123–4) |
|---|---|
| Chimbuk Hotel | 16 C4 |
| Hotel Agrabad | 17 B5 |
| Hotel Al-Faisal | 18 C3 |
| Hotel Bandargaon | 19 C3 |

| | |
|---|---|
| Hotel Golden Inn | 20 C4 |
| Hotel Hawaii | 21 A4 |
| Hotel Hoque Tower | 22 A4 |
| Hotel Manila | (see 23) |
| Hotel Midtown | (see 23) |
| Hotel Miskha | 23 C4 |
| Hotel Saint Martin | 24 A4 |
| Hotel Samrat | 25 D4 |
| Hotel Sylhet Super | 26 B4 |
| Landmark Hotel | 27 A5 |
| Meridian Hotel | 28 B2 |
| Shaikat Hotel | 29 C4 |

| EATING | (p124) |
|---|---|
| Asian Spice Restaurant | 30 D1 |
| Blossom Garden | 31 B2 |
| Chin Lung | 32 C4 |
| Chung King Restaurant | 33 A4 |
| Dhaba | 34 B2 |
| Hong Kong Restaurant | 35 C5 |
| Pizzaland | (see 46) |
| Sayeman | 36 B2 |
| Shaad Snacks | (see 3) |
| Tai Wah | 37 C3 |
| Zaman | 38 B2 |

| DRINKING | (p124) |
|---|---|
| Railway Men's Store | (see 26) |

| TRANSPORT | (pp124–5) |
|---|---|
| Bardarhat Bus Station | 39 D1 |
| Biman Airlines | 40 C1 |
| BIWTC Boat Terminal | 41 C5 |
| BRTC Bus Station | 42 B4 |
| Bus Station for Dhaka | 43 B4 |
| Cinema Palace Bus Station | 44 B3 |
| Dhaka Buses | 45 B2 |
| Dhaka Buses | (see 20) |
| GMG Airlines | 46 B2 |
| GMG Airlines | (see 17) |
| Kadamtale Bus Station | 47 B4 |
| Modapur Bus Station | 48 C1 |
| Society Market Bus Station | 49 C4 |

| OTHER | |
|---|---|
| Bangladesh Ecotours | 50 C4 |
| Biplob Uddyan (Revolution Park) | 51 B1 |
| Chittagong Public Library | 52 B2 |
| Forestry Department Office | 53 C4 |
| International Telephone Office | 54 C4 |
| Medical College Hospital | 55 C2 |
| New Market | 56 C4 |
| Standard Chartered Bank | 57 A5 |
| Standard Chartered Bank | 58 B3 |
| Telephone & Telegraph Office | 59 A5 |

## INTERNET ACCESS

GEC Circle has a couple of Internet cafés, usually more costly than those on Station and Jubilee Rds.

**SM International Internet Café** (Station Rd; per hr Tk 30) Opposite New Market.

## MONEY

There are lots of banks in the Agrabad Commercial Area.

**HSBC** Near the Ethnological Museum, with an ATM.

**Standard Chartered Bank** Central Bazar (Station Rd); Nasirabad (CDA Ave) 24hr ATM.

## POST

**Main post office** (Suhrawardi Rd; ☉ 8am-8.30pm Sat-Thu, 3-9pm Fri)

## TOURIST INFORMATION

**Parjatan** (Shaikat Hotel, Station Rd) Not very forthcoming. You'll get a brochure if you're lucky.

## Sights & Activities

### OLD CITY

As in Dhaka, the city's oldest area is the waterfront area called Sadarghat. The early arrival of the Portuguese is evinced by the proximity of the Paterghatta district, just next to Sadarghat, which remains a Christian area. There isn't much to see in Paterghatta, but it's a quiet, clean place to walk around – until you get into the slums of the prawn-sellers around the waterfront near Feringhee Bazar, which will leave an enduring stench on your shoes. A rowboat back to Sadarghat costs anything from Tk 5.

You can hire a boat from the boat terminal to go across the river (Tk 20, 10 minutes) to the **fish harbour and market**. The **Marine Fisheries Academy** is housed in a new building with a small museum. It has a few fish specimens to look at, if you need to add a little excitement to your day and think this will do it.

**Shahi Jama-e-Masjid**, in Anderkilla (inner fort), was built in 1670 on a hillock and hence looks a bit like a fort. The mosque has a tall minaret, Saracenic or Turkish in design, which looms up out of the shops that have since surrounded it. In the early 1950s it was greatly enlarged and most of its original features altered, though a number of original inscriptions are still embedded in the walls.

The **Chilla of Badar Shah** derives its name from a Sufi who came to Chittagong in 1336.

It is a modest-sized place with a courtyard and worship area built around the grave of Badar Shah, and is walking distance from the Shahi-Jama-e-Masjid. There are several *mazars* (graves) in the area, so make sure you're directed to the right one – ask for 'Badar Shah Chilla'. On the same road are interesting shops that make traditional tablas (musical instruments).

### BRITISH CITY

The British originally occupied the area just northwest of Sadarghat, a slightly hilly section where they built their usual collection of administrative and cultural edifices: a hospital, the secretariat and the High Court. Station Rd, with its brightly lit stalls, forms the boundary with the old city.

The British city has become the central business district of Chittagong. The area retains its colonial air and sense of order and cleanliness.

The massive **circuit house** (Shahid Saiffuddin Khaled Rd) was where President Zia Rahman was machine-gunned by soldiers in May 1981. Built in 1913 in the style of a Tudor manor house, it originally stood amid 35 acres of landscaped gardens and lawns. It is one of the few remaining timber structures in the country. The building now houses the **Zia Memorial Museum** ( ☉ 10.30am-4.30pm Sat-Wed, 3.30-7.30pm Fri). Among its much-revered collection is the microphone and transmitter with which President Zia proclaimed the country's Independence in 1971. The museum attracts around a thousand visitors per week and is still undergoing renovations to further glorify the general's memory.

The **Chandanpura Mosque** is north of the city centre on the road to Kaptai, near Dewan Bazar. It has no historical importance but is an attractive sight with its delicate design.

**Fairy Hill** is said to be named for the fairies and genies that were believed to occupy it when the Sufi saint Badar Shah first came to Chittagong. Legend says that he made a number of requests to the fairies before they would allow him to build a place of worship. It's behind the main post office and New Market – climb the path leading off Jubilee Rd just north of the pedestrian bridge near New Market. Ask directions for the **High Court**, the building on top of the hill – Fairy Hill was the common name during the Raj era and is rapidly being forgotten.

Atop **DC Hill** is the district commissioner's residence, but the surrounding area is open to the public. It is a pleasant place with many old trees.

The peaceful, well-maintained **WWII Memorial Cemetery** (Fazul Rd) contains the graves of soldiers from both Allied and Japanese forces who died on the Burma front.

## MODERN CITY

Agrabad, the modern commercial section with banks, large hotels and corporate offices, is quite in keeping with the trends of a 21st-century city. The outer reaches of the city have become industrialised; the only steel mill and oil refinery in Bangladesh are in Chittagong.

Just around the corner from the Hotel Agrabad, the interesting **Ethnological Museum** ( 9am-1pm & 1.30-4pm Mon-Wed, 9am-noon Thu) has displays on Bangladesh's tribal people. Unfortunately, it isn't always open when it should be. Some of the exhibits are looking a bit tattered, but it covers all the major tribal groups of the nearby Chittagong Hill Tracts. The museum's assumption that these cultures are doomed is depressing.

## QADAM MUBARAK MOSQUE

Built in 1719 in the Rahmatganj area, the late-Mughal **Qadam Mubarak Mosque** derives its name from a slab that bears an impression of the Prophet's foot *(mubarak)*.

## PAHARTALI LAKE

Also known as **Foy's Lake**, this area has boating facilities and is a popular picnic spot; things get hectic on weekends. Early in the morning is a nice time to visit. On a cool day, walking is pleasant in the denuded hills around the lake. There is a zoo here, but it's a wretched place. A high hill near the lake's edge affords grand views of Chittagong and the Bay of Bengal. You can get to the lake by rickshaw (Tk 10) or tempo (Tk 3) from the junction of CDA Ave and Zakir Hossain Rd.

## Sleeping
### BUDGET
**Chimbuk Hotel** ( 619 028; Jubilee Rd; s with attached/shared bathroom Tk 90/70, d with bathroom Tk 160) One of the best budget hotels: the staff are friendly, there's a TV in the pleasant reception area, and a balcony overlooking the city's busiest intersection.

**Hotel Samrat** ( 637 648; s/d Tk 50/150) Singles have shared bathroom, doubles have attached bathrooms. Located down a dirt road opposite Fairy Hill.

**Hotel Hoque Tower** (Sheikh Mujib Rahman Rd; r Tk 300) Good value, but can get noisy.

**Hotel Miskha** ( 610 923; 95 Station Rd; s/d with bathroom Tk 175/250, d with TV Tk 300) Mosquito nets aren't supplied. There's also a decent restaurant here.

**Hotel Midtown** ( 617 236; 85 Station Rd; s/d/t with bathroom Tk 100/150/200) The rooms here aren't so clean.

**Hotel Manila** ( 614 098; Station Rd; s/d Tk 170/220) Expensive for what you get and some rooms are much better than others.

### MID-RANGE
There is a concentration of mid-range hotels on Station Rd, though some aren't too foreigner-friendly.

**Hotel Golden Inn** ( 611 004; 336 Station Rd; economy s/d Tk 400/650, standard d Tk 725, executive d Tk 1000) About 300m west of the train station, this is one of the best options. Staff are friendly, but be warned that they 'reserve the right to cancel the reservation in case of any misdeclaration regarding family'. Make your marriages convincing. Rooms are a little overpriced, but there are some handy features, such as international power points in all rooms. The standard double is a good option, and only differs from the executive room for its want of AC and dubiously odorous carpets. Specify upfront whether you would like a squat or a sit-down toilet. There is a restaurant, a rooftop courtyard with good views and a travel agency at the front of the building, convenient for buying domestic-airline tickets.

**Hotel Sylhet Super** ( 632 265; 16 Station Rd; r Tk 275-1000) Countless bright and impressively clean rooms. Opposite the Golden Inn.

**Hotel Al-Faisal** ( 710 048; 1050 Nur Ahmed Rd; s Tk 350-500, d Tk 500-1200, t 750-1200) The best rooms are the newly renovated ones on the top floor, with hot water and sit-down toilets.

**Hotel Bandargaon** ( 637 686; 875 Nur Ahmed Rd; d Tk 550) Clean, larger-than-average rooms with attached bathrooms (squat toilets and no hot water). The manager is obliging.

**Hotel Hawaii** ( 724 057; s/d Tk 375/500, deluxe s/d Tk 625/1000) On the same road as the Ethnological Museum, this labyrinthine hotel has everything you could need, though the décor is tired and it can be a hike to your room.

**Shaikat Hotel** ( ☎ 619 514; Station Rd; r Tk 600-2000). This place is unusually grotty for a Parjatan. Staff may apologetically direct you to alternative accommodation across the road.

**TOP END**
In recent years there has been a boom in top-end hotels in Chittagong.

**Hotel Agrabad** ( ☎ 713 311; s/d US$110/120, royal ste US$415) This mammoth luxury hotel in the Agrabad Commercial Area is *plush*. It has a couple of restaurants, a swimming pool, one of the few bars in the city and Internet access, which costs an unfathomable Tk 500 per hour. The rooms are looking dated, but the 1960s décor adds some charm to the Trishita Bar. Rickshaw-wallahs will charge more if they think you're staying here, so walk up the street from the hotel to catch a cheaper ride.

**Landmark Hotel** ( ☎ 727 299; landmark@bbts.net; 3072 Sheikh Mujib Rahman Rd; s/d/t Tk 2300/3400/4000) This is a new arrival on the top-end scene. All rooms have a plastic luxury feel. Its **restaurant** (dishes Tk 250) is an asset with exotic Bangladeshi/Chinese/Thai options. The 'lunchbox' options for each cuisine are good value for Tk 125/145/155.

**Meridian Hotel** ( ☎ 654 000; meridian@abnetbd .com; 1367 CDA Ave; economy/deluxe r US$35/40, ste US$45) Something of a fading starlet, given the young competition. The location is great and all the facilities are there, but rooms are a little pokey and certainly eclipsed in value by the alternatives.

**Hotel Saint Martin** ( ☎ 725 961; fax 710 659; 25 Sheikh Mujib Rahman Rd; r US$50-125) This is the Bangladeshi businessman's choice. It has absolutely nothing in common with St Martin's Island, except maybe its size.

## Eating
Jubilee Rd is one of the best restaurant areas; even the cheap eateries are pretty good by Bangladeshi standards. Many of the upmarket restaurants cater to East Asian businesspeople.

**Zaman** (GEC Circle) Opposite the Meridian Hotel, this mammoth four-storey restaurant has sensational Bangladeshi food in a classy but comfortable atmosphere.

**Blossom Garden** (CDA Ave; dishes around Tk 120) Offers outside garden dining, complete with a waterless water-feature. There is also

the option of indoor dining. The fresh and tasty food is mainly Chinese, with a few subcontinental dishes thrown in. The menu is swimming in seafood.

**Chung King Restaurant** (Sheikh Mujib Rahman Rd) One of the oldest establishments that's reputed to have the best Chinese food in town, as well as Indonesian, Thai and Indian selections.

There are two **Sayeman** (CDA Ave; dishes Tk 150-250) restaurants across the road from each other. The one on the same side as the Blossom Garden is Chittagong's best-known Mughal restaurant. The other one has sensational Thai clear soup with prawns.

Other recommendations:

**Pizzaland** (GEC Circle; pizza Tk 115-190) Decent fast food with a very cosy atmosphere.

**Chin Lung** (Suhrawardi Rd) Opposite the main post office, this Chinese restaurant is just above average in quality and prices.

**Tai Wah** (Nur Ahmed Rd; mains around Tk 120) Popular with Korean businessmen.

**Dhaba** (CDA Ave) Laid-back café, where all the girls in jeans are hiding.

**Shaad Snacks** (Suhrawardi Rd) Good for a quick bite.

**Asian Spice Restaurant** (CDA Ave) Near the Modapur and Bardarhat bus stations, it's good if you're waiting for a bus. Chicken chilli curry is Tk 80.

**Hong Kong Restaurant** (Strand Rd) Handy if you're waiting for a boat. Unremarkable food, but you've never seen a redder building in your life.

## Drinking
At last – a drinking section! Alcohol in Chittagong isn't too hard to come by. In addition to the bar at the Hotel Agrabad (left), there's the extremely discreet Railway Men's Store, a crowded and dimly lit bar, thick with an air of mischief. To find it, head through the fruit market to the right of Hotel Sylhet Super. Follow the road around to the right and carry on until you see a guarded entrance on your left. You'll have to play it cool with security; women on their own will have an especially hard time getting in and an even harder time once they're in there. Beer costs Tk 170. Spirits are also available.

It's also possible to buy a beer (Tk 150) at the Hong Kong Restaurant (above).

## Getting There & Away
The Dhaka-Chittagong Hwy is probably the busiest in the country and prone to

bumper-to-bumper traffic jams. Travelling to Dhaka by train is far less nerve-racking.

### AIR
**GMG Airlines** ( ☎ 718 147; Hotel Agrabad) has five flights a day to/from Dhaka (Tk 2600, 50 minutes) and to Cox's Bazar (Tk 1000, 30 minutes) on Monday, Thursday, Friday and Saturday. There's another **GMG office** ( ☎ 655 659; CDA Ave) near the Aarong store.

**Biman** ( ☎ 650 7671; CDA Ave) has two to four flights daily to Dhaka, as well as flights to Cox's Bazar (depart 9.45am Sunday and Thursday). Prices for both routes are comparable to GMG's.

It has recently become possible to fly to select international destinations from Chittagong. Biman has twice-weekly flights to Kolkata, and Thai now has return flights to Bangkok, Chiang Mai and Phuket.

### BOAT
The Bangladesh Inland Waterway Transport Corporation (BIWTC) terminal is near the end of Sadarghat Rd, a few hundred metres to the west along the river bank. The administration office is clearly marked in English, but tickets are sold from a nondescript building just before the office. Book early if you want a 1st-class cabin.

Launches go to Barisal (1st/2nd/inter/deck class Tk 850/560/175/120, 24 hours, depart 9am Monday).

There is also a service to Hatiya Island (1st/2nd/inter class Tk 994/449/114, depart 9am Saturday and Wednesday).

### BUS
The largest bus station is **Bardarhat** (Cox's Bazar Rd), 4km north of the city centre. To get there, take a local bus (Tk 5) or rickshaw (Tk 10) from Nur Ahmed Rd. From here, buses leave for Cox's Bazar (Tk 110, four hours) and Bandarban (Tk 50, three hours) every 15 minutes between 6am and 6pm.

Buses for Rangamati (Tk 50, 2½ hours) and Kaptai (Tk 30, two hours, half-hourly 7am to 7pm) leave from **Modapur bus station** (CDA Ave).

Most Dhaka-bound private-bus companies operate out of the old **BRTC bus station** (Station Rd). There are AC chair coaches to Dhaka (Tk 250 to Tk 350, five to six hours). There are also coach companies around the Hotel Golden Inn and the Blossom Garden

restaurant that operate non-AC buses to Dhaka (Tk 190, 6½ hours, every 20 minutes between 5.45am and 5pm).

Coaches to Cox's Bazar (Tk 110, four hours, every 15 minutes between 5.30am and 7.30pm) and Comilla (Tk 80, 5½ hours, every 20 minutes between 6.45am and 1pm) leave from **Cinema Palace bus station** (Nur Ahmed Rd). For express buses to Comilla, head to Kadamtale bus station over the railway lines at the western end of Station Rd.

There are no direct buses to Sylhet; you must change in Comilla.

### TRAIN
The four intercity (IC) trains a day to Dhaka (1st/*sulob* class Tk 290/125, six hours, depart 7am, 7.15am, 2pm and 11pm) pass through Comilla (1st/*sulob* class Tk 140/60). There is a sleeper option (Tk 660) on night trains. Trains tickets should be booked at least two or three days in advance.

There is an IC train to Sylhet (1st/*sulob* class Tk 490/190, 10 hours, departs 7.45am).

## Getting Around
### TO/FROM THE AIRPORT
There isn't always a bus to meet incoming flights and the airport is a long way out from town – baby taxis cost around Tk 100. You could try catching a bus to New Market (Tk 10) at the T-junction, 500m from the airport.

### LOCAL TRANSPORT
Rickshaws and baby taxis are plentiful, and cost about the same as in Dhaka. Tempos and buses are cheaper, but are cramped and can be frustrating if you don't speak Bangla – routes aren't easy to decipher.

## AROUND CHITTAGONG
A few sites are challenging to get to but worth the effort.

### Shakpura
This small village, 24km south of the city, has Buddhist and Hindu temples. The **Nindam Kanon Temple** is a meditation centre. Buses (Tk 20, eight a day) leave from Bardarhat bus station in Chittagong.

### Patenga Beach
About 24km along the airport road south of Chittagong, this public beach is adjacent to

an industrial area, so it's hard to recommend it to sun-seekers. The fare is over Tk 100 by baby taxi. You might try finding a public bus (BIWTC bus No 1 from the BIWTC boat terminal reportedly travels there).

Bird-watching enthusiasts will find the mud flats near Patenga Beach an excellent high-tide roost for waders, the occasional spoon-billed sandpiper, Nordman's green-shank and good numbers of great-knot and grey-rumped tattlers.

To get to the mud flats, take a baby taxi to the Steel Mill Colony (housing development) on the way to Patenga. From there walk to the beach and head north a short distance to the mud flats.

### Ship-Breaking Yards

Along the shore north of Chittagong, every kind of ocean-going vessel, from super-tankers to tugboats, is dismantled – all with manual labour. At any one time there can be 30 ships beached on the shoreline be-tween the towns of Bhatiara and Sitakunda. Armies of workers use blowtorches, sledge-hammers and plain brute force to tear them apart. It's such a bizarre sight that the ship-breaking yards have become a popular set-ting in Bangladeshi movies; typically as bad-guy hang-outs.

This experience is dependent on whether you can get in, a task made all the more difficult by a series of critical media reports that have made supervisors reticent to let anyone wander around (particularly with a camera). If you're game enough to try, take bus No 6 or a tempo from Station Rd. It might help to ask for the ship-breaking yards near Madam Bibirhat. Once you're there, walk five minutes to the waterfront and try to smile your way through which-ever gate you arrive at. If you are rejected at one, try another. Some have reported

---

success at the southernmost yards; from the main road, turn left at a sign reading 'Ocean Steels'.

This is not an entirely safe undertak-ing because there is a complete absence of sensible workplace practices. It can also be a dirty process, given that you're at a (de)construction site.

### Sitakunda

About 36km north of Chittagong, this sleepy town has one attraction – the historic Hindu **Chandranath Temple**. There are great views from the top, which can be a real treat in flat Bangladesh. Unless you have a par-ticular interest in Hindu temples and don't mind an hour's uphill climb, it's only really worth visiting during the Shiva Chaturdasi Festival, held for 10 days in February and attracting thousands of Hindu pilgrims.

To get there, take a bus for Feni (Tk 20, 45 minutes) from the Kadamtale bus sta-tion in Chittagong.

### Ramgarh

It's a little-known fact that there are **tea estates** in the Chittagong area, some as large as those in Sylhet. One of the best places to see them is northeast of Ramgarh. Two of the country's largest tea estates are located here, and you can walk around at your leisure. Ramgarh is most accessible by bicycle or private vehicle. You could also take a bus to Feni (Tk 20, 45 minutes) and get a Ramgarh-bound bus from there.

### Rauzan

About halfway along the road from Chit-tagong to Rangamati, the area around the town of Rauzan is the centre of the Bang-ladeshi Buddhist community. The commu-nity is often known by the name Barua, the surname that nearly all its members share. The most famous Buddhist temple in the area is **Mahamuni**, a huge cement replica of the original Mahamuni image, which, in the 19th century, was taken to Mandalay in Myanmar as booty.

## CHITTAGONG HILL TRACTS

Decidedly untypical of Bangladesh topog-raphy and culture, the 13,180 sq km of the Hill Tracts comprises a mass of hills, ra-vines and cliffs covered with dense jungle, bamboo, creepers and shrubs.

---

**SHIPSHAPE?**

Ship-breaking is a controversial industry. It threatens public health, the environment and the rights and lives of workers. Green-peace and other organisations have taken issue with the industry; for more informa-tion on its stance on Chittagong's ship-breaking yards, visit www.greenpeaceweb .org/shipbreak/bangladesh.asp.

**WARNING**

The safety situation in the Chittagong Hill Tracts is constantly changing. Reliable information is hard to find, but find it you must. In the absence of a centralised source of information, it is difficult to canvas an accurate picture between travel-advisory overstatements and tourist-operator understatements. It is a fact that the Hill Tracts can be very dangerous. The importance of exploring the region with a reputable tour operator has certainly increased in light of this, but even this is no guarantee – a group of travellers on tour were held up at gunpoint in February 2004.

But don't let the exaggerations, conspiracy theories and dangers of the Chittagong Hill Tracts dissuade you from putting in the time and effort to get a balanced understanding of what is happening. It's well worth your while, not just for your own safety but also as a means of subverting attempts to keep foreigners unaware of injustices being perpetrated.

Always check newspapers and government-advisory websites before setting out to the Hill Tracts. At the time of research, the Chittagong Hill Tracts Regional Council was proposing to launch a website containing travel advice for foreigners. Hopefully www.cipd-cht.org has since become operational.

About half the tribal population are Chakma, and the remainder are mostly Marma (who represent about a third) or Tripura. Among the 11 much smaller groups (Mru, Tengchangya, Bohmong, Khumi, Mizo, Pankhu, Sak, Bawm, Mogh, Kuki and Reang), the Mru (called Murung by Bangladeshis) stand out as the most ancient inhabitants of the area.

The culture and lifestyle of the Adivasis (tribal people) is very different from that of the Bangladeshi farmers of the plains. Some tribes are matriarchal and all have similar housing – made entirely of bamboo and covered by thatched roofs of dried leaves. In most other respects, the tribes are quite different, each having its own distinctive rites, rituals, dialect and dress, eg Chakma women wear indigo-and-red striped sarongs.

The women are particularly skilled in making handicrafts, while some of the men still take pride in hunting with bows and arrows.

## History

Under the British, the Hill Tracts had special status and only Adivasis could own land there, but the Pakistani government abolished the special status of the Hill Tracts as a 'tribal area' in 1964. The construction of the Kaptai Lake for hydroelectricity in 1960 was an earlier blow, submerging 40% of the land used by the Adivasis for cultivation, and displacing 100,000 people. The land provided for resettlement was not sufficient and many tribal people became refugees in neighbouring northeastern India.

During the Liberation War, the then Chakma king sided with the Pakistanis, so when Independence came, the Adivasis' plea for special status fell on deaf ears. The Chakma king left for Pakistan and later became that country's ambassador to Argentina.

Meanwhile, more and more Bengalis were migrating into the area, usurping the land. In 1973 the Adivasis initiated an insurgency. To counter it, the government, in 1979, started issuing permits to landless Bengalis to settle there, with title to tribal land. This practice continued for six years and resulted in a mass migration of approximately 400,000 people into the area – almost as many as all the tribal groups combined. Countless human-rights abuses occurred as the army tried to put down the revolt.

From 1973 until 1997 the Hill Tracts area was the scene of a guerrilla war between the Bangladeshi army and the Shanti Bahini rebels. The troubles stemmed from the cultural clash between the tribal groups and the plains people.

Sheikh Hasina's government cemented an internationally acclaimed peace accord in December 1997 with tribal leader Jyotirindriyo Bodhipriya (Shantu) Larma. Rebel fighters were given land, Tk 50,000 and a range of other benefits in return for handing in their weapons. The peace deal handed much of the administration of Khagrachhari, Rangamati and Bandarban districts to a regional council. The struggle to have the accord fully honoured continues today.

## Information

Whether a permit is required to visit the Hill Tracts can change from month to month. At the time of writing, permits were absolutely required.

To obtain a permit, fax your details to the district commissioner (DC) of the district you intend to visit three days before you enter the region. The DC should forward your details to the relevant 'foreigner checkpoints', but this doesn't always happen. You must provide your name, native country, passport number, district you intend to visit, purpose of visit, duration of stay, occupation, mode of transport, probable date of visit, expected date of return and signature.

It is a good idea to type your details and keep the original on your person – it will look far more official to checkpoint police than a handwritten application. Also try to procure some sort of receipt to show that you have faxed the information in good time. It's also sensible to fax the same details to the relevant superintendent of police (see below). None of this guarantees that you'll be allowed to visit, but it will increase your chances.

Fax numbers:

**Rangamati**
**District commissioner** 0351-63020
**Superintendent of police** 0351-63127

**Bandarban**
**District commissioner** 0361-62509

**Khagrachhari**
**District commissioner** 0371-61674
**Superintendent of police** 0371-61755

## Tours

**Bangladesh Ecotours** ( ☎ 31-637 657; www.bangla deshecotours.com; 263 Jubilee Rd, Chittagong; US$75-120) One of the best tour companies, this professional organisation takes a genuinely eco-aware approach and prides itself on being able to tailor tours.
**Bangladesh Expeditions** ( ☎ 01-822 7387; www .expeditions-bd.com; 2nd fl, Sheraton Hotel, Dhaka)
**Bengal Tours** ( ☎ 02-882 0716; www.bengaltours.com; House 66, Rd 10, Block D, Banani)
**Guide Tours** ( ☎ 02-988 6983; www.guidetours.com; Darpan Complex, 1st fl, Gulshan Circle II, Dhaka) In addition to tours, it has also recently opened the Hillside Resort (p131), 4km from Bandarban.
**Unique Tours & Travels** ( ☎ 02-988 5116; unique@ bangla.net; 51B Kemal Ataturk Ave, Banani, Dhaka)

## Rangamati

☎ 0351

Rangamati, 77km east of Chittagong, is beautifully situated over a series of islands in Kaptai Lake. The town was laid out as an administrative centre and modern-day hill station in the 1960s, after the damming of the Karnaphuli River. The town's fleet of noisy, smoky baby taxis detracts from the charm, but the surrounding countryside is lush, undulating and verdant.

The vast majority of Adivasis here are Chakma, and much of their ancestral land is flooded by the lake. The population of the town is, however, overwhelmingly Bangladeshi, and tourists from the cities descend on the town en masse at weekends.

### ORIENTATION

Rangamati extends for about 7km from the army checkpoint to the Parjatan Motel. The main road passes banks, the fish market and Hotel Sufia before it crosses a long causeway, at the end of which is a traffic circle (roundabout). The road to the right leads to the Parjatan Motel (after crossing a steel bridge), while the road to the left leads to the main bazar and the main launch ghat.

### SIGHTS & ACTIVITIES

The small **Tribal Cultural Institute** ( ⊙ 10am-4pm Sun-Thu) has displays on the tribes of the Hill Tracts, including costumes, bamboo flutes, coins and silver-and-ivory necklaces. There is also a map showing where the different tribes live. The institute is about 1.5km past the army checkpoint.

There are several modern Buddhist *viharas* (monasteries) in and around the town. The biggest is the **Bana Vihara**, on a headland at the northern end of town. In one open-walled hall there are elaborate thrones for the head abbot, in the form of a Naga serpent.

The Chakma king has his rajbari on a neighbouring island. The rajbari is not open to visitors but the **Raja Vihara** on the same island has a large bronze statue of Shakyamuni (the historical Buddha) overseen by a small and friendly monastic community. The island is reached by small launches at the end of the lane that runs between the Tribal Cultural Institute and the Sabarang Restaurant; the boat also goes to the Bana Vihara.

A **boat trip** on Kaptai Lake, the country's largest artificial lake, with stops at tribal villages along the way, is the highlight of a visit here. The lake is ringed with banana plantations and thinning patches of tropical and semi-evergreen forests. The level of the lake varies considerably throughout the year. When it starts to fall in March, the emerging land is farmed before the lake rises again in the monsoonal season.

While the lake itself is beautiful, the villages you'll see around it make the trip special. Bring binoculars for bird-watching and better viewing of some of the thatched villages and fishing boats. Tourist boats usually stop at Chakma villages, allowing you to see traditional bamboo houses and small Buddhist shrines made of bamboo.

There are three main places from which to hire a boat: across the hanging bridge near Parjatan Motel; at the main ghat; and at Tobulchuri ghat. The latter is probably the best, while the first is unquestionably the most expensive. An hour in a boat should cost around Tk 200.

Foreigners may be told by various sources (such as hotel staff) that they must report to the police station so they can be issued

with armed escorts for boat rides, though few can explain why. Armed escorts won't cost anything, other than your freedom of movement. Having armed police on board may ward off elusive dangers, but they may also prevent you from visiting the town of Kaptai. In practical terms, you will have greater liberty without escorts, but the risks are entirely yours. The other consideration is that it may be your boatman who's reprimanded by authorities for not having escorts on board.

If you don't manage to get out to Kaptai, there are still plenty of interesting villages within 30 minutes of Rangamati. A good place to visit is the Buddhist monastery, **Jawnasouk Mountain Vihara**, across the lake from Rangamati. Another interesting journey is through the narrow, steep-sided waterway that leads into the lake's upper basin, where you can also swim.

### SLEEPING
**Peda Ting Ting** ( ☎ 62082; cottages Tk 1000) One of the nicest ways to absorb the charms of the area is to stay at this resort, a 20-minute boat ride from Tobulchuri ghat, 5km east

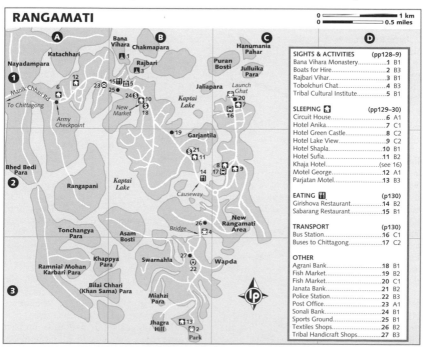

## RANGAMATI

0 _____ 1 km
0 _____ 0.5 miles

| SIGHTS & ACTIVITIES | (pp128–9) |
| --- | --- |
| Bana Vihara Monastery | 1  B1 |
| Boats for Hire | 2  B3 |
| Rajbari Vihar | 3  B1 |
| Tobolchuri Chat | 4  B3 |
| Tribal Cultural Institute | 5  B1 |

| SLEEPING 🛏 | (pp129–30) |
| --- | --- |
| Circuit House | 6  A1 |
| Hotel Anika | 7  C1 |
| Hotel Green Castle | 8  C2 |
| Hotel Lake View | 9  C2 |
| Hotel Shapla | 10  B1 |
| Hotel Sufia | 11  B2 |
| Khaja Hotel | (see 16) |
| Motel George | 12  A1 |
| Parjatan Motel | 13  B3 |

| EATING 🍴 | (p130) |
| --- | --- |
| Girishova Restaurant | 14  B2 |
| Sabarang Restaurant | 15  B1 |

| TRANSPORT | (p130) |
| --- | --- |
| Bus Station | 16  C1 |
| Buses to Chittagong | 17  C2 |

| OTHER | |
| --- | --- |
| Agrani Bank | 18  B1 |
| Fish Market | 19  B2 |
| Fish Market | 20  C1 |
| Janata Bank | 21  B2 |
| Police Station | 22  B3 |
| Post Office | 23  A1 |
| Sonali Bank | 24  B1 |
| Sports Ground | 25  B1 |
| Textiles Shops | 26  B2 |
| Tribal Handicraft Shops | 27  B3 |

of Rangamati. This indigenous venture also offers tours of the region. The two-bedroom bamboo cottages face the lake, and have a bathroom and a veranda. There's also a **restaurant** (meals Tk 160) that serves traditional indigenous fare. The captivating ambience of the island is only interrupted by disconcerting signs that warn of biting fish, prohibit swimming 'in birthday suit' and advise you to 'Cry for help before you are drowned'.

**Parjatan Motel** ( ☎ 63126; d with/without AC Tk 1200/600, 4-/8-bed cottage Tk 1000/1500) This place is becoming run-down but it hasn't dropped its prices accordingly. Rooms aren't spectacular, though the setting is. The cottages aren't as quaint as you'd expect a 'cottage' to be. The area can be crowded and noisy given the busloads of tourists. The Parjatan has also recently opened a bar, discretely hidden behind the cottages.

**Hotel Sufia** (s/d Tk 300/400) A sensible option on the main road, just before the causeway. Rooms have balconies overlooking a small portion of the lake. There is no hot water, but staff will bring buckets on request. Service at the rooftop restaurant is slow but the food that eventually arrives is great. Better rooms for steeper prices may be pending, given the current renovations.

**Hotel Green Castle** (s with/without AC Tk 400/300, d Tk 750/500) This new hotel with friendly staff has fans and satellite TV. There's also a clean restaurant and a nice common balcony out the back.

**Motel George** (s Tk 100-400, d Tk 350-600) The George boasts that it is the 'best in town'. This is debatable, but it isn't bad. Rooms are big, quaint and quiet.

Other options:

**Hotel Lake View** (s/d Tk 80/200) Adequate and centrally located. Also known as Hotel Al-Amin.

**Hotel Anika** (s/d Tk 80/150) The communal balcony out the back is perfect for watching the water turn to gold at sunrise. There's a very clean restaurant downstairs.

**Khaja Hotel** (r Tk 300) At the bus station, so it can be noisy.

**Hotel Shapla** (s/d Tk 80/200) Women will be hard pressed getting a room.

**Circuit house** An unlikely option given the presence of a Parjatan, but worth a shot, if you're after accommodation that's worthy of its surrounds.

### EATING
Around the main ghat is a gaggle of cheap restaurants selling the usual stuff for the usual prices.

**Sabarang Restaurant** (dishes Tk 150; ✆ dinner) Next to the Tribal Cultural Institute, Sabarang is an initiative of the Chakma raja. Local specialities include curried eel and snails with their shells, but not all of the exotic choices are always available. The waiters speak English and can acquire some Chakma liquor if you ask. There is also a Chinese and Bangladeshi menu.

You can't beat the view at Girishova Restaurant, which literally hangs off the causeway. Here you'll also find good Bangladeshi food with some curious Chinese concoctions thrown in. Armed guards sit ominously out the front.

### GETTING THERE & AWAY
Buses from Chittagong leave for Rangamati (Tk 50, three hours) periodically from Modapur bus station. You'll pass a couple of security checkpoints en route, where you are called off to fill out formalities and prove you have applied for a permit.

From Rangamati, buses for Chittagong leave from outside Hotel Green Castle throughout the day from around 7am. Buses also leave from the more manic bus station outside Khaja Hotel. There is no direct route to Kaptai; you'll have to go back to Chittagong to catch a bus from there.

There are also two public launches a day leaving Rangamati for the town of Kaptai; they depart at 8.30am and 3.30pm but verify the schedule to be sure. The trip takes 1½ hours (four hours return). There is also a speedboat that does the round trip in two hours. These boats leave from the main launch ghat.

### GETTING AROUND
Due to its hilly topography Rangamati is a rare example of a Bangladeshi town without rickshaws. Baby taxis operate as share taxis (five or six passengers); the cost is usually Tk 30 divided by the number of passengers, regardless of where you're going. The other option is to jump on a passing bus.

## Kaptai
Once a hunting ground for wild animals, Kaptai is 64km east of Chittagong, at the southern end of Kaptai Lake. Sadly, it's the site for a 50m dam wall and a hydroelectricity plant, and the atmosphere is rather oppressive (signs say there should be no photography or

'unauthorised movement'). The Kaptai ghat looks quite picturesque at night, however.

Kaptai is a flat town with one main street where you'll find all eateries, hotels, boarding houses, teahouses and general stores. At the dam wall there's a **crane** that lifts stacks of bamboo, ferried in rafts across the lake, over and into the Karnaphuli River, from where they float down to Chittagong.

Approximately 4km from Kaptai, on the Chittagong Rd, is the village of **Chitmorong**, home to the Buddhist Marma tribe, where there are richly adorned Buddhist sculptures, a monastery and a stupa on the side of a hill. A **Buddhist festival** is held here every Bangladeshi New Year around mid-April.

### SLEEPING

There is a government circuit house in Kaptai. As always you'll need permission from the district commissioner to stay; his office is nearby. Otherwise, there are some very basic boarding houses, most of which are clean and cheap.

### GETTING THERE & AWAY

Unless you have a private vehicle, you cannot travel here straight from Rangamati; instead you'll have to head back to Chittagong for the bus. Direct buses to Kaptai (Tk 30) leave from Chittagong's Modapur bus station throughout the day. You might also be able to get a launch from Rangamati, but check it out carefully as the situation changes frequently.

## Bandarban

Bandarban lies on the Sangu River, 92km from Chittagong. The river is the centre of local life: bamboo craft carry goods downstream, while country boats make leisurely trips to neighbouring villages. Most inhabitants belong to the Buddhist Marma tribe.

The small **Tribal Cultural Institute** has a museum and library. Opening hours are vague but the curator is very knowledgeable. The **Bohmong Rajbari** is the residence of the Bohmong king.

There is a **tribal bazar** ( Wed & Sun), where trading is conducted in Marma rather than Bangla.

At the checkpoint before coming into town, officials may request that you call upon the district commissioner. His office is just around the corner from the Hotel Purabi.

There is an **Internet café** (per hr Tk 80) under Hotel Greenhill.

### SLEEPING & EATING

**Hillside Resort** (Milonchhori; ☎ 02-988 6983; Chimbuk Rd; dm Tk 100-150, basic tribal s/d/t cottages Tk 400/700/850, modern s/d/t cottages Tk 750/1000/1200) Without a doubt, this is the best place to stay. Run by Guide Tours, it is 4km from Bandarban in the thick of lush greenery. There are stunning cottages of authentic bounce-as-you-walk bamboo, with electric fans and lights. The modern cottages have hot water. Security has been stepped up after armed gunmen stormed the resort in February 2004. The resort restaurant boasts a variety of surprisingly reasonably priced food. Try to book ahead at Guide Tour's Dhaka office (p128).

Otherwise there are some basic places in the town itself. **Hotel Greenhill** (s/d Tk 80/150) is on the main intersection, while **Hotel Purabi** (s Tk 80-100, d Tk 160) has a friendly manager. **Hotel Hillbird** (s/d Tk 150/200) is close to the bus station but looks nicer from the outside than it is inside. Staff may need convincing to let you stay.

Eating options are limited; there are some basic restaurants and teahouses on the main street.

### GETTING THERE & AWAY

Buses leave from Chittagong's Bardarhat bus station for Bandarban (Tk 50, three hours) throughout the day.

Purbani Coach Service at the Bandarban bus station has buses to Cox's Bazar (Tk 75, depart 7.30am and 4pm).

The checkpoints on the way in to Bandarban can be frustrating. The bus may continue without you so it doesn't have to wait the 45 minutes it takes you to convince officials that you have applied for a permit.

## COX'S BAZAR
☎ 0341

Welcome to beach life, Bangladeshi style. The usual question, 'Why have you come here?' doesn't get asked because the answer is obvious – you've come to be at the seaside. Cox's Bazar is both loved and loathed. On the one hand, it has an impressive beach. On the other, it is becoming carelessly over-developed and there are criminal elements to watch out for. Don't come expecting Goa; just surrender to the enthusiasm of Bangladeshi holiday-makers. There is a good range of hotels, which give generous discounts in the winter season. Alcohol is readily available.

The surrounding area, adjacent to the Chittagong Hill Tracts, runs south down the coastline to the Myanmar border. The culture here is less overtly Muslim, or even Hindu for that matter; it has a more Burmese-Buddhist atmosphere.

## History
This region was a favourite of the Mogh pirates who, with the Portuguese, ravaged the Bay of Bengal in the 17th century. The Moghs have remained, maintaining their tribal ways through handicrafts and cottage industries, while to some degree also assimilating into the dominant Muslim culture.

When the area was taken over by the British in 1760, Captain Hiram Cox founded the town as a refuge for the Arakanese, who were fleeing their homeland after being conquered by the Burmese. These new refugee Mogh settlers erected a number of stupas on the low hills around town. In recent years there has been a new influx from Arakan, now known as Rakhine state in Myanmar. In the early 1990s at least 250,000 Rohingyas (Muslims from Rakhine) fled to Bangladesh to escape persecution by Myanmar's military regime. There has also been an influx of migrant workers from Rakhine, attracted by the relatively better wages and security. Many work as labourers and rickshaw drivers.

## Information
### EMERGENCY
**Tourist Police** ( ☎ 64060)

### INTERNET ACCESS
**Cyber Café** (per hr Tk 30)
**Niloy Cyber Café** (per hr Tk 40) On the main road.

### MONEY
**Agrani Bank** ( ☎ 63259; Ramu Rd) The best place to change money.

### POST
**Post office** (Motel Rd) On the edge of the Hotel Shaibal grounds. It's poorly marked – look for the letter box outside.

### TOURIST INFORMATION
**Hotel Silver Shine** ( ☎ 64893) Tour desk at reception.
**Parjatan** (Motel Upal) More useful than most.

## Dangers & Annoyances
Foreign women in swimsuits may be hassled (and photographed) by men. Bangladeshi women who swim do so in their *salwar kameez* (long, dress-like tunic worn over baggy trousers) and you'd be very wise to do the same.

The northern end of the beach next to the airport may be invitingly quiet, but armed robberies have occurred here, even in daylight. The entire beach is not safe at night.

## Sights & Activities
The main reason to come to Cox's Bazar is the **beach**. The route to the beach, along Sea Beach Rd, can be crowded and dirty. Once you're there you can rent a sun lounge and umbrella (Tk 5 to Tk 10), and staff will offer security so you can leave your belongings unattended while you go for a dip. You could also plant yourself in front of a big hotel, where guards will watch over your gear if you go swimming, and shoo away kids selling shell necklaces. They will also deal with the crowds of gawkers, if they get too intrusive.

If you're intrigued by the wooden fishing boats chugging along the shore, you can check them out from the Bakhali River on the north side of town, where they're moored. Some of the boats look uncannily like pirate ships; and given that piracy is on the rise in the Bay of Bengal there's the possibility that they might be!

The colourful **Buddhist Water Festival** takes place here each year (13–18 April).

### AGGAMEDA KHYANG
This Buddhist **monastery**, at the eastern end of town, is representative of Burmese-style architecture. Its distinctive appearance would stand out anywhere, but nestled among trees in the middle of Cox's Bazar it's all the more fascinating. The main sanctuary is built around massive timber columns. The teak flooring adds an air of timelessness to the place.

You may be asked for a donation at Aggameda Khyang (and Maha Thin Daw Gree). Tk 10 is reasonable.

### MAHA THIN DAW GREE
Behind Aggameda Khyang is **Maha Thin Daw Gree**, a vast spread of Buddhist buildings amid the trees. Almost invisible from the

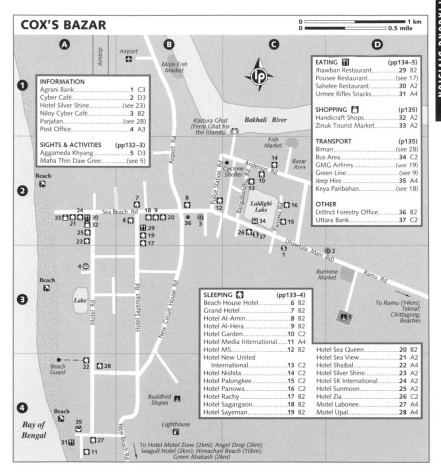

**COX'S BAZAR**

road, this interesting display of Buddhas was built in 1790, though some monks believe it is 400 years old.

## Sleeping
### BUDGET
There are some cheap dives in the town centre around Laldighi Lake.

**Hotel Al-Amin** ( ☎ 3420; Sea Beach Rd; s/d with bathroom Tk 50/100) This place is quite a distance from the beach.

**Hotel New United International** ( ☎ 63753; Bangabandhu Rd; s with shared/attached bathroom Tk 60/100, d Tk 100/200) A good-value budget choice. It's cleaner and brighter than some of its contemporaries, and far enough away for you to get some shuteye.

**Hotel Sagargaon** ( ☎ 63445; Sea Beach Rd; s/d with bathroom Tk 150/300) A large multistorey edifice with friendly management. The front rooms will be loud, as much for the TV-addicted neighbours as for the traffic outside.

**Hotel Panowa** ( ☎ 63282; s/d/t with bathroom Tk 120/250/450) Down a lane to the east of Laldighi Lake, the Panowa has small but clean rooms.

**Hotel Zia** ( ☎ 64497; Ramu Rd; s with shared bathroom Tk 100, d with bathroom Tk 250) Right across from the bus station, Hotel Zia is ageing badly. Women may not be allowed to stay here.

**Hotel Sunmoon** ( ☎ 63231; Motel Rd; s/d Tk 150/200) A cheerful place that's smaller than most. Doubles with access to the large balcony cost Tk 300.

**Beach House Hotel** (s/d Tk 100/150) In a town where things are getting bigger and shinier by the day, there's something comforting about the continuing existence of places that seem as though they have actively maintained their run-down look.

Other decent budget options:

**Hotel SK International** ( ☎ 63830; Sea Beach Rd; r with shared/attached bathroom Tk 200/350)

**Hotel Nishita** ( ☎ 64362; Anderson Rd; s/d Tk 150/300)

**Hotel Palongkee** ( ☎ 63873; Panowa Rd; s/d Tk 300/500)

**Hotel Garden** ( ☎ 63589; Anderson Rd; s/d/t Tk 100/200/300)

### MID-RANGE

**Hotel Silver Shine** ( ☎ 64893; Motel Rd; r Tk 450-1450) One of the best mid-range options. TV, fridge and hot water are available in all but the cheapest rooms. There are also lifts and a swimming pool on the rooftop!

**Hotel Sea View** ( ☎ 64491; Sea Beach Rd; d with/without AC Tk 795/395, d with TV & hot water Tk 495) It really does have sea views. It's also clean and professionally run. All rooms have balconies facing the sea, and there is a rooftop garden.

**Hotel Rachy** ( ☎ 64452; Hotel Sayeman Rd; s/d Tk 300/600, 2-bedroom deluxe r Tk 800) One of the best value-for-taka places. All bathrooms have cold water, and some have balconies but no view.

**Hotel Sea Queen** ( ☎ 63789; r Tk 250-1200) Rooms aren't bright but the price is right. The most expensive rooms have such luxuries as hot water and AC.

**Grand Hotel** ( ☎ 64709; Sea Beach Rd; r with/without AC Tk 1000/600) Discounts come thick and fast, though you could do better closer to the beach and off the noisy main road. There's a bar.

**Motel Upal** ( ☎ 64258 r with/without AC including breakfast Tk 1450/950) A long-standing establishment, complete with a kitsch karaoke room. Doubles have balconies.

**Motel Labonee** ( ☎ 64703; fax 64202; r Tk 500-700) Parjatan in name but not in character. The cheapest rooms at this low-key establishment have only cold water and squat toilets. Staff are often tourism students doing practical training.

At the lower end of this price range are **Hotel Al-Hera** ( ☎ 64840; Sea Beach Rd; s/d/t Tk 350/500/600) and **Hotel MS** ( ☎ 63930; Police Station Rd; s/d/t Tk 200/350/650). The Parjatan-affiliated **Green Abakash** ( ☎ 647 445; abakash@bttb.net.bd; r Tk 200-800) is cheaper than the hotels in its vicinity.

### TOP END

Cox's Bazar is rapidly turning into the Las Vegas of Bangladesh. If you follow New Beach Rd, you will find yourself in the gaudy Hotel Motel Zone, with far too many homogenous hotels to mention. Most start at Tk 800 and push Tk 5000.

**Seagull Hotel** ( ☎ 624 8091; www.seagullhotelbd.com; s/d/ste Tk 1600/2000/5000) The most monstrous of the glitzy range. All rooms are pristine. Unless you're going to get a suite with a balcony, it probably isn't worth the money, though it has a private piece of beach.

**Hotel Sayeman** ( ☎ 63235; fax 64231; Hotel Sayeman Rd; r Tk 490-1250) Everyone knows the Sayeman; even rickshaw-wallahs will hand you a business card. Like other centrally located top-end hotels, it's been overshadowed by those in the Hotel Motel Zone. It's still reasonable value, however, and its well-furnished rooms have decent space and facilities. There's also a swimming pool on the premises.

**Hotel Shaibal** ( ☎ 63274; fax 64202; Motel Rd; r Tk 1000-3500) The new hotels in town have demoted this Parjatan establishment from being luxurious to merely being comfortable. It has some catching up to do. It has a path to a private beach and a discreet bar. Other facilities include a tennis court and barbecue. There's a small lake, in which, some complain, mosquitoes breed, as they also do in the irregularly cleaned swimming pool.

**Hotel Media International** ( ☎ 62047) At the time of research, the Media was about to throw open its enormous doors for business, and looks as though it'll give the Seagull a run for its money.

## Eating

**Angel Drop** ( ☎ 0171-441 416; Marine Dve; ⏰ 10am-10pm) One of the most memorable places to eat in all of Bangladesh. Follow New Beach Rd south; it's literally on the beach. This fabulous two-storey, open-air construction is so special that the food (mostly snacks and drinks) is irrelevant (but very good). A cup of coffee is around Tk 20, and a plate of chips around Tk 40. Places like this should prove to developers that you don't need slabs of concrete to create something special. It's the sort of place that will let you hang around after they've turned out the lights.

**Pousee Restaurant** ( ☎ 62343; meals Tk 50) The popular Pousee, next to Hotel Rachy and just as clean, serves up great Bangladeshi food. There is no menu but staff will wait patiently as you gesticulate what you want. This is a great place to sample some traditional Bangladeshi fish.

**Jhawban Restaurant** ( ☎ 018-821 987; Hotel Sayeman Rd; meals Tk 50) The Jhawban comes highly recommended by locals.

Drinks and fast snacks are surprisingly cheap at Urmee Rifles Snacks, a pleasant beach-side eatery.

There are many good local restaurants around the western end of Sea Beach Rd. The **Sahelee Restaurant** ( ☎ 0171-303 113; dishes around Tk 60) is clean and spacious. Its motto is 'economy food with aristocracy'.

Almost all mid-range and top-end hotels have restaurants. For an upmarket meal, try an upmarket hotel such as the Seagull.

## Shopping

The **Zinuk Tourist Market** (Sea Beach Rd), next to Hotel Sea View, sells an array of trinkets made from seashells. There are other handicrafts and Burmese shops near Aggameda Khyang, selling hand-woven fabrics, saris, cheroots, jewellery and conch-shell bangles.

## Getting There & Away

### AIR

**Biman** ( ☎ 63461; Motel Upal) operates afternoon flights to Dhaka (Tk 2925, 1½ hours) on Thursday, Saturday and Sunday. Try for a seat on the right-hand side of the plane because the views are good.

**GMG Airlines** ( ☎ 63900; Hotel Sayeman) has flights to/from Dhaka (Tk 3370) and Chittagong (Tk 1370) on Thursday and Saturday.

### BUS

Most buses leave from around the Laldighi Lake area. Express buses to Dhaka (Tk 160, eight to 10 hours) leave throughout the day. Non-AC chair coaches cost around Tk 300, the last one leaving around 7pm.

Buses to Chittagong (Tk 110, four hours) leave regularly until 4.30pm. Express buses to Teknaf (Tk 60, three hours) depart until 6pm.

For an AC chair coach, check the offices of **Keya Paribahan** ( ☎ 64248; Hotel Sagargaon) or **Green Line** ( ☎ 62533; info@greenlinebd.com; Hotel Al-Hera). On Friday, Keya has buses to Dhaka (Tk 470) and Chittagong (Tk 170). Green Line has daily buses to Dhaka (Tk 500, 10am and 7pm) and Chittagong (Tk 180, 10am and 7pm).

## Getting Around

Some rickshaw drivers are hotel touts; be clear where you want to go and how much you want to pay. On the other hand, not all their hotel recommendations are bad ones.

For trips further afield you can hire jeeps for rides along the beach, although they aren't cheap. A ride just to Himachari, 10km south of town, costs Tk 700. Head south on Motel Rd, and right at the T-junction. Walk towards the beach and you won't be able to miss the Jeeps. Shinier models from the Hotel Shaibal cost Tk 2500 per day. Hotel SK International can arrange motorbike hire for around Tk 1500 per day.

## AROUND COX'S BAZAR

The road from Cox's Bazar, south along the seashore to Teknaf, is controversial because of the deforestation caused along the way.

The evergreen and semi-evergreen tropical rainforest bordering this stretch of beach is still some of the best in the country, despite the recent heavy pressure from the Rohingya refugees and others who have settled in the area.

This forest is home to a wealth of plant and animal life. Bird-watching, especially in the patches of forest on the low hills running off the beach, just south of Cox's Bazar and around Teknaf, should reveal quite a number of interesting species. The staff at the district forestry office in Cox's Bazar are happy to give more information about local species to watch out for.

## Inani Beach

Inani Beach, one of Bangladesh's claims to fame, is considered the world's longest and broadest beach: 180m at high tide and 300m at low tide. Even here, 30km south of Cox's Bazar, it's not completely deserted, so don't be surprised if you attract a small audience.

There's a **Forestry Department Guest House** (r Tk 300) on the beach, just south of Inani Beach, with fine views of the sea. It has three guest rooms with common facilities. The entire guesthouse can be rented for Tk 1500. You have to take your own food and the facilities are limited, but it is furnished. Book through the **district forestry office** ( ☎ 63409) in Cox's Bazar.

To get here, take a bus to Teknaf and get off at Court Bazar (30km), a tiny village 2km before Ukhia. From there, you can rickshaw or tempo west to the beach, 10km away. If you're headed for the guesthouse, ask the rickshaw driver to let you off at the tiny village of Sonarpara. From there, walk south until you reach the guesthouse.

Alternatively, hire a Jeep from Cox's Bazar to take you directly to Inani using the scenic beach route.

## Ramu & Lamapara

Ramu and Lamapara are noted for their Buddhist khyangs (temples). Ramu is an undistinguished town 14km east of Cox's Bazar, just off the Chittagong road. Some hills in this area are topped with pagodas.

In addition to its khyangs, Ramu, a subsidiary capital of the Arakan kingdom for nearly three centuries, is noted for a beautiful **monastery** containing images of Buddha in bronze, silver and gold inlaid with precious and semiprecious stones. Start at the far end of the street of Buddhist buildings, at the lovely **U Chitsan Rakhina Temple**, and work your way back towards the town centre.

The beautiful Burmese **Bara Khyang** at Lamapara has the country's largest bronze Buddha statue. The temple's three wooden buildings house a number of precious Buddhist images in silver and gold, set with gems. Lamapara is a palm-shaded village about 5km from Ramu, and accessible only by zigzagging paved village paths. It's impossible to find it on your own, so take a rickshaw or a baby taxi (from Tk 100 to Tk 150 return).

About 2km from Lamapara, at the village of Ramkot, there are **Buddhist and Hindu temples** perched on adjacent forested hills.

In Ramu you can stay at **Bungalow Abakash** ( ☎ 64744; r Tk 800-1500).

Buses and tempos to Ramu (Tk 8, 30 minutes) leave Cox's Bazar a few blocks east of the bus stand on Sea Beach Rd.

## Sonadia Island

According to legend, a ship laden with gold sunk here centuries ago during an attack by Portuguese pirates and an island formed around the shipwreck. The tiny, 4.63-sq-km island, 7km from Cox's Bazar, was once renowned for pink pearls, but more profitable commercial fishing has seen this tradition slowly fade away. Fishermen set up camp in winter, and Bangladeshi tourists make the trip here to buy dried pomfret fish.

Sonadia acts as a temporary sanctuary for migrating birds such as petrels, geese, curlews, ducks and other waterfowl. The western side of the island is a beach known for interesting seashells. There is a small **bazar** selling seashell crafts. There are no public launches, so you'll have to hire a boat (Tk 700 or more for a day trip) at Kastura ghat, or around the port, ask if any fishermen are heading that way. A speedboat from Kastura ghat costs around Tk 2000 and takes around 10 minutes.

## Maheskhali Island

About 6km northwest of Cox's Bazar, Maheskhali (mosh-khal-ee) Island makes a pleasant day trip. If there are any festivals underway among its mixed Buddhist, Hindu and Muslim population, you might be invited to stay and watch.

Walking along the jetty into the town of Ghoroghata, you'll see a **hill** to the north, about a 20-minute rickshaw ride away. This holy spot is the principal tourist attraction, with a famous stupa on top. The climb takes five minutes and affords a good view of the island from the top.

A few hundred metres away is a wooded area that hides **Adinath**, a mandir and ashram dedicated to Shiva. It's a delightfully serene place set in a beautiful garden.

If it's the dry season and you have the time, you might consider some hiking. There are paths along the top of the cliffs that line the eastern side of the island. Swimming is also an option, particularly at the sandy beaches on the island's western side.

When you return to town, ask to be pointed towards the small fishing settlement nearby, where you can watch **boat-building** activity. During the dry season you can also watch people fishing and drying their catch. During the festive season of Falgoon (March to April), a visit here can be most interesting.

In the north of the island, the little town of Hohanak has a **betel bazar** on Monday and Thursday evening.

If you're not content to do a day trip from Cox's Bazar, there are three sleeping options in Ghoroghata, none of which are particularly good. There's the big blue government rest house, which is usually full of government or NGO workers and requires the district commissioner's permission. Alternatively, there's **Hotel Bhai Bhai** (s/d Tk 40/80) and **Hotel Sea Guard** (s with shared bathroom Tk 60 d with shared/attached bathroom Tk 120/150). The hotels face each other on the main road near the bazar. They are unsigned, so you will need to ask around with the buzzword 'hotel'. There are a few reasonable restaurants.

To reach the island, take a speedboat from Kastura ghat in Cox's Bazar, which will leave when there are about 10 people on board (Tk 50, 15 minutes). You will have to pay Tk 2 to get onto the impressively rickety pier at Kastura ghat. Also be prepared to clamber over wooden boats tied together as a makeshift pier extension when the tide is out. The last speedboat leaves from the island at around 6pm.

# TEKNAF

This bustling smugglers' town is on the southern tip of the narrow strip of land adjoining Myanmar, 92km south of Cox's Bazar. The Bangladesh-Myanmar border is formed by the Naaf River, a branch of which divides the town. Most of the town is a crowded area of narrow alleys. From the main road, where the bus stops, a narrow street runs east, downhill and across the creek. Over the bridge, a left turn leads up to the marketplace, where you'll find food stalls and smuggled Burmese merchandise. Some travellers report a slightly menacing atmosphere in Teknaf, but as long as you don't stick your nose into the local import-export business and keep your head down during hartals, it's safe enough.

It is illegal to cross into Myanmar from here, and since its army has planted mine-fields along the border to deter illegal immigrants and smugglers, it's not wise to try.

## Sights & Activities

Just south of the market and police station you'll find Jeeps that provide transport to surrounding villages. The last village on the mainland, **Shahpuri**, is a bumpy 30-minute ride. Its main attractions are the beautiful view from the embankment through the mangrove swamps to the Myanmar coast. Another option is a ride south to Badarmokam at the tip of the peninsula, where the white sandy beach is quite deserted and particularly nice at sunset.

In 1994 some visitors walked from Teknaf all the way to Cox's Bazar, a trip that took three days but is better done in four. Finding a place to sleep was apparently not a major problem. On one or two nights, villagers reportedly welcomed them into their homes, offering board and lodging. A hike similar to this might be worth considering, except during the rainy season.

The main reason for visiting Teknaf is to reach St Martin's Island (below), 38km south.

## Sleeping & Eating

**Hotel Ne-Taung** (r with/without AC Tk 1000/500) Close to the ferry, this Parjatan-run hotel is the only one in town that has hot water. Its restaurant serves reasonably priced Bangladeshi food.

**Hotel Dwip Plaza** (d Tk 400) This place is new and clean; rooms have squat toilets.

**Hotel Skyview** (s/d Tk 150/300) is cruder than the Plaza but sufficient. The next step down in price and quality is the **Hilltop** (s/d Tk 100/200), followed by the even-cheaper **Hotel Raj Mahal** (s/d Tk 80/150) in front of Zame Mosque.

Finding cheap food is no problem, but don't expect culinary excellence. There are some basic restaurants near the market and on the main highway, just west of the bridge over the creek.

## Getting There & Away

Buses run between Cox's Bazar and Teknaf (Tk 60, 70km, hourly until 6pm). Expect three arse-aching hours.

# ST MARTIN'S ISLAND

Some 10km south of the Teknaf peninsula tip, St Martin's is the country's only coral island, and one of its highlights. Between 1890 and 1900, about 60 people settled on the island, which has now grown to a population of around 7000. The majority of the island's inhabitants are Islamic, and live primarily off fishing.

Named after a British provincial governor, and called Narikel Jinjira (Coconut Island) by the locals, the dumbbell-shaped island has an area of about 8 sq km, which reduces to about 5 sq km during high tide. The main island to the north, Uttar Para, gradually narrows several kilometres southward, to a point where it's roughly 100m wide. Three smaller islands, Zinjira, Galachira and Ciradia, are located just south of the main island. At low tide they're essentially one body of land, connected to the main island by a narrow strip of land.

St Martin's Island is a special place. There is no question of its enormous potential as a tourist destination, but far less certain is how it will establish a sustainable tourist infrastructure without compromising the things that attract tourists in the first place, such as unspoilt beaches, amiable islanders and the absence of soulless concrete buildings. The occasional boisterousness of young holiday-makers that already disrupts the serenity may prove to be something of a prophecy. Entrepreneurs are increasingly becoming aware of the island's economic potential and environmental and cultural vulnerability, but only time will tell whether their eco-promises are kept.

### Activities

Locals assert that St Martin's is a better place to dive and snorkel than Australia's Great Barrier Reef. This might not be the case, but there is certainly the option of doing both. A new diving business, **Oceanic** ( ☎ 0171-867 911), has recently opened. To find it, take a left at the small road at the end of the restaurant strip on the beach; it's a couple of hundred metres along on the right. Prices are yet to be fixed and are therefore still negotiable. Its proprietor is an ex-navy diver (with a great yarn about a Bengal tiger). Make sure you pick your time for optimal visibility – not too soon after rain.

### Sleeping & Eating

**Eco Resorts** (r with bathroom Tk 200) A place with big plans; time will tell whether it lives up to the 'eco' in its title. This spacious and homely hotel is very much a work in progress. The highlight is the restaurant, where those who have heard the rumours congregate at night for spectacular meals at great prices (the prawns and salad are fantastic). Eco Resorts also has plans to open a similar establishment on the other side of the island.

**Hotel Nijhum** (dm Tk 90, d/t with bathroom Tk 350/400) At the end of the main road with access to a nice piece of beach, this Parjatan-owned hotel is popular with Bangladeshi holiday-makers. There are also some more expensive cottage options. The affiliated Appayan Restaurant is equally popular (and crowded).

**Paradise Hotel** (r Tk 1000) The first hotel you'll see immediately as you step onto the island is this very nice one. Rooms are clean

and have a balcony. This is a good example of the type of hotels under construction, and some would say demonstrative of the sad direction the island is taking.

Next door to Eco Resorts is the tiny **Bay of Bengal Lodge** (r with bathroom Tk 200), run by a delightful elderly man, who will be milling around. You might not want to use the attached bathroom. For the same price you can stay at Hotel Prabal, but it might get lonely in the dark. There is a common bathroom outside the main building.

There is no dearth of shops and tea-houses on St Martin's. As you step off the pier you'll walk through a strip of seemingly makeshift restaurants. Their fierce competitiveness makes for some great meals.

Among other things smuggled from Myanmar, through St Martin's, is Burmese Beer. Ask quietly and you may be able to acquire a bottle.

### Getting There & Away

Getting to St Martin's Island from Teknaf and back again can be a hassle. There is a lack of consensus concerning departure times and fares, though once you're on a boat, the three-hour voyage along the coast of Myanmar is a real privilege.

A ferry is supposed to leave the island at 10am, but get there at 9am and be prepared to wait until 11am. Keari Sindbad runs an efficient service between St Martin's and Teknaf (1st-/2nd-class return Tk 350/300, October to March). Its boats leave Teknaf at 9.30am and St Martin's at 3.30pm.

The alternative is to charter a small boat (Tk 1200), which, divided among a group, can be a small price to pay for the flexible departure time.

The **Green Abakash** ( ☎ 647 445) arranges boats from Cox's Bazar for its large numbers of guests. You could try to hitch a ride through it.

## COMILLA
☎ 081
Comilla is 90km southeast of Dhaka, a few kilometres west of the Indian state of Tripura. It is the base for visitors to the nearby Buddhist ruins of Mainimati (p140).

### Orientation

The heart of Comilla is Kandirpar Circle, from which four major arteries extend.

# COMILLA

0 — 2 km
0 — 1 mile

**INFORMATION**
EarthNet-Bd...........................**1** C3
One Click Cyber Café...............**2** C3

**SIGHTS & ACTIVITIES**    (pp140–1)
Ananda Vihara......................**3** A5
Charpatra Mura.....................**4** A3
Hindu Temples......................**5** D5
Mainimati Museum.................**6** A6
Maynamati War Cemetery........**7** A3
Mosque..............................**8** D5
Rupban Mura........................**9** A6
Salban Vihara.......................**10** A6

**SLEEPING**    (pp140–1)
Hotel Abedin.......................**11** C4
Hotel Ashik.........................**12** B3
Hotel Lilufa.........................**13** D3

Hotel Mainimati....................**14** C4
Hotel Meraj.........................**15** C3
Hotel Noorjahan....................**16** B6
Nirapad Guest House..............**17** C3
Salbon Vihara Archaeological
   Rest House...................(see 6)

**EATING**    (p140)
Biroti Restaurant...................**18** B4
China Garden.......................**19** C3
Diana Hotel.........................**20** C3
Kakoli Restaurant..................**21** A3
Silver Spoon........................**22** C3

**TRANSPORT**    (pp140–1)
Bus Station (for Chittagong).......**23** D5
Main Bus Station (for Dhaka & Sylhet)...**24** B4
Tisha Bus...........................**25** B4

**OTHER**
Chowk Bazar.....................(see 23)
Coca Cola Plant....................**26** B4
Colonial-Era Mansions............**27** C5
Medical Centre.....................**28** C4
Military Hospital....................**29** C3
New Market.........................**30** D3
Pharmacies.........................**31** C4
Post Office..........................**32** D3
Rajshinda Market...................**33** D5
Sonali Bank.........................**34** C3
Sonali Bank.........................**35** D4

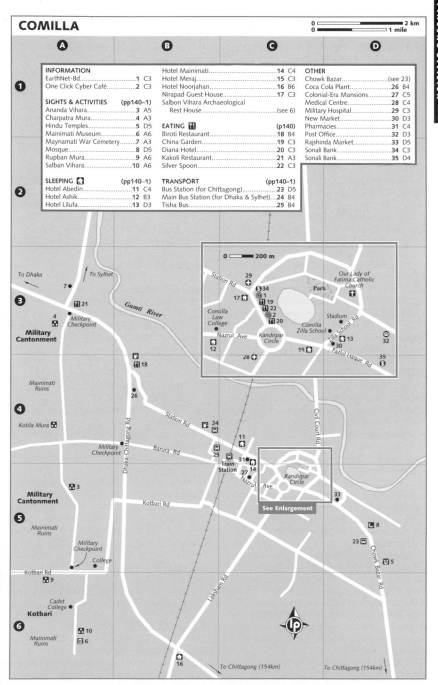

Fazlul Haque Rd heads eastward, eventually becoming Chowk Bazar Rd and the road to Chittagong. Heading east along this street you'll come to Rajshinda Market and Chowk Bazar, a major commercial area.

## Information

### INTERNET ACCESS

**One Click Cyber Café** (3rd fl, Hazi Taru Miah Poura Market; per hr Tk 25)

**EarthNet-Bd** (per hr Tk 30) Faster connections.

## Sights

On the northwestern outskirts of town, along the road north to Sylhet and 1km off the Dhaka road, the beautifully maintained **Maynamati War Cemetery** is one of the city's principal attractions. British, African, Indian and Australian troops from WWII are all buried here. Japanese troops also penetrated the area and 40 Japanese soldiers are among the hundreds buried in the manicured grounds.

Just past Chowk Bazar, on the outskirts of town, are some impressive **Hindu temples**.

## Sleeping

**Hotel Noorjahan** (Dhaka-Chittagong Rd; d Tk 1200-2500) Just out of town, the enormous Noorjahan has large doubles complete with hot water, sit-down toilet, a bathtub, a fridge and horrendously kitsch ornaments. This is as luxurious as Comilla gets. It also has three restaurants.

**Hotel Ashik** (Nazrul Ave; r with bathroom Tk 400) Unusually large, comfortable rooms with tables and sit-down toilets.

**Hotel Abedin** (Station Rd; s/d with shared bathroom Tk 60/120) The poorly marked Abedin has a dilapidated exterior but is OK inside. Smaller singles/doubles, minus trimmings such as reading chairs and mosquito nets, are available for Tk 50/80.

Other options:

**Nirapad Guest House** (Station Rd; s/d with shared bathroom Tk 45/90) A dumpy two-storey structure; its tiny rooms have fans.

**Hotel Meraj** (Hotel Meraz; Fazlal Haque Rd; s/d Tk 100/180) Staff aren't overly comfortable with foreigners staying.

**Hotel Lilufa** (d Tk 300) Friendly enough staff, but prices seem to fluctuate mid-quote. Rooms on the top floor are supposedly new, but the bathroom grime seems old enough.

**Hotel Mainimati** (Station Rd; s/d Tk 100/200) A good budget option.

## Eating

For cheap Bangladeshi food, the area around the train station, in the centre of town, has several good restaurants.

**Diana Hotel** (Kandirpar Circle) Real Bangladeshi food in atypically clean surrounds. The curries are delectable and the naan is piping-hot perfection.

**China Garden** (Station Rd; meals Tk 40-150) has decent Chinese fare. Nearby, with comparable prices but better food, is the **Silver Spoon** (Station Rd), with a menu sensibly divided into single, half and full serves.

There are a couple of upmarket restaurants on the northwestern outskirts of town: the Biroti Restaurant and Kakoli Restaurant are carpeted and have AC. Both offer Bangladeshi and Chinese menus in the Tk 80-plus range.

## Getting There & Away

### BUS

Buses for Dhaka (Tk 40, two hours), and other cities to the north, leave from Station Rd, just west of the railway line. **Tisha Bus** ( ☎ 65856; Wapda Rd), off Station St, operates coaches to Dhaka (Tk 75, every 20 minutes between 5.40am and 7pm).

Buses for Chittagong (Tk 100, four hours, every 20 minutes between 5.30am and 5.30pm) and other towns to the south leave from the Chowk Bazar Rd bus station, about 2km east of Kandirpar Circle.

If you're heading to Mymensingh and don't want to go via Dhaka, go north to Bhairab Bazar, in Dhaka division, and pick up connections there.

### TRAIN

Comilla is on the Dhaka–Chittagong line. There are two daily IC trains to Dhaka (1st/*sulob* class Tk 170/75, five hours, depart 1.53am and 9.54am) and one to Sylhet (Tk 195/120, seven hours, departs 10.38am). There's also a train to Chittagong (1st/*sulob* class Tk 140/60, departs 10.30am and noon).

There are also mail trains running at various times throughout the day.

## MAINIMATI RUINS

The Mainimati–Lalmai ridge is a 20km range of low hills, 8km west of Comilla. Famous as an important centre of Buddhist culture from the 6th to 13th centuries, the buildings excavated in the area were wholly made of baked bricks. The three most important of the 50-odd Buddhist sites are Salban Vihara, Kotila Mura and Charpatra Mura.

A large section of Mainimati is a military cantonment. It was while the army was clearing the area with bulldozers that the archaeological site in the Kotbari area was discovered. Some of the major ruins are within the cantonment, and cannot be visited without permission from military officers. For this reason, most visitors see only the museum and the ruins outside the cantonment.

## Sights
### MAINIMATI MUSEUM
The best place to start explorations is at **Mainimati Museum** (admission Tk 2; 9am-1.30pm & 2.30-5pm Sun-Fri Oct-Mar, 10am-1pm & 2-6pm Sun-Fri Apr-Sep). The collection includes terracotta plaques, bronze statues, 4th-century silver and gold coins, jewellery, kitchen utensils and votive stupas embossed with Buddhist inscriptions. The marvellous terracotta plaques reveal a rural Buddhist art alive with animation and vivid natural realism.

Also on display is an unusually large bronze bell from one of the Buddhist temples and large, black-stone carvings of Hindu gods and goddesses, including Vishnu, Ganesh and Parvati.

The museum's custodian, Mr Pramanik Abdul Latif, is happy to chat. His office is opposite the museum.

### SALBAN VIHARA
While **Salban Vihara** lacks Paharpur's imposing stupa, the remains give a better idea of the extent of the structure, as they were rebuilt more recently.

This 170-sq-metre monastery has 115 cells for monks, facing a temple in the centre of the courtyard. The royal copper plates of Deva kings and a terracotta seal bearing a royal inscription found here indicate that the monastery was built by Sri Bhava Deva in the first half of the 8th century. The original cruciform plan of the central temple was reduced in scale during subsequent rebuilding. The entire basement wall was heavily embellished with decorative elements such as terracotta plaques and ornamental bricks.

### KOTILA MURA
Like all the ruins in the cantonment, **Kotila Mura** cannot be visited without permission from the military. Situated 5km north of Salban Vihara, it comprises three large stupas representing Buddha, Dharma and Sangha, the 'Three Jewels of Buddhism', plus some secondary stupas, all enclosed by a massive boundary wall. The ground plan of the central stupa is in the shape of a *dharma chakra*, or 'wheel of the law'. The hub of the wheel is represented by a deep shaft in the centre, and the spokes by eight brick cells. The two stupas on either side each contain a sealed relic-chamber that has yielded hundreds of miniature clay stupas.

### CHARPATRA MURA
Situated 2km north of Kotila Mura, **Charpatra Mura** is another oblong Buddhist shrine perched on a hilltop in the cantonment. The main prayer chamber of the shrine is to the west, and is approached from a spacious hall to the east through a covered passage. The roof was originally supported on four thick brick columns, and a covered entrance led to the prayer chamber.

### ANANDA VIHARA
Also in the cantonment, 1.5km south of Kotila Mura, this **mound** is the largest of the ancient sites on the ridge, occupying over 100 sq metres. Similar in plan to Salban Vihara, it was badly damaged and plundered during WWII, so there's not much to see. You could have a quick look on your way to Kotila Mura.

## Sleeping
If you're a ruin fanatic, it may be possible to stay at **Salban Vihara Archaeological Rest House** (r Tk 200), across from the Mainimati Museum. You'll need permission from the **Director of Ecology** ( 812 6817) in Dhaka.

## Getting There & Away
From Kandirpar Circle, you can get a tempo to Kotbari for Tk 7. Most rickshaw drivers aren't interested in the long trip to Mainimati, but if you go down Laksham Rd to the intersection with Kotbari Rd (where there's a petrol station), you'll find lots of drivers willing to make the 5km trip for between Tk 15 and Tk 30.

# Sylhet Division

**SYLHET DIVISION**

**HIGHLIGHTS**

- **Cycling** (p151) through the gently rolling tea estates around Srimangal

- Joining the thousands of daily pilgrims to the **Shrine of Hazrat Shah Jalal** (p145), the 14th-century Sufi mystic

- Hearing and maybe seeing gibbons swing through the trees of the densely veg-etated **Lowacherra Forest Reserve** (p152)

Sylhet division is a broad valley, fringed by the Khasi and Jaintia Hills to the north and the hills of Tripura to the south. The countryside is covered with terraced tea estates, patches of tropical forest, pineapple plantations and orange groves. Sylhet division produces over 30 million kg of tea annually, with more than 150 tea estates spread over 40,000 hectares.

This division has the best climate in the country – temperate and cool with clean, crisp air in winter. It's moderately warm in summer, but has an annual rainfall of 5000mm, the highest in the country.

The Surma River passes through the city of Sylhet and eventually joins the mighty Meghna further south. The valley is dotted with broad shallow natural depressions known as *haors* (wetlands; *how*-ar), which are sanctuaries for migratory birds from places as far away as Siberia.

The area along the northern border, at the foot of the Khasi-Jaintia hills, is tribal land. There are also tribal communities scattered through the southern hills. The Khashia (or Khasi), Pangou and Tripura people tend to shun regular contact with the outside world, venturing only occasionally from their settlements. The Monipuri (Manipuri) are the exception. They have become artisans, jewellers and businesspeople, and have entered into the general Bangladeshi community. The best-known feature of Monipuri culture is the tribe's classical dance, dedicated to the worship of Radha-Krishna; centred on the tale of Krishna's love affair with the female cowherd Radha. She symbolises human spirituality, while Krishna is the embodiment of divine love.

**SYLHET DIVISION**

## SYLHET
☎ 0821

At first glance, Sylhet seems to be a prosperous city, with new shopping centres and restaurants opening all the time. However, the wealth of Sylheti émigrés and their relatives is starkly contrasted with that of the wider community, some of whom resent the fact that money received from abroad goes towards mosques, shrines and shopping centres rather than into developing local industry.

Former residences and social structures in Sylhet seem to have weathered the transition from Independence better than many other pieces of British Raj flotsam. Colonnaded residences are still fronted by neatly trimmed lawns and verandas with delicately arranged armchairs.

Sylhet has Muslim, Hindu and Buddhist festivals. The Hindu melas (festivals), the Laspurnima, Jolung Jatra, and Rota Jatra, all dedicated to Radha-Krishna, are the most colourful. Monipuri dances are held during Hindu melas.

## Orientation & Information
On the south side of the Surma River you'll find the train and bus stations, but not much more. The river is traversed by two bridges. Kean Bridge, the more central one, was repaired after being damaged by Pakistani bombers during the Liberation War. In making the crossing, rickshaw-pullers are aided by rickshaw-pushers; these 'assistants' are paid Tk 2 for their service.

Zinda Bazar Rd is littered with restaurants and shopping centres, as is the intersection of Telihaor and Taltala Rds. There's a small **bookshop** (Zinda Bazar Rd), next to the Agra Hotel & Restaurant, with some English-language titles.

There are Internet cafés dotted around town, with more on the way. **Cyber Point** (cnr Jaintiapur & Shaikh Ghat Rds; per hr Tk 24) serves drinks and has fast computers. There are cheaper ones on Amberkhana Rd at the northern end of town.

There is a **Standard Chartered Bank** (Airport Rd) with an ATM opposite Darga Gate, and other banks closer to the river.

# SYLHET

0 _____ 1 km
0 _____ 0.5 miles

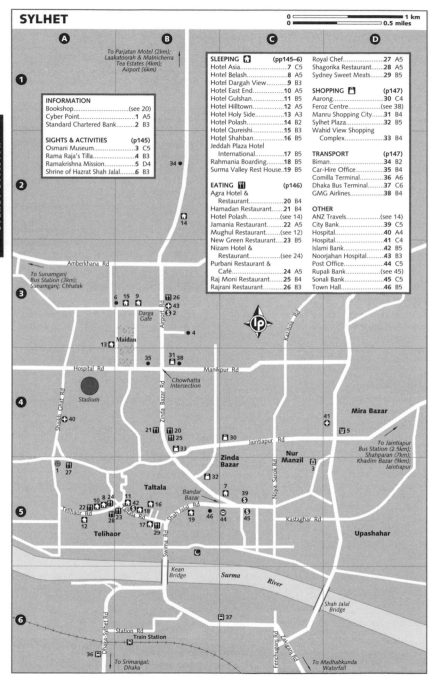

**SLEEPING** (pp145–6)
Hotel Asia.......................7 C5
Hotel Belash.....................8 A5
Hotel Dargah View..........9 B3
Hotel East End................10 A5
Hotel Gulshan.................11 B5
Hotel Hilltown................12 A5
Hotel Holy Side.............13 A3
Hotel Polash...................14 B2
Hotel Qureishi................15 B3
Hotel Shahban................16 B5
Jeddah Plaza Hotel
   International...............17 B5
Rahmania Boarding........18 B5
Surma Valley Rest House.19 B5

**EATING** (p146)
Agra Hotel &
   Restaurant..................20 B4
Hamadan Restaurant......21 B4
Hotel Polash.............(see 14)
Jamania Restaurant........22 A5
Mughul Restaurant........(see 12)
New Green Restaurant...23 B5
Nizam Hotel &
   Restaurant.............(see 24)
Purbani Restaurant &
   Café...........................24 A5
Raj Moni Restaurant......25 B4
Rajrani Restaurant..........26 B3

Royal Chef......................27 A5
Shagorika Restaurant.......28 A5
Sydney Sweet Meats.......29 B5

**SHOPPING** (p147)
Aarong..........................30 C4
Feroz Centre.................(see 38)
Manru Shopping City.....31 B4
Sylhet Plaza...................32 B5
Wahid View Shopping
   Complex....................33 B4

**TRANSPORT** (p147)
Biman............................34 B2
Car-Hire Office..............35 B4
Comilla Terminal............36 A6
Dhaka Bus Terminal.......37 C6
GMG Airlines.................38 B4

**OTHER**
ANZ Travels..................(see 14)
City Bank.......................39 C5
Hospital.........................40 A4
Hospital.........................41 C4
Islami Bank....................42 B5
Noorjahan Hospital........43 B3
Post Office.....................44 C5
Rupali Bank...............(see 45)
Sonali Bank...................45 C5
Town Hall......................46 B5

**INFORMATION**
Bookshop.....................(see 20)
Cyber Point......................1 A5
Standard Chartered Bank........2 B3

**SIGHTS & ACTIVITIES** (p145)
Osmani Museum..................3 C5
Rama Raja's Tilla.................4 B3
Ramakrishna Mission............5 D4
Shrine of Hazrat Shah Jalal........6 B3

To Parjatan Motel (2km);
Laakatoorah & Malnicherra
Tea Estates (4km);
Airport (6km)

To Sunamganj
Bus Station (3km);
Sunamganj; Chhatak

Amberkhana Rd

Darga Gate

Maidan

Hospital Rd

Chowhatta Intersection

Manikpur Rd

Stadium

Airport Rd

Zinda Bazar Rd

Shaikh Ghat Rd

Mira Bazar

Jaintiapur Rd

To Jaintiapur
Bus Station (2.5km);
Shahparan (7km);
Khadim Bazar (9km);
Jaintiapur

Zinda Bazar

Nur Manzil

Kazitola Rd

Noya Sarok Rd

Taltala

Bandar Bazar

Telihaor Rd

Taltala Rd

Shah Jalal Rd

Swina Rd

Telihaor

Kastaghar Rd

Upashahar

Kean Bridge

Surma River

Shah Jalal Bridge

Station Rd

Train Station

Dhaka-Sylhet Rd

Fenchuganj Rd

Zakiganj Rd

To Srimangal;
Dhaka

To Madhabkunda
Waterfall

SYLHET DIVISION

## Sights

### SHRINE OF HAZRAT SHAH JALAL

In the north of the city, off Airport Rd, lies the region's holiest place, the **Shrine of Hazrat Shah Jalal**. The 14th-century Sufi saint Shah Jalal is buried here, making it a major pilgrimage site for Bangladeshi Muslims. Being buried near the saint is considered a great honour. Shah Jalal's sword and robes are preserved within the large new mosque, but aren't on display. The tomb is covered with rich brocade, and at night the space around it is illuminated with candles – it is quite magical. It's never entirely clear whether non-Muslims can visit the shrine. If you are invited to see the tomb, behave with appropriate solemnity.

The pond in front of the shrine complex is filled with sacred catfish that are fed by pilgrims and are, according to legend, metamorphosed black magicians of the Hindu raja Gour Govinda, who was defeated by Shah Jalal in 1303.

Nearby, on a hillock named **Rama Raja's Tilla**, you can get some partially blocked views of the city. Legend has it a Hindu temple that once stood here was destroyed by an earthquake, instigated by Shah Jalal.

### OSMANI MUSEUM

In Nur Manzil, near the centre of town and east of Noya Sarok Rd, is the **Osmani Museum** ( 10.30am-4.30pm Sat-Wed, 3.30-7.30pm Fri). This small, colonial-era house is dedicated to General Osmani, a key figure in the Liberation War.

A block to the northeast is the **Ramakrishna Mission**, where Hindu melas are often held.

## Tours

Organised tours that operate out of Sylhet are less guided tours than car-hire services. For that reason, you might want to consider hiring a vehicle and driver independently (see p147).

**ANZ Travels** (Hotel Polash) offers tours to Madhabkunda Waterfall (Tk 2200), Tamabil and some tea estates en route (Tk 1800) and Sunamganj (Tk 1400).

**Hilltown Hotel** ( 716 077; Telihaor Rd) also offers car-hire programmes for similar prices: Madhabkunda Waterfall (Tk 2000), Jaflang via Tamabil and Jaintiapur (Tk 1500) and Sunamganj (Tk 1500).

## Sleeping

### BUDGET & MID-RANGE

A number of budget hotels are in the centre of town, in Taltala, along Taltala Rd, and the adjoining Telihaor area.

**Hotel Gulshan** ( 716 437; Taltala Rd; s/d Tk 350/500) A long-time favourite with visitors to Sylhet, the four-storey Hotel Gulshan is well managed; it also has rooms with an enormous sitting room and bedding for three people for Tk 800. All rooms are clean, and some have sit-down toilets and TV but only the most-expensive ones have hot water. The restaurant doesn't have an atmosphere worth partaking in.

**Hotel Asia** ( 717 713; Bandar Bazar; s Tk 75-100, d Tk 140) A modern five-storey building in Bandar Bazar, this presentable hotel features a small reception area with TV. Rooms are clean with fans, mosquito nets and squat toilets. Some have a small desk and relatively soft beds.

**Hotel East End** ( 719 210; Telihaor Rd; s Tk 150-250, d Tk 250-1000) Some rooms have sit-down toilets and TVs. Rooms are very clean and carpeted. The hotel also offers Internet access and has a decent restaurant.

**Parjatan Motel** ( 712 426; r Tk 500-1200) Its distance from town is the upside and the downside to staying at the Parjatan. The building is also starting to look a tad rundown both inside and out. Some rooms have nice views, some have views of power lines. Still, it's a decent place to stay if you want to be isolated. The most expensive rooms have hot water and AC.

**Hotel Hilltown** ( 716 077; s Tk 175-750, d Tk 280-3500) A range of rooms to match the range of prices. Rooms are tiled and clean but lack character, and corridors can be a bit long and lonely. You can arrange car hire from here, and there's a good restaurant (see p146).

**Hotel Belash** ( 714 659; Telihaor Rd; s Tk 60-70, d Tk 120-600) Next to the Nanditha Cinema, the four-storey Hotel Belash is good value. The economical units are reasonably clean and not too cramped, while the deluxe rooms have carpets, comfortable armchairs and large bathrooms with sit-down toilets.

There are a couple of options at Darga Gate. **Hotel Qureishi** (s Tk 150-170, d Tk 250-700) is a decent choice, particularly if you are travelling with more than two people. There are also rooms with three beds (Tk 375), four beds (Tk 500) and even five beds (Tk 550).

In the same area, **Hotel Dargah View** (Shahjalal complex; s Tk 160, d Tk 250-800) has a range of room options.

Other recommendations:

**Hotel Sufia** ( ☎ 714 697; Telihaor Rd; r Tk 80-250) Opposite Hotel Gulshan, the rooms can be grubby, but they are reasonably spacious with large beds and bathrooms.

**Hotel Shahban** ( ☎ 718 040; r Tk 100-650) Off Taltala Rd.

**Jeddah Plaza Hotel International** ( ☎ 712 124; Taltala Rd; s Tk 50-120, d Tk 120-200) Tiled floors ensure there is no dank hotel smell.

**Rahmania Boarding** ( ☎ 714 939; Taltala Rd; s Tk 50-65, d Tk 100-120) The cheapest hotel in the area and a friendly place.

### TOP END

**Hotel Holy Side** ( ☎ 722 278; holyside@xirus.net; s Tk 650-800, d Tk 950-1700) One of the nicer places to stay; all rooms have AC, hot water and satellite TV. The restaurant is very pleasant and the staff are hospitable. The only downside is its proximity to the noisy maidan (open grassed area); sometimes the loudspeakers bleat away through the night.

**Surma Valley Rest House** ( ☎ 712 671; Shah Jalal Rd; r with breakfast Tk 950-1300) Rooms at this small hotel have hot water, colour TV and laundry service. Rooms are nicely lit and some have tiled bathrooms, telephones, minibars and comfortable chairs. They aren't huge, but the space is nicely used.

**Hotel Polash** ( ☎ 718 811; Airport Rd; s Tk 230-1725, d Tk 345-1840, t Tk 632-2070) Modern, well-run and comfortable, with large airy rooms. It's probably the cheapest place to get facilities like hot water. Staff may lie about the availability of economy rooms, so ask again. Also be clear if you want a room with hot water. Deluxe rooms include breakfast in the price.

**Anurag Hotel** (s Tk 800-1200, d Tk 1200-2500) Fake marble to its very core, and the more taka, the more tacky. All rooms have TV and hot water, some even with an inviting bathtub. A big downside (apart from the décor) is the lack of natural lighting. There are some great restaurants downstairs.

**Laakatoorah Tea Estate** ( ☎ 716 216; r Tk 750) A tentative option, even if you book ahead. Your chances depend on whether there are any company-related VIPs in town. Rooms have no hot water or AC.

### Eating

**Raj Moni Restaurant** (Zinda Bazar Rd; meals Tk 60) A nice escape from the streets, with plenty of space upstairs and down. The food, which the staff patiently help you order, is clean, varied and delicious.

**Agra Hotel & Restaurant** (Zinda Bazar Rd; meals around Tk 30) As full of character as it is full of characters, this popular restaurant, tucked away in a corner, won't give you much privacy with its cramped quarters, but will give you great food.

**Rajrani Restaurant** (Airport Rd) Similar to the Agra, this well-marked restaurant is a good budget option.

**Hamadan Restaurant** ( ☎ 722 457; 4th fl, Al-Hamra Shopping Centre, Zinda Bazar Rd; dishes from Tk 150) This comfortably plush restaurant serves Chinese and Thai dishes. The *tom yum*, in all its flaming glory, is indeed yum. There is a menu page dedicated to Bangladeshi food for Bangladeshi prices – a smart way to escape the 'real Bangladesh', while taking its food with you. To find it, take the escalators (yes, escalators) to the third floor and climb the stairwell at the back left-hand corner of the building.

**Royal Chef** (dishes Tk 80-150) Another Thai and Chinese option. Staff are proud of the food, and rightly so. Even the French fries (Tk 50) are memorable.

**Hotel Polash** (dishes Tk 80-150) The restaurant at the Polash has the usual stuff (chicken korma) and the not-so-usual stuff (pigeon-roast special). Staff ignore you when you want to order, but watch you eat when your food arrives.

**Hotel Hilltown** ( ☎ 716 077) The restaurant at the Hilltown does good Bangladeshi dishes (beef kebab for Tk 20) with a smattering of miscellaneous items (milkshakes for Tk 20).

If you're staying in the Telihaor area, you'll have lots of choices, including the friendly **New Green Restaurant** (meals Tk 20-25), **Shagorika Restaurant** (meals Tk 20-25) and the well-marked **Jamania Restaurant** (meals Tk 20-25), all of which are on Telihaor Rd. You can get delicious hot *puris* (flat dough that puffs up when deep-fried) at the Banani and good vegetable kebabs at the New Green. Jamania has received even better reviews from travellers. The Purbani Restaurant & Café and the Nizam Hotel & Restaurant are also good options around this area.

There are lots of similar places closer to Kean Bridge, at Surma Market, including the popular **Sydney Sweet Meats** (Taltala Rd).

## Shopping

The city's liveliest area is Bandar Bazar, in the heart of town, where you'll find just about anything. Smuggled products from India, such as cosmetics, confectionery and saris, are widely available.

The best selection of handicrafts and textiles is available at **Aarong** (Jaintiapur Rd), a block east of Zinda Bazar Rd.

The city also has some ultra-modern shopping establishments:

**Sylhet Plaza** (Zinda Bazar Rd)
**Feroz Centre** (Manikpur Rd) East of Chowhatta intersection.
**Manru Shopping City** (Manikpur Rd)
**Wahid View Shopping Complex** (Jaintiapur Rd)

## Getting There & Away

### AIR

Both **Biman** ( ☎ 717 076; Airport Rd), 1km north of Amberkhana Rd, and **GMG Airlines** ( ☎ 711 225; Feroz Centre, Manikpur Rd) have frequent flights to Dhaka (Tk 2500).

### BICYCLE

The best route for cycling from Sylhet to Dhaka is via Mymensingh. The less-travelled route is via Chhatak, Sunamganj and Mohanganj, all of which have hotels. The trip to Mymensingh takes three or four days.

At Sunamganj, take back roads and dirt tracks southwest to Mohanganj (frequently asking directions), or catch a launch on the Surma River to Jaysiri (seven hours), about 15km from Mohanganj, the halfway point between Sunamganj and Mymensingh.

### BUS

A daytime bus trip between Dhaka and Sylhet is an interesting journey through varied countryside.

Buses for Dhaka (Tk 200, seven hours, 346km, every 30 minutes between 6am and 11.30pm) leave from the large bus station south of the river, often referred to as Dhaka terminal.

There are no direct buses to Chittagong. Those to Comilla (Tk 180, 7½ hours, 257km, every 15 minutes between 6am and 10.30pm) leave from **Comilla terminal** (Dhaka-Sylhet Rd), south of the railway station. The last bus costs Tk 190.

Buses to Sunamganj (Tk 45, 2½ hours, every 20 minutes between 6am and 8.30pm) leave from the bus station a few kilometres northwest of town, along Amberhkana Rd.

Buses northeast to Jaintiapur (Tk 22, three hours, between 6.45am and 5.35pm) and Tamabil (Tk 40, 2½ hours) leave from the small **Jaintiapur bus station** (Jaintiapur Rd), several kilometres east of the town centre.

### TRAIN

The **train station** ( ☎ 83968) is on the south side of town. There are three daily express trains for Dhaka (1st/*sulob* class Tk 270/150, between 7½ and nine hours, depart at 7.30am, 3pm and 10pm). The night train also has a sleeping car (AC/fan Tk 610/425). There is also a mail train (10.30pm), which takes 11½ hours.

Trains to Chittagong (1st/*sulob* class Tk 320/190, 10 hours, depart 10.15am, 7.20pm and 8.40pm) also stop at Comilla (1st/*sulob* class Tk 195/120). Only the 10.15am train is an express.

There are IC trains to Srimangal (1st/*sulob* class Tk 90/50, two hours, depart 7.30am, 10.15am, 3pm and 10pm).

## Getting Around

### TO/FROM THE AIRPORT

Located 7km north of town, the airport has numerous taxis and baby taxis waiting outside. For a vehicle into town, expect to pay about Tk 200 for a taxi, Tk 100 for a baby taxi and Tk 10 for a seat in a tempo.

### CAR

Renting a vehicle at the Parjatan Motel or Hotel Polash will cost between Tk 1500 and Tk 2200 a day, including petrol and driver. You could also arrange car hire at the airport.

There is a makeshift **car-hire office** (Hospital Rd) in town. Drivers are affiliated, so don't feel bad about going with one over another. Be prepared for the bargaining process. The group you negotiate with will use ferry crossings and petrol for leverage. Do the same; itemise the costs they throw at you and come up with a sensible total. A fair price would be Tk 1500 per day, including petrol and ferry crossings.

## AROUND SYLHET
### Tea Estates

Tea-estate managers haven't cottoned on to their tourist potential, so don't expect a tour on a dune buggy followed by a complimentary cuppa. At best, you'll get permission to be there, and maybe a quick tour with a staff member.

There are a couple of tea estates just beyond the city's northern outskirts on Airport Rd. If you can smile your way past the humourless guard at the gate of **Malnicherra** (dating back to 1854), the manager at the general office may be able to provide you with a guide. The other one to try is the **Laakatoorah Tea Estate**, where the manager may lecture you on the history of tea production in exchange for a tour of the factory.

Just east of Sylhet are the **Khadim Tea Gardens**. Take a tempo from Khadim Bazar, 10km east of town. Around 23km further east, 7km before Jaintiapur, you'll pass **Lalakal Tea Estates** on the right-hand side of the road; its staff seem accustomed to receiving visitors.

The largest number of tea estates in the northern half of Sylhet Division are further on, around **Jaflang**, near the Indian border. This is one of the most scenic parts of Sylhet division, and a major tribal area, where many Khasi are found. The bus from Sylhet takes 2½ hours to Tamabil and another 30 minutes to Jaflang. Remind the bus-wallah that you want to get off at Jaflang – it's easy to miss.

## Shrine of Shah Paran

Around 8km east of Sylhet, just off the highway to Jaintiapur, is the **Shrine of Shah Paran** in the tiny village of Shahparan. It's a single-domed mosque that attracts about 2000 pilgrims a day; you'll see charter buses from Dhaka all around the place.

## Madhabkunda Waterfall

A three-hour drive southeast of Sylhet (and equally accessible from Srimangal by road and rail), and a 3km rickshaw ride from Dakshinbagh train station, is the famous **waterfall** of Madhabkunda. It is popular with busloads of Bangladeshi tourists and their truckloads of litter. You may also be able to find some elephants, which are still being used to haul huge logs, in this general area. There's a Parjatan tourist spot nearby, with a restaurant, picnic area and toilet facilities.

## TAMABIL

The Tamabil border crossing (open between 9am and 6pm), 55km from Sylhet, is primarily used to import coal from India,

though foreigners occasionally cross here. Getting to the border can be messy – some travellers have reported being confused as to where the official crossing actually is, but all declare the hassle well worth the scenery between Dawki and Shillong in India: it's spectacular. Coming from India, Sylhet division is a nice way to ease yourself into Bangladesh.

To cross from Tamabil to Dawki, you *must* deposit Tk 500 departure tax into any Sonali Bank. Once you have done this, you are required to show your deposit receipt to border officials. The closest Sonali Bank is in Jaintiapur, 13km from Tamabil.

Plan in advance to have some rupee/taka on you – there is nowhere to change money in Tamabil, and the bank at Dawki is none too cooperative.

## Getting There & Away
### FROM BANGLADESH
Buses run from Sylhet to Tamabil (Tk 40, 2½ hours). From here, it's a 15-minute hike to the border. The other alternative is a private car (Tk 400 to Tk 500).

Once in India, it's a 1.5km walk to the town of Dawki, from where buses run to Shillong (Rs 40, 3½ hours). If you are stranded in Dawki, there is a small hotel on the hill, above the Sikh temple. It costs Rs 200 for a grubby room with no running water but the overnight stay might be a justifiable sacrifice for the daytime view it will afford of the scenery to Shillong.

The last bus leaves Tamabil for Shillong sometime between 10am and 1pm. If you miss it, there are a number of taxis eager to take you the two hours to Shillong, but at high rates (Rs 800 to Rs 1200).

### FROM INDIA
The border post is at Dawki in Meghalaya, accessible by bus from Shillong, 70km away. From Dawki, it's a 1.5km walk to Tamabil, where formal but friendly border officials may be able to help you negotiate a car to Sylhet, which shouldn't cost more than Tk 500. There is nowhere to stay the night in Tamabil, but nearby Jaflang has a couple of budget hotels and restaurants. It is also easier to organise onward transport from here. For the sake of safety and scenery, you're better off taking a daytime bus to Sylhet (Tk 50, 2½ hours).

## SUNAMGANJ
☎ 0871

Approximately 70km west of Sylhet, this small town offers little for tourists. However, the local *haors* are rife with bird life. From mid-winter through to the end of March, and sometimes April, migrants, winter birds and residents all get together for a big bird party. Varieties of rails, raptors, ducks, sandpipers and others congregate.

The three *haors* that seem to be the best for bird-watching are several hours upriver from the Sunamganj River. Visiting all of them is a four-day affair, which, except for true bird enthusiasts, is probably more than most travellers want. An overnight trip would get you into some of the most fascinating rural areas in Bangladesh.

### Tours
To arrange a trip into the *haor* area, visit the **Bangladesh Boat Owner's Association** ( ☎ 55996) at least a day before you plan to go. This small office is halfway along the strip of shops on the waterfront of Sachna ghat. Ask to speak to the proprietor, MD Farouk Miah. The association has two boats: the *Alamin Express* and the *Rubia Express*. Four can sleep comfortably on board. Boat hire will cost around Tk 1500 per day. Food costs extra, and will have to be pre-organised. You will need to provide a cash advance for petrol and other necessities. Remember to take water, bedding of some description, a torch (flashlight), mosquito net and binoculars.

### Sleeping
In the Sachna ghat area there are a couple of spartan but acceptable hotels. In town, the best accommodation is at the **circuit house**.

### Getting There & Away
From Sylhet, there are regular buses to Sunamganj (Tk 45, 2½ hours), leaving from **Sunamganj bus station** (Amberkhana Rd). Buses from Sunamganj to Sylhet depart approximately every 20 minutes from the bus station.

## SRIMANGAL
☎ 08626

Around 75km south of Sylhet, Srimangal (or Sreemongal) is the tea centre of Bangladesh. This hilly area, with tea estates, lemon orchards and pineapple plantations, is one of the most picturesque parts of the country. For miles around, tea estates form a perennially green carpet on the sloping hills. It's the one area (besides the Sundarbans) where it is possible to look around and not see another human being. Visits to forest reserves, tea estates and tribal villages are the main attractions of Srimangal.

The town itself is quite small. The Dhaka-Sylhet Rd passes from one end to the other, with a four-way intersection in the middle. It has the bare essentials, including several banks, a restaurant or two, some tourist operators and friendly locals.

### Information
**INTERNET ACCESS**
**Cyber Corner** (per hr Tk 25) At the end of the long corridor under the Hotel Mukta.
**Cyber Zone** (per hr Tk 40) On the 3rd floor of the shopping strip next to Hotel Plaza.

**MONEY**
Within a stone's throw of each other on the main drag is a Rupali Bank, Sonali Bank and IFIC Bank.

### Tours
The most professional tour company by far is **Classic Tours & Travel** ( ☎ 706; www.classictours-bd.com/aboutus/aboutus.htm). Its founder, Mr Razu, is planning to revolutionise tourism in Bangladesh and has made a good start in Srimangal. Mr Razu runs a series of trips throughout the area, covering tea and pineapple plantations, the Lowacherra Forest Reserve and Monipuri and Khashia tribal villages. He offers set programmes of various lengths, and can tailor trips. Classic Tours also rents bicycles (Tk 100 per day).

It's also likely you'll be approached by a few amateur operators, who offer fairly competitive prices. One is Mr Rashed Husan. If he doesn't find you, you can find him through his brother, who manages Hotel Tea Town.

### Sleeping
**Hotel Tea Town** ( ☎ 370; Dhaka-Sylhet Rd; r Tk 250-950) The newest and best place to stay, Hotel Tea Town opened in December 2003 and is so clean you can see your reflection in the floors. Rooms are devoid of personality, but the staff certainly make up for it. It's the only place in town where you'll find hot water.

**Hotel Taj Mahal** ( ☎ 480; Dhaka-Sylhet Rd; s with shared bathroom Tk 40, d with shared/attached bathroom

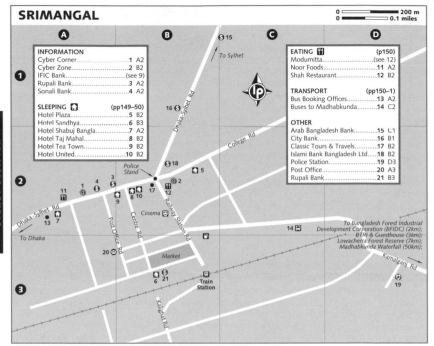

## SRIMANGAL

| | |
|---|---|
| INFORMATION | |
| Cyber Corner.................................1 A2 | |
| Cyber Zone..................................2 B2 | |
| IFIC Bank..................................(see 9) | |
| Rupali Bank.................................3 A2 | |
| Sonali Bank.................................4 A2 | |
| | |
| SLEEPING (pp149–50) | |
| Hotel Plaza..................................5 B2 | |
| Hotel Sandhya.............................6 B3 | |
| Hotel Shabuj Bangla...................7 A2 | |
| Hotel Taj Mahal..........................8 B2 | |
| Hotel Tea Town..........................9 B2 | |
| Hotel United..............................10 B2 | |

| | |
|---|---|
| EATING (p150) | |
| Modumitta..............................(see 12) | |
| Noor Foods..............................11 A2 | |
| Shah Restaurant.......................12 B2 | |
| | |
| TRANSPORT (pp150–1) | |
| Bus Booking Offices.................13 A2 | |
| Buses to Madhabkunda...........14 C2 | |
| | |
| OTHER | |
| Arab Bangladesh Bank............15 C1 | |
| City Bank.................................16 B1 | |
| Classic Tours & Travels............17 B2 | |
| Islami Bank Bangladesh Ltd....18 B2 | |
| Police Station...........................19 D3 | |
| Post Office................................20 A3 | |
| Rupali Bank..............................21 B3 | |

To Sylhet

Dhaka-Sylhet Rd

College Rd

Police Stand

Dhaka-Sylhet Rd

To Dhaka

Post Office Rd

Centre Rd

Cinema

Railway Station Rd

Market

To Bangladesh Forest Industrial Development Corporation (BFIDC) (2km); BTRI & Guesthouse (3km); Lowacherra Forest Reserve (7km); Madhabkunda Waterfall (50km);

Kamalganj Rd

Train Station

Kalighat Rd

Tk 80/100) Renovations are underway to increase facilities, and possibly prices.

**Hotel United** ( ☎ 419; Dhaka-Sylhet Rd; s with shared/attached bathroom Tk 50/70, d Tk 80/100) Next door to the Taj Mahal, Hotel United offers rooms that are clean and good value, though there is a lack of natural light.

**Hotel Plaza** ( ☎ 525; College Rd; s/d Tk 100/150, larger r with AC Tk 350-450) All rooms are reasonably spacious.

**Hotel Sandhya** ( ☎ 243, 439; s/d Tk 300/600) On the south side of the large concrete market building, the Sandhya has furnished AC rooms with comfortable beds and decent bathrooms. There are cheaper rooms on the floors below, but they are minus all the trimmings that make it a place worth staying.

**Hotel Shabuj Bangla** (Dhaka-Sylhet Rd; s with shared/attached bathroom Tk 40/60, d with bathroom Tk 120) At the western end of town, this hotel has small but clean rooms with fans and mosquito nets.

## Eating

**Shah Restaurant** (Railway Station Rd; meals around Tk 50) In the heart of town, a few doors south of the main intersection, the Shah turns out filling and tasty meals.

**Modumitta** (meals around Tk 50) Next door to the Shah, with similarly good food.

There are a couple of nice restaurants on Dhaka-Sylhet Rd. **Noor Foods** (meals around Tk 40) is one of the most popular, with enormous and delicious meals. The fish is particularly good, as is the cha. There's a small sign in English.

Miraculously, there are no Chinese restaurants in Srimangal.

## Getting There & Away

### BUS

To take a local bus to Dhaka (Tk 90, five hours) or Sylhet (Tk 60, three hours) you will have to hail one on the road. You can try the same for Comilla (Tk 120, 6 hours). Buses for Kamalganj (Tk 10) and Madhabkunda (Tk 30) leave from Kamalganj Rd.

There are three booking offices for coaches along the main road in close proximity to each other. These service Dhaka (non-AC/AC Tk 200/300, five hours, every 30 minutes) and Chittagong (Tk 300, 12 hours).

Buses for Sylhet also have offices on the main drag near the main intersection.

### TRAIN

Three are three trains a day to Dhaka (1st/ *sulob* class Tk 200/110, 5½ hours, depart 9.50am, 5.03pm and 12.20am), except for Sunday, Wednesday and Tuesday when there are only two. Afternoon trains also have AC compartments (Tk 300) and the evening train has sleepers (Tk 500).

Trains leave Dhaka for Srimangal at 6.40am, 12.45pm and 9.30pm.

## AROUND SRIMANGAL
### Cycling

The area around Srimangal is one of the best in Bangladesh for cycling. Despite the rolling terrain, the roads are reasonably level; if overly encumbered rickshaw-wallahs can do it, then so can you, even on the ubiquitous one-speed Chinese bike.

There's an intricate network of roads connecting all the tea estates to the main highways. Only the major routes are tarred or bricked, but the dirt roads are in good

condition. Even if you just head east out of town on Kamalganj Rd and stay on the main roads, you will find yourself weaving in and out of heaven in no time.

It can be difficult to determine where one estate stops and another starts. Bear in mind that you might inadvertently pedal into private property. Though you will find that most people are more likely to treat you like a guest than a trespasser, it is appropriate to seek management's permission to be there. You can try your luck in asking for accommodation at the tea estates, but don't assume you'll be successful – allow enough daylight hours to get back to town.

### Tea Estates

There are so many tea estates that it's not easy to determine which are the best for visiting. Some are more receptive to visitors than others.

One of the most frequently visited estates is **Madabpore Tea Gardens**. It has a lake on the premises that hasn't been treated with the respect that its scenic potential deserves, but is pleasant nonetheless. The turn-off for

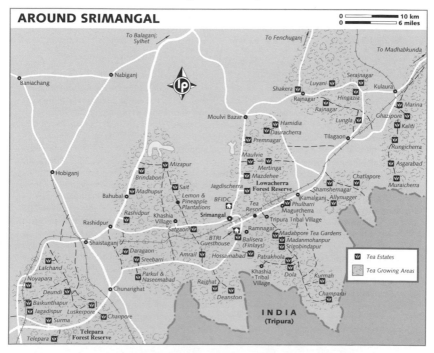

SYLHET DIVISION

the gardens is about 1.75km beyond the Tea Resort compound.

The sprawling **Finlays** estate is reportedly not so hospitable. Politely pleading ignorance and leaving should be enough to deal with irate estate managers.

Sadly, tea-estate managers aren't overly interested in providing accommodation for travellers, though one suspects that the first to do so won't be the last. However, all estates have guesthouse facilities for friends, family and visiting VIPs; given Bangladeshi hospitality you may be lucky enough to be considered within one, if not all, categories.

**Tea Resort** ( ☎ /fax 207; r Tk 1400, 2-/3-person bungalow Tk 3200/4800) At the time of research, this pleasant oasis, 3km from Srimangal was in the throes of being handed over to the Bangladesh Tea Board from the Department for International Development. All rooms have hot water and AC. There is also a swimming pool and tennis and badminton courts. Food costs an extra Tk 750 per day. Bills must be paid in taka. You must book a week or two in advance; faxing the estate manager is probably the most efficient way to do so.

**Bangladesh Tea Research Institute Guesthouse** (BTRI; ☎ 225; r Tk 300-400) It is possible to stay at the BTRI as long as it isn't full. Meals are available for around Tk 200 per day. The guesthouse is charming, with a veranda to relax on in the evenings. Again, it's a good idea to book in advance.

It is also possible, but rare, to stay at the Bangladesh Forest Industrial Development Corporation, 4km from town, for around the same price as the BTRI.

## Lowacherra Forest Reserve

Around 8km east of Srimangal, on the road to Kamalganj, **Lowacherra Forest** (known to locals as Shaymoli) is worth a visit if you're in the area. It extends for only a few kilometres, but the terrain is hilly and the vegetation fairly thick. Fortunately, this forest is in an area that's not heavily populated. Consequently, it's less threatened than Madhupur Forest in Dhaka division.

There are trails to follow and you can wander off without fear of getting lost. Look for wild orchids growing in the upper branches of trees, and keep an eye out for gibbons that make lots of noise as their troupe swings through the branches of the upper canopy. The blue-bearded bee-eater and the red-breasted trogon are a couple of interesting birds to watch out for. Take care during the wet season, as leeches are not unheard of.

### TEA GARDENS & TEA ESTATES

Tea production in Bangladesh dates from 1854, when Malnicherra Tea Estate, just north of Sylhet, was set up by the British. The tea grew well here and by the end of the century there were around 150 tea estates, almost all under British ownership. About the same number exist today but, since Independence, less than half are British-owned. The rest mainly belong to wealthy Bangladeshis and, to a lesser extent, the government's Tea Board.

When the British began growing tea in Sylhet, they didn't bother training the indigenous people. Rather, they brought experienced Indian labourers, mainly from tea estates in Bihar, Orissa and Bangla (West Bengal). Today, virtually all of the labourers, or 'coolies', are descendants of these original Hindus. Small Hindu shrines are a common feature of tea estates with worker colonies.

Each estate provides an elementary school and a doctor. Since many of the estates are in remote locations, few of the workers' children are able to go beyond the primary grades. However, the tea workers have the only trade union in Bangladesh that effectively bargains with management, so their contracts often include special privileges, such as a festival allowance. New Year's Eve is one of the most festive times, in part because the tea season is over. Hinduism does not ban alcohol and many workers get a bit tipsy at festival time. Several private 'clubs' outside Srimangal cater to the owners and managers year round. Faced with these long-standing traditions, the government looks the other way.

When you are visiting a tea estate, as you must, don't make the mistake of touring on a Friday, the day of rest, or visiting between mid-December and the start of March, as everything will be at a standstill. The picking season is during the wetter months, from early March to early December, when the factories are in full operation.

To access the reserve from Srimangal, take the paved road east towards Kamalganj. The poorly marked turn-off to your left (north), which is easy to miss, is about 4.75km past the Tea Resort compound and another 2.75km beyond the well-marked turn-off for the Nurjahan and Madabpore tea estates. The dirt road into the forests, which crosses the railroad tracks, is less than 1km long and an easy walk. A bus from Srimangal should cost between Tk 5 and Tk 7.

## Tribal Villages

There are 11 Khashia villages (called *punji*) and several Monipuri villages (called *para*) scattered among the tea plantations in the Srimangal area. Khashia villages are usually on hilltops surrounded by betel-nut trees, which is their cash crop. When visiting a Khashia village you should first call in on the local chief, as the community will not extend full hospitality without his permission. The Khashia *punji* **Magurcherra** is on the edge of the ruined Magurcherra gas field, 8km from Srimangal on the road to Kamalganj. The gas field caught fire in 1997 and was ablaze for three months, laying waste to betel-nut plantations and tea estates in the vicinity.

There is a Monipuri village called **Ramnagar** close to the Bangladesh Tea Research Institute; if you call in on the institute you will be able to get directions.

## Telepara Forest Reserve

About 60km southwest of Srimangal on the Dhaka–Sylhet highway is the small **Telepara Forest Reserve**. This reserve has become less

> **WARNING**
>
> Foreigners are requested to inform the Forestry Department before entering the Lowacherra Forest Reserve, but there is rarely anyone checking that you've done so. The same is not true of Telepara Forest Reserve, where travellers have reported being turned away after the 60km journey there. Increased security is largely in response to government concern about the welfare of tourists. Details about the source of the threat are sketchy. Many locals warn of bandits operating in the forests, so it's best not to get too intrepid.

popular than the Lowacherra Forest Reserve because of the need to apply for permits a week in advance from Sylhet and the likelihood of being turned away without one. Similar to Lowacherra, this reserve provides a good habitat for a number of forest birds and small animals. If you do go, it's wise to stay on discernable paths.

The forest is on the south side of the main road, about 1km east of the Satcheri bus stop and Telepara Tea Estate, where the highway takes a sharp left (hairpin) bend. You could get the driver of the Dhaka–Sylhet bus to drop you here, if you don't mind missing the early hours when bird-watching is best. Alternatively, get a bus from Srimangal and walk to the trailhead 1km away. To return to Srimangal, flag down one of the Dhaka–Sylhet buses, or walk back to Telepara Tea Estate and catch one there.

# Directory

## CONTENTS

### PRACTICALITIES

- The *Daily Star*'s supplementary magazine on Fridays is a good source of information on what's going on in Dhaka.
- Almost every TV is satellite TV.
- Electricity (when there is electricity) is 220V, 50 Hz AC – two-pronged connection with round rather than flat holes.
- Officially Bangladesh is metric, but some local measures are still used. For instance, a *seer* equals 850g and a *maund* is 37kg. Yards are interchanged with metres and miles are often confused with kilometres.

## ACCOMMODATION

There are international-standard hotels in Dhaka, but most accommodation is well down the price scale.

Unmarried couples won't find things as difficult as in some Muslim countries, but some hotels, particularly in remote villages, are unwilling to condone unmarried couples sharing a room. Prices are often characterised as AC (air-conditioning) or non-AC, and the latter is often significantly cheaper. Outside of this major distinction, prices vary according to whether there is a TV and/or an attached bathroom. If you're trying to save taka, be sure to specify that you don't want these amenities.

### Government Rest Houses & Circuit Houses

There are government rest houses and circuit houses in every district. They aren't officially accessible to travellers but if there are rooms available and you come across with suitable poise and dignity, the district commissioner may let you stay. Your chances are greater if there are few alternative accommodation options around.

The Archaeology Department has rest houses at Paharpur, Mainimati and Mahasthan. They accept travellers if there's a room. The rooms are basic but cheap at typically Tk 200 for a double.

### Hotels

The word 'hotel' denotes a hotel or restaurant; the correct term for hotel is 'residential hotel'. Lower-end establishments often make this distinction on their signs, and you'll avoid confusion if you use this term when asking for directions.

Many hotels don't have English signs and some buildings look like hotels but aren't. You'll save yourself time and trouble if you learn to recognise the word 'hotel' in Bangla script.

Bottom-end accommodation usually consists of a tiny room with fan, shared bathroom and maybe mosquito nets. This typically costs around Tk 50/70 for a single/double. Apart from space and hygiene deficiencies, these places sometimes refuse to accept foreigners; you'll usually be told that there is no room. You could try hanging around the foyer for a while.

The biggest hassles with cheap hotels are the over-friendly room boys who constantly bang on your door offering mosquito spray or cha or something else, when all you want is privacy. A firm word with the manager may help.

Mid-range hotels are better value and there are an increasing number of them. Expect to pay around Tk 100/200 (or more in Dhaka) for a single/double with attached bathroom. For this you will usually get a small room with a reasonably soft bed, and a clean (though often wet) bathroom with a cold shower and squat toilet. Double this price will usually get you a larger room, softer beds and, if you're lucky, hot water.

Government-run Parjatan hotels are expensive by Bangladeshi standards (between Tk 500 and Tk 1200 per room) but are usually modern and have decent restaurants.

## ACTIVITIES
### Cycling
Bangladesh's lazy terrain makes it an ideal place for cycling. Even the slightly more hilly areas aren't arduous, they're just scenic. Good places for cycling include Srimangal (p151) in Sylhet division and Thakurgaon (p109) in Rajshahi division.

There are also some nice trips to do outside of Dhaka (p54). For information about cycling in general, see p171.

### Hiking
The best places to do some hiking are forest reserves and national parks. Some, like Telepara Forest (p153) and Lowacherra Forest (p152) in Sylhet, require special permits, though it is sometimes possible to sneak in without them. Do be mindful though of the dangers that such regulations are trying to guard against. Certainly don't go beating your own path or linger after dusk.

Unquestionably the best place for fully fledged hikes is the Chittagong Hill Tracts (p126). The Adivasis (tribal people) in this area are generally hospitable and the landscape in which they live is unforgettable. Again there are serious safety issues that must be considered (p127). Before embarking on an expedition, seek out the advice of

reputable travel advisories. You are unwise to trek in the Hill Tracts without a reputable guide.

### River Trips
Although river trips in Bangladesh are unavoidable if you're doing any sort of extensive travel, it's also worth putting in the effort to do a good one. There are some river trips you can do around Dhaka either independently or through an organised tour company. See p55 for details.

Try to tie a Rocket ride in with your travel plans. Once you have gone through the rigmarole of getting your ticket, the trip will be one of your most relaxing and interesting in Bangladesh. See p172 for more details.

## BUSINESS HOURS
Banking hours on Saturday to Wednesday are 9am to 3pm, and on Thursday 9am until 2pm. The official day off is Friday. Select ATMs, like those attached to Standard Chartered Bank or the less-common HSBC, are open 24 hours or at least very late.

Government offices are open Saturday to Thursday from 9am until 2pm. Private businesses generally operate between 9am and 4pm (closed Friday), while shops, including bazars, tend to vary from 9am or 10am to 8pm or 10pm. Some shops and bazars are open for half a day on Friday.

## CHILDREN
Children are an integral part of Bangladeshi life, and foreign children are especially fascinating. You may find yourself fending off would-be nannies who want to show their village to your child, or rather show your child to the village. On the other hand, you may find yourself happily taking advantage of the impromptu childcare service! Older children will find instant playmates wherever they go.

From a health standpoint, dishes of boiled rice and unspiced *dahl* (yellow lentils), scrambled or boiled eggs, oatmeal and a variety of fruits and vegetables should be enough to keep kids happy.

You'll be hard pressed coming across highchairs and nappy-changing facilities but formula and disposable nappies can be found at some supermarkets in towns and cities.

Lonely Planet's *Travel with Children* is a collection of experiences from travelling families, and includes practical advice on how to avoid hassles and have a fun travel experience with kids.

## CLIMATE CHARTS

The climate in Bangladesh is dramatic to say the least. It is subtropical and tropical with temperatures ranging from as low as 3°C overnight in the cold season to a daytime top of 40°C in the hot season. Annual rainfall varies from 1000mm in the west to 2500mm in the southeast, and up to 5000mm in the north, near the hills of Assam.

Three-quarters of the annual rainfall occurs between June and September. The 90% to 95% humidity in this season is almost unbearable.

In the cold season the weather is drier and fresh, with average daytime temperatures of 21°C. Rainfall is negligible, although

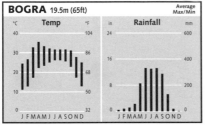

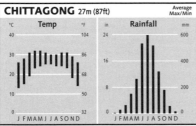

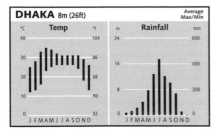

even in winter a brief thunder shower may come along.

While early March can still be pleasant, by April, as the monsoon approaches, humidity increases and lethal hailstorms aren't uncommon. The monsoonal season usually starts between late May and mid-June. It doesn't rain solidly all day – there tends to be an initial downpour, followed by clear skies.

See also When to Go (p9).

## COURSES

The best place for learning Bangla is **HEED** (Health, Education, Economic Development; Map pp60-1; ☎ 881 2390, 989 6028; hlc@agni.com; House 104, Rd 12, Block E, Banani, Dhaka). The centre, which teaches both spoken and written Bangla, is open from Sunday to Thursday from 8am to 4pm. Group classes run for two hours and cost Tk 5500 per month. Private classes cost Tk 300 per hour. There is also a Tk 1000 registration fee.

HEED also has a guesthouse on its premises. A standard single/double room costs Tk 400/600, or more with AC.

The **Effective Bangla Learning Centre** (EBLC; Map pp60-1; ☎ 245 193; House 16A, Rd 25A, Banani, Dhaka) has also been recommended.

## CUSTOMS

The usual '200 cigarettes, 1L of alcohol' rule applies, though a relatively casual approach is employed at border crossings. Foreigners are permitted to bring in US$5000 without declaring it and Bangladeshis can bring in US$2500.

On departure tourists are allowed to reconvert 25% of the total foreign currency encashed in the country. This is only possible at the airport in Dhaka, and you will need to have your encashment slips with you as proof.

## DANGERS & ANNOYANCES

By and large Bangladesh is overwhelmingly friendly and hospitable. The biggest annoyance you will probably have to face is unabating friendliness – interested crowds are everywhere and questions about your nationality, religion and marital status never cease.

Having said that, there are some very rare but very real dangers in Bangladesh; foreigners have been robbed, raped and kidnapped.

Pickpocketing on crowded buses is not as endemic as in some other Asian countries, but dacoity (armed robbery) on buses, particularly at night, is on the increase – crude weapons such as knives, acid bulbs and home-made shotguns are popular. You're in more danger from bag-snatching, although even this isn't particularly common.

We have had reports of harassment of foreigners in the form of pushing, stone throwing and spitting. Such incidents are rare, but seem to relate to the global political climate. American travellers have reported no particular hostility.

There are also ripples of terrorist activity, targeted assassinations, politically motivated attacks and, sometimes, violent religious rivalry. In December of 2002, bombs exploded in four movie theatres in Mymensingh. A similar attack occurred in September 2002 in the town of Satkira. Foreigners have never been targeted in these incidents, but many travel advisories warn foreign nationals to stay away from large gatherings to cut down on the 'wrong-place, wrong-time' possibility.

Hartals (strikes) can also turn violent, and many people have been killed or seriously injured as a result. The National Day of Mourning (21 February) is a potentially chaotic day (see p160).

The Sundarbans has its own set of problems with banditry (p89), and the Chittagong Hill Tracts is especially volatile (p127). Both areas are worth putting in the time and effort to assess the situation before heading off.

You should keep yourself informed as to what's going on in the country by regularly consulting travel advisories and newspapers.

Also see Dangers & Annoyances in the Dhaka chapter (p46).

### Scams

Tourism has not really established itself in Bangladesh, and nor have tourist-related scams. It is actually difficult not to become overly complacent in the face of daily kindnesses. However, as with anywhere in the world, not everyone is a good guy.

The most common scam you will encounter is short-changing for small transactions. The best guard against this is vigilance when you're receiving change, or a polite query about unlikely restaurant bills. A similar scam is bus boys conveniently 'forgetting' to give you your change,

even though they have a fistful of taka. Nine times out of 10 you're more likely to be chased because *you've* forgotten, but keep it at the back of your mind.

Some travellers have reported being approached by dubious charities, initially appearing legitimate. Some professional beggars wave fraudulent or at least out-of-date pharmaceutical prescriptions asking for assistance in purchasing medicine for children.

Finally, there are the usual hassles with rickshaw, baby taxi (mini three-wheeled auto-rickshaws) and taxi drivers. Rickshaw-wallahs may take you on a sightseeing tour rather than to your desired destination, and baby-taxi and standard-taxi drivers may say that the meter doesn't work, or take you on the long route because it does. Before you climb into a taxi, always ask whether the meter 'works' – and try elsewhere if it doesn't. However, often it isn't equitable to use the meter where distances are short but time-consuming, so it may be fair to negotiate a reasonable price before you start out.

## DISABLED TRAVELLERS

Putting it bluntly, disabled travellers will struggle in Bangladesh. Some footpaths are difficult for even the able-bodied to traverse. In fact, with its squat toilets, over-crowded buses and absence of elevators in all but the finest of buildings in Dhaka, it would seem that the country has contrived to keep out all but the most fit and able.

On the other hand, hiring help to check out accessible hotels and restaurants, toilets and other facilities and to help you get around is going to be quite cheap. Also, Bangladeshis are good at coming to the aid of foreigners before they are even asked.

Several organisations offer general advice on travel for disabled people, though none have specific information on Bangladesh. They include the following:

**Holiday Care Service** ( ☎ 0129-377 4535; www .holidaycare.org.uk; 2nd fl, Imperial Buildings, Victoria Rd, Horley, Surrey RH6 7PZ, UK)

**Mobility International USA** ( ☎ 541-343 1284; www .miusa.org; PO Box 10767, Eugene, Oregon, 97440, USA)

## EMBASSIES & CONSULATES
### Bangladeshi Embassies & Consulates

**Australia** Canberra ( ☎ 02-6290 0511/22/33; www.users .cyberone.com.au/bdeshact; 21 Culgoa Circuit, O'Malley ACT 2606)

**Belgium** Brussels ( ☎ 02-640 5500; fax 02-646 5998; 29-31 Rue Jacques Jordaens 1000)

**Bhutan** Thimphu ( ☎ 02-322539; fax 02-322629; Plot No HIG-3, Upper Chubachu)

**Brazil** Brasilía DF ( ☎ 61-248 4830; fax 61-248 4609; SHIS, QL-7, Conj 01, Casa 17, 70468 900)

**Canada** Ottawa ( ☎ 613-236 0138; www.iosphere .net/~bhc; Ste 302, 275 Bank St, Ontario K2P 2L6)

**China** Beijing ( ☎ 10-4651 9033; fax 10-6532 4346; 42 Guang Hua Lu, 100600)

**France** Paris ( ☎ 01 46 51 90 33; fax 01 46 51 90 25; 39 Rue Erlanger, 75016)

**Germany** Berlin ( ☎ 30-3989 750; fax 30 3989 7510; Dovestrasse 1, 10587)

**Hong Kong** Wanchai ( ☎ 2827 4278/9; fax 2827 1916; Room 3807, China Resources Bldg, 26 Harbour Rd)

**India** Agartala ( ☎ 22-4807; fax 22-4807; Colonel Chowmuhoni, West Tripura, 799001); Kolkata ( ☎ 33-347 5208/9; fax 33-247 0941; 9 Bangabandhu Sheikh Mujib Sarani, 700017); New Delhi ( ☎ 11-683 4668; fax 11-684 0596; 56 Ring Rd, Lajpat Nagar III, 110024)

**Indonesia** Jakarta ( ☎ 21-525 1986; fax 21-526 1807; Jalan Denpasar Raya No 3, Block A,13 KAV 10, Kuningan)

**Italy** Rome ( ☎ 06-808 3595; fax 06-808 4853; Via Antonio Bertoloni 14, 00197)

**Japan** Tokyo ( ☎ 03-5704 0216-8; fax 03-5704 1696; 4-15-15 Meguro, Meguro-ku, 153-0063)

**Malaysia** Kuala Lumpur ( ☎ 03-2148 7940; fax 03-2141 3381; Block 1, Lorong Damai 7, Jalan Damai, 55000)

**Myanmar (Burma)** Sittwe ( ☎ 043-23968; 56 Main Rd, South Lanmadaw); Yangon ( ☎ 01-515275, 526144; fax 01-515273; 11/B Than Lwin Rd)

**Nepal** Kathmandu ( ☎ 01-372 843; fax 01-373 265; Maharajganj, Chakrapath (Ring Rd), Narayan Gopal Chowk)

**Netherlands** The Hague ( ☎ 70-328 37 22; fax 70-328 35 24; Wassenaarseweg 39, 2596 CG)

**Pakistan** Islamabad ( ☎ 051-2279267; fax 051-2279266; House No 1, St No 5, F-6/3); Karachi ( ☎ 21-5855238; fax 21-2414322; House No 31/3, St No 27, Phase V, Defence Housing Authority)

**Philippines** Manila ( ☎ 02-817 5001; fax 02-816 4941; 2nd fl, Universal Re Bldg, 106 Paseo De Roxas, Makati, Metro)

**Republic of Korea** Seoul ( ☎ 2-796 4056/7; fax 2-790 5313; 1-67, 1-92 Dongbinggo-dong, Yongsan-KU, 140-230)

**Russia** Moscow ( ☎ 95-246 7900; fax 95-248 3185; Zemledelcheski Pereulok 6, 119121)

**Singapore** Singapore ( ☎ 65-6255 0075; fax 65-6255 1824; 05-04 United Sq, 101 Thompson Rd, 307591)

**South Africa** Pretoria ( ☎ 27-12 343 2105-7; fax 27-12 343 5222; 410 Farenden St, Sunnyside, 0002)

**Sri Lanka** Colombo 7 ( ☎ 00941-681310-2; fax 00941-681309; 47 Sir Ernest De Silva Mawatha)

**Sweden** Stockholm ( ☎ 08-679 9555; fax 08-611 9817; 1st fl, Anderstorpvagen 12, 17154 Solna)

**Switzerland** Geneva ( ☎ 22-449 340; 7 Rue Henry Veyrassat, 1202)

**Thailand** Bangkok ( ☎ 02 392 9437/8; fax 02 391 8070; House No 727, Thonglor, Soi-55, Sukhumvit Rd, 10110)

**United Kingdom** Birmingham ( ☎ 0121-643 2386; fax 0121-643 9004; 31-33 Guildhall Bldg 12, Navigation St, B2 4BT); London ( ☎ 0171-584 0081, fax 0171-225 2130; 28 Queen's Gate, SW7 5JA); Manchester ( ☎ 0161-236 4853; fax 0161-236 1064; 28-32 Princess St, M1 4LB)

**USA** Los Angeles ( ☎ 323-932 0100; fax 323-932 9703; 4201 Wilshire Blvd, Ste 605, 90010); New York ( ☎ 212-599 6767; fax 212-682 9211; 211 E 43rd St, Ste 502, 10017); Washington DC ( ☎ 202-244 0183; fax 202-244 5366; 3510 International Dr NW, 20008)

## Embassies & Consulates in Bangladesh

If you are going to spend a considerable length of time in a remote area, it is a good idea to register with your embassy.

**Australia** (Map pp60-1; ☎ 881 3101-5; fax 811 125; 184 Gulshan Ave, Gulshan II)

**Bhutan** (Map pp60-1; ☎ 882 6863; fax 882 3939; House 12, Rd 107, Gulshan II)

**Canada** (Map pp60-1; ☎ 988 7091-7; fax 882 3043; House 16/A, Rd 48, Gulshan II)

**China** (Map pp60-1; ☎ 882 4862; fax 882 3004; House 2 & 4, Rd 3, Block 1, Baridhara)

**Denmark** (Map pp60-1; ☎ 882 1799; fax 882 3638; House 1, Rd 51, Gulshan)

**France** (Map pp60-1; ☎ 881 3811-4; fax 882 3612; House 18, Rd 108, Gulshan)

**Germany** (Map pp60-1; ☎ 882 4735-7; fax 882 3141; 178 Gulshan Ave, Gulshan II)

**India** (Map pp60-1; ☎ 988 9339; fax 881 7487; House 2, Rd 142, Gulshan I)

**Italy** (Map pp60-1; ☎ 882 2781-3; fax 882 2578; Plot 2/3, cnr Rds 74 & 79, Gulshan II)

**Japan** (Map pp60-1; ☎ 881 0087; fax 882 6737; Plot 5 & 7, Dutabash Rd, Baridhara)

**Malaysia** (Map pp60-1; ☎ 882 7759-60; fax 882 3115; Plot 1, United Nations Rd, Baridhara)

**Myanmar (Burma)** (Map pp60-1; ☎ 989 6373; fax 882 3740; House 3, Rd 84, Gulshan II)

**Nepal** (Map pp60-1; ☎ 989 2490; fax 882 6401; cnr United Nations Rd & Rd 2, Baridhara)

**Netherlands** (Map pp60-1; ☎ 882 2715-8; fax 882 3362; House 49, Rd 90, Gulshan II)

**Norway** (Map pp60-1; ☎ 882 3065; fax 882 3661; House 9, Rd 111, Gulshan)

**Pakistan** (Map pp60-1; ☎ 882 5387-9; fax 882 3677; House 2, Rd 71, Gulshan)

**Russia** (Map pp60-1; ☎ 882 8147; fax 882 3735; House 9, Rd 79, Gulshan)

**Sweden** (Map pp60-1; ☎ 882 4761-4; fax 882 398; House 1, Rd 51, Gulshan II)

Switzerland (Map pp60-1; ☎ 881 2874-6; fax 882 3588; House 31/B, Rd 18, Banani)
Thailand (Map pp60-1; ☎ 881 2795-6; fax 882 3588; House 4, cnr Rds 58 & 62, Gulshan II)
UK (Map pp60-1; ☎ 882 2705-9; fax 882 3437; 13 United Nations Rd at Dutabash Rd, Baridhara)
US (Map pp60-1; ☎ 882 4700-22; fax 882 3744; Madani Ave, Baridhara)

## FESTIVALS & EVENTS

A festival in Bangladesh is usually called a mela. Melas are generally times when all religions – Muslims, Hindus, Buddhists and Christians – join in the celebrations. Festivals may be related to harvests and other religious rites and ceremonies of the Hindus and Buddhists. Minor melas are mainly related to weddings, exhibition fairs or even election victories.

### Islamic Festivals

Muslim holidays, known as Eids, follow a lunar calendar. The dates depend on the phases of the moon, and fall about 11 days earlier each successive year. Along with public holidays, these special events are observed nationally, with government offices, banks and most businesses closing.

#### January–March

**Eid-ul-Azha** Known as the Eid of Sacrifice or, informally, Bloody Eid, this two-day festival falls 69 days after Eid-ul-Fitr. It remembers Abraham's sacrifice of his son Ishmael, celebrated with the slaughter of a cow, sheep or goat. After the morning prayers the head of the family takes the animal out to the entrance of the house, faces it toward Mecca and kills it with a quick slash of the throat. The meat is divided among the poor, friends and family. During the week preceding the festival, open-air fairs do a brisk trade in cattle and goats. The animals are brightly adorned with ribbons, garlands and tassels. This festival also marks the beginning of the hajj (pilgrimage) to Mecca.

**Ashura** The Ashura festival (also called Muharram) takes place in the Muslim month of Muharram. It commemorates the martyrdom of Hussain, grandson of the prophet Mohammed, on the battlefield of Kerbala in modern-day Iraq in the Christian year 680.

#### April–June

**Eid-e-Miladunnabi** Birth of the Prophet Mohammed.

#### September–November

**Shab-e-Barat** This holiday marks the sighting of the full moon 14 days before the start of Ramadan. The night of barat (record), according to Mohammed, is the time that God registers all the actions men are to perform in the ensuing year. It is a sacred night when alms and sweets are distributed to the poor.

**Jamat-ul-Wida** Start of the month of Ramadan and the fasting period.

**Ramadan** Referred to as Ramzan in Bangladesh. Fasting, the third pillar of Islam, incurs merit whenever observed, but is an absolute duty during Ramzan. For the entire month, between sunrise and sunset, abstinence from food, liquids (including swallowing one's own saliva), smoking, impure thoughts and physical pleasures is obligatory. Fasting begins at dawn and is broken when the evening call to prayer is heard. The *iftar* (meal) taken when the fast is broken includes samosa (a pastry triangle stuffed with spiced vegetables or minced meat), *shingara* (similar to samosa but round and with a heavier filling), *piaju* (deep-fried lentil-and-onion balls), *beguni* (eggplant fritters made with chickpea flour), *alur chop* (fried potato cutlet), various kebabs, and *moori* (aniseed) and *cheera* (flattened rice) preparations. For many reasons, extreme poverty being the best one, many Bangladeshis do not fast during Ramzan. Snack shops in the larger cities will stay open during the day, but put up curtains so diners have a little anonymity. In smaller villages it may be more difficult to find a meal during the day. Plan accordingly.

#### November–December

**Eid-ul-Fitr** One of the two major Muslim holidays, it celebrates the end of Ramzan with the sighting of the new moon. It's a holiday as important to Muslims as Christmas is to many Westerners. The festival is characterised by alms-giving and prayer, feasting, merriment and gifts. Eid Mubarrak or Happy Eid are the common greetings.

### Hindu Festivals

Hindu holidays follow a different calendar but they generally fall at much the same date each year. They usually mark the changing of the seasons.

#### January–February

**Saraswati Puja** Towards the end of January clay statues of Brahma's consort Saraswati are made in preparation for this ceremony, held around the beginning of February. The goddess of knowledge is always depicted playing a *veena* (an Indian stringed instrument) and accompanied by a swan, but outside these limitations there's a lot of variety.

#### February–March

**Holi** The Festival of Colours is celebrated in late February/early March. Commonly known as the spring festival, it is celebrated, less so here than in other countries, with the throwing of coloured water and powders and the consumption of foodstuffs containing bhang (powdered marijuana).

**June–July**
**Rath Jatra** This festival celebrates Jagannath, the lord of the world and a form of Krishna, along with his brother and sister. These three images are set upon a Jagannath (chariot) and pulled through the streets by devotees. The 7m chariot in Dhamrai, 32km northwest of Dhaka, is typical.

**October**
**Durga Puja** The most important Hindu festival celebrated in Bangladesh. Statues of the goddess Durga astride a lion, with her 10 hands holding 10 different weapons, are placed in every Hindu temple. Celebrations last for four days, culminating on the day of the full moon when the statue is carried into the water after sunset. A huge festival takes place along the Buriganga in Dhaka (see also p56).

## GAY & LESBIAN TRAVELLERS

There is a high degree of sexual repression (and frustration) in Bangladesh. Authorities generally deny the existence of homosexuality; you may even hear suggestions that gays in Bangladesh are a product of Western cultural pollution. The criminal code left by the Raj punishes male homosexual acts with deportation, fines and/or prison, but these laws are hardly ever used. Lesbianism is studiously denied by the legal system.

Unofficially, many believe homosexuality is quite prevalent. Bangladeshi society can be privately tolerant towards homosexuality among young men, but only if it is a 'phase' that doesn't interfere with marriage prospects. Lesbians have to stay even deeper in the closet.

The great irony is that in a country where it is largely inappropriate for men and women to shake hands, it is socially acceptable for two men to hold hands. Such public displays of affection between men are common, but don't signify a nonplatonic relationship.

Gay travellers are wise to be discreet in Bangladesh. The upside is that you will be spared the hassles that many unmarried heterosexual couples have in checking into hotels, given the assumption that you are just friends.

## HOLIDAYS
### Public Holidays

The following holidays are observed nationally, and government offices, banks and most businesses are closed.
**Amar Ekushe** (Shaheed Day; National Day of Mourning) 21 February. This holiday is a tribute to the students who successfully opposed the government's attempts to deny Bangla the status of state language. On 21 February 1952 several students from the Language Movement were killed, and subsequently given martyr status. This day celebrates a crucial event on the path to independence but also legitimises student protest, and all the rival factions attempt to claim the mantle of saviours of the country.
**Birthday of the Father of the Nation** (Sheikh Mujibur Rahman's birthday) 17 March
**Independence Day** 26 March
**Pohela Boisakh** (Bangladeshi New Year) 14 April
**May Day** 1 May
**Bank Holiday** 30 June
**National Mourning Day** (Anniversary of the death of Sheikh Mujibur Rahman) 15 August
**National Revolution Day** 7 November
**Biganj Dibash** (Victory Day) 16 December
**Christmas Day** 25 December. Known as Bara Din (Big Day), churches are adorned with lights and some churches hold cultural evenings with dances and prayers.
**Bank Holiday** 31 December

## INSURANCE

Any policy you get should cover medical expenses and an emergency flight home. Always check the fine print. Some policies exclude coverage of 'dangerous activities', which can include motorcycling and trekking.

For theft and loss you will require documentation from the Bangladeshi police; getting it can be a hassle, often requires a 'fee' and even then your insurance company may not honour it.

See also p179 for health insurance details.

## INTERNET ACCESS

Many top-end hotels provide universal power adaptors in rooms, but outside of those rare cases you'll need to bring your own. If you are travelling with a laptop or some other electronic device, remember to bring a 220V, 50 Hz AC adaptor. If you forget to bring one, you may be able to track one down in Dhaka. The Stadium Market would be a good bet.

Any connection you can get in a hotel room won't be reliable, and it certainly won't be cheap. Thankfully Internet cafés are popping up everywhere in Bangladesh – even small towns are getting tech savvy. They are usually cheap and open till quite late. The cheapest price is around Tk 20 per hour; the average is Tk 30.

## LEGAL MATTERS

Drug offences are taken seriously in Bangladesh and can result in the death penalty if considerable quantities are seized. Anyone, including foreigners, caught smuggling virtually any amount of drugs or gold often ends up with a prison sentence for life. As a matter of practice, courts permit those charged to have access to a lawyer.

Under the Vienna Convention on Consular Relations, to which Bangladesh is a signatory, any foreign national under detention has a right to request that their embassy be notified of their situation.

## MAPS

The best two map publishers are **Graphosman** (Map pp52-4; ☎ 955 2394; graphos@bangla .net; 1st fl, Karim Mansion, 3/3C Purana Pultan) and **Mappa** (Map pp52-4; ☎ 881 6710; www.themappa .com; 112 Green Rd, Farmgate). These two publishers produce numerous English-language maps, which are updated regularly. All are available at bookshops and New Market (Map pp52–4), and on occasion from street vendors.

The Parjatan Corporation also produces a Dhaka city map and a Bangladesh map. Though not as detailed as the professionally produced maps, they can be useful references. These are available at the **Parjatan Tourist Office** (Map pp52-4; ☎ 811 7855-9; 233 Airport Rd) and occasionally at Parjatan Hotels.

## MONEY

The local currency of Bangladesh is the taka (Tk; rhymes with Dhaka), which is further divided into 100 paisas. There are 10, 20 and 50 paisa, and Tk 1, Tk 2 and Tk 5 coins. There are notes in denominations of Tk 1, Tk 2, Tk 5, Tk 10, Tk 20, Tk 50, Tk 100 and Tk 500.

Torn notes may refused by merchants. Most banks will exchange them for you.

For information on costs see p10, and on exchange rates see Quick Reference on the inside front cover.

### ATMs

Major towns and cities have ATMs, and there appear to be more on the way. The most common is Standard Chartered Bank, which has extremely reliable ATMs, usually an open-all-hours guarded booth that accepts all cards. Less common but just as reliable are HSBC ATMs, although these only accept Visa and Plus cards; they do not accept Cirrus cards.

## Cash

It is a good idea to bring US dollars with you to change into local currency when you can't change travellers cheques or use a credit card. US dollars are the preferred currency, with British pounds running a very distant second. American Express, Standard Chartered Bank and HSBC have branches in Dhaka and Chittagong. The Standard Chartered empire is expanding to cities like Khulna, Sylhet and even Bogra. The government-owned Sonali and Janata banks usually change money, although some rural branches won't. Uttara, Agrani and Pubali will often change money; other private commercial banks include Al Bar aka Bank, Arab Bangladesh Bank, National Bank and the City Bank.

At some banks you may have to show your passport even when changing cash.

### Credit Cards

Visa, MasterCard and American Express are usually accepted by major hotels and restaurants in Dhaka and Chittagong.

American Express cardholders can obtain cash or travellers cheques with their cards. Cash advances on credit cards can be made at Standard Chartered and HSBC banks. HSBC ATMs do not accept Cirrus cards.

### Moneychangers

There are an obscene number of authorised moneychangers that legally convert cash on the spot at good rates. They're open all hours and can convert taka into US dollars as well. If it looks like a well-run establishment, chances are it is.

With the liberalisation of the economy, there is essentially no black market.

### Tipping

Baksheesh (*bohk*-sheesh), in the sense of a tip or gift rather than a bribe (an admittedly fine line), is part of life in Bangladesh. Don't see it as begging; it's part of Islamic morality that rich people give part of their income to those less fortunate. There are some peculiarities to this system though; if you're going to be repeatedly using a service, an initial tip ensures that decent standards will be kept up.

Don't feel persecuted – well-to-do locals also have to pay baksheesh. Always be conscious of the expectations that will be placed on the next foreigner in light of the amount you give and don't feel embarrassed about not giving baksheesh to someone who rendered absolutely no service at all.

In expensive restaurants in Dhaka that are mostly frequented by foreigners, waiters often expect a small tip, typically about 5%.

### Travellers Cheques

Standard Chartered Bank is the best place to change travellers cheques. Other banks may do it, but at a higher commission. You will need to show your passport when changing travellers cheques, and some banks may even require a receipt showing proof of purchase.

### POST

Bangladesh's postal system works well. You may be sceptical when you're watching an old man weigh your letter on a set of scales that should be in an antique shop, but rest assured it will get sent and arrive in around 10 to 15 days.

If you've overdone the shopping, consider mailing stuff home to yourself – it's amazingly cheap. Sending 10kg by sea costs around Tk 300 and will take two or three months. Sending 10kg by air will cost around Tk 1000 and take 15 days.

Receiving mail can be more frustrating. The poste restante service in Dhaka is at the **main post office** (Map pp52–4). If your stuff isn't in the box that you are given to riffle through, ask to see the 'other box'. For more information, see p45.

### SHOPPING

You don't get hassled to buy things here, mainly because there isn't very much produced with the tourist market in mind. Even quality postcards are hard to come by.

Things not to buy are products made from wild animals and reptiles, all of which are under pressure to survive in this crowded country. Even if a leopard skin for sale really is 20 years old, how do you think the stock will be replenished if you buy it? There is also trade in the country's artistic treasures, which are often plundered from Hindu temples.

### Handicrafts

Souvenirs include jewellery, garments, brasswork, leatherwork, ceramics, jute products, artwork, woodcarvings and clay or metal sculptural work. Unique items include pink pearls, fine *jamdani* (loom-embroidered muslin or silk) saris, jute doormats, wall pieces, glass bangles, seashells, conch shell bangles and reed mats. Quality is generally high and the prices generally low.

Jute carpets, if you have the room, are a real deal. The better ones look exactly like and feel similar to Oriental wool carpets. They don't last as long as the real thing, but a 2m-by-3m (6ft-by-9ft) jute carpet costing US$50 will last five or more years.

The chain of Aarong shops has a range of high-quality goods, although the fixed prices are higher than what could be bargained for in markets.

### Clothing

You may decide to replace everything in your backpack. The Bangladeshi garment industry is one of the biggest producers of Western clothing, and you can buy seconds and overruns at the enormous Banga Bazar (Map p47), sometimes referred to as Gulistan Hawker's Market. There's also a good range at New Market (Map pp52–4). Clothing ranges from Calvin Klein jeans to baby rompers. See p63 for more information.

### Rickshaw Art

One distinctly Bangladeshi souvenir is a piece of authentic rickshaw art. It's lightweight and easy to pack in the flat of your bag or backpack. Rickshaw art is not a tourist industry, so you'll have to shop where the rickshaw-wallahs shop. The few centrally located shops are on Bicycle St in Dhaka, a local name for the area where most bicycle parts and a few whole bicycles are sold. See p50 for details. Quality varies among shops, but expect to pay Tk 50/100 for a tin/vinyl piece. You could also splash out and get some personalised rickshaw art (see p64).

### SOLO TRAVELLERS

Those who are travelling alone on the assumption that they will meet other travellers on the road should think again. You may, but you'll probably be able to count them on one hand. To increase your chances, you could sign up for a language course, join a short tour to suss out candidates or ask around at embassy clubs.

Travelling alone through Bangladesh can be a rewarding experience, and won't cost you much more money than travelling with company – basic single rooms are often less than half the cost of a double. Then again it may be worthwhile splashing out on a cabin or sleeper on a boat or train for peace of mind. On your own you will have to stay particularly alert, and exercise a greater degree of caution with regards to where you go and when.

## TELEPHONE

Though there are a surprising number of mobile phones floating around Bangladesh, some towns still don't have land lines. Don't expect that every hotel and restaurant will have a phone number.

International calls are easy to make. Many phones have direct-dial service via satellite. Rates are 25% lower all day Friday and on other days from 11pm to 8am. Local calls present no problems, but between cities it is often difficult to hear the other end. The only way to make a 'public' phone call is to use the telephone and fax services available at numerous small business centres. Charges are roughly Tk 120/130/140 per minute to Australia/Europe/America, ie roughly double the actual rate. Major hotels charge two or three times as much. The numbers for long-distance information are ☎ 103 (domestic) and ☎ 162 (international). International operators speak English; others usually don't.

### Mobile Phones

Some mobile phones can only be called from other mobile phones. Business centres cater for this.

To call a country outside of Bangladesh using a mobile phone, press the key for international dialling (+), followed by the country code, the city code and then the number.

To call a mobile phone in Bangladesh from outside the country, dial country code ☎ 880, followed by the mobile number without the leading 0.

Some service providers have global roaming facilities, usually for hefty fees. You may want to inquire about this at home if you are thinking of bringing your mobile.

### Phone Codes

To call a number in Bangladesh from outside the country, dial country code ☎ 880, followed by the city or cell code without the leading 0, and then the number.

To call another country from Bangladesh, dial ☎ 00 followed by the country code and city code.

To call a different city from within Bangladesh, dial the city code (Nation Wide Dialling) including the leading zero, followed by the number.

City codes can be found in phone books, and, for major cities, in this guide under the city headings in each regional chapter.

### Phonecards

There is an increasing number of phonecards appearing on the market, which can be bought at some small business centres and phone shops in large cities. Shop around for the best deal for the country you'll be calling most.

## TIME

Bangladesh has one time zone: an hour behind Thailand, half an hour ahead of India, six hours ahead of GMT, 10 hours ahead of New York (11 during daylight savings time), four hours behind EST in Australia and five hours ahead of France.

## TOILETS

In mid-range and top-end establishments you'll find sit-down toilets that flush, but most toilets are mildly malodorous squat types. Sit-down toilets are sometimes described as 'high commode' and squat toilets as 'Indian style'.

The ritual in squat toilets is to use your left hand and water. A strategically placed tap and jug is usually at hand. If you can't master the local method or don't even want to try, toilet paper is widely available. Sometimes a basket is provided where paper and tampons can be discarded.

Some women report that when trying to use toilets in cheap restaurants, they've been told the facilities are unsuitable. Polite protestations that they're more suitable than the floor may help.

There are very few facilities at bus stations and other public places, and what facilities there are, are pretty horrific. It pays to do your thing back at your hotel. By and large you will find that Bangladeshi hospitality extends to letting you use a toilet, if you ask nicely enough, or you could simply buy a drink at a nice hotel for an excuse to sit down (pun absolutely intended).

In rural areas it can be difficult to find both toilets and privacy. For women in a desperate situation, a long skirt will make this awkward position a little less so.

## TOURIST INFORMATION

The national tourist office is the Bangladesh Parjatan Corporation. It has more of a presence in terms of nationwide hotels than nationwide information. It also theoretically runs tours, but private-sector operators have eclipsed its tour service. Outside of the **Parjatan main office** (Map pp52-4; ☎ 811 7855-9; www.bangladeshtourism.org; 233 Airport Rd, Tejgaon), information counters at hotels have little to offer but brochures, though they are often the nicest place to stay in town.

Parjatan hotels can be found in Benapole, Bogra, Chittagong, Cox's Bazar, Dhaka, Dinajpur, Kuakata, Madhabkunda, Mongla, Rangamati, Rangpur, Rajshahi, Sylhet, Teknaf and Tungipara.

The Parjatan website is also extremely good. For other useful tourist-oriented Internet resources see p10.

## VISAS

With some obscure exceptions, visas are required for citizens of all countries.

Airport visas (landing permits) are no longer available upon arrival by air, though this situation seems to change periodically. If entering by land, a 15-day visa is usually issued.

Visas valid for six months from the date of issue, and good for stays of three months, are the norm. If you don't request a three-month visa, you may end up with a visa valid for only one month. Visa fees vary according to nationality and whether you are seeking single or multiple entry. Requests for visas for stays longer than three months are usually denied. See p157 for a list of embassies and consulates.

If you decide to extend your stay, extensions can be obtained, though this requires tangling with Bangladeshi bureaucracy.

### Visa Extensions & Change of Route Permits

To apply for visa extensions and change of route permits you will need to visit the **Immigration and Passport Office** (Map pp52-4; ☎ 889 750; Agargaon Rd; ☺ Sat-Thu), near the National Assembly Building in Dhaka. This is also the office where long-term visitors are required to register.

Travellers have reported poor service and misinformation at this office. You will need to be both persistent and patient.

If you overstay your visa, you will be fined for each extra day. In some cases travellers have been charged even more, given no receipt and the extra charge has not been explained.

Extensions up to a total stay of three months are generally easy to obtain. If you've been in Bangladesh for three months and wish to extend beyond that, the process can take up to a week or more, and there is no assurance that you'll receive an extension. The more convincing your reasons for wanting an extension, the better your chances of getting one.

Processing of requests to stay longer than three months is notoriously inefficient, so start the process early – at least a week before the expiration date, if you've already been there three months.

If you exit Bangladesh by means other than that by which you entered (ie you flew in but are leaving by land), you will need a change of route permit, also sometimes referred to as a road permit. Change of route permits shouldn't take more than 24 hours, but sometimes take up to 72 so start the process early. The permit is free. You will need a couple of passport photos.

## WOMEN TRAVELLERS

Bangladeshi opinions about Western women are still being formed. By and large the default response to the bewildering sight of you is respect, so don't do anything that would make you less than worthy of it. Bangladesh is safer than a lot of Muslim countries, but it's wise to be careful. How you carry yourself subtly determines how you are treated. Women who are tentative, appear unsure or seem to be helpless are potential targets for harassment. A woman who is politely assertive can ask for space and usually gets it. The other side of the harassment coin, and almost as much of a nuisance, is that people are constantly making elaborate arrangements to protect you from harassment.

Dressing like a local is not obligatory but it will certainly impact on the way you are treated. You will still get attention, but the attention you get will be more respectful and appreciative of the fact that you have gone to the effort. Invest in a *salwar kameez* (a long dress-like tunic worn over baggy trousers). A dupatta (long scarf) to cover your head increases the appearance of modesty and is a handy accessory. You can get away with wearing baggy trousers and a long loose-fitting shirt in most parts of the country. Long, loose skirts are also acceptable and provide the added advantage of a modicum of privacy in the absence of a public toilet. Make sure you wear a headscarf at places of worship. Most mosques don't allow women inside, although some have a special women's gallery. If in doubt, ask.

Keep in mind that in this society, women are not touched by men, but because you're a foreigner, it might happen. A clear yet tactful objection should end the matter.

Tampons are available from some upmarket supermarkets (like Agora) for around Tk 60 a packet. Sanitary napkins and panty liners are widely available, but you might want to bring your favourite products with you. Be sure to carry adequate supplies if you're travelling away from major cities.

A good place to take a breather from the patriarchal streets is Adda, an informal space for women to eat and chat, at Narigrantha Prabartana, the feminist bookshop run by Unnayan Bikalper Nitinirdharoni Gobeshona (UBINIG; Policy Research for Development Alternatives) in Dhaka. Men are welcome, so long as they are accompanied by a woman. See p44 for further details.

## Eating

In a Bangladeshi middle-class home you would most likely be expected to eat first with the men while the women of the household tuck themselves away in another part of the house or dutifully serve the meal. In rural areas you might not eat with either, but be served first, and separately, as a gesture of respect. Accept either graciously. Protest would cause great embarrassment on the part of your host.

In restaurants you may be shown to the curtained women's rooms. This is a courteous offer that you can decline, though you may find that the curtain provides something of a respite from the eyes that will be on you if you sit elsewhere.

## Getting Around

On buses, unaccompanied women are expected to sit at the front. If you are travelling with 'your husband' you are expected to sit on the window side away from the aisle. Avoid travelling alone at night; Bangladeshi women avoid going out alone at night as much as possible.

## Sleeping

Women, with or without men, are sometimes unwelcome in budget hotels, usually because the manager thinks the hotel is not suitable. This knee-jerk reaction can sometimes be overcome if you hang around long enough. On the other hand, staying in one of these cheaper establishments, especially if you are going solo, can be more trouble than it is worth. Mid-range hotels that are accustomed to foreigners are the best bet. Unmarried couples are better off simply saying they're married.

# Transport

## CONTENTS

# GETTING THERE & AWAY

## ENTERING THE COUNTRY

To enter Bangladesh you will need a passport that's valid for at least six months beyond the duration of your stay, an onward/return ticket and a visa.

Rules and procedures for entering and exiting Bangladesh seem to be in a constant state of flux. At the time of writing it was not possible to get an airport visa (landing permit) on arrival. There have been reports of people being refused entry at the airport. Play it safe and make sure you arrive with a visa and your passport in order. See p164 for more information.

If entering by land it is theoretically possible to get a 15-day visa on arrival. You would be wise, though, to arrange your visa from India or Myanmar (Burma) before trying to enter (see p157).

If you are exiting by land but entered by air, a 'change of route' permit is required (see p164). Note that Bangladesh currently refuses entry to Israeli passport holders.

## AIR
### Airports & Airlines

There are three international airports in Bangladesh. Osmani International (ZYL) in Sylhet, Patenga (CGP) in Chittagong and

Zia International Airport (DAC) in Dhaka. **Zia International Airport** ( ☎ 02-819 4350) is the busiest of the three. Located 12km north of the city centre, on the road to Uttara, it doesn't have 'gateway to the world' written on it, but it does have a bank, some duty-free shops and a couple of restaurants.

Bangladesh has two major airlines, which largely cover the same routes for roughly the same prices. Biman runs domestic flights to all cities, and has select international flights. GMG is much the same but newer. Both get good reports, though GMG is generally hailed as the classier of the two.

The US Federal Aviation Administration has classified Biman as category 2, which means that it is not in absolute compliance with international aviation safety standards.

Airlines flying to and from Bangladesh:
**Aeroflot** (SU; ☎ 02-861 3391; www.aeroflot.org; hub Sheremetyevo-2 International Airport, Moscow)
**Air France** (AF; ☎ 02-956 8277; www.airfrance.com; hub Paris-Charles de Gaulle 2)
**Biman** (BG; ☎ 02-891 4771; www.bangladeshonline .com/biman/; hub Zia International Airport, Dhaka)
**British Airways** (BA; ☎ 02-881 5111-5; www.british airways.com; hub Heathrow Airport, London)
**Dragon Air** (KA; ☎ 02-912 2935; www.dragonair.com; hub Hong Kong International Airport)
**Druk Air** (Bhutan Airlines; KB; ☎ 02-882 7969; www .drukair.com.bt/; hub Paro Airport)
**Emirates** (EK; ☎ 02-956 3825-9; www.emirates.com; hub Dubai International Airport)
**GMG Airlines** (Z5; ☎ 02-881 4236-7; www.gmgairlines .com; hub Zia International Airport, Dhaka)
**Gulf Air** (GF; ☎ 02-811 3221; www.gulfairco.com; hub Bahrain Airport)

**Indian Airlines** (IC; ☎ 02-955 5915; www.indian-airlines
.nic.in; hub Indira Gandhi International Airport, Delhi)
**KLM** (KL; ☎ 02-912 0421-5; www.klm.com; hub Schiphol
Airport, Amsterdam)
**Malaysia Airlines** (MH; ☎ 02-862 1557-64; www.malay
siaairlines.com; hub Kuala Lumpur International Airport)
**Pakistan International Airways** (PK; ☎ 02-831 2985;
www.piac.com.pk; hub Quaid-e-Azam International Airport,
Karachi)
**Royal Nepal Airlines** (RA; ☎ 02-955 0423; www
.royalnepal.com; hub Kathmandu Airport)
**Singapore Airlines** (SQ; ☎ 02-881 1504; www
.singaporeair.com; hub Changi Airport)
**Thai International** (TG; ☎ 02-813 4711-20; www
.thaiair.com; hub Bangkok International Airport)

## Tickets

While fares from Europe and Bangkok are
often bargains, fares out of Bangladesh can
be pricey. Compared to fares for flights
originating in India, those from Dhaka
seem even more expensive. In general, fares
out of India are half those originating in
Dhaka, so if you're headed from Dhaka to,
say, Karachi, you'll save big money going to
Kolkata and purchasing your ticket there.

There are many good travel agents in
Dhaka. Those listed in the Dhaka chapter
accept payment by credit card or travellers
cheques (see p46).

## Asia

There are flights to/from all neighbouring
Asian countries. Most connections are direct to Dhaka's Zia International Airport,
except for Biman flights between Chittagong and India or Thailand. During hajj
(the pilgrimage to Mecca), airlines usually
increase their services so that it is even possible to fly directly out of Sylhet.

### BHUTAN

Druk Air offers the only service between
Dhaka and Paro, and the fare is high
(US$190/380 one way/return). There are
only two flights a week. If the schedule isn't
convenient, you could fly to Paro via Kolkata,
using Druk Air and Biman; connections are
good and the cost is only marginally more.

### INDIA

Biman and Indian Airlines have frequent
flights between Dhaka and Kolkata and
Delhi. Both airlines charge the same, but tickets are less if they are purchased in India.

---

> ### DEPARTURE TAX
>
> New airport departure taxes have been in-
> troduced at Zia International Airport. Pas-
> sengers heading to Europe and the USA
> must pay Tk 2500, while those bound for
> Asia must pay Tk 1800. Payment can only
> be made in taka, so bring enough. Some-
> times travel tax is included in the price of a
> ticket – check this out when you're making
> your purchase.

From India expect to pay around
US$65/115 for a one-way/return flight
from Kolkata or US$235/470 from Delhi to
Dhaka.

Biman also has twice-weekly flights between Chittagong and Kolkata for around
US$85.

### MYANMAR

The only direct flight between Yangon
(Rangoon) and Dhaka is Biman's weekly
flight every Sunday. The one-way fare for
the 90-minute flight is US$190. Flying via
Bangkok, which you can do almost daily,
costs almost 65% more.

### NEPAL

There are flights five days a week between
Dhaka and Kathmandu; Biman and Royal
Nepal Airlines serve this route. The flight
takes 65 minutes and the one-way fare is
around US$110 on either airline.

### THAILAND

Thai Airlines, Biman and Druk Air fly
Bangkok to Dhaka. Thai Airlines has flights
every day and Biman has almost as many.
Thai charges US$245 (one way) to Dhaka
and US$206 to Chittagong.

If you purchase your ticket from one of
the many discount agencies in Bangkok,
you'll get a much better deal.

## Australia

The easiest way to get to Bangladesh from
Australia is to fly to Bangkok, Singapore
or Kuala Lumpur, and fly from there to
Dhaka, or to fly to Kolkata in India, and
fly or travel by land into Bangladesh. See
left for more details on flights from Bangkok or Kolkata. Advance-purchase airfares
from the east coast to Bangkok cost from

TRANSPORT

A$800 one way, or A$1350 return on Malaysia Airlines. You should be able to find similar fares, without the advance-purchase restrictions, through travel agents.

Quite a few travel offices specialise in discount air tickets. Some travel agents, particularly smaller ones, advertise cheap fares in the travel sections of weekend newspapers such as the *Age* in Melbourne and the *Sydney Morning Herald*.

Reputable agents with branches throughout Australia:

**Flight Centre Australia** ( ☎ 133 133; www.flightcentre
.com.au)

**STA Travel Australia** ( ☎ 1300 733 035; www.statravel
.com.au)

## Continental Europe

Though London is the travel discount capital of Europe, there are several other cities where you can find a range of good deals. Generally there is not much variation in airfares for departures from the main European cities. All the major airlines usually offer some sort of deal, and travel agents generally have a number of deals on offer, so shop around.

Good places to start:

**STA Travel** ( ☎ 0870 160 0599; www.statravel.co.uk)
**Trailfinders** ( ☎ 020-7937 1234; www.trailfinders.co.uk)

The best airlines serving Dhaka from Europe are British Airways and KLM. Quite a few Middle Eastern airlines, such as Gulf Air, have connections between Europe and Bangladesh, with a stop in their home country.

## The UK & Ireland

Airline-ticket discounters are known as 'bucket shops' in the UK. Despite the somewhat disreputable name, there is nothing under-the-counter about them. Discount air travel is big business in London. Advertisements for many travel agents appear in the travel pages of the weekend broadsheets, such as the *Independent* on Saturday, and the *Sunday Times*. Look out for the free magazines, such as *TNT*, that are widely available in London – start by looking outside the main railway and underground stations.

Good starting points:

**STA Travel** ( ☎ 0870 160 0599; www.statravel.co.uk)
**Trailfinders** ( ☎ 020-7937 1234; www.trailfinders.co.uk)

## The USA

Discount travel agents in the USA are commonly known as consolidators (although you won't see a sign on the door saying 'consolidator'). San Francisco is the consolidator capital of America, although some good deals can be found in Los Angeles, New York and other big cities. Consolidators can be found through the *Yellow Pages* or the major daily newspapers. The *New York Times*, the *Los Angeles Times*, the *Chicago Tribune* and the *San Francisco Examiner* all produce weekly travel sections in which you will find travel-agency ads.

There are basically two ways to get to Bangladesh from the USA. From the west coast virtually everyone flies to Dhaka via Bangkok or Singapore. You can also fly direct to India and connect from there, but it will cost more.

From the east coast most people fly via Europe. Biman has the only direct flights from North America to Dhaka, and Gulf Air offers the best deals. Biman's DC 10s depart from New York and stop en route at Brussels, or Amsterdam and Delhi, without requiring you to change planes.

Gulf Air offers lower fares from New York and its service is reputedly better. You must switch planes en route but connections are good.

If you live near a city serviced by British Airways or KLM, you can often get special return excursion fares flying all the way with those airlines for around US$1400. For instance, you could fly with KLM to Amsterdam and connect there with its twice-weekly flights to Dhaka, or on British Airways to London and connect with one of its four flights a week from London to Dhaka.

Well-known travel agents:

**Council Travel** ( ☎ 880-226 8624; www.ciee.org)
**STA Travel** ( ☎ 800-781 4040; www.statravel.com)

## LAND
## Border Crossings

There are numerous points to cross into India, but only a few of these are set up with immigration facilities to service foreigners.

Theoretically the same system is supposed to be in place for all of these crossings, but in practice this isn't the case. Travellers have reported having to pay travel tax at some borders and not at others. There have also been reports of people managing to leave without a change of route permit, and others being turned back for not having one. A change of route permit is officially required if you have entered Bangladesh by air and leave via a land crossing. These can be obtained at the Immigration and Passport Office (p164). Customs are fairly lax with foreigners. The same rules regarding what you can bring into the country (in the way of cigarettes and alcohol) apply at border crossings as at airports, though in practice a blind eye is usually turned to your luggage at land crossings.

At the time of research there was talk of privatising land port management, except for that at Benapole, which would remain under state control. If this occurs, it may increase the efficiency and array of facilities available.

### AKHAURA/AGARTALA
This border is close to Dhaka, along Akhaura Rd, 4km west of Agartala in India. This is a convenient border to use if you need to extend an Indian tourist visa in a hurry, though there have been reports of attempted bribes. The border is open from 8am to 6pm daily.

Officials on both sides operate an unofficial money-changing service, which may be necessary for a small amount to get you to Akhaura, if you're coming into Bangladesh. The distance between Dhaka and Agartala (in India's Tripura state) is 155km.

In India it is cheap to fly from Kolkata to Agartala, from where a Bangladeshi visa can be issued. The border is a couple of kilometres from Agartala (around Rs 10 for a rickshaw).

Coming into Bangladesh you will find plenty of transport to the town of Akhaura, 5km away. From Akhaura you can get a train (Tk 110, 2½ hours) or a bus (Tk 80, four hours) to Dhaka.

### BENAPOLE
Officials at this border seem to be particularly prone to request change of route permits. Without one, you run a big risk of being turned back.

For more information on crossing this border, see p80.

In India **Shyamoli Paribahan** (Bangladesh Road Transport Corporation; ☎ 033-2252 4503; fax 033-2229

13715; 8 Marquis St; ☺ 10am-5pm) also runs a daily Jeep service to Benapole in Bangladesh (Rs 500 one way), leaving at 5am.

### BURIMARI
Burimari is 13km northwest of the village of Patgram. It can be reached by direct bus from Dhaka or Rangpur. Since the Chilahati border closed in 2002, more foreigners have been crossing here.

For more information, see p110.

### GODAGARI
To get to the Godagari border from Rajshahi, take a Nawabganj-bound bus. In the town of Godagari, the border is quite well marked.

The towns of Godagari and Lalgola are separated by the Padma River. In the dry season it is possible to walk across it, otherwise there will be boats waiting to take you across. In the town of Lalgola, on the Indian side, there is a train station.

### HILI
Much trade between Bangladesh and India goes on via this border. The Indian town of Balurghat is 25km from Hili, on the state highway. The border can be seen from the side of the road – it's usually lined with hundreds of trucks.

In Badurghat, on the Indian side, there are a few places to stay, including the state-owned **PWD Bungalow** ( ☎ 55267; d with bathroom Rs 180). Beside the children's park is the **Irrigation Bungalow** ( ☎ 56031; d Rs 165). Cheapest and closest to the border is **Atithi Nibas** ( ☎ 50262; r Rs 50).

### TAMABIL
The catch with crossing at this border is the need to present a receipt that shows you have deposited a travel tax of Tk 500 into a Sonali Bank. Travellers have been turned back because they have failed to do so.

For more information on crossing this border see p148.

## Bus
There are both government- and private-bus companies that run between Bangladesh and India. With private companies you will be required to disembark at the border to be processed and reboard another bus on the other side. The Bangladesh Road Transport

**TRANSPORT**

Corporation (BRTC), a government service, is said to be extremely efficient.

If you are travelling from Bangladesh into India, no exit permit is required to leave Bangladesh. However, you will require a change of route permit if you arrived by air. You will also need to make your own visa arrangements (p164).

### DHAKA TO KOLKATA
Since 1999 the **BRTC** ( ☎ 02-933 3803, 835 7757) has been operating a service from Dhaka to Kolkata, which is by far the most convenient way of crossing into India.

From Dhaka, AC coaches leave Kamlapur station at 7am, 8.45pm and 10pm, and arrive at Kolkata's Salt Lake City some 12 hours later (one way/return Tk 600/1200).

From Kolkata, buses bound for Dhaka leave Karunamoyee International bus depot at Salt Lake on Wednesday, Thursday and Saturday at 7am, arriving in Dhaka at around 7.30pm (return around Rs 1000). You can purchase the Kolkata–Dhaka bus ticket from **Shyamoli Paribahan** (BRTC; ☎ 033-2252 4503; 8 Marquis St; ☻ 10am-5pm). There is also a branch at 51 Mirza Ghalib St, next to the Hotel VIP International, and another at **Kamlapur station** ( ☎ 02-933 3803).

---

**FROM MYANMAR**

Overland routes between the subcontinent and Myanmar have been closed since the early 1950s. Even if the border were to be opened to foreigners in the future (it is periodically opened for Bangladeshis), roads across the frontier are in bad condition. However, the laying of the foundation stone for the Bangladesh-Myanmar Friendship Bridge in April 2004 might be a sign of changes to come. It is expected to take some 1½ years to complete the 133km bridge.

In the meantime it is not possible to cross from or into Myanmar. Given the forbidden-fruit fascination that off-limits border areas have for many travellers, some people have been tempted to make a discreet trek across the Bangladeshi border into Rakhine (Arakan) state. While this may have been fun in the past, and the punishment not too severe, things are different now: Myanmar's army has planted minefields along the border.

---

### DHAKA TO AGARTALA
The route between Dhaka and Agartala in India has only been operating since late 2003. Though still in a teething stage, the service is reportedly efficient. There are two buses daily from the Bangladeshi side, and only one bus, six days a week, from the Indian side.

The service currently costs US$10 (plus Tk 500 travel tax), but this may be reduced, as it has been met with heavy criticism.

## Car
To drive in Bangladesh, you will need an International Driver's Licence. The import of a vehicle requires a *carnet de passage en douane* (a document from the motoring organisation in the country in which the vehicle is registered, which says you will not sell the vehicle abroad without paying import duties) and an entry permit from the Bangladeshi consulate in Kolkata or the high commission in New Delhi (see p157).

## Train
At the time of writing there was talk of a train, commencing in 2004, from Kolkata to Dhaka via Benapole.

# GETTING AROUND

Internal transport in Bangladesh is so cheap that everyone uses it all the time, whether it be air, land or water transport. The rule is: if you want a seat, get there early and learn to shove, kick and gouge like the rest of your travelling companions.

The distinguishing feature of internal travel in Bangladesh is the presence of a well-developed and well-used system of water transport. Rivers and streams outstretch roads in total distance, making water transport very interesting, especially on the smaller rivers where you can watch life along the banks.

Nevertheless, travelling by boat is slow compared to travelling by bus and it's usually avoidable, so many travellers never go out of their way to take a long trip, settling instead for a short ferry ride across a river or two. This is a big mistake – going to Bangladesh and not taking a trip down a river is like going to the Alps and not skiing or hiking. Travelling on river boats is a high point of a visit to Bangladesh for many travellers.

## AIR
### Airlines in Bangladesh
Bangladesh currently has two domestic airlines: Biman and GMG Airlines.

Biman's planes have done an awful lot of air miles and the interiors are a bit tattered, but the pilots are enormously experienced. Some expatriates recommend Biman if you have to fly during the stormy monsoonal season.

The privately owned GMG is classier, operating Canadian-built Dash 8 turboprop aircraft fitted out with comfy leather seats. GMG also wins for punctuality and service.

Airlines mostly fly between Dhaka and regional cities; there are only a couple of direct flights between regional cities, including Cox's Bazar–Chittagong, and Saidpur–Rajshahi.

## BICYCLE
Bangladesh is great for cycling and this is an interesting way to see the country. With the exception of the tea-estate regions in the Sylhet division, the Chittagong Hill Tracts and the road between Chittagong and Teknaf, Bangladesh is perfectly flat – you can pedal around very easily with a single-gear bike.

Cities, particularly Dhaka and Chittagong, are not easy or safe places to ride given manic traffic and pollution. If you leave early, say 5.30am, you should be able to get out of the city without incident. Alternatively, you can put your bike on the roof of a baby taxi (three-wheeled autorickshaw) or bus. Some travellers have reported not being allowed to take their bikes on board trains.

The trick to cycling in Bangladesh is to avoid major highways as much as possible; look for back streets that will get you to the same destination. Unfortunately maps of Bangladesh aren't detailed enough to be of much use, so be prepared for some interesting though unintentional detours.

Most paths are bricked and in good condition, and even if it's just a dirt path, bikes will be able to pass during the dry season. A river won't hinder your travel, since there's invariably a boat of some sort to take you across. At major bridges a sympathetic truck driver is likely to pile both you and your bike in the back for the crossing.

The ideal time to go cycling is in the dry season from mid-October to late March;

during the monsoon many tracks become impassable.

Though cycling can by and large be a relaxing way to explore Bangladesh, don't get complacent about your belongings; snatches from saddlebags are not unheard of.

### Hire
Some tourist operators have a bike-hire service, but usually only for short trips in select areas. If you're planning to cycle cross-country, your best bet is to buy a bike and resell it when you're done.

### Purchase
New Chinese bikes cost from around Tk 3000 to Tk 5000. Bicycle St (p50) in Old Dhaka is the best of several places to look. When you leave the country, there's a good chance that you will be able to sell it for about half the price you paid, perhaps to the person you bought it from, if you arrange it during the sale. Parts and repair services are available virtually everywhere to cater for rickshaws.

## BOAT
### Ferry
The river is the traditional means of transport in a country that has 8000km of navigable rivers, though schedules, even for the ferries crossing the innumerable rivers, are prone to disruption. During the monsoon, rivers become very turbulent and flooding might mean relocation of ghats (landings); during the dry season, riverbeds choked with silt can make routes impassable. Winter fogs can cause long delays, and mechanical problems on the often poorly maintained boats are not unknown.

The main routes are covered by the Bangladesh Inland Waterway Transport Corporation (BIWTC), but there are many private companies operating on shorter routes and some competing with the BIWTC on the main ones. Private boats tend to be slower and less comfortable but cheaper than BIWTC boats.

Bangladesh averages about five major ferry sinkings a year, frequently at night and with an average of 100 people drowning each time.

### CLASSES
There are four classes of ticket on Bangladeshi boats: 1st, 2nd, inter and deck class.

TRANSPORT

Deck class simply means a space on deck, for which you'll need to bring your own bedding, mattress, food and water. Inter stands for intermediate, and gives you a berth in a cabin with 10 to 16 wooden-slat bunks. In deck class you may find your ability to sleep in cramped, noisy spaces stretched to the limit. Bedding is provided only in 1st class. It's quite unusual for a foreigner to use either the intermediate or deck classes.

On all craft with 1st-class tickets you must book in advance to be assured of a cabin. On popular routes, especially the Rocket (paddle-wheel) route between Dhaka and Khulna, you may have to book a couple of weeks ahead during the dry season. If you're catching a boat at one of the smaller stops, your reservation for a 1st-class cabin will have to be telegraphed to another office, and may take some time. Inter- and deck-class tickets can be bought on board, so there's always a scramble for room.

If you haven't managed to book a 1st-class cabin, it's worth boarding anyway and buying a deck-class ticket, as you may be offered a crew member's cabin. Renting a crew cabin is a common and accepted practice, but it's technically against the rules, so there's scope for rip-offs. Don't necessarily believe the crew member when they tell you that the fee you pay them is all that you will have to pay – you need to buy at least a deck-class ticket to get out of the ghat at the other end of the trip, and other hastily thought of hidden charges may crop up. Some travellers have even had these sorts of problems when renting the captain's cabin.

It's a hassle finding the ship assistant, but if you want to avoid the possibility of minor rip-offs, involve him in negotiations for a crew cabin. He is responsible for matters relating to passengers and accommodation.

If you travel deck or inter class (and having a crew berth counts as deck class), you can't use the pleasant 1st-class deck, from where the best views are to be had. You might of course be able to sneak in, but don't complain too loudly if you're thrown out.

Travellers on a really tight budget, who can't even afford the crew berth, might try going up to the 1st-class dining room to sleep there, if you can fit in between all the staff. Once again, it's a bit arrogant to complain if you're thrown out.

Prices in this book are generally for 1st/2nd/inter/deck class.

## TIPS

In winter, thick fog can turn a 12-hour trip into a 24-hour one, although the captain sometimes doesn't decide that it's unsafe to proceed until he has a very close encounter with a riverbank. If you're travelling deck class, make sure that you're sleeping in a spot where you won't roll off the boat if it comes to a sudden stop!

Porters waiting to leap on docking ferries jostle and fidget like swimmers on the starting blocks – if you don't fancy a swim, don't stand in front of them.

Watching the countryside drift by is amazing and relaxing. If you're lucky, you may spot a sluggish Gangetic river dolphin. Sometimes you find yourself gliding over thick growths of water hyacinth close to the jungle-covered bank; at other times you're churning along a river so wide that neither of the banks are visible.

## The Rocket

Rocket is the generic name that is given to special BIWTC boats that run daily between Dhaka and Khulna, stopping at Chandpur, Barisal, Mongla and many other lesser ports en route. During the 2002–03 financial year some 20 million people travelled by Rocket.

The BIWTC is in the throes of trying to procure more Rockets, given the chequered history of the four in its possession. As the result of some major incidents that have left hundreds dead, the boating community is becoming more and more conscious of safety on the waterways.

If you're heading to the Sundarbans, Kolkata or the ruins at Bagerhat, travelling by Rocket is a great way to go for a major part of the journey. The north–south journey all the way to Khulna takes less than 30 hours, departing from Dhaka at 6pm and arriving at 8pm the following night. Going in the other direction, the Rocket leaves Khulna at 3am and arrives in Dhaka at 5.40am.

### CLASSES

Inter and deck classes are similar to those in ferries, and again, foreigners are highly unlikely to be sold tickets in either of these classes.

Rockets are not particularly glamorous by Mississippi paddle-wheel standards, but they do have paddle wheels. All have two levels. The front half of the upper deck of the old paddle wheel steamer is reserved for 1st-class passengers, most of them, typically, Bangladeshis – this is not a tourist boat. There are eight cabins in this section – four doubles and four singles. Inside, floors are carpeted and each cabin has a washbasin and a narrow bunk bed or two with reasonably comfortable mattresses, freshly painted white walls, wood panelling and good lighting. Bathrooms with toilets and showers are shared. Bathrooms get progressively less clean as the trip goes on.

The central room has overhead fans, a long sofa and dining tables where meals are eaten. Meals are not included in ticket prices. There are both Bangladeshi and Western options, or you can go for a walk into the lower-class areas, where you can buy cheaper snacks.

The real highlight of 1st class, though, is the outside deck at the front of the boat, where you can sit while stewards serve tea and biscuits, and the Padma flows by.

Second class is at the back of the boat. Rooms are smaller than those in first, and have no washbasin and no bed linen. There are small fans, though, and some chairs outside your door for scenery-gazing. If you are staying back here, it might be possible for you to dine in 1st class, for a fee, naturally.

In Dhaka tickets are available from the well-marked BIWTC office (Map pp52–4) in the modern commercial district of Motijheel. Book your tickets in advance. The boat leaves from Sadarghat terminal on the Buriganga River and, on rare occasions, from Badam Tole, a pier 1km north. When leaving from Khulna, you should be allowed to sleep the night before in your cabin as departure is at 3am. They move the boat to a different anchorage for the night, so get aboard early. Sometime after midnight the boat steams back to the loading dock.

Prices in this book are generally for 1st/ 2nd/inter/deck class.

## Traditional River Boats

There are about 60 types of boats plying the rivers of Bangladesh. Steamers are only one type – the remaining 59-odd are traditional wooden boats of all shapes and sizes, some

with sails but most without. These smaller boats plying the smaller rivers are the only way to see life along the riverbanks. On a bigger boat out on the wide Padma, you'll see lots of big launches, traditional boats and maybe some river dolphins, but you might not see people fishing with their nets, children waving from the shore, farmers working in unimaginably green paddy fields and women brightening up the river banks with their colourful saris.

The problem with taking boats on the minor rivers, and the reason why travellers almost never do this, is finding out where to board them and where they're heading. There is no 'system'; you simply have to ask around. If you see two towns on a map with a river connecting them, you can be sure that boats travel between them, and if there's no obvious road connecting them, there will be lots of passenger boats plying the route.

A great river for taking a cruise on, right in the Dhaka area, is the Tongi (*tong*-gee). See p55 for details.

## BUS

The number of buses on the highways is hard to believe. Travelling between Dhaka and Comilla (a two-hour trip), you'll pass about 500 – an average of four buses every minute! Bus travel is cheap and, though it might not seem it, relatively efficient. A six-hour trip on a coach costs around Tk 200, and about half as much for a local bus.

The country has an extensive system of passable roads. When your bus encounters a river crossing, it generally comes on the ferry with you, and the smoky queues of buses waiting to be loaded is one of the more frustrating aspects of travel here. If you don't mind paying another fare, you can always leave your bus and get on one at the head of the queue.

For the lengthy ferry crossings of the mighty Padma, you may have to leave your bus and pick up another one from the same company waiting on the other side. These major inland ghats are a mass of boats, people and vehicles, so expect to be confused – pick out someone on your bus and follow them off the ferry. In any case, the bus assistant continues with the passengers, so you're unlikely to get left behind if you take a while finding your bus after the crossing.

TRANSPORT

**RUSHING ROULETTE**

Bus travel in Bangladesh is something of a 'rushing roulette'. The astounding number of accidents that occur every day attests to the fact that Bangladeshi bus drivers are among the most reckless in the world. You may even be advised that buses are simply too dangerous to catch, and that the only safe way to travel between cities is to fly.

If you're not involved in an accident, you will most likely witness one, or at least its aftermath. The main problem is that roads aren't really wide enough for two buses to pass without pulling onto the verge, which is inevitably crowded with rickshaws and pedestrians. All this swerving, yelling and honking can amount to the most exhausting and stressful experience you're likely to have sitting down.

Exercise some judgment. The law of probabilities suggests that a local bus covered with thorns will continue to be. Coaches, on the other hand, tend to be more looked after. If you find yourself on a bus with a driver who is more reckless than the average reckless driver, don't be bashful about just getting off. Far better to be stranded on the side of the road than lying on it.

It's illegal to ride on top of a bus, like the locals do, but the police won't stop you. If you do ride on top, though, remember that low trees kill quite a few people each year.

Most bus stations are located on the outskirts of towns, often with different stations for different destinations. This helps reduce traffic jams in town (if you've come from India you'll appreciate the difference), but it often means quite a trek to find your bus. Chair-coach companies, however, usually have their own individual offices, often in the centre of town, and it's at these offices, not at the major terminals, that you must reserve your seat.

## Chair Coaches

The safest and most comfortable options are chair coaches, which are distinguished by their adjustable seats and extra leg room. Where possible, take one of these large modern buses on journeys of more than three or four hours. They are not faster on the road – nothing could possibly go faster

than the usually out-of-control ordinary buses! However, departure hours are fixed and seats must be reserved in advance, so unlike regular buses, there's no time wasted filling up the seats and aisles. In addition they are less crowded, often with no people in the aisles and, most importantly for taller people (ie more than about 180cm tall), there's plenty of leg room.

Most chair-coach services travelling between Dhaka and cities on the western side of the country operate at night, typically departing sometime between 5pm and 9pm and arriving in Dhaka at or before dawn. Chair coaches plying the Dhaka–Chittagong route, however, travel mostly during the day.

There are two classes of chair coach – those with AC and those without. Those with AC cost about twice those without. All chair coaches are express buses, but not vice versa. Some serve snacks and drinks on board, and occasionally screen videos!

Some of the best chair-coach companies are **Eagle Paribahan** ( ☎ 02-801 7320), **Green Line** ( ☎ 02-933 9623), **Hanif Enterprise** ( ☎ 02-831 3869), **National** ( ☎ 02-812 4427), **Silk Line** ( ☎ 02-710 2461), **Shohagh Paribahan** ( ☎ 02-933 4152) and **Soudia** ( ☎ 02-801 8445).

## Ordinary Buses

Among the ordinary buses there are express buses and local ones, which stop en route. The latter charge about 25% less but are slow. In more remote areas local buses may be your only option. Most buses are large, but there are a few minivans (coasters).

The BRTC, whose buses generally leave from a separate station, is being driven out of business by private companies. It may be just as well, as BRTC buses tend to be in much worse condition.

Ordinary buses are seemingly made for the vertically challenged – the leg room does not allow anyone to sit with their knees forward. On long trips this can be exceedingly uncomfortable, so try and get an aisle seat.

Women travelling alone sit together up the front, separate from the men. Women travelling with their husbands normally sit in the main section, preferably on the window side. On long-distance bus trips cha stops can be agonisingly infrequent and a real hassle for women travellers – toilet facilities are rare indeed and sometimes hard to find when they do exist.

One of the most under-appreciated professions would have to be that of bus-wallah. These are the men who half hang out the door helping people on and off, load goats onto the roof, bang on the side of the bus telling the driver to stop and go, and uncannily keep track of who needs how much change. They are usually extremely helpful – they often rearrange things so you are comfortably seated and rarely fail to let you know when the bus has arrived at your destination.

## CAR

It's sad to say, but if you're in a serious or fatal traffic accident (and, God forbid, you're responsible), the local custom is to flee, if you can. No-one has much faith in the justice system, so there is an element of self-law in the form of an angry crowd. Newspaper reports of road accidents typically end with words like 'the driver absconded on foot' or 'miscreants beat the driver to a bloody pulp'.

Travelling by car has two possibilities: either you'll be driving your own vehicle or you'll be the passenger in a rental car, which comes complete with its own driver.

### Hire

Self-drive rental cars are not available in Bangladesh, and that's probably a good thing. Fortunately, renting cars with drivers has become very easy and the price is lower than in Europe and North America. Considering the ease and low cost of renting cars in Bangladesh, it's surprising how rarely travellers do it.

In Dhaka there are innumerable companies in the rental business; the best ones are recommended on p67. Expect to pay about Tk 2000/1500 a day for a car with/without AC, plus petrol (which costs only Tk 35 a litre). There's only one other extra: when you stay out of town overnight, you must pay for the driver's lodging (about Tk 80 a night) and food (Tk 50 a meal is reasonable). They don't try to hide this, but make sure you determine beforehand what those rates will be, so as to avoid any misunderstandings. Insurance isn't required because you aren't the driver.

Outside of Dhaka, the cost of renting vehicles is typically less (around Tk 1200 a day plus petrol for a non-AC van), if you don't go through the government tourist-organisation, Parjatan. You negotiate with the driver, but if you go through Parjatan, it takes a percentage of the driver's price.

Where no information is available, your best bet is to go to the top hotel in town and ask the manager. If this approach fails, try a development organisation in the area – chances are staff or their drivers will know of someone in the business. Outside of Dhaka any taxi is also a rental car, but there are so few taxis available that finding one can be difficult – try the airport when a plane arrives.

### Owner-Drivers

Driving in Bangladesh, especially on the Dhaka-Chittagong Hwy or within 100km of Dhaka , takes a bit of guts (stupidity?). On the major highways, you'll be pushed onto the curb every few minutes by large buses hurtling down the road. Dhaka presents its own unique driving perils because of the vast number of rickshaws and baby taxis.

It's a far better – and safer – option to hire a car and driver (see left).

## HITCHING

Hitching is never entirely safe in any country in the world, and we don't recommend it. Travellers who decide to hitch should understand that they are taking a small but potentially serious risk. People who do choose to hitch will be safer if they travel in pairs, and let someone know where they are planning to go. Solo women are particularly unwise to hitchhike.

## LOCAL TRANSPORT

Bangladesh has an amazing range of vehicles – on any highway you can see buses, cars, trucks, rickshaws, baby taxis, tempos (auto-rickshaws), tractors with trays laden with people, motorbikes, scooters, bicycles carrying four people, bullock and water-buffalo carts, and bizarre home-made vehicles all competing for space. One local favourite in Rajshahi division is a sort of mini-tractor powered by incredibly noisy irrigation pump motors.

In Dhaka and Chittagong motorised transportation has increased tremendously over the last 10 years and traffic jams in Central Dhaka are a nightmare. The problem continues to be due more to rickshaws than cars, but motorised vehicles are now also causing traffic jams.

What is most disturbing to people is the total chaos that seems to pervade the streets, with drivers doing anything they please – certainly the police can't control them. Accidents do happen and sometimes people are killed, but the odds of your being involved are still fairly slim.

Where possible it can be wise to negotiate fares beforehand so as to avoid hassles at the other end, though you will be surprised at how often people don't overcharge you on principle. If you are hassled, a good strategy is to keep the discussion going long enough for a crowd to form, which won't be long. This crowd of strangers is something of a people's court, and more often than not is an impressively fair adjudicator. Once deliberations are over and the court has handed down its verdict, the honourable thing for both parties to do is graciously acquiesce.

## Baby Taxi

In Bangladesh three-wheeled auto-rickshaws are called baby taxis. As with the rickshaw-wallahs, baby-taxi drivers almost never own their vehicles. They're owned by powerful fleet-owners called *mohajons*, who rent them out on an eight-hour basis. Also like rickshaws they're designed to take two or three people, but entire families can and do fit. However, unlike rickshaws, they pollute the air.

In Dhaka and Chittagong baby taxis are everywhere – most people use these instead of regular taxis. Faster and more comfortable than rickshaws on most trips, baby taxis cost about twice as much. You'll also find them at Dhaka and Chittagong airports, and they charge less than half the taxi fare. Outside of these two metropolises, baby taxis are much rarer. In towns such as Rangpur, Dinajpur and Barisal they virtually do not exist.

In Dhaka baby taxis are metered and start at Tk 12. You can go from one side of Dhaka to the other for around Tk 100. For distances that won't clock over Tk 20, you are better off taking a rickshaw, or negotiating a reasonable fare with the baby-taxi driver, who probably won't feel satisfied with the fee according to the meter.

In addition to colourful baby taxis, every so often you'll see a *mishuk* (mee-*shuk*), which is a similar vehicle that is slightly narrower and, if you look closely, is driven by a motorised chain like that on a bicycle.

## Boat

Given that there are some 8433km of navigable inland waterways, boats are a common means of getting around. You may have to pay a few taka here and there to be ferried from one side of a river to the other, or hire a wooden boat to get from town to town.

## Bus

The only real difference between local buses and long-distance buses is how you catch them – in the case of local buses, literally. It can be something of a death-defying process. Firstly, assess whether the bus will get you to your desired destination by screaming the name of the destination to the man hanging out the door. If he responds in the affirmative, run towards him, grab firmly onto a handle, if there is one, or him if there isn't, and jump aboard, remembering to check for oncoming traffic.

## Rickshaw

In Bangladesh all rickshaws are bicycle driven – there are none of the human-puller variety. Rickshaw-wallahs usually do not speak English and often don't know much of the layout of their town beyond their own area, so if you'll be going a good distance and you're not sure where you're going, don't expect them to be able to help much in locating your destination – you probably won't be able to explain yourself anyway. There are some English-speaking wallahs, who hang around outside top-end hotels, but they are sometimes shifty operators.

To hail a rickshaw, stick your arm straight out and wave your hand downwards – the usual way of waving your arm upwards used in the West appears to a Bangladeshi as 'Go away! To hell with you!'.

Fares vary a lot, and you must bargain if you care about paying twice as much as locals, although it still isn't very expensive. In any case it is unrealistic to expect to pay exactly what Bangladeshis do. If you can get away with paying a 25% premium, you'll be doing exceptionally well. At the other end of the paying spectrum, there is sometimes a temptation to be overly generous. Try not to succumb to the warm feeling you know you'll get from doing so, and just be reasonable. Around Tk 30 per hour or Tk 3 per km, with a minimum fare of Tk 5 (and up to double that in Dhaka), is normal.

When you're negotiating, don't do so on the assumption that a rickshaw-wallah is trying to rip you off. People have been surprised at how proud and honest these hard-working men can be.

## Taxi

Taxis are abundant in Dhaka. You might be able to hail one down on the side of the road if they are on their way to their usual hang-out, but if they're all occupied you are better off heading straight to an intersection or top-end hotel, where you will find a fleet waiting. Taxis are all metered, the yellow ones beginning at Tk 20 and the smaller, more dinted black taxis at Tk 15.

**Capital Cab Company** ( ☎ 02-935 2847-9) is a recently established radio-controlled service.

Outside of Dhaka there are precious few taxis in Bangladesh. In Chittagong you'll find a few at the airport, at large hotels like the Agrabad and around GEC Circle. In Sylhet, Khulna, Saidpur and possibly Rajshahi you'll see no taxis except for a few at the airport. They are not marked, so you'll have to ask someone to point them out to you.

## Tempo

This is a larger version of a baby taxi, with a cabin in the back. Tempos run set routes, like buses, and while they cost far less than baby taxis, they're more uncomfortable because of the small space into which the dozen or so passengers are squeezed. On the other hand they're a lot faster than rickshaws and as cheap or cheaper. Outside Dhaka and Chittagong they're a lot more plentiful than baby taxis – you will find them even in relatively small towns.

## TRAIN

Trains are a lot easier on the nerves, knees and backside than buses, and those plying the major routes aren't too bad, at least in 1st class. However, travel is slowed down by unbridged rivers requiring ferry crossings, circuitous routing and different gauges. This means that a train ride can take up to twice as long as a bus ride, or take exactly the same time.

At the time of writing the train system was in something of a state of revamp, with the introduction of computerised ticketing.

## Classes

Intercity (IC) trains are frequent, relatively fast, clean and reasonably punctual, especially in the eastern zone. Fares in 1st class are fairly high (about a third more than an AC chair coach), but in *sulob* (2nd class with reserved seating and better carriages than ordinary 2nd class) the fare is comparable to that in a non-AC chair coach, and the trip is a lot more pleasant.

There really isn't much difference between 1st class and *sulob* except space – 1st class has three seats across, facing each other and separated by a table, while *sulob* has four seats across without tables. Some IC trains also have an AC 1st class, which is popular but limited – you'll have to reserve at least several days in advance to get a seat or berth.

There are generally no buffet cars, but sandwiches, Indian snacks and drinks are available from attendants.

Second-class cars with unreserved seating are always an over-crowded mess and on mail trains (which do allow for some passenger cargo) your trip will be even slower than on an IC train. However, you may come out of the experience with a few good stories.

The only sleepers are on night trains, and the fare is about 40% more than 1st class.

On the poorly maintained local trains, 2nd class is crowded and uncomfortable, though remarkably cheap – less than a third the price of 1st class. Unreserved 2nd class has so many class categories and combinations above it (1st class, *sulob*, seating, sleeping, AC, non-AC) that it's technically lower than 3rd class and it feels like it. On some trains, such as those between Dhaka and Mymensingh, there are only 2nd-class compartments.

## Costs

As a rough indication, the 259km journey from Rajshahi to Dhaka costs Tk 630 for a 1st-class AC berth, Tk 425 for a 1st-class AC seat, Tk 290 for a 1st-class non-AC seat and Tk 165 for *sulob*.

Prices in this book are generally for 1st/ *sulob* class, and 1st-class prices are usually for AC seats.

## Reservations

For IC and mail trains, ticket clerks will naturally assume that you, as a seemingly rich foreigner, want the most expensive seats, unless you make it clear otherwise. Buying tickets on local trains is a drag because they don't go on sale until the train is about to arrive, which means that while you're battling the ticket queue all the seats are being filled by hordes of locals. It's almost always better to take a bus than a local train.

Printed timetables are not available, so understanding the convoluted rules of train travel is not easy, even for railway staff. It usually isn't too difficult to find a stationmaster who speaks English. Dhaka's modern Kamlapur station is the exception – schedules are clearly marked on large signs in Bangla and English, but you'll have to double-check to make sure they are correct. Some schedules, particularly on the Dhaka–Sylhet route, change by half an hour or so between the summer and winter seasons, and the signs may not have been updated. You can phone the station, but inquiries in person are more likely to yield a reliable result. When making inquiries it's best to keep things as simple as possible: specify when and where you want to go, and which type of train you want to catch.

If your queries are too much for counter staff, try the District Information Officer (DIO) at Kamlapur station (in the administration annexe just south of the main station building).

If the crowds that silently follow you around the platform get you down (and they will), ask for the waiting room to be unlocked, or establish yourself in the office of an official who speaks English. Rural railway stations are prone to power failures – hang onto your luggage if the lights go out.

Some useful contact numbers:

| City | Reservations | General Inquiries |
| --- | --- | --- |
| Dhaka | ☎ 413 137 (IC)<br>☎ 409 686 (Mail) | ☎ 831 5857 |
| Chittagong | ☎ 616 366 | ☎ 635 126 |
| Sylhet | ☎ 713 990 | ☎ 713 061 |
| Rajshahi | ☎ 774 043 | |
| Khulna | ☎ 721 091 | |

# Health

## CONTENTS

Travellers tend to worry about contracting infectious diseases in this part of the world, but infections are a rare cause of *serious* illness or death in travellers. Pre-existing medical conditions such as heart disease, and accidental injury (especially traffic accidents), account for most life-threatening problems. Becoming ill in some way, however, is very common.

Environmental issues such as heat and pollution can cause health problems. Hygiene is generally poor throughout the region so food- and waterborne illnesses are common. Many insect-borne diseases are present, particularly in tropical areas. Fortunately most travellers' illnesses can either be prevented with some common-sense behaviour or be treated easily with a well-stocked traveller's medical kit. Medical care remains basic so it is essential to be well prepared before travelling to Bangladesh.

The following advice is a general guide only and does not replace the advice of a doctor trained in travel medicine.

## BEFORE YOU GO

Pack medications in their original, clearly labelled, containers. A signed and dated letter from your physician describing your medical conditions and medications, including generic names, is very useful. If carrying syringes or needles, be sure to have a physician's letter documenting their medical necessity. If you have a heart condition, bring a copy of your ECG taken just prior to travelling.

If you take any regular medication, bring double your needs in case of loss or theft. In most South Asian countries, including Bangladesh, you can buy many medications over the counter without a doctor's prescription, but it can be difficult to find some of the newer drugs, particularly the latest anti-depressant drugs, blood-pressure medications and contraceptive pills, in particular outside Dhaka.

### INSURANCE

Even if you are fit and healthy, don't travel without health insurance – accidents do happen. Declare any existing medical conditions you have – the insurance company *will* check if your problem is pre-existing and will not cover you if it is undeclared. You may require extra cover for adventure activities such as rock climbing. If your health insurance doesn't cover you for medical expenses abroad, consider getting extra insurance. If you're uninsured emergency evacuation is expensive.

Find out in advance if your insurance plan will make payments directly to providers, or whether the company will reimburse you later for your overseas health expenditures. (In many countries, including Bangladesh, doctors expect payment in cash.) Some insurance policies offer lower and higher medical-expense options; the higher ones are primarily for countries that have extremely high medical costs, such as the USA. You may prefer a policy that pays doctors or hospitals directly rather than you having to pay on the spot and make a claim later. If you have to claim later, make sure you keep all documentation. Some policies ask you to call back (reverse charges) to a centre in your home country, where an immediate assessment of your problem is made.

# VACCINATIONS

Specialised travel-medicine clinics are your best source of information; they stock all available vaccines and will be able to give specific recommendations for you and your trip. The doctors will take into account factors such as your vaccination history, the length of your trip, activities you may be undertaking and underlying medical conditions, such as pregnancy.

Most vaccines don't produce immunity until at least two weeks after they're given, so visit a doctor four to eight weeks before departure. Ask your doctor for an International Certificate of Vaccination (otherwise known as 'the yellow booklet'), which will list all the vaccinations you've received.

## Recommended Vaccinations

The World Health Organization (WHO) recommends the following vaccinations for travellers to South Asia:

**Adult diphtheria & tetanus** Single booster recommended if none in the previous 10 years. Side effects include sore arm and fever.

**Hepatitis A** Provides almost 100% protection for up to a year; a booster after 12 months provides at least another 20 years' protection. Mild side effects such as headache and sore arm occur in 5% to 10% of people.

**Hepatitis B** Now considered routine for most travellers. Given as three shots over six months. A rapid schedule is also available, as is a combined vaccination with Hepatitis A. Side effects are mild and uncommon, usually headache and sore arm. In 95% of people, lifetime protection results.

**Measles, mumps & rubella** Two doses of MMR are required unless you have had the diseases. Occasionally a rash and flu-like illness can develop a week after receiving the vaccine. Many young adults require a booster.

**Polio** In 2003 polio was still present in Nepal, India and Pakistan but it has been eradicated in Bangladesh. Only one booster is required as an adult for lifetime protection. Inactivated polio vaccine is safe during pregnancy.

**Typhoid** Recommended for all travellers to Bangladesh, even if you only visit urban areas. The vaccine offers around 70% protection, lasts for two to three years and comes as a single shot. Tablets are also available, however the injection is usually recommended as it has fewer side effects. Sore arm and fever may occur.

**Varicella** If you haven't had chickenpox, discuss this vaccination with your doctor.

These immunisations are recommended for long-term travellers (more than one month) or those at special risk:

**Japanese B Encephalitis** Three injections in all. Booster recommended after two years. Sore arm and headache are the most-common side effects. Rarely an allergic reaction comprising hives and swelling can occur up to 10 days after any of the three doses.

**Meningitis** Single injection. There are two types of vaccination: the quadravalent vaccine gives two to three years' protection; meningitis group C vaccine gives around 10 years' protection. Recommended for long-term backpackers aged under 25.

**Rabies** Three injections in all. A booster after one year will then provide 10 years protection. Side effects are rare – occasionally headache and sore arm.

**Tuberculosis** A complex issue. Long-term adult travellers are usually recommended to have a TB skin test before and after travel, rather than vaccination. Only one vaccine given in a lifetime.

## Required Vaccinations

The only vaccine required by international regulations is yellow fever. Proof of vaccination will only be required if you have visited a country in the yellow-fever zone within the six days prior to entering Bangladesh. If you are travelling to Bangladesh from Africa or South America, you should check to see if you will require proof of vaccination.

## MEDICAL CHECKLIST

Recommended items for a personal medical kit:

- Antibacterial cream, eg Muciprocin
- Antibiotic for skin infections, eg Amoxicillin/Clavulanate or Cephalexin
- Antibiotics for diarrhoea include Norfloxacin or Ciprofloxacin; for bacterial diarrhoea, Azithromycin; for giardia or amoebic dysentery, Tinidazole
- Antifungal cream, eg Clotrimazole
- Antihistamine – there are many options, eg Cetrizine for daytime and Promethazine for night
- Antiseptic, eg Betadine
- Anti-spasmodic for stomach cramps, eg Buscopa
- Contraceptive method
- Decongestant, eg Pseudoephedrine
- DEET-based insect repellent
- Diarrhoea – consider an oral rehydration solution (eg Gastrolyte), diarrhoea 'stopper' (eg Loperamide) and anti-nausea medication (eg Prochlorperazine)
- First-aid items such as scissors, elastoplasts, bandages, gauze, thermometer (but

not mercury), sterile needles and syringes, safety pins and tweezers

- Ibuprofen or another anti-inflammatory
- Indigestion tablets, eg Quick Eze or Mylanta
- Iodine tablets (unless you are pregnant or have a thyroid problem) to purify water
- Laxative, eg Coloxyl
- Migraine medicine – take your personal medicine
- Paracetamol
- Permethrin to impregnate clothing and mosquito nets
- Steroid cream for allergic/itchy rashes, eg 1% to 2% hydrocortisone
- Sunscreen and hat
- Throat lozenges
- Thrush (vaginal yeast infection) treatment, eg Clotrimazole pessaries or Diflucan tablet
- Ural or equivalent, if prone to urine infections

## ONLINE RESOURCES

There is a wealth of travel health advice on the Internet. For further information, **Lonely Planet** (www.lonelyplanet.com) is a good place to start. The **World Health Organization** (WHO; www.who.int/ith/) publishes a superb book called *International Travel & Health*, which is revised annually and available online at no cost. Another website of general interest is **MD Travel Health** (www.mdtravelhealth.com), which provides complete travel-health recommendations for every country and is updated daily. The **Centers for Disease Control and Prevention** (CDC; www.cdc.gov) website also has good general information.

---

**HEALTH ADVISORIES**

It's usually a good idea to consult your government's travel-health website before departure, if one is available:

**Australia** (www.dfat.gov.au/travel/)
**Canada** (www.travelhealth.gc.ca)
**New Zealand** (www.mfat.govt.nz/travel)
**South Africa** (www.dfa.gov.za/consular/travel_advice.htm)
**UK** (www.dh.gov.uk/PolicyAndGuidance/HealthAdviceforTravellers/fs/en/)
**USA** (www.cdc.gov/travel/)

---

## FURTHER READING

Lonely Planet's *Healthy Travel – Asia & India* is a handy pocket size and packed with useful information including pretrip planning, emergency first aid, immunisation and disease information and what to do if you get sick on the road. Other recommended references include *Traveller's Health* by Dr Richard Dawood and *Travelling Well* by Dr Deborah Mills – check out the website (www.travellingwell.com.au).

# IN TRANSIT

## DEEP VEIN THROMBOSIS

Deep vein thrombosis (DVT) occurs when blood clots form in the legs during plane flights, chiefly because of prolonged immobility. The longer the flight, the greater the risk. Though most blood clots are reabsorbed uneventfully, some may break off and travel through the blood vessels to the lungs, where they may cause life-threatening complications.

The chief symptom of DVT is swelling or pain of the foot, ankle or calf, usually but not always on just one side. When a blood clot travels to the lungs, it may cause chest pain and difficulty in breathing. Travellers with any of these symptoms should immediately seek medical attention.

To prevent the development of DVT on long flights you should walk about the cabin, perform isometric compressions of the leg muscles (ie contract the leg muscles while sitting), drink plenty of fluids, and avoid alcohol and tobacco.

## JET LAG & MOTION SICKNESS

Jet lag is common when crossing more than five time zones; it results in insomnia, fatigue, malaise or nausea. To avoid jet lag try drinking plenty of fluids (non-alcoholic) and eating light meals. Upon arrival, seek exposure to natural sunlight and readjust your schedule (for meals, sleep etc) as soon as possible.

Antihistamines such as dimenhydrinate (Dramamine), promethazine (Phenergan) and meclizine (Antivert, Bonine) are usually the first choice for treating motion sickness. Their main side effect is drowsiness. A herbal alternative is ginger, which works like a charm for some people.

# IN BANGLADESH

## AVAILABILITY OF HEALTH CARE

In general, medical facilities are not up to international standards and serious cases are likely to be evacuated. Facilities are severely limited outside the major cities and, as a result, it can be difficult to find reliable medical care in rural areas. Your embassy and insurance company can be good contacts. Recommended clinics are listed on p45 in the Dhaka chapter.

Self-treatment may be appropriate if your problem is minor (eg traveller's diarrhoea), you are carrying the relevant medication and you cannot attend a recommended clinic. If you think you may have a serious disease, especially malaria (see opposite), do not waste time – travel to the nearest quality facility to receive attention.

Buying medication over the counter is not recommended, as fake medications and drugs that have been poorly stored or are out-of-date are common.

## INFECTIOUS DISEASES
### Coughs, Colds & Chest Infections

Respiratory infections are common in Bangladesh. This usually starts as a virus and is exacerbated by environmental conditions such as pollution in the cities, or cold and altitude in the mountains. Commonly a secondary bacterial infection will intervene – marked by fever, chest pain and coughing up discoloured or blood-tinged sputum. If you have the symptoms of an infection, seek medical advice or commence a general antibiotic.

### Dengue Fever

This mosquito-borne disease is becomingly increasingly problematic in the tropical world, especially in the cities. As there is no vaccine available it can only be prevented by avoiding mosquito bites. The mosquito that carries dengue bites day and night, so use insect avoidance measures at all times. Symptoms include high fever, severe headache and body ache (dengue was previously known as 'breakbone fever'). Some people develop a rash and experience diarrhoea. There is no specific treatment, just rest and paracetamol – do not take aspirin as it increases the likelihood of haemorrhaging. See a doctor to be diagnosed and monitored.

### Hepatitis A

A problem throughout the region, this food- and waterborne virus infects the liver, causing jaundice (yellow skin and eyes), nausea and lethargy. There is no specific treatment for hepatitis A, you just need to allow time for the liver to heal. All travellers to South Asia should be vaccinated against hepatitis A.

### Hepatitis B

The only sexually transmitted disease that can be prevented by vaccination, hepatitis B is spread by body fluids, including sexual contact. In some parts of South Asia up to 20% of the population are carriers of hepatitis B, and usually are unaware of this. In Bangladesh the number of carriers is just below 10%. The long-term consequences can include liver cancer and cirrhosis.

### Hepatitis E

Transmitted through contaminated food and water, hepatitis E has similar symptoms to hepatitis A, but is far less common. It is a severe problem in pregnant women and can result in the death of both mother and baby. There is currently no vaccine, and prevention is by following safe eating and drinking guidelines.

### HIV

HIV is spread via contaminated body fluids. Avoid unsafe sex, unsterile needles (including those in medical facilities) and procedures such as tattoos. The rate of HIV infection in South Asia is growing more rapidly than anywhere else in the world.

### Influenza

Present year-round in the tropics, influenza (flu) symptoms include high fever, muscle aches, runny nose, cough and sore throat. It can be very severe in people over the age of 65 or in those with underlying medical conditions such as heart disease or diabetes – vaccination is recommended for these individuals. There is no specific treatment, just rest and paracetamol.

### Japanese B Encephalitis

This viral disease is transmitted by mosquitoes and is rare in travellers. Like most mosquito-borne diseases it is becoming a more common problem in affected countries. Most cases occur in rural areas and vaccination is recommended for travellers spending more than one month outside of cities. There is no treatment, and a third of infected people will die, while another third will suffer permanent brain damage.

## Malaria

For such a serious and potentially deadly disease, there is an enormous amount of misinformation concerning malaria. You must get expert advice as to whether your trip puts you at risk. Outside Dhaka, the risk of contracting malaria far outweighs the risk of any tablet side effects. Remember that malaria can be fatal. Before you travel, seek medical advice on the right medication and dosage for you. Malaria in South Asia, including Bangladesh, is chloroquine resistant.

Malaria is caused by a parasite, transmitted through the bite of an infected mosquito. The most important symptom of malaria is fever, but general symptoms such as headache, diarrhoea, cough or chills may also occur. A diagnosis can only be made by taking a blood sample.

Two strategies should be combined to prevent malaria – mosquito avoidance, and anti-malaria medications. Most people who catch malaria are taking inadequate or no anti-malarial medication.

Travellers are advised to prevent mosquito bites by taking these steps:

- Use a DEET-containing insect repellent on exposed skin. Wash this off at night, as long as you are sleeping under a mosquito net. Natural repellents such as citronella can be effective, but must be applied more frequently than products containing DEET.
- Sleep under a mosquito net impregnated with permethrin
- Choose accommodation with screens and fans (if not air-conditioned)
- Impregnate clothing with permethrin in high-risk areas
- Wear long sleeves and trousers in light colours
- Use mosquito coils
- Spray your room with insect repellent before going out for your evening meal

There are a variety of medications available:
**Lariam (Mefloquine)** Lariam has received much bad press, some of it justified, some not. This weekly tablet suits many people. Serious side effects are rare but include depression, anxiety, psychosis and having fits. Anyone with a history of depression, anxiety, other psychological disorders or epilepsy should not take Lariam. It is considered safe in the second and third trimesters of pregnancy. Tablets must be taken for four weeks after leaving the risk area.

**Doxycycline** This daily tablet is a broad-spectrum antibiotic that has the added benefit of helping to prevent a variety of tropical diseases including leptospirosis, tick-borne diseases and typhus. The potential side effects include photosensitivity (a tendency to sunburn), thrush in women, indigestion, heartburn, nausea and interference with the contraceptive pill. More serious side effects include ulceration of the oesophagus – you can help prevent this by taking your tablet with a meal and a large glass of water, and never lying down within half an hour of taking it. It must be taken for four weeks after leaving the risk area.

**Malarone** This new drug is a combination of Atovaquone and Proguanil. Side effects are uncommon and mild, most commonly nausea and headache. It is the best tablet for scuba divers and for those on short trips to high-risk areas. It must be taken for one week after leaving the risk area.

A final option is to take no preventive medication but to have a supply of emergency medication should you develop the symptoms of malaria. This is less than ideal, and you'll need to get to a good medical facility within 24 hours of developing a fever. If you choose this option the most effective and safest treatment is Malarone (four tablets once daily for three days). Other options include Mefloquine and Quinine but the side effects of these drugs at treatment doses make them less desirable. Fansidar is no longer recommended.

## Measles

Measles remains a significant problem in Bangladesh. This highly contagious bacterial infection is spread via coughing and sneezing. Most people born before 1966 are immune as they had the disease in childhood. Measles starts with a high fever and rash, and can be complicated by pneumonia and brain disease. There is no specific treatment.

## Rabies

This is a common problem in South Asia. Around 30,000 people die in India alone each year from rabies, and there are more than 2000 deaths annually in Bangladesh. This uniformly fatal disease is spread by the bite or lick of an infected animal – most commonly a dog or monkey. You should seek medical advice immediately after any animal bite and commence post-exposure treatment. Having pre-travel vaccination means the post-bite treatment is greatly simplified. If an animal bites you, gently wash the wound with soap and water, and apply iodine-based antiseptic. If you are not previously vaccinated, you will need to receive rabies immunoglobulin as soon as possible. This is very difficult to obtain outside Dhaka.

## STDs
Sexually transmitted diseases most common in Bangladesh include herpes, warts, syphilis, gonorrhoea and chlamydia. People carrying these diseases often have no signs of infection. Condoms will prevent gonorrhoea and chlamydia but not warts or herpes. If, after a sexual encounter, you develop any rash, lumps, discharge or pain when passing urine, seek immediate medical attention. If you have been sexually active during your travels, have an STD check on your return home.

## Tuberculosis
While TB is rare in travellers, those who have significant contact with the local population, such as medical and aid workers, and long-term travellers, should take precautions. Vaccination is usually only given to children under the age of five, but adults at risk are recommended to have pre- and post-travel TB testing. The main symptoms are fever, cough, weight loss, night sweats and tiredness.

## Typhoid
This serious bacterial infection is also spread via food and water. It gives a high and slowly progressive fever and headache, and may be accompanied by a dry cough and stomach pain. It is diagnosed by blood tests and treated with antibiotics. Vaccination is recommended for all travellers spending more than a week in South Asia. India and Nepal pose a particularly high risk and have the added problem of significant antibiotic resistance. In Bangladesh the risk is medium level but the infection is also antibiotic resistant. Be aware that vaccination is not 100% effective, so you must still be careful with what you eat and drink.

## TRAVELLER'S DIARRHOEA
Traveller's diarrhoea is by far the most common problem affecting travellers – between 30% and 70% of people will suffer from it within two weeks of starting their trip. In over 80% of cases, traveller's diarrhoea is caused by a bacteria, and therefore responds promptly to treatment with antibiotics. Treatment with antibiotics will depend on your situation – how sick you are, how quickly you need to get better, where you are etc.

Traveller's diarrhoea is defined as the passage of more than three watery bowel-actions within 24 hours, plus at least one other symptom such as fever, cramps, nausea, vomiting or generally feeling unwell.

Treatment consists of staying well hydrated; rehydration solutions such as Gastrolyte are the best for this. Antibiotics such as Norfloxacin, Ciprofloxacin or Azithromycin will kill the bacteria quickly.

Loperamide is just a 'stopper' and doesn't get to the cause of the problem. It can be helpful, for example if you have to go on a long bus ride. Don't take Loperamide if you have a fever, or blood in your stools. Seek medical attention quickly if you do not respond to an appropriate antibiotic.

### Amoebic Dysentery
Amoebic dysentery is rare in travellers but is often misdiagnosed by poor-quality labs in South Asia. Symptoms are similar to bacterial diarrhoea, ie fever, bloody diarrhoea and generally feeling unwell. You should always seek reliable medical care if you have blood in your diarrhoea. Treatment involves two drugs: Tinidazole or Metronidazole to kill the parasite in your gut, and then a second drug to kill the cysts. If left untreated, complications such as liver or gut abscesses can occur. Bacterial dysentery is more common.

### Giardiasis
Giardia is a parasite that is relatively common in travellers. Symptoms include nausea, bloating, excess gas, fatigue and intermittent diarrhoea. 'Eggy' burps are often attributed solely to giardia, but work in Nepal has shown that they are not specific to giardia. The parasite will eventually go away if left untreated but this can take months. The treatment of choice is Tinidazole, with Metronidazole being a second-line option.

## ENVIRONMENTAL HAZARDS
### Air Pollution
If you have severe respiratory problems, speak with your doctor before travelling to any heavily polluted urban centres. Dhaka is one of the most polluted cities in the world. This pollution also causes minor respiratory problems such as sinusitis, dry throat and irritated eyes. If troubled by the pollution, leave the city for a few days and get some fresh air.

### Food
Eating in restaurants is the biggest risk factor for contracting traveller's diarrhoea. Ways to avoid it include eating only freshly cooked food, and avoiding shellfish and food that has been sitting around in buffets. Peel all fruit, cook vegetables, and soak salads in iodine water for at least 20 minutes. Eat in busy restaurants with a high turnover of customers.

### Heat
Parts of Bangladesh are hot and humid throughout the year. For most people it takes at least two weeks to adapt to the hot climate. Swelling of the feet and ankles is common, as are muscle cramps caused by excessive sweating. Prevent these by avoiding dehydration and excessive activity in the heat. Take it easy when you first arrive. Don't eat salt tablets (they aggravate the gut), but drinking rehydration solution or eating salty food helps. Treat cramps by stopping activity, resting, rehydrating with double-strength rehydration solution, and gently stretching.

Dehydration is the main contributor to heat exhaustion. Symptoms include feeling weak, headache, irritability, nausea or vomiting, sweaty skin, a fast weak pulse and a normal or slightly elevated body temperature. Treatment involves getting out of the heat and/or sun; fanning the victim and applying cool wet cloths to the skin; laying the victim flat with their legs raised; and rehydrating with water containing ¼ teaspoon of salt per litre. Recovery is usually rapid but it is common to feel weak for some days afterwards.

Heatstroke is a serious medical emergency. Symptoms come on suddenly and include weakness, nausea, a hot, dry body with a temperature of over 41°C, dizzi-

ness, confusion, loss of coordination, fits and eventually collapse and loss of consciousness. Seek medical help and commence cooling by getting the person out of the heat, removing their clothes, fanning them, and applying cool wet cloths or ice to their body, especially to the groin and armpits.

Prickly heat is a common skin rash in the tropics, caused by sweat being trapped under the skin. The result is an itchy rash of tiny lumps. Treat by moving out of the heat and into an air-conditioned area for a few hours and by having cool showers. Creams and ointments clog the skin, so they should be avoided. Locally bought prickly-heat powder can be helpful.

Tropical fatigue is common in long-term expatriates based in the tropics. It's rarely due to disease and is caused by the climate, inadequate mental rest, excessive alcohol intake and the demands of daily work in a different culture.

### Insect Bites & Stings
Bedbugs don't carry disease but their bites are very itchy. They live in the cracks of furniture and walls, and then migrate to the bed at night to feed on you. You can treat the itch with an antihistamine.

Lice inhabit various parts of your body but most commonly your head and pubic area. Transmission is via close contact with an infected person. They can be difficult to

### DRINKING WATER
- Never drink tap water
- Bottled water is generally safe – check the seal is intact at purchase
- Avoid ice
- Avoid fresh juices – they may have been watered down
- Boiling water is the most efficient method of purifying it
- The best chemical purifier is iodine. It should not be used by pregnant women or those with thyroid problems.
- Water filters should also filter out viruses. Ensure your filter has a chemical barrier such as iodine and a small pore size, eg less than four microns.

treat and you may need numerous applications of an anti-lice shampoo such as permethrin. Pubic lice are usually contracted from sexual contact.

Ticks are contracted after walking in rural areas. They are commonly found behind the ears, on the belly and in armpits. If you have had a tick bite and experience symptoms such as a rash at the site of the bite or elsewhere, fever or muscle aches, you should see a doctor. Doxycycline prevents tick-borne diseases.

Leeches are found in humid rainforest areas. They do not transmit any disease but their bites are often intensely itchy for weeks afterwards and can easily become infected. Apply an iodine-based antiseptic to any leech bite to help prevent infection.

### Skin Problems

Fungal rashes are common in humid climates. There are two common fungal rashes that affect travellers. The first occurs in moist areas that get less air such as the groin, armpits and between the toes. It starts as a red patch that slowly spreads and is usually itchy. Treatment involves keeping the skin dry, avoiding chafing and using an antifungal cream such as Clotrimazole or Lamisil. *Tinea versicolor* is also common – this fungus causes small, light-coloured patches, most commonly on the back, chest and shoulders. Consult a doctor.

Cuts and scratches become easily infected in humid climates. Take meticulous care of any cuts and scratches to prevent complications such as abscesses. Immediately wash all wounds in clean water and apply antiseptic. If you develop signs of infection (increasing pain and redness), see a doctor. Divers and surfers should be particularly careful with coral cuts as they become easily infected.

### Sunburn

Even on a cloudy day sunburn can occur rapidly. Always use a strong sunscreen (at least factor 30), making sure to reapply after a swim, and always wear a wide-brimmed hat and sunglasses outdoors. Avoid lying in the sun during the hottest part of the day (10am to 2pm). If you become sunburnt, stay out of the sun until you have recovered, apply cool compresses and take painkillers for the discomfort. One percent hydrocortisone cream applied twice daily is also helpful.

## WOMEN'S HEALTH

Pregnant women should receive specialised advice before travelling. The ideal time to travel is in the second trimester (between 16 and 28 weeks), when the risk of pregnancy-related problems are at their lowest and pregnant women generally feel at their best. During the first trimester there is a risk of miscarriage and in the third trimester complications such as premature labour and high blood pressure are possible. It's wise to travel with a companion. Always carry a list of quality medical facilities available at your destination and ensure you continue your standard antenatal care at these facilities. Avoid rural travel in areas with poor transportation and medical facilities. Most of all, ensure travel insurance covers all pregnancy-related possibilities, including premature labour.

Malaria is a high-risk disease in pregnancy. WHO recommends that pregnant women do not travel to areas with Chloroquine-resistant malaria. None of the more effective anti-malaria drugs are completely safe in pregnancy.

Hepatitis E is a particular problem for pregnant women – if it is contracted in the third trimester, 30% of women and their babies will die.

Traveller's diarrhoea can quickly lead to dehydration and result in inadequate blood flow to the placenta. Many of the drugs used to treat various diarrhoea bugs are not recommended in pregnancy. Azithromycin is considered safe.

In the urban areas of Bangladesh, supplies of sanitary products are readily available. Birth control options may be limited so bring adequate supplies of your own form of contraception. Heat, humidity and antibiotics can all contribute to thrush. Treatment is with antifungal creams and pessaries such as Clotrimazole. A practical alternative is a single tablet of Fluconazole (Diflucan). Urinary tract infections can be precipitated by dehydration or long bus journeys without toilet stops; bring suitable antibiotics.

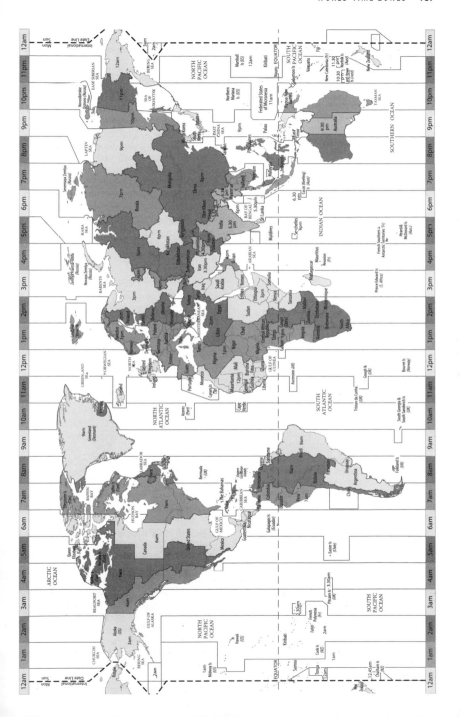

# Language

## CONTENTS

Bangla (also widely known as Bengali) is the national language of Bangladesh and the official language of the state of West Bengal in India. Bangla is the easternmost of the Indo-European languages with its roots in Prakrit, the vernacular (ie commonly spoken) form of Pali, which was the original language of the Buddhist scriptures. In addition to Arabic, Urdu and Persian words, the Sanskrit of Brahmin Hindus was assimilated into the local speech, giving Bangla a strong resemblance to Hindi, with some variation in pronunciation. The vocabulary was further expanded through contact with European traders and merchants. Today, Bangla has a number of regional variations, but remains essentially the same throughout Bangladesh.

## HISTORY

The modern development of Bangla as a symbol of the cultural individuality of Bangladesh began under the British. In keeping with the Raj's policy of working within local cultures, Bangla was taught to officers, who used it in their dealings with locals. This resulted in the fusion of the vernacular of the peasants with high-caste literary Bangla, which had fallen into disuse under Muslim rulers, who favoured Urdu. The Hindus took to Bangla with enthusiasm, seeing it as a means toward reasserting their cultural heritage, and the 19th century saw a renaissance in Bangla literature. Author Rabindranath Tagore gave Bangla literature kudos when he won the Nobel Prize for literature (see p31).

It wasn't until partition, and the departure of most of the Hindu ruling class, that Bangladeshi intellectuals felt the need for Bangla as a means of defining their culture and nationalism.

There is a much lower proportion of English speakers in Bangladesh than in India. It's surprising how many conversations you can have in which you think that you're being understood. English has lapsed for three main reasons: there aren't distinct regional languages which make a lingua franca (common language) necessary; the symbolic importance of Bangla in the independence movement; and the many weaknesses in the public education system. In recent years, however, the value of English has risen considerably, especially if the number of colleges and schools advertising tuition is anything to go by.

Making the effort to learn some Bangla will not only be greatly appreciated; at times it's your only hope. You'll find that most billboards and street signs are written in Bangla script only.

Lonely Planet's *Bengali Phrasebook* provides a far more in-depth guide to the language, with a selection of useful words and phrases to cover most travel situations. There are a few Bangla phrasebooks available in Dhaka in the New Market bookshops, although the standard of English in some isn't very good. The Heed Language Centre in Dhaka produces a useful Bangla-English/English-Bangla dictionary and a basic course instruction booklet. See Courses (p156) in the Directory chapter for information on learning Bangla while you're in the country.

## PRONUNCIATION

Pronunciation of Bangla is made difficult by the fact that the language includes a variety of subtle sounds with no equivalents in English. To make this language guide easier to use for basic communication we haven't tried to cover all the sounds, instead using nearest English equivalents – you're unlikely to have any trouble making yourself understood.

With regard to word stress, a good rule of thumb is to place the emphasis on the first and last syllables of words.

| | |
|---|---|
| a | as in 'father' |
| b | as English 'b' or 'v' |
| ch | as in 'chant' |
| e | as in 'bet' |
| i | as in 'police' |
| j | as in 'jet' |
| o | similar to the 'o' in 'hold' |
| th | as in 'thing' |
| u | as in 'put' |
| v/w | a cross between English 'v' and 'w' |
| y | as in 'boy' |

## USEFUL VERBS

Two verbs that will undoubtedly come in very handy are *achhe* (there is, has), and *lagbe* (need). You can ask *khana a·che?* (Is there food?) or *bangti a·che?* (Do you have change?) The negative form of *a·che* is simply *nai*. Saying *baksheesh nai* means you don't have any baksheesh to give. You can say *pani lagbe* (lit: water is needed), or say *lagbe na* (lit: don't need) to turn down any unwanted offer.

## ACHA

*Acha*, the subcontinent's ambiguous 'OK/ Yes/I see' is used widely, but the local slang equivalent is *tik assay* or just *tik*. The words *ji* or *ha* are more positive – if the rickshaw-wallah answers *acha* to your offered price, expect problems at the other end; if it's *tik* or *ji* he's unlikely to demand more money.

## ACCOMMODATION

| | |
|---|---|
| Is there a hotel/ guesthouse nearby? | kache kono hotel/guesthouse a·che ki? |
| Do you have a room? | rum a·che? |
| May I see the room? | rum dekte pari? |
| Is there a toilet? | paikana a·che? |
| mosquito net | moshari |
| towel | toale |
| | |
| I'd like to book a room ... | ami ekta rum buk ... korbo |
| for one person | ekjon thakbe |
| for two people | duijon thakbe |

| How much is it ...? | ... thakte koto taka lagbe? |
|---|---|
| per person | ek jon |
| per night | ek ra·te |
| per week | ek soptaho |

## CONVERSATION & ESSENTIALS

Men might hear people greet them with *bahadur*, an honorific implying that you're wise and wealthy and should pay top price. Married or otherwise 'respectable' women might be addressed as *begum*, roughly the equivalent of 'Madam'. However, in most situations you'll be referred to as *bondhu*, meaning 'friend'.

'Please' and 'Thank you' are rarely used in Bangla. Instead, these sentiments are expressed indirectly in polite conversation. The absence of these shouldn't be misread as rudeness. If you want to thank someone, you may use the Bangla equivalent for 'Thank you (very much)', *(onek) donyobad*, or, alternatively, pay them a compliment.

| | |
|---|---|
| Hello. (Muslim greeting) | asalam walekum |
| (response) | walekum asalam |
| Hello. (Hindu greeting) | nomashkar |
| Goodbye. | khuda hafiz |
| See you later. | po·re dakha ho·be |
| See you again. | abar deka ho·be |
| Excuse/Forgive me. | maf korun |
| Thank you (very much). | (onek) don·nobad |
| Yes. | ji (polite)/ha (commonly used, with the 'a' given a very nasal pronunciation) |
| No. | na |
| How are you? | (apni) kamon achen? |
| I'm well. | bhalo achi |
| friend (often used in greetings) | bondhu |
| What's your name? | apnar nam ki? |
| My name is ... | amar nam ... |
| Where are you from? | apnar desh ki? |
| My country is ... | amar desh ... |
| Not any/None. | nai |
| It's all right/ No problem. | tik a·che |
| How old are you? | koto boyosh? |
| Do you like ...? | apnar ... bhalo lagge? |
| I like it (very much). | amar eta (khub) bhalo lagge |
| I don't like ... | amar ... bhalo lagge na |
| What do you want? | ki lagbe? |
| Do you smoke? | cigarette khaben? |
| It's available. | pawa jai |
| It's not available. | pawa jai na |

**BANGLA GREETINGS**

Greetings vary in Bangla according to religion and custom. The Muslim greeting is *asalam walekum* (peace be on you). The response is *walekum asalam* (unto you, also peace). Hindus say *nomashkar* when greeting and saying goodbye. This is accompanied by the gesture of joining the open palms of both hands and bringing them close to the chest.

## DIRECTIONS

| | |
|---|---|
| Where is ...? | ... kotai? |
| How far is ...? | ... koto dur? |
| I want to go to Dhaka. | ami dhaka jabo |
| I'm going to Chittagong. | chittagong jachi |
| Go straight ahead. | shoja jan |
| | |
| left | ba·me |
| right | da·ne |
| here | ekha·ne |
| | |
| there | okhane |
| before | a·ge |
| after | po·re |
| above | upo·re |
| below | ni·che |
| north | uttor |
| south | dokkin |
| east | purbodik |
| west | posh-chim |

**SIGNS**

| | |
|---|---|
| ভিতর | Enter |
| বাহির | Exit |
| ধুমপান নিষেদ | No Smoking |
| হোটেল | Hotel |
| বাস | Bus |
| শৌচাগার | Toilets |
| মহিলা | Ladies (also bus seats reserved for women) |
| পুরুষ | Men |

**Cities**

| | |
|---|---|
| ঢাকা | Dhaka |
| খুলনা | Khulna |
| রাজশাহি | Rajshahi |
| সিলেট | Sylhet |
| চট্রগ্রাম | Chittagong |
| বরিশাল | Barisal |

## EMERGENCIES

| | |
|---|---|
| Please help me! | amake shahajjo koren! |
| Go away! | jao! |
| Call a doctor/the police! | daktar/pulish lagbe! |
| I've been robbed. (of things) | amar jinnish churi hoyecheh |
| I've been robbed. (of money) | amar taka churi hoyecheh |
| I'm lost. | ami hariye ghechi |
| Where is the toilet? | paikhana kotai? |

## HEALTH

| | |
|---|---|
| I need/(My friend needs) a doctor. | amar/(amar bondhur) daktar lagbe |
| I'm a (diabetic/ epileptic). | amar (diabetes/mirghi rog) a·che |
| I'm allergic to antibiotics/ penicillin. | amar (antibiotikeh/penisillineh) allergy a·che |
| I'm pregnant. | ami pregnant |
| | |
| antiseptic | savlon |
| aspirin | aspirin |
| condom | kondom |
| nausea | bomi-bhab |
| sanitary napkins | softex/modess (brand names) |

## LANGUAGE DIFFICULTIES

| | |
|---|---|
| I understand. | ami bujhi |
| I don't understand. | ami bujhi na |
| Do you speak English? | apni english/ingreji bolte paren? |
| I speak a little Bangla. | ami ektu bangla bolte pari |
| Please write it down. | likhte paren |
| How do you say ... in Bangla? | banglai ... ki bo·le? |

## NUMBERS

Counting up to 20 is easy, but after that it becomes complicated, as the terms do not follow sequentially. In Bangla 21 isn't *bish-ek* or *ek-bish* as you might expect, but *ekush*; 45 is actually *poy-tal·lish*, but the simpler *pach-chollish* is understood.

| 0 | shun·no | ০ |
|---|---|---|
| 1 | ek | ১ |
| 2 | dui | ২ |
| 3 | tin | ৩ |
| 4 | char | ৪ |
| 5 | pach | ৫ |
| 6 | ch-hoy | ৬ |

| | | |
|---|---|---|
| 7 | shat | ৭ |
| 8 | at | ৮ |
| 9 | noy | ৯ |
| 10 | dosh | ১০ |
| 11 | egaro | ১১ |
| 12 | baro | ১২ |
| 13 | tero | ১৩ |
| 14 | chod·do | ১৪ |
| 15 | ponero | ১৫ |
| 16 | sholo | ১৬ |
| 17 | shotero | ১৭ |
| 18 | at·haro | ১৮ |
| 19 | unish | ১৯ |
| 20 | bish | ২০ |
| 30 | tirish | ৩০ |
| 40 | chollish | ৪০ |
| 50 | ponchash | ৫০ |
| 60 | shatt | ৬০ |
| 70 | shottur | ৭০ |
| 80 | ashi | ৮০ |
| 90 | nob·boi | ৯০ |
| 100 | eksho | ১০০ |
| 1000 | ek hajar | ১০০০ |
| 100,000 | ek lakh | ১০০০০০ |
| 10 million | ek koti | ১০০০০০০০ |

| | |
|---|---|
| ½ | sha·re |
| 1½ | der |
| 2½ | arai |

After two, the word *sha·re* is used before the number to indicate half, eg 3½ is *sha·re tin*.

## SHOPPING & SERVICES

For many words, such as 'station', 'hotel' and 'post office', the English word will be understood.

| | |
|---|---|
| **Where is the ...?** | ... kotai? |
| **bank** | bank |
| **bookshop** | boyer dokan |
| **chemist/pharmacy** | oshuder dokan |
| **clothing store** | kaporer dokan |
| **change** (eg from a large banknote) | bhangti |
| **embassy** | embassy |
| **hospital** | hashpatal |
| **laundry** | kapor dhobar dokan |
| **market** | bajar |
| **mosque** | moshjid |
| **palace** | rajbari |
| **post office** | post offish |
| **temple (Hindu)** | mondir |

| | |
|---|---|
| **town** | taun |
| **village** | gram |
| **What time does it open/close?** | kokhon khole/bondo-hoy? |
| **Where is the toilet?** | paikhana kotai? |
| **What is this?** | eta ki? |
| **How much is it?** | dam koto? |
| **It's too expensive.** | eta onek beshi dam |

## TIME & DATES

| | |
|---|---|
| **What is the time?** | koto ba·je? |
| **When?** | kokhon? |
| **2.45** | po·ne tin ta (quarter to three) |
| **1.30** | der ta (one thirty) |
| **4.15** | shoa char ta (quarter past four) |
| **hour** | ghonta |
| **day** | din |
| **week** | shopta |
| **month** | mash |
| **year** | bochor |

| | |
|---|---|
| **date** (calendar) | tarikh |
| **today** | aj |
| **tonight** | aj ra·te |
| **tomorrow** | agamikal |
| **yesterday** | gotokal |
| **in the morning** | shokale |
| **in the afternoon** | bika·le |
| **night** | rat |
| **every day** | proti din |
| **always** | shob shomoy |
| **now** | ekhon |
| **later** | po·re |

| | |
|---|---|
| **Monday** | shombar |
| **Tuesday** | mongolbar |
| **Wednesday** | budhbar |
| **Thursday** | brihoshpotibar |
| **Friday** | shukrobar |
| **Saturday** | shonibar |
| **Sunday** | robibar |

## TRANSPORT

| | |
|---|---|
| **I want to go to ...** | ami ... jabo |
| **Where is this bus going?** | ey bas kotai ja·be? |
| **When does the ... leave/arrive?** | kokhon ... charbe/pochabe? |
| **boat** | nouka/launch |
| **bus** | bas |
| **car** | gari |
| **rickshaw** | riksha |
| **train** | tren |

LANGUAGE

# Glossary

**AC** – air-conditioning
**Adivasis** – tribal people

**baby taxis** – mini auto-rickshaws
**baksheesh** – donation, tip or bribe, depending on the context
**Bangla** – the national language of Bangladesh (see Bengali); also the new name for the Indian state of West Bengal
**bangla** – architectural style associated with the Pre-Mauryan and Mauryan period (312–232 BC); exemplified by a bamboo-thatched hut with a distinctively curved roof
**baras** – old houseboats
**bawalis** – timber workers in the Sundarbans
**Bengali** – the national language of Bangladesh, where it is known as Bangla, and the official language of the state of Bangla (formerly West Bengal) in India
**BIWTC** – Bangladesh Inland Waterway Transport Corporation
**BNP** – Bangladesh Nationalist Party
**BRAC** – Bangladesh Rural Advancement Committee
**BRTC** – Bangladesh Road Transport Corporation

**cha** – tea, usually served with milk and sugar
**chair coach** – modern bus with adjustable seats and lots of leg room
**char** – a river or delta island made of silt; highly fertile but highly susceptible to flooding and erosion
**chaturmukhar** – a structure with all four walls decorated with stone images of gods
**chilla** – place of meditation

**DC** – District Commissioner

**Eid** – Muslim holiday

**ghat** – steps or landing on a river
**guarni jaur** – cyclone

**hammam** – a sort of bathroom
**haors** – wetlands
**hartals** – strikes, ranging from local to national
**hazrat** – Muslim saint

**jamdani** – ornamental loom-embroidered muslin or silk
**jatra** – folk theatre
**jor bangla** – twin hut architectural style

**kameez** – long, dress-like tunic worn by women over a *salwar*
**kantha** – traditional indigo-dyed muslin

**khyang** – Buddhist temple
**kuthi** – factories

**mahavihara** – large monastery
**maidan** – open grassed area in a town or city, used as a parade ground during the Raj
**mandir** – temple
**mau** – honey; also *madhu*
**maualis** – honey-gatherers in the Sundarbans
**mazars** – graves
**mela** – festival
**mihrab** – niche in a mosque positioned to face Mecca; Muslims face in this direction when they pray
**mishuk** – smaller, less-colourful version of a baby taxi
**mohajons** – rickshaw- or taxi-fleet owners
**Mughal** – the Muslim dynasty of Indian emperors from Babur to Aurangzeb (16th–18th century)
**mullah** – Muslim scholar, teacher or cleric
**mustan** – Mafia-style bosses who demand, and receive, payment from baby-taxi drivers, roadside vendors and people living on public land

**nava-ratna** – nine towered; used to describe certain mosques
**nawab** – Muslim prince

**paisa** – unit of currency; there are 100 paisa in a taka
**Parjatan** – the official Bangladesh-government tourist organisation
**pir** – a Sufi religious leader

**Raj** – also called the British Raj; the period of British government in the Indian Subcontinent, roughly from the mid-18th century to the mid-20th century
**raj** – rule or sovereignty
**raja** – ruler, landlord or king
**rajbari** – Raj-era palace built by a *zamindar*
**rekha** – buildings with a square sanctum on a raised platform
**rest house** – government-owned guesthouse
**rickshaw** – small, three-wheeled bicycle-driven passenger vehicle
**rickshaw-wallah** – rickshaw driver
**Rocket** – paddle-steamer

**salwar** – baggy trousers worn under a *kameez*
**salwar kameez** – a long, dress-like tunic *(kameez)* worn by women over a pair of baggy trousers *(salwar)*
**shankhari** – Hindu artisan
**Shi'ia** – Islamic sect that sees the authority of Mohammed as continuing through Ali, his son-in-law

**Shiva** – Hindu god; the destroyer, the creator
**stupa** – Buddhist religious monument
**Sufi** – ascetic Muslim mystic
**sulob** – upper-2nd class on a train (with reserved seating)
**Sunni** – school of Islamic thought that sees the authority of Mohammed as continuing through Abu Bakr, the former governor of Syria

**taka** – currency of Bangladesh
**tea estate** – terraced hillside where tea is grown; also tea garden

**tempo** – auto-rickshaw
**thana** – the lowest political administrative division in Bangladesh; divisions (like a state or province) are divided into *zilas*, and *zilas* are divided into *thanas*
**tolars** – motorised passenger boats

**vihara** – monastery

**zamindar** – landlord; also the name of the feudal-landowner system itself
**zila** – district

# Behind the Scenes

## THIS BOOK

This 5th edition of *Bangladesh* was researched and written by Marika McAdam. The boxed text 'Chars of the Brahmaputra' in the Rajshahi Division chapter was written by Bangladesh expert Bruno de Cordier. The Health chapter was written by Dr Trish Bachelor. Jose Santiago was the author of the 1st edition, way back in 1985. Jon Murray researched the 2nd edition, Betsy Wagenhauser and Alex Newton researched the 3rd, and Richard Plunkett researched the 4th edition.

## THANKS FROM THE AUTHOR

**Marika McAdam** Thank you to the people of Bangladesh, who overwhelmed me every day with their hospitality.

Sincere appreciation to travellers who took the time to write in; special thanks must go to Bruno de Cordier.

Thanks to the colourful characters I met on the road, both for their insight and their company. Michael Walzak, Damian Brosnan, Stephen Harris, Duncan and Juliet, Wouter Velthuis, Sriti Driever, Frans van Wittmarschen and Amine van Lieshout – it was a pleasure to cross paths with you.

Much appreciation also to Ashfaq Khan at the Daily Star, Glennis Neilson at the Bagha club, Neil Sanderson at the Australian High Commission, Ian Marsh of Global Drift, Didar of Bangladesh Ecotours and Mr Razu of Classic Tours and Travels.

Big thanks to Janine Eberle, Shahara Ahmed, Piers Kelly, Alex Landragin, Anna Bolger and other folk at Lonely Planet who gave me support or just gave me a chance.

And finally, thank you to Mum and Dad for taking me on the trips that led to this one. To Johann Aigner for being there – brother for a fortnight, friend forever. And Andrew Lockwood – tech support/life support; thank you for turning Bangladesh and every other challenge into a great adventure.

## CREDITS

*Bangladesh 5* was commissioned and developed in Lonely Planet's Melbourne office by Janine Eberle and Virginia Maxwell. Susie Ashworth wrote the brief. Cartography for this guide was developed by Shahara Ahmed. The Project Managers were Ray Thomson and Kieran Grogan. Editing was coordinated by Andrea Dobbin, with assistance from Andrew Bain, Victoria Harrison, Jane Thompson and Sasha Baskett. Cartography was coordinated by Julie Sheridan, with assistance from Jenny Jones. Bruce Evans was the Managing Editor. The book was laid out by Adam Bextream, with colour pages laid out by Margie Jung. Nic Lehman designed the cover. The artwork was done by Nic Lehman and Candice Jacobus. Quentin Frayne compiled the language chapter.

## THANKS FROM LONELY PLANET

**Many thanks to the travellers who used the last edition and wrote to us with helpful hints, useful advice and interesting anecdotes:**
**A** A Ahad, Pulak Ahmed, Celine Ali, Martin Arker
**B** Karen Baker, Andy Baschong, Sabine Beck, Luke Bell, M Shakil I Bhuiyan, Laurent Bianchi, Andrew Bisson, Barry Black, Andrew Boland,

---

### THE LONELY PLANET STORY

The story begins with a classic travel adventure: Tony and Maureen Wheeler's 1972 journey across Europe and Asia to Australia. There was no useful information about the overland trail then, so Tony and Maureen published the first Lonely Planet guidebook to meet a growing need.

From a kitchen table, Lonely Planet has grown to become the largest independent travel publisher in the world, with offices in Melbourne (Australia), Oakland (USA), London (UK) and Paris (France).

Today Lonely Planet guidebooks cover the globe. There is an ever-growing list of books and information in a variety of media. Some things haven't changed. The main aim is still to make it possible for adventurous travellers to get out there – to explore and better understand the world.

At Lonely Planet we believe travellers can make a positive contribution to the countries they visit – if they respect their host communities and spend their money wisely.

Yvonne Briggs, David Buckley **C** Rosalba Cafolla, Andrea Corgnier, Ranald Coyne **D** Tobias Dahl Hansson, Bruno de Cordier, Nathan de Klepper, Maria Decker, Jennifer Denomy, Mike Douse, Con Dritsas, Janine Dunlop **E** Mike Eaton, Amanda Ebdy, Duncan Edmondson, Rachel Edwards, Magali Elhuyar, Jonathan Eriksson, Kerstin Eyrich **F** Cathy Jo Faruque, Lauren Finemore, Carolynn & Patrick Fischer, Les Fitt, Pernille & Kennet Foh, Hans Folke, Mike Fox **G** Kane Gilmour, Peter Goltermann, Helen Gregory **H** Paul Haddock, Kristin Hanssen, Reid Harvey, Julie Hassman, Graham & Mary Head, Carolyn Hitter **I** Otto Insam **J** Jessica Jacobson, Michiel Jehee **K** Rinku Kamal, Takahiro Kamijo, Yoichi Kaneko, Jennifer Kavanagh, Christine Kent, John A Kerr, Moshiur Khandaker, C Kim, Joshua King **L** Lotte Ladegaard, Justin Lawson, Sara LeRoy, Mark Levitin, Leslie & Robert Lewinter-Suskind, Annette Leyden, Scott Loo **M** Markus Mannheim, Bill Mansoor, Eric Marshall, Samuel Martin, Andreas Mattheiss, Philipp Mattle, Su Mi, Sarah Michael, Nicholas Mleczko **N** Andrew Nash **O** Robert Oldfield, Dennis Olds, Berend Onnes **P** Rachel Parr, Marcus Pennekamp, Riku Perhoniemi, Julia Perry, Alexis Peters, David A Peterson, Daniel Philipp, Manirat Pitarangsi, Bjorn Prevaas **R** Sadiqur Rahman, Safa Rahman, Alan Reimer, Edward Richards, Michelle Rowan, Jay Ruchamkin **S** Sheikh Sadiquelwady, Judith W Schrafft, Cinderella Servranckx, Kerry Shaw, Ben Silverman, Astrid Noreng Sjolie, Tessa Skoczylas, Ken R. Smith, Valerie Solomon, Tanja Stucki, Anders Svensson **T** Ito Takumi, Ben W Tettlebaum, Georgina Thomas, Fredrik Tukk **U** Jakub Urbanski **V** Annemiek va Schie, Erwin van Veen, Chelsea Vaughn, Wouter Velthuis, Freddy von Rabenau **W** Richard Wareham, Christie & Zach Warren, Kelly Welch, Wendy Werner, Christian Wieners, Craig & Kerry Wishart, Leigh Wright, Robin Wyatt **Z** Bla Zabukovec, Anna Zarebska, Ellinor Zeino-Mahmalat, Patrick Zoll, Dagmar Zwebe, Liz Zylinski

## ACKNOWLEDGEMENTS

Globe on back cover © Mountain High Maps 1993 Digital Wisdom, Inc.

### SEND US YOUR FEEDBACK

We love to hear from travellers – your comments keep us on our toes and help make our books better. Our well-travelled team reads every word on what you loved or loathed about this book. Although we cannot reply individually to postal submissions, we always guarantee that your feedback goes straight to the appropriate authors, in time for the next edition. Each person who sends us information is thanked in the next edition – and the most useful submissions are rewarded with a free book.

To send us your updates – and find out about LP events, newsletters and travel news – visit our award-winning website: **www.lonelyplanet.com**.

Note: We may edit, reproduce and incorporate your comments in Lonely Planet products such as guidebooks, websites and digital products, so let us know if you don't want your comments reproduced or your name acknowledged. For a copy of our privacy policy visit www.lonelyplanet.com/privacy.

# Index

**000** Map pages
**000** Location of colour photographs

INDEX

200

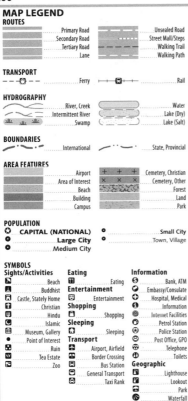

## MAP LEGEND

**ROUTES**
Primary Road — Unsealed Road
Secondary Road — Street Mall/Steps
Tertiary Road — Walking Trail
Lane — Walking Path

**TRANSPORT**
Ferry — Rail

**HYDROGRAPHY**
River, Creek — Water
Intermittent River — Lake (Dry)
Swamp — Lake (Salt)

**BOUNDARIES**
International — State, Provincial

**AREA FEATURES**
Airport — Cemetery, Christian
Area of Interest — Cemetery, Other
Beach — Forest
Building — Land
Campus — Park

**POPULATION**
⊙ CAPITAL (NATIONAL)  ● Small City
● Large City  ● Town, Village
● Medium City

**SYMBOLS**

*Sights/Activities*
Beach, Buddhist, Castle, Stately Home, Christian, Hindu, Islamic, Museum, Gallery, Point of Interest, Ruin, Tea Estate, Zoo

*Eating*
Eating

*Entertainment*
Entertainment

*Shopping*
Shopping

*Sleeping*
Sleeping

*Transport*
Airport, Airfield, Border Crossing, Bus Station, General Transport, Taxi Rank

*Information*
Bank, ATM, Embassy/Consulate, Hospital, Medical, Information, Internet Facilities, Petrol Station, Police Station, Post Office, GPO, Telephone, Toilets

*Geographic*
Lighthouse, Lookout, Park, Waterfall

## LONELY PLANET OFFICES

**Australia**
Head Office
Locked Bag 1, Footscray, Victoria 3011
☎ 03 8379 8000, fax 03 8379 8111
talk2us@lonelyplanet.com.au

**USA**
150 Linden St, Oakland, CA 94607
☎ 510 893 8555, toll free 800 275 8555
fax 510 893 8572, info@lonelyplanet.com

**UK**
72–82 Rosebery Ave,
Clerkenwell, London EC1R 4RW
☎ 020 7841 9000, fax 020 7841 9001
go@lonelyplanet.co.uk

**Published by Lonely Planet Publications Pty Ltd**
ABN 36 005 607 983

© Lonely Planet 2004

© photographers as indicated 2004

Cover photographs: Coconut sellers on Meghna River in wooden nouka boat Bangladesh, Nicholas Pitt/Alamy Images (front); Saffron for sale at the Kaliakur market, Richard I'Anson/Lonely Planet Images (back). Many of the images in this guide are available for licensing from Lonely Planet Images: www.lonelyplanetimages.com.